"Why do so many people find it diffi
young people seem indifferent and ev
proclaim the gospel in a secular age? If you are asking questions such as
these, read *The Truth Will Make You Free*. Fr. Robert Leavitt explains how
our secular society came about and how a new evangelization might
address it. This is a book we have needed for a long time."

> — Frank J. Matera
> Professor Emeritus
> The Catholic University of America

"This book is the most in-depth and erudite treatment of secularization
and the new evangelization available. Fr. Robert F. Leavitt displays an
incredible depth and breadth of knowledge as he analyzes the current
state of affairs in the world and the role the new evangelization can play
in it. He takes his cue from Vatican II's call to discern the 'signs of the
times,' adds insights from the formidable Canadian philosopher Charles
Taylor, among others, and sets forth a comprehensive and perceptive
analysis of religion in the secular age. Anyone concerned about the new
evangelization—and why it is desperately needed—need look no further
for a reliable guide."

> — Ronald D. Witherup, PSS, former professor of sacred scripture,
> superior general of the Sulpicians and the author of
> *Saint Paul and the New Evangelization*

"Robert Leavitt provides an in-depth presentation of the Catholic
church's 'missionary discipleship' by challenging its oft-stated rejection
of the so-called secular world. Tracing major turning points in the history
of Christian and cultural development, accompanied by analysis of
philosophical traditions that recognize the healthy importance of
'options,' he suggests that our secular age is a sign of the times. As such,
it can be a vehicle, not an obstacle, to the 'new evangelization,' the
proclamation of the Gospel. Leavitt has given his contemporary Catholic
readers every reason for joyful passion (*thymos*). This timely book shows
us how this might be achieved."

> — Francis J. Moloney, SDB
> Catholic Theological College
> University of Divinity, Melbourne
> Victoria, Australia

"Drawing on his own expertise as a theologian and theological educator, Robert Leavitt has tackled an important and complex topic—the church's response to 'secularism.' After an initial burst of enthusiasm for engaging the world sparked by Vatican II, the church's leadership has tended to warn against the corrosive threat of secular values. Leavitt, however, argues that there have also been salutary effects from modern secularism, such as helping the church purify itself from its own fascination with secular power and prestige. An authentic evangelical spirit, driven by a passionate desire to give witness to the gospel, Leavitt argues, both challenges and learns from the values of the secular world. This is a book that requires careful thought on the part of the reader and one that can bring wisdom to religious and civic leaders who respect the role of religion as well as the requirements of living in a secular and pluralistic world."

> — Donald Senior, CP
> President Emeritus, Catholic Theological Union

"Fr. Robert Leavitt has written an invaluable and indispensable book. *The Truth Will Make You Free* explores the development and goals of the 'New Evangelization' in the face of the challenges of secularism and pluralism within our contemporary world. What is remarkable is the clarity of his exposition, his insights into diverse issues, and his advocacy for a constructive engagement of the church in proclaiming and living the Gospel today. If I had to recommend one book for students, seminarians, and priests, it would be this remarkable treatment."

> — Francis Schüssler Fiorenza
> Stillman Professor of Roman Catholic Theological Studies
> Harvard Divinity School

"This is an important book because it casts a light on the link between the history and nature of the modern secular age and the most pressing issue for the future of the Church—the new evangelization. The secular age is here a new opportunity for faith. Highly recommended for a clearer understanding of the challenges for Christianity in our contemporary world."

> — Massimo Faggioli
> Professor of Historical Theology
> Villanova University

# The Truth Will Make You Free

## The New Evangelization for a Secular Age

### A STUDY IN DEVELOPMENT

*For Kevin Manning,*
*Thanks for your kind words.*
*In admiration of your great work*
*at St Joann. Best regards.*

*Robert F. Leavitt, PSS*

*Palm Sunday*
*2019*

**LITURGICAL PRESS**
**ACADEMIC**

Collegeville, Minnesota
www.litpress.org

Cover design by Jodi Hendrickson. Image courtesy of W. P. Wittman Photography.

Scripture quotations are from New Revised Standard Version Bible © 1989 National Council of the Churches of Christ in the United States of America. Used by permission. All rights reserved worldwide.

Excerpts from the English translation of *The Roman Missal* © 2010, International Commission on English in the Liturgy Corporation. All rights reserved.

Excerpts from the Magisterium of Pope Francis and Pope Benedict XVI © Libreria Editrice Vaticana. Used with permission.

Excerpts from documents of the Second Vatican Council are from *Vatican Council II: Constitutions, Decrees, Declarations; The Basic Sixteen Documents*, edited by Austin Flannery, OP, © 1996. Used with permission of Liturgical Press, Collegeville, Minnesota.

"From Mythology" from THE COLLECTED POEMS: 1956–1998 by ZBIGNIEW HERBERT. Translated & Edited by Alissa Valles. Copyright © 2007 The Estate of Zbigniew Herbert. Translation copyright © 2007 by HarperCollins Publishers LLC. Reprinted by permission of HarperCollins Publishers.

© 2019 by Order of Saint Benedict, Collegeville, Minnesota. All rights reserved. No part of this book may be used or reproduced in any manner whatsoever, except brief quotations in reviews, without written permission of Liturgical Press, Saint John's Abbey, PO Box 7500, Collegeville, MN 56321-7500. Printed in the United States of America.

1    2    3    4    5    6    7    8    9

**Library of Congress Cataloging-in-Publication Data**

Names: Leavitt, Robert F., author.
Title: The truth will make you free : the new evangelization for a secular age / Robert F. Leavitt, P.S.S.
Description: Collegeville, Minnesota : Liturgical Press, 2019. | Includes bibliographical references.
Identifiers: LCCN 2018024089 (print) | LCCN 2018041691 (ebook) | ISBN 9780814646922 (ebook) | ISBN 9780814646687
Subjects: LCSH: Evangelistic work—Catholic Church. | Christianity and culture. | Secularism. | Catholic Church—Doctrines.
Classification: LCC BX2347.4 (ebook) | LCC BX2347.4 .L43 2019 (print) | DDC 266/.209051—dc23
LC record available at https://lccn.loc.gov/2018024089

If you continue in my word,
you will truly be my disciples;
and you will know the truth,
and the truth will make you free.

—John 8:31-32

To my former teachers, colleagues, students, and friends
at St. Mary's Seminary & University
Baltimore, Maryland

*Ave, Maria, gratia plena, Dominus tecum,*
*Benedicta tu in mulieribus*
*et benedictus fructus ventris tui, Jesus*

# Contents

# Acknowledgments

A theologian accumulates enough intellectual debts to others after fifty years of teaching, and it's not possible to itemize them, much less to pay them back. I feel obligated, nevertheless, to open this book by gratefully acknowledging a few of them.

I begin with the gratitude I feel for having both Raymond E. Brown, SS (1928–98), and Paul Ricoeur (1913–2005) as teachers when I began my priesthood. At the same moment the Catholic Church was itself taking cognizance of the diverse challenges of the modern world, these figures found ways to reconcile the ancient and ever-new revelation of God with critical methods and philosophical reason. When an aged John Paul II presented the Pope Paul VI Award to Paul Ricoeur, the Holy Father graciously acknowledged what this extraordinary French Protestant philosopher had contributed to a contemporary Christian humanism. If there's a common language where Christian faith and the secular world might find ways to recognize each other, it will be forged, I believe, in humanistic philosophies capable of doing full justice to the truth of the human person.

The purpose of this book is to clarify the meaning(s) of secularization in relation to modern culture and faith. For the inspiration to attempt that, I have a special indebtedness to the thought of Daniel Bell (1919–2011) and Charles Taylor (1931– ). Their analyses of the sources and meanings of secularization, different as they are, constitute two of the best in print. Charles Taylor's genealogy of modern self-identity in *Sources of the Self* and of secularization in *A Secular Age* suggested a way to weave an analysis of the new evangelization in its concerns with secularism with new forms of philosophical argumentation. I could name many others, but the four authors I've just mentioned outrank them all.

Closer to my spiritual and academic world, I must express an undying gratitude to the Society of St. Sulpice and to my friends and colleagues at St. Mary's Seminary & University for my education and continuing formation as a priest, theologian, and senior administrator. This study is a minor dividend on a considerable institutional investment in one priest. Without Howard P. Bleichner, PSS, I probably would not have encountered the writings of his former professor at Dartmouth College, Eugen Rosenstock-Huessy. This brilliant and idiosyncratic émigré German historian possessed an extraordinary range of insights into the enduring truth of Christianity which anyone inclined to a non-religious worldview should take to heart. To the Rev. Msgr. David I. Fulton, Fisher Professor of Moral Theology and Director of Priest Programs in the Center for Continuing Formation at St. Mary's Seminary & University, I express gratitude for annual invitations to speak on the new evangelization and the secular age in his program for young pastors. A few years ago, I was invited by the late Robert L. Beloin to deliver a lecture on religion and secularization to faculty and students at the St. Thomas More Center and Chapel at Yale University. Posthumous thanks go to this intelligent and gracious priest for his hospitality to me.

When the time arrived to cease lecturing and devote myself to writing, my Sulpician colleague, Richard M. Gula, PSS, offered helpful and trenchant criticisms of early drafts of this book. Phillip J. Brown, PSS, read parts as well, suggesting ways to make my points stronger. To the president-rector of St. Mary's Seminary & University, Philip J. Brown, PSS, and to his immediate predecessor, Thomas R. Hurst, PSS, I express my continuing gratitude for the appointment to the France-Merrick University Chair in Theology and for the precious opportunity they extended to me to continue teaching theology to future priests.

Having served as professor of theology and president-rector of St. Mary's Seminary & University myself for nearly three decades, a period which coincides with the inauguration and maturation of the new evangelization movement in the church, I am acutely conscious of the many obligations I owe to very capable faculty, administrators, staff, and trustees at the seminary whose efforts brought such blessings to my alma mater during those years. To those seminarians and other students who sat in my classes as I was working out my ideas on faith in the secular age, I hope what I taught helped them cope better with their own faith struggles on the way to the altar and later. In that connection, I am happy to name seminary trustee Dr. Paul R. McHugh, University Distinguished Professor of Psychiatry at the Johns Hopkins School of Medicine, for encouraging me in this project and for delightful conversations about the book's topic with him and his lovely wife, Jean.

The close friendships I have formed with remarkable men and women in Baltimore over the course of a half-century of priestly ministry in that city have left an indelible mark of affection on my heart and soul. To the librarians in the Marion Burk Knott Library, who have never failed to offer me whatever assistance I needed, I express my sincere gratitude.

Finally, nothing like this study would have seen the light of day, despite the intellectual debts and spiritual blessings I've mentioned, much less of a desire to employ them for explaining in a new fashion the opportunities and obstacles of religious faith in a secular age, were it not for the interest and support of Hans Christoffersen of Liturgical Press. For his patience and the competency of the production editor, Stephanie Lancour, as well as the other staff at Liturgical Press, I express my respect and appreciation.

# Introduction

# Signs of the Times

In a saying of Jesus, he criticizes some listeners for their inability to "read the signs of the times." He was not talking about future trends in Roman or Jewish society. Romans read entrails of animals for that and some Jews read apocalyptic. He was talking about his miracles, which, if those judges could see them as true portents, would tell them the kingdom of God had arrived.

The miracles of science, technology, markets and their own identity are what fascinate the modern mind, not the miraculous cures recounted in the gospels. Miracles happen daily at Johns Hopkins Medical Center. Crippled people now walk, and the blind can see again. Kids get a new iPhone and enter a magical kingdom more enchanting than hillside homilies by the rabbi from Nazareth. Possessed people in our society receive psychotropic medications. An "act of God" is now a euphemism for a tornado or a flood, not a deliverance from them.

Truth be told, few in the great secular centers of science and culture expect much from any religion that could seriously change what's happening in human life. After September 11, 2001, and the clergy abuse scandals, if they expect anything from the passionate convictions of religion, it would be hatred and more hypocrisy. So, what can the new evangelization in the Catholic Church mean for a world that feels it has seen enough of what religion is all about?

In this book, I explore the meanings of the new evangelization against the horizon of what the philosopher Charles Taylor means by the secular age. So, let me briefly set the table for the reader. In the largest and best sense of the word, I regard the secular as providential for the authentic mission of the church. What I mean by that is that

1

the birth of the idea of a secular state emancipated the church from its quest for worldly power. Bringing that to pass required the combined effects of the fifteenth-century humanist movement in Italy, the sixteenth-century Protestant Reformation in Germany, England, and France, the seventeenth-century wars of religion in Europe and the emergence of the idea of religious toleration, and the eighteenth-century Romantic movement and the European Enlightenment. It did not happen overnight. These events served to liberate the truth of the Gospel from its captivity to the dream of worldly power. Christendom had to die so that the church, more closely modeled on the Paschal Mystery and the missionary ministry of St. Paul, could come to life. Byzantine and Anglican models of caesaropapism, where the head of state is the head of the church, had no real basis in the New Testament. But, so were Catholic theo-politics of "throne and altar."

The secular ideal achieved formal expression at the Peace of Westphalia (1648) and, in principle, separated politics from religion and its passions. Christianity gained two things from that. First, it allowed the church to see itself no longer as an ally of political protectors or the status quo, but as a prophetic institution. Second, it enabled the church to rediscover the power of the image of Christ Crucified for its own ecclesial identity and mission. Individual Christians are called by the Gospel to a "change of heart." That is a wrenching experience for anyone, much more for the church as a powerful cultural and political institution in the West. The evangelical significance of a death like Christ's, as the way to new life like his, applies as much to the church as it does to individual believers. That is the Christian meaning of reform.

This vision of the church's new identity for the modern world came to expression in two major documents of Vatican II—*Lumen Gentium* and *Gaudium et Spes*. The new evangelization builds on them. It is a second-generation development of themes of the renewal and rebirth of the church at the Second Vatican Council. What was then known generally as "the modern world" is probably more accurately described as "a secular age." The meaning of that is what I try to explain in this book.

The threat to the new evangelization, which is often disguised as its very soul, is any version of a Christian "culture war." The biblical background of "holy war" makes such metaphors morally unstable and dangerous. Invoking such images arises from some deep resentment at Christianity (either Catholic or Protestant fundamentalist) having lost political authority in the secular age. The moral problems of the secular order, and there are many of them, will not be solved by a return to some form of Christendom, as if that were even possible again. The evangelization of culture cannot happen when the church transforms itself into a political actor. The basic paradox is that the secular order, in crucially important ways, painfully liberated the church from its own ambitions to resemble more closely, in its inner life and mission, the figure of Christ and the apostle to the Gentiles.

The new evangelization is not a concept everyone absolutely agrees on in the church because Catholics still disagree about the essential meaning of the texts of Vatican II and how to translate into the church's institutional life what they call for. In addition to the contestable hermeneutics of the council, there remain abiding questions about the meanings (because there are many meanings involved) of cultural modernity and secularity. So, this book tackles two controversial questions buried in one phrase: What is the new evangelization as part of the post-conciliar debates on the identity of the church, and what is the secular age which shapes our cultural and moral identities as modern human beings? I will weave my theological points into a narrative context to shed light on both questions.

Which is to say that the theological referendum about the meaning of the Second Vatican Council is now prolonged in discussions about the new evangelization. This is where the Spirit is at work within the spiritual, intellectual, and pastoral life of the church. The sociological and philosophical debates over the meanings of modernity are also far from over.

If the church drew its truth from all the Scriptures and from the figure of Christ in the gospels, it did not enclose itself in a textual fundamentalism at all. It not only borrowed categories from Greek philosophy to interpret the inspired Word of God but adopted cultural models as well. The church was not reluctant to admit there were "seeds of the Word" (*semina Verbi*) in the world (*mundum* and *saeculum* both) which were deposited in creation and culture for its instruction. The parable of the Sower became a parable of the church drawing upon the beauty of nature and the wisdom of culture to understand God's revelation. Looking back over the past five centuries, one could at least speculate that the Protestant Reformation, in some crucial respects, was good seed scattered in the church. If the struggles to renew biblical hermeneutics in the church are seen in a similar light, then good seed was planted by the methods of the historical-reconstructive sciences and literary criticism in reading the sacred documents of the Christian faith. Is it too far-fetched to suggest that the birth of the secular order of life and the emergence of a modern human identity in culture, despite all the problems and grievous errors in them, create a seedbed which can be harvested appropriately by the Christian faith? And, does not the very creation of the secular principle of religious freedom, starting from Hugo Grotius and John Locke and crystalizing in the European Enlightenment, and which in its own form the church itself approved at Vatican II, amount to a seed of the Word in a secular age? These are the seeds of the Word which bear the fruit that make the new evangelization for a secular age possible.

## Signs of the Times

In one of its most well-known passages, Vatican Council II alluded to an expression Jesus used for those Pharisees who failed to see the meaning of his mission. His critics, he said, know perfectly well how to forecast the weather, but they could not read in Jesus' actions "the signs of the times" (Matt 16:4 and parallels). The council wrote: "In every age, the church carries the responsibility of reading the signs of the times and of interpreting them in the light of the Gospel, if it is to carry out its task" (Pastoral Constitution on the Church in the Modern World, 4).

Interpreting the "signs of the times" is always controversial. Signs do not interpret themselves. What does 9/11 really mean? What did the financial crisis of 2008 tell us? What do empty pews in our parishes suggest? How did the crisis of clergy abuse come about and what explains the cover-ups by bishops in the church? An astute observer of the culture wars claims that American society is now caught in a rampant pluralism within a weakened cultural consensus.[1] Others suggest that "identity politics" are eroding the very bases of a pluralistic liberal democracy in a political tribalism. Whose in-

---

[1] James Davison Hunter, "The Culture War and the Sacred/Secular Divide: The Problem of Pluralism and Weak Hegemony," in *Social Research* 76, no. 4 (Winter 2009): 1307–22.

terpretation of the signs of the times sheds the greatest light on them? In his poem "The Second Coming" (1919), composed in the immediate aftermath of World War I and the troubles in Ireland, William Butler Yeats penned these famous words:

> The falcon cannot hear the falconer;
> Things fall apart; the centre cannot hold;
> Mere anarchy is loosed upon the world . . .
> The best lack all conviction, while the worst
> Are full of passionate intensity.

Who are the best who supposedly "lack all conviction"? Could some be the secular scientists and cultural elites who abandoned religious faith to secure the modern world on other foundations and wound up in a dangerous moral relativism? And who are the worst "full of passionate intensity"? Some of them bought tickets on flights from Boston on September 11, 2001. No question about that. But, why? Oversimplifications by the secular left about the nature of religion and resentments of seculars by fundamentalist religion are among the signs of the times we are still struggling to decipher despite all the information at our disposal. Some ancients read portents in the sky or in the entrails of poultry to interpret the future and the hidden signs of the times. Moderns read blogs and their favorite pundits. Fundamentalists scour the Scriptures for hidden meanings about the last days.

## Apocalyptic Sign Reading for a Secular Age

One of the fascinating signs of the times today is that both secular and neo-conservative commentators, for very different reasons, see some troubling evidence that our culture is going off the rails or even veering toward catastrophe. The biblical canon contains examples of "apocalyptic" such as the book of Daniel. Let me share a few contemporary examples of this genre.

A secular example of it can be found in *An Inquiry into the Human Prospect* (1974), written by Robert L. Heilbroner (1919–2005) which appeared the same year Paul VI called the first World Synod on Evangelization. Heilbroner was then the Norman Thomas Professor of Economics at the New School of Social Research in New York. The question that opened the book sounded ominously apocalyptic: "Is there hope for man?"[2] Based on his own reading of the signs of the times economically in the early 1970s, Heilbroner had serious doubts about it. "For some time, observers skeptical of the panacea of growth have wondered why their contemporaries, who were three or five or ten times richer than their grandparents, or great-grandparents, or Pilgrim forebears, did not seem to be three or five or ten times happier or more content or more richly developed as individual human beings."[3] Had we, the wealthiest nation in the world, banked too much on the wrong solutions to the quest for happiness?

The 1974 case he built hung loosely on a concatenation of what he called major "confidence-shaking events" in social and political life (Vietnam, street crime, race riots, airline hijackings, political assassinations, etc.) and the demoralizing disconnect in the experience of shared moral values between the postwar generation and their offspring. To these, he added "attitudinal changes" (less confidence in the "course of social events" and "the limits of rational planning" in shaping progress) and "fear" that the immediate postwar growth curve could not be sustained indefinitely. Within this mixture was the growing sense of a possible "ceiling on industrial production." Looming over everything came a word that the philosopher Charles Taylor, among others, has used. "The civilizational malaise, in a word, reflects the inability of a civilization directed to material improvement—higher incomes, better diets, miracles of medicine, triumphs of applied physics and chemistry—to satisfy the human spirit."[4] This economist started to sound like a preacher.

The civilizational malaise, according to Heilbroner, left us with the uncomfortable feeling that "the values of an industrial civilization, which has for two centuries given us not only material advance but also a sense of élan and purpose, now seem to be losing their self-evident justification."[5] Heilbroner did not believe that those addicted to the material benefits of the status quo could change, especially those at the summit of political and economic culture who held so much capital on the wrong solutions. In the light of the "inertial

---

[2] Robert L. Heilbroner, *An Inquiry into the Human Prospect* (New York: W. W. Norton & Company, 1974), 13. The third edition was published in 1991 as *An Inquiry into the Human Prospect: Looked at Again for the 1990s.*

[3] Ibid., 20.

[4] Ibid., 21.

[5] Ibid.

momentum" of the powerful and productive industrial age, he expected that most would take his reactions to events to be just worrisome overreactions. So, he concluded that only a "storm of crisis problems" could force "convulsive change" on us in the United States and around the world.[6] Issues like those Heilbroner posed in 1974 partly explain and certainly dwarf the church's pastoral problems, serious as they are. But, now clergy abuse has unleashed its own "storm of crises" which threaten the viability of the church herself as an institution of trust.

America is one thing, but global civilization is another. The third edition of *An Inquiry into the Human Prospect* (1991) coincided with the publication of a major work in international politics, *The Clash of Civilizations and the Remaking of World Order*. Its author is Samuel Huntington, chairman of the Harvard Academy for International and Area Studies, who was also coeditor of the journal *Foreign Policy*. Henry Kissinger called *The Clash of Civilizations* one of the most important books on global politics since the end of the Cold War. Huntington tried to convey what an emerging world order would look like as a multi-civilizational reality. We're now staring that in the face.

> Modernization has generally enhanced the material level of Civilization throughout the world. But has it also enhanced the moral and cultural dimensions of Civilization? In some respects, this appears to be the case. Slavery, torture, vicious abuse of individuals, have become less and less acceptable in the contemporary world. Is this, however, simply the result of the impact of Western civilization on other cultures and hence will a moral reversion occur as Western power declines? Much evidence exists in the 1990s for the relevance of the "sheer chaos" paradigm of world affairs: a global breakdown of law and order, failed states and increasing anarchy in many parts of the world. A global crime wave, transnational mafias and drug cartels, increasing drug addiction in many societies, a general weakening of the family, a decline in trust and social solidarity in many countries, ethnic, religious, and civilizational violence and rule by the gun prevalent in much of the world.[7]

[6] Ibid., 132.

[7] Samuel P. Huntington, *The Clash of Civilizations and the Remaking of World Order* (New York: Simon & Schuster, 1996), 321.

In the end, Huntington agrees with Lester Pearson that we are entering a "new age" of different civilizations (Far East, Indian, Middle East, African, and the West, etc.) which must "learn to live side by side in peaceful interchange, learning from each other, studying each other's history and ideals and art and culture, mutually enriching each other's lives. The alternative, in this overcrowded little world, is misunderstanding, tension, clash, and catastrophe."[8] A possible global clash of civilizations was looming over us. Clearly Western secularism as we know it will not prevail everywhere on the planet as it has prevailed in the United States and Europe. The worries about culture and world affairs surveyed in *Gaudium et Spes* at Vatican II and in papal encyclicals since seem prescient in relation to such secular judgments.

Turning again to the American scene, social commentators on the religious right and secular left seem to agree on one thing now: something in American culture has gone badly wrong. Virginia Wolfe's epigram in *Mr. Bennett and Mrs. Brown* "On or about 1910, human character changed!" could as easily apply to the interpretations of the signs of the times from the very different perspectives of Rod Dreher and Kurt Anderson.

Rod Dreher has written a compelling moral tale from the perspective of neo-conservative evangelical Christianity. For 1910 when Virginia Wolfe claimed human character changed, he would supply Friday, June 26, 2015, when the Obergefell v. Hodges decision by the Supreme Court constitutionally recognized same-sex marriage in the United States. The secularist Kurt Anderson sees things exactly the opposite. If a precise date were needed for what explains how America, as he says, "went haywire," he would no doubt opt for Tuesday, November 8, 2016, when a narcissistic billionaire reality television personality and golf course, casino, and real estate developer, with no political experience or even a coherent political philosophy, was elected president of the United States. For seculars and evangelicals both, and for very different reasons, something seems to have gone terribly wrong here. Let me briefly say what Dreher and Anderson are trying to tell us. Rod Dreher makes his evangelical case against the culture wars and for the faithful Christian as willing exile

---

[8] Ibid.

from the secular age in *The Benedict Option*.[9] As senior editor at *The American Conservative*, Dreher reflects the intuitions of many religious conservatives troubled by secular culture's willingness to slough off traditional moral values. Relying on the philosopher Alasdair MacIntyre, Dreher blames late medieval nominalism (from the Latin *nomen*) for rupturing the syntax of theological and moral reason. It first severed truth and moral values from the given nature of things. From this distant discordance between language and reality, Dreher draws his moral consequences. Heterosexual marriage which biological nature dictates for reproduction is redefined in Obergefell v. Hodges. Marriage can be whatever the Supreme Court says it is. Dreher sees this as the final salvo in the culture wars. Christians lost. The only option to preserve the faith now will be in a Christian ghetto of sorts. That leads Dreher to embrace what he calls a "Benedict Option" version of the church: mission to the world reverts to flight from the world as some modern Christian version of an Amish existence. Dreher intends his book to be a religious "survival manual" and "rule of life" for the true believer as a religious exile from secular culture.

Some might scoff at Dreher's conclusions and the stark choices he sets before us, but *New York Times* columnist David Brooks has called *The Benedict Option* the most important religious book of the decade. Dreher sees himself as a biblical sentinel sounding the trumpet of retreat for those sleepwalking out of faith into secularism. Because culture is toxic the only way for the faith to survive is to live apart from it.

For a dyspeptic secularist like Kurt Anderson, America has exactly the opposite problem. It has too much faith and not enough hard-headed doubt about it. A public radio host for *Studio 360*, Anderson peppers his prose with metaphor like Dreher. He recently published *Fantasyland: How America Went Haywire—A 500-Year History* that was abridged in *The Atlantic* as "How America Lost Its Mind."[10] In Anderson's narrative, it all begins at Plymouth Rock with Puritans searching for the biblical City on a Hill—a new religious utopia.

---

[9] Rod Dreher, *The Benedict Option: A Strategy for Christians in a Post-Christian Nation* (New York: Penguin, 2017).

[10] Kurt Anderson, "How America Lost Its Mind," in *The Atlantic* (September 2017): 76–91. This is adapted from *Fantasyland: How America Went Haywire—a 500-Year History* (New York: Random House, 2017).

Anderson strings together an off-beat story of a culture so hungry for belief, for God's hand at work in puritanical purification or for some kind of magical moment somewhere or some ecstatic release, that people will fall for anything. It could be UFOs, drugs, free sex, political conspiracies, almost anything that taps into the insatiable need for strong belief in something. It came ashore with the Puritans. Now it can be found on cable news, and far right and far left websites, and tweeted by a president who calls responsible journalism "fake news" and who is something of a circus figure himself. The unbelievable, Anderson claims, is precisely what America finds most worthy of belief! Only the Enlightenment and hardheaded secular reason with all the blinkers off can save us. Steven Pinker makes the same case.

For Anderson, the 1960s offered Americans the ripe "low-hanging fruit" of the incredible which became suddenly very believable: conspiracy theories about John F. Kennedy's assassination, Timothy Leary's "turn on, tune in, and drop out" culture, sightings of Elvis. The taste for the incredible went haywire. Serious politicians now contest scientific evidence of climate change. It is not just religious or moral truth that is contested; even scientific facts are. America has become, for Anderson, *Fantasyland*. Is it Dreher or Anderson or both in some strange coincidence of opposites who read the signs of the times correctly? If the truth will set us free, what is the truth about the times we're living in?

An enlightening and humorous take on that question can be found in a small book by the philosopher Harry Frankfurt called (with all due respect for the truth!) *On Bullshit*.[11] This was no wisecrack but a serious piece of language analysis related to truth-seeking by a respected philosopher. Frankfurt claimed that when people speak of something called "bullshit" they are not speaking about the cognitive or moral distortions of error or lying, but of something far more serious. They are saying the issue of truth is not even in question. The "bullshitter," Frankfurt says, is simply indifferent to the whole idea of truth, to evidence, to facts which contradict his opinions. Pope Benedict XVI continually stressed the essential epistemic and moral

---

[11] See Harry G. Frankfurt, *On Bullshit* (Princeton, NJ: Princeton University Press, 2005). The issue of truth emphasized repeatedly by Joseph Ratzinger/Benedict XVI is not "Catholic" dogmatism. It is crucial for discourse in all public life.

necessity of truth and serious truth-claims in the spheres of ethics and religious belief. If the whole idea of truth in these realms are contested as they are, what will we be left with? The issue of truth is what drives the human mind and spirit. We want to know what really happened and what is really the case. Harry Frankfurt, in some ways, makes a more compelling case for truth than the pope himself. Without respected cultural and political referees whose wisdom can help us distinguish truth from sincere mistakes or fabrications, where would we be? In religion and philosophy, no one gets far without some dependence on reliable and trusted referees as well.

In this book, I will tell the reader who my referees are in reading the signs of the times. One of them is Charles Taylor, whose writings on the modern identity and the secular age many consider one of the most intelligent and ecumenical assessments of the times we live in over the past fifty years. Before getting into that, let me provide some background on secularization.

## Sociology and the Signs of Secularization

Sociology is a science concerned with the structures and functions of human social life.[12] Its methods can vary from techniques to analyze large macro institutions that wrap a social "skin" around the self, such as work and family and leisure time, to the phenomenology of microsocial rituals of everyday life such as how people in a given culture bid someone goodbye, or even apologize.[13] We feel these social rituals as if they were instinctive, but they are actually socially transmitted and legitimated. One breaks them at a price. When sociology moves beyond statistics, trends, and microsocial rituals in everyday life, it leans toward more philosophical subspecialties like the history of mentalities, cultural anthropology, and the sociology of knowledge and religion. These subspecialties in the discipline of sociology reveal the hidden plausibility structures in social life that

[12] Auguste Comte is considered the French founder of sociology, which he defined as one of his new positivist (fact-based empirical sciences) sciences and which he once called praxeology.

[13] See Erving Goffman, *Relations in Public: Microstudies of the Public Order* (New York: Basic Books, 1974). Goffman is credited with founding a school of sociology known as microsociology. He applied phenomenological method to social rituals that structured the "presentation of the self" in everyday life.

tell us something is believable or not. At the beginning of the twentieth century, careful observers of social life in Europe began noting a decline in religious belief and adherence. They called it "secularization."

Emile Durkheim, Max Weber, Ernst Troeltsch, and, later, the American Talcott Parsons offered various interpretations about the causes and prognosis of secularization.[14] Max Weber linked it to nineteenth-century urbanization, modernization, and industrialization in Europe. The factory and city were to blame for the decline in religious practice, not the village atheist. Weber referred to the negative effects of modernization on religious faith as *Entzauberung* or disenchantment. Atheism was not what was emptying the pews. Engineering was. It was logical to think that the more that technical science and modern business spread, the more religion would eventually dry up. The imaginary patina of transcendence religion painted

---

[14] Secularization theory is beyond the scope of this book. Allow me, however, to include in an opening footnote a few of the major thinkers who have helped to define the issue. The classic is Max Weber's *The Protestant Ethic and Spirit of Capitalism* (1904) and all subsequent theories are effectively footnotes to Weber's comprehensive survey in this groundbreaking study of economic progress and certain forms of Protestantism. Along with Weber, Emile Durkheim merits a place in the pantheon of secularization theorists with his *The Elementary Forms of the Religious Life* (1912). An ardent secularist himself, Durkheim nevertheless held that some concept of the sacred was necessary as glue for social and cultural life. In America, Peter Berger applied principles from the sociology of knowledge to religious belief in *The Sacred Canopy: Elements of a Sociological Theory of Religion* (1967). A social world (whether traditional or modern) is a humanly constructed entity unlike the natural organic world. The medieval world was sheltered from absurdity by a canopy of meaning based on divine justice overarched by a Platonic-Ptolemaic imaginary. Secularized cultures abandon that canopy, and its key ingredients like the supernatural, grace, and sacraments, for human justice rather than divine providence. Daniel Bell in *The Cultural Contradictions of Capitalism* (1976) proposed disaggregating economics and politics from culture whose "axial principle" is existential and religious by nature. In 2007, Charles Taylor published *A Secular Age* to counter the current "substitution" theory of secularization, where science grows as religion wanes in a society with his "master reform" narrative of secularization, which I will explain in the book. The literature on secularization is vast, but I can single out for those interested the following: Stephen Bruce, *God Is Dead: Secularization in the West* (Oxford: Blackwell, 2002); John Milbank, *Theology and Social Theory*, 2nd ed. (Oxford: Oxford University Press, 2005); John Milbank, *Beyond Secular Order: The Representation of Being and the Representation of the People* (Chichester: John Wiley & Sons, 2013); Christian Smith, "Introduction," in *The Secular Revolution: Power, Interests, and Conflict in the Secularization of American Public Life*, ed. Christian Smith (Berkeley: University of California Press, 2003).

on the world for believers was being scratched off like the plastic film on a lottery ticket. Underneath the scratch card were the magic numbers—science and progress. Place your bets there!

For a century, secularization theory was the unchallenged axiom about the future of religion which every college undergraduate took in Sociology 101. But recent scholarship, working with better statistics, longer narratives, and more subtle concepts and theories about religion and secularization, is changing the old theory. The association of social science with the prognosis of religious morbidity among many in our culture, however, stuck like a dogma. Consider a story Leo Tolstoy wrote in 1902 called "The Overthrow of Hell and Its Restoration."[15] In Tolstoy's tale, a devil returns from this world to the underworld where he brags to Beelzebub, the prince of devils, that he's figured out how a new science he invented called sociology will lead people away from Jesus Christ. Sociology, he says, tells them that societies always got better when religious beliefs no longer held them back. Religion was simply an impediment to progress. Secularization got society past that. Since 9/11, we've witnessed the terror that religious beliefs—from radical Islam to fundamentalist Christian—can create. Can we blame people for following Tolstoy's junior demon away from religion, then?

The year the Second Vatican Council ended—1965—was the same year that Harvey Cox, a liberal Baptist theologian teaching at Harvard, introduced the word "secular" into the vocabulary of modern theology in a book entitled *The Secular City*.[16] The "secular city" was Max Weber baptized and anointed for confirmation by Cox. Some Catholics didn't like his conclusions. The priest sociologist and sometime novelist Andrew M. Greeley wrote *Unsecular Man: The Persistence of Religion* (1972) in response, making his case against Cox by drawing

[15] On Tolstoy's short story and sociology, see Hans Joas, "The Church in a World of Options," in *Renewing the Church in a Secular Age: Holistic Dialogue and Kenotic Vision*, ed. Charles Taylor, José Casanova, George F. McLean, and Joao J. Vila-Cha (Washington, DC: The Council for Research in Values and Philosophy, 2016), 86.

[16] Harvey Cox, *The Secular City* (New York: Macmillan, 1965). For a conservative Catholic counterattack on Cox, see James Hitchcock, *What Is Secular Humanism? Why Humanism Became Secular and How It Is Changing Our World* (Ann Arbor, MI: Servant Books, 1982), 11–17. The American Humanist Association published its humanist creed in 1933 in the first *Humanist Manifesto*. *Humanist Manifesto II* was published in 1973. Hitchcock's presentation of secular humanism reflects the understanding of a Roman Catholic traditionalist thinker.

on better scientific sociology. Religion, according to Greeley's take on the "signs of the times," was rebounding from its first defeat and would rebound again. The "secular city" be damned.

Between the publication and notoriety of Cox's *The Secular City* and Greeley's apologetic for religious consciousness in *Unsecular Man*, the Lutheran sociologist Peter Berger came out with what many still consider the American classic on religion and secularization, *The Sacred Canopy: Elements of a Sociological Theory of Religion* (1967).[17] Berger clarified how the symbolic scaffolding of religion, which had once given meaning to human suffering and death, was coming apart. Berger went deeper into things than Weber, Cox, or Greeley. In my judgment, it should be part of the required curriculum of every seminary. With an infuriating knack for keeping his own disciples perplexed, Berger followed up *The Sacred Canopy* with a little essay titled *A Rumor of Angels: Modern Society and the Rediscovery of the Supernatural* (1969).[18] Here's how he ended that provocative trial balloon:

> In the religious view of reality, all phenomena point toward that which transcends them, and this transcendence actively impinges from all sides on the empirical sphere of human existence. It was only with the onset of secularization that the divine fullness began to recede, until the point was reached when the empirical sphere became both all-encompassing and perfectly closed in upon itself. At that point man was truly alone in reality. We have come a long way from the gods and from the angels. The breaches of this-worldly reality which these mighty figures embodied have increasingly vanished from our consciousness as serious possibilities. They linger on as fairy tales, nostalgias, perhaps as vague symbols of some sort.[19]

---

[17] Peter Berger, *The Sacred Canopy: Elements of a Sociological Theory of Religion* (New York: Anchor Books, 1990). Originally published in 1967. Berger subsequently published and edited a number of extraordinarily insightful books and essays treating secularization and its effects on religion or on religion's resistance to secularization in the following: *A Rumor of Angels: Modern Society and the Rediscovery of the Supernatural* (Garden City, NY: Anchor Books, 1970); *A Far Glory: The Quest for Faith in an Age of Credulity* (New York: The Free Press, 1992); Peter Berger, ed., *The Desecularization of the World: Resurgent Religion and World Politics* (Grand Rapid, MI: Eerdmans, 1999); Peter Berger, ed., *Between Relativism and Fundamentalism: Religious Resources for a Middle Position* (Grand Rapids, MI: Eerdmans, 2010).

[18] Berger, *A Rumor of Angels*.

[19] Berger, *A Rumor of Angels*, 94.

The theological provocateur side of the sociologist of religion then added:

> This book has not been about angels. At best, it might be a preface to angelology, if by that one meant a study of God's messengers as His signals in reality. We are, whether we like it or not, in a situation in which transcendence has been reduced to a rumor. We cannot escape our situation with one magical jump. We cannot readily, and probably should not wish to, return to an earlier situation in the history of man's grappling with reality. For this reason, I have taken pains, at a number of points in my argument, to stress that what I am advocating is neither esoteric nor "reactionary." But I have also tried to show that our situation is not an inexorable fate and that secularized consciousness is not the absolute it presents itself as. We must begin in the situation in which we find ourselves, but we must not submit to it as to an irresistible tyranny. If the signals of transcendence have become rumors in our time, then we can set out to explore these rumors—and perhaps to follow them to their source.[20]

The religious believer today exists without a robust sacred canopy as his or her ancestor had, but somehow porous enough, as Charles Taylor might say, to still sense the uncanniness of life even in a secular age.

## Signs of the Times:
## The Easy Way into Faith and Out of It

One doesn't need the subtle promptings of Tolstoy's junior devil to abandon a faith. The sacrament of confirmation on its own will do that for you. You heard me right! If trends continue about teenage indifference, the new evangelization in the Catholic Church won't have much material to work with. Pope Paul VI put the re-evangelization of the young at the top of the church's agenda forty years ago. Some were transformed, but most were not. The World Youth Days tried to pump up enthusiasm for the faith in young people (aged sixteen to twenty-nine). The October 2018 World Synod of Bishops on Young People, the Faith, and Vocational Discernment

---

[20] Ibid., 95.

could not have come at a more pressing time. It will be interesting to see what comes of it.

Last fall, my niece called in a panic to tell me her fourteen-year-old son had just declared himself an atheist and didn't want to be confirmed.[21] Let me be clear. I do not fault the boy's honesty. On the contrary, I admire his candor. He told the truth. My bet is that a good number of his confirmation classmates just went through the motions. At least he had the strength of his convictions, such as they were at age fourteen. As the sacrament that completes Christian initiation into the church, confirmation is supposed to be the beginning of a serious teenage pivot to an adult faith in Christ, the Holy Spirit, and the church. More often than we care to admit, it gets a wink and a nod, a rite of passage right out of the faith with parents and grandparents proudly looking.

No bishop or pastor scrutinizing what's going on here can fail to see the annual irony involved in anointing so much adolescent indifference to religion. Those kids who take confirmation seriously are themselves a pastoral windfall, and, in some places, thanks to great pastoral leadership and parental encouragement, they are growing. But the trend to religious indifference and nonbelief among young people is statistically overwhelming. The intergenerational transmission of religion in America—whether Catholic or Protestant or Jew or Muslim—is in serious trouble. Many teens who received confirmation will soon make church attendance a seasonal affair if they haven't done so already. The transition into collegiate agnosticism will seal the case for the implausibility of belief.

All I know is that my great-nephew never asked his uncle-priest-theologian-seminary president about God or Jesus Christ or the Holy Spirit or the meaning of anything remotely smacking of religion. Of course, I baptized him and gave him his First Holy Communion and remember the simple joy on his face when enchantment about faith's mysteries still had some purchase on his naïve imagination. One

---

[21] See Christian Smith with Melinda Lundquist Denton, *Soul Searching: The Religious and Spiritual Lives of American Teenagers* (New York: Oxford University Press, 2005). Smith uses the formula "moralistic therapeutic deism" (MTD) to describe the generic nonbiblical, nonliturgical, nondoctrinal all-purpose religion of American teens today. Smith's summary of MTD provides some of the sociological fuel for Ron Dreher's best-selling conservative manifesto, *The Benedict Option.*

Christmas when he was much younger, he was wearing blue pajamas and serving as my acolyte. I also know that whatever belief he harbored in his soul at ten did not buckle suddenly at fourteen under the weight of Nietzsche's arguments or those of Richard Dawkins, although I do not deny it could have. No. It was easy to leave. The difficult part of it was telling his parents and knowing it would upset them. Which, of course, it did, and knowing how things are at fourteen, he most probably relished the frisson of *schadenfreude* he got from doing it.

My niece responded to all of this as any mom whose uncle is a priest would. She insisted her son speak with me right away, which, in this case, would have required his father to chauffeur him three hundred miles for a pointless bit of emergency apologetics. What teenage atheist wants to face his priest uncle who once baptized him and gave him his First Holy Communion to say why he doesn't believe in God anymore? Why he thinks, although he would not put it like this, that my vocation is built on a big mistake about the nature of reality? What priest wants to treat his great-nephew as some juvenile religious delinquent? What's the point of emergency religion at all? It is not my great-nephew's disbelief but the social conditions that made it possible—one could say even inevitable—for him to check out of the church that I want to explain in this book.

Perhaps his parents could have done a better job of teaching him the rudiments of religion. It doesn't matter. They shouldn't blame themselves for their son's atheism. Nietzsche's father was a Lutheran minister, after all. Faith does not come in the genes or in driving kids to CCD. For a long time, kids have sensed that their parents were trying to believe, struggling with it for one reason or another, or more or less faking it so their children could be exposed to moral lessons in church. Some sociologists started calling this "vicarious religion"— mommy and daddy pretend to believe because believing is good and makes kids want better values, but no one takes it very seriously. Like reading poetry, religious discourse in a secular age is passing from the status of commonplace usage and recognition into the "deep freeze of academicism."[22] Even smart laypersons can't figure out what exegetes and theologians are up to.

[22] George Steiner, "Text and Context," in *On Difficulty and Other Essays* (New York: Oxford University Press, 1978), 9.

Discussions about faith and secularization were already taking place among intellectuals before my niece herself was born and baptized. She got married when Charles Taylor was preparing his Gifford Lectures on the secular age. As the bishops who approved the Pastoral Constitution on the Church in the Modern World (*Gaudium et Spes*) were packing their bags to leave Vatican City in 1965, the modern world was re-christened a "secular" world.

My great-nephew, at his age, hardly knows what life is about, much less the Christian faith. What he puts his trust in are equations, mathematics, all the means available to calculate and control material reality. He will learn eventually that much of human life depends on trust in some incalculable factors—deep love of a friend or spouse, a social cause worth giving one's life to even if the outcome is uncertain. The larger the bet anyone places on something or someone, the more it approaches religious trust.

Human trust and social faith are what allow us to place an "anticipatory confidence" in social institutions, government, the church, one's business partner or spouse. In marriage, even love is called fidelity (trust). Trust is what whole societies are built on.[23] My great-nephew who says he has no faith will discover places in his soul that can only be filled by faith. Christianity holds that faith is the first of the supernatural virtues for good reason. The greatest of the virtues, as St. Paul writes in 1 Corinthians 13, may be love. But without faith no one would undertake the commitment that real love requires. Eugen Rosenstock-Huessy put it well in words even a teenage atheist might understand: "He who believes in nothing still needs a girl to believe in him."[24] Cynics teach us nothing. No worldview of serious intent can do without belief. None can last long without exposure to critiques and challenges coming from other belief systems. To believe in linear progress, as many once did, is quite a stretch now, says Robert Heilbroner. To believe that the American model of the secular order must inevitably prevail in other cultures as it has here does not

---

[23] See Francis Fukuyama, *Trust: The Social Virtues and the Creation of Prosperity* (New York: The Free Press, 1996). The social contract is built on trust. We always ante up more in the game of life than we can possibly know in advance will work in our favor. Lying undercuts trust in all social institutions where people indulge in it, including business, politics, and religion.

[24] *Life Lines: Quotations from the Work of Eugen Rosenstock-Huessy*, ed. Clinton Gardner (Norwich, VT: Argo Books, 1988), 1.

seem likely, according to Samuel Huntington. Many others are now asking if society is on the cusp of a post-secular age which will demand greater humility in the search for truth. The age of ideologies and false absolutes of all kinds yields to Socratic cross-examination and prophetic irony.

## The New Evangelization for a Secular Age

So, these are some of the "signs of the times" in a secular age. What is the new evangelization, in case you're one of those who haven't heard of it? I will spend much of the first part of the book explaining it, so I won't go into that here. But, suffice to say that it stands for ecclesial renewal on steroids. The sudden rise of religious indifference coming on the heels of Vatican II is what drove it. One cause for such indifference was said to be secularism. Lots of books have been written on what the new evangelization is and how to do it. The Catholic religious book market is saturated with the new evangelization.[25] Amazon currently lists over four hundred titles on the new evangelization, covering every aspect of it from serious theological, biblical, liturgical, and homiletic explanations to popularizations slanted toward a culture war to off-the-shelf/turn-key programs backed up by catechetical series, and even videos on the beautiful art treasures of the Vatican. It's all geared to reigniting faith and religious observance in the church at a time when too many Catholics are either ignorant of their faith or barely interested in it. I recognize the problem such publications are trying to address. But, this book on the new evangelization is different.

---

[25] There are many excellent approaches available to rejuvenate religious practice in a struggling parish. Often dioceses will have selected a new evangelization approach based on the USCCB website for pastors. For another Catholic approach to evangelization, adapted from successful evangelical congregations, see Michael White and Tom Corcoran, *Rebuilt: The Story of a Catholic Parish; Awakening the Faithful, Reaching the Lost, Making Church Matter* (Notre Dame, IN: Ave Maria Press, 2013). The experience of the megachurches and free nondenominational congregations in reaching the unchurched and de-churched in modern American culture has important lessons for Catholic pastors. From a historical perspective, Protestantism fractured into multiple confessions, which became denominationalism in America and which Hans Joas now describes as a state of trans-confessionalism.

I intend to clarify both the development of the new evangelization and the philosophical-moral target much of the new evangelization is challenged to meet called the secular age. Frankly, I have not run across many treatments of the new evangelization that do much justice to the history and nature of the modern secular age.[26] In my view, a more deliberate historical account of how and why the new evangelization got underway in the first place and what we should make of such words as modernity, the modern moral order, the making of the modern identity, and the arrival of the secular age are needed.

The United States Conference of Catholic Bishops (USCCB) and its Committee on Catechesis and the New Evangelization continue to provide national leadership in communicating a vision and practical resources for diocesan and parish new evangelization efforts around the country.[27] Virtually every international ecclesial initiative since the end of Vatican II, and especially during the lengthy pontificate of Pope John Paul II, has been devoted to one or another aspect of the new evangelization. In 2010, Pope Benedict XVI established the Pontifical Council for the Promotion of the New Evangelization to coordinate new evangelization initiatives in the Catholic Church worldwide. That same pontifical council published a massive *Compendium on the New Evangelization* in preparation for the 2012 synod which contained every passage in pre-conciliar, conciliar, and post-conciliar papal teaching about this subject going back as far as Pope Pius XII. The Compendium is the major source for all the papal

[26] For a more thoughtful approach to secularization, based on Christian Smith and Charles Taylor, and the effects "moral therapeutic deism" have on a liturgical faith, see Timothy P. O'Malley, *Liturgy and the New Evangelization: Practicing the Art of Self-Giving Love* (Collegeville, MN: Liturgical Press, 2014), 35–50.

[27] See *Compendium on the New Evangelization: Texts of the Pontifical and Conciliar Magisterium 1939–2012* (Washington, DC: United States Conference of Catholic Bishops, 2014). The Compendium was prepared by the Pontifical Council for the Promotion of the New Evangelization in conjunction with the 2012 World Synod of Bishops on the New Evangelization for the Transmission of the Christian Faith. It covers all relevant papal and conciliar references to mission, evangelization, and new evangelization from Pope Pius XII to Pope Benedict XVI. It does not contain the writings of Pope Francis on the subject since it was initially assembled prior to his pontificate. The Compendium contains an introduction by Archbishop Rino Fisichella, president of the Pontifical Council for the Promotion of the New Evangelization, and a thorough index of themes.

documentation about the new evangelization during the last four pontificates. Its index reveals the breadth and depth of this concept. It references all the major themes in the movement, including the ones I am interested in here.

This book belongs in a special category of new evangelization literature. Its niche is not in piety or catechetics, but in the larger historical and philosophical narratives which are the contexts for them. Because a vague secularism was baked into the concept of the new evangelization from the beginning, anyone was free to define it as he or she wished. This book is at pains to examine it much more carefully as the default worldview of the average parishioner living in a modern situation. I intentionally bracket the moral issues religious people ordinarily associate with secularism. My concern is the horizon of values moderns take for granted. Secularism is one dimension of the secular age and the modern social imaginary. Let me briefly run through the chapters to follow.

In the beginning I set the table, so to speak, with a sketch of some of the problems and challenges the church faces today. My aim is only to sketch out in broad strokes how and why the new evangelization began, what the secular challenges were that provoked it, and why a new interpretation of the default secular condition of believers requires a new approach to homiletics. I then try to explain the background of religious indifference which is what impedes evangelization and undercuts one of its crucial concepts—missionary discipleship. In subsequent chapters I offer a retrospective about how the church first met the challenges of the modern world from the late eighteenth century through Vatican II and a possible way to reconstruct the new evangelization movement as a referendum on the council and the meaning of secularism with its moral byproducts. The final chapters of the book are the most difficult since they seek to explain complicated historical and sociological concepts which give us a better grasp on what modernity and secularity are all about. I pay particular attention here to the analysis of the modern identity and the secular age by the philosopher Charles Taylor. At the end of the book, I explain what Pope Francis has written in his interpretation of the new evangelization, The Joy of the Gospel. After offering remarks on each of its five chapters, I take up the thematic core of the pope's treatment of evangelization in the word "joy." What at first appears to be no more than a superficial spiritual enthusiasm in the word "joy," in fact opens reflection on the Platonic concept of *thymos*, which passes through psychiatry as hyperthymic feelings of human exuberance to biblical and theological correlatives to philosophical claims about the roots of joy in the very ontology of the human person. In short, I attempt in the final part of the last chapter to offer a deeper explanation of the evangelical significance of joy than the word itself might suggest. *Thymos* refers to the psychic reservoir in human persons which powers indignation at injustices, defensive intervention on behalf of victims, and courage in the face of danger. It is the source in human nature that the message of the Gospel first transforms and then directs toward the values of the kingdom of God.

In the book's conclusion, I offer some personal reflections on Christian spirituality understood as a religious inflection of thymotic desire. Then, I turn to the issue of religious freedom which demands philosophical distinctions about the treatment and practices of religion in a secular state. Given the moral and religious diversity in secular culture today, the issues of rights, respect, and recognition have become the paramount moral language for human identity. For that reason, I follow up my earlier comments on the concept of *thymos* which Francis Fukuyama introduced in *The End of History and the Last Man* with his more recent reflections on it in his latest work, *Identity: The Demand for Dignity and the Politics of Resentment*. The final pages of the book return to the pastoral challenges priests face pastoring their sheep in the secular age.

Preaching the new evangelization to laypersons, who desire to live faithfully in a secular age, should require that priests fulfill what *Gaudium et Spes* 4 requires of them. Namely, first to read the "signs of the times" as carefully and thoroughly as possible. I hope what I offer in the book about modernity and secularity helps them do that more responsibly. Second, evangelization also demands of Catholics a faithful reading and translation of the revealed Word of God in Scripture and tradition. If the truth alone makes us free, as Jesus says in the Gospel of John, then the truth about ourselves as believers living in a secular age is one truth we cannot afford to overlook.

# Chapter 1

# The Nature of Our Problems

Why do teens quit attending church? Why do some declare themselves atheists out of the blue, or just fake being religious at confirmation and communion for the sake of their parents? Parishioners rightly turn to priests for answers. When parishioners ask me about these issues, they usually begin by telling me their children attended Catholic schools, had religious instruction, received all the sacraments, and were even once active in the faith. They are proud that their adult children have turned out to be loving parents, hardworking and often successful individuals. As a mitigating circumstance for missing Mass, they admit life is too busy now for families with two working parents or a single parent raising kids. I wait for them to tell me soccer schedules make church attendance hard in springtime. That's how weak the attachment to religious observance has become for ordinary, good Catholics.

In response to their question about lapsed practice, I attempt to put it in context. I want to say "secularization," as I will explain it in the book, but I don't, because they would mistake what I mean for a moral indictment. What I tell them is that religious practice is down across the board in America. In comparison with some Protestant churches, many Catholic parishes are doing rather well, soccer notwithstanding. Free evangelical churches in some places seem to be prospering. But, when all the figures are totaled on American religious practice, the only cohort standing with a significant increase in percentages in recent years is the cohort marking the choice in the census about religious affiliation, "No Religious Affiliation." Sociologists label these folks the "Nones." Presently, Nones count for almost a quarter of the U.S. population.[1] They are heterogeneous. A very small percentage of Nones are outright atheists. Some Nones are agnostics or secularists. Other Nones fall into the diffuse category of spiritual seekers and searchers who have not yet landed on a religious or non-religious choice. They are keeping their options open. While America remains predominantly Christian, with the largest percentage of religiously affiliated being Roman Catholic (which does not mean they go to church at all), the country is becoming both religiously and irreligiously more pluralistic than ever. Will Herberg's classic from the 1950s, *Catholic, Protestant, Jew,* is hopelessly out of date.

The point I want to stress is that secularization is a two-way turnstile. It may take some out of religious faith only to release them to explore a tolerant agnosticism, to shop for something that feels religious in some vague sense without necessarily needing a god, a church, or a particular dogma. If we factor into this native religious pluralism, the new immigrants from Latin America, Africa, the Middle East, and the Far East, many large American cities are a thriving metropolis of religious beliefs. America remains what it has been for two hundred years—a liberal democratic experiment in religious freedom characterized by diverse ethnicities, beliefs, and moral sensibilities. Today that freedom also means the freedom *not to believe.* And, many enthusiastic nonbelievers are not as shy about their secular nonbelief as Catholics—devout or indifferent—are about the faith that is in them. And, if Catholics only believe what seculars already believe, then what is the point of their religious practice at all?

The fact is that all belief now is somehow optional belief. The non-religious option has been gaining more ground with some Nones, but attachment to religion in America is still in our cultural DNA. The European path into non-religious secularism, unlike the optional belief cherished in America, is different. It is called *laïcisme* in France.

---

[1] See Robert D. Putnam and David E. Campbell, with the assistance of Shaylyn Romney Garrett, *American Grace: How Religion Divides and Unites Us* (New York: Simon and Shuster, 2010). The authors hold that American Christianity went through one "shock" and two "after-shocks" since the 1960s, largely over sexuality and politics. Religious identification shifted from strict doctrine to new cultural markers of identity such as ethnicity, gender, and political affiliation.

American secularism is unlike the European version. Hans Joas claims that for a secular age like ours, all faith is effectively "optional."[2] And, paradoxical as it seems, an optional religious faith, partly engendered by the Reformation and fostered by the secular age, whatever problems it holds for Catholic theology, has more going for it in psychological, social, and political terms than any conceivable version of enforced belief.

Even when Catholics you know stop attending the parish, you can bet some have joined another parish or possibly an evangelical megachurch. If some simply opt out of organized religion, they may have embraced transcendental meditation in a search for a higher mindfulness. A few have joined a fitness club of earnest fellow seekers for "the best body you ever had." In the secular age, all that feels vaguely spiritual if not traditionally religious. Secular seekers may not be seeking Jesus, but many are seeking more from life than money and a new car. Disappointment with your standard run-of-the-mill parish Catholicism may lead some Catholic seekers to a monastery and contemplative prayer. The 2017 Man Booker Prize winner George Saunders (*Lincoln in the Bardo*) was raised Catholic but is now a practicing Buddhist. Read his 2013 commencement address at Syracuse University on compassion. He and Pope Francis are on the same page. If you want more spirituality in your life, and you don't like how your own church is doing it, in America people are free to look elsewhere for something religious or do it themselves.

The pastoral entrepreneur can open a storefront church in Baltimore, Maryland, or build a mega-congregation in the county. In the land of opportunity, religion is another business. In France, that doesn't happen. Here, a "techy" money manager with a knack for talking and organization can build her own congregation. Certification by a seminary is okay, but that's optional too. You can buy an "officiant" who got ordained online for your wedding. The French, as it turns out, have a great word for such types—a *bricoleur*. In religion, a *bricoleur* is someone who cobbles together a church using the pastoral and liturgical spare parts of other churches. No bishop or judicatory heads get in the way. One can pick and choose all the accoutrements. Christianity, oddly enough, did something like that when the early church borrowed the Hebrew Scriptures as a preface

---

[2] Hans Joas, *Faith as an Option* (Stanford, CA: Stanford University Press, 2014).

to its own New Testament and retooled a Passover service for its own worship. Later, in the Roman imperial context, the birth of Jesus as the Son of God was celebrated on the pagan festival of the sun god, Sol Invictus—December 25.[3] Christianity itself is a *bricoleur*. Joseph Smith started Mormonism cobbling pieces of the Old Testament and the New Testament together in the Book of Mormon.

The zip codes of the contemporary urban/suburban parish life are more ecumenical, interreligious, and secular/non-religious than ever before. Upscale supermarkets today shelve the spices and cuisines of New Delhi, Tokyo, Tuscany, and Mexico City. The religious market is much the same. Secularization, in that sense, doesn't finish off religion, as some have supposed or wished; it pluralizes and metastasizes it in multiple ways. Those who blame the lack of religious practice among Catholics today solely on catechetical misadventures in the 1970s are not entirely wrong, but they always miss the larger point.

## The New Evangelization: A Brief History

I will get into more of this in later chapters, but to start I want to offer a brief overview of the new evangelization. The immediate aftermath of Vatican II in America was marked, as older priests know, by many changes that upended the settled symbolic structures in "Baltimore Catechism Catholicism." Introducing the vernacular into a Latinized liturgy was always culturally risky. Upsetting settled customs in life or rituals does not go down easy. Today English is the custom for Mass and few think twice about it. The sixteen documents of Vatican II included farseeing if still immature trajectories for church life and ministry. Harmonizing the old church with the new trajectories, putting new wine in old wineskins, is not a magic trick; it takes a long time and some wineskins will burst.

It fell to an inveterate worrier, Paul VI, to implement the Vatican reforms while maintaining the ecclesial equilibrium they threatened

---

[3] Rémi Brague argues that the condemnation of the Marcionite heresy in the second century was a decisive hermeneutical event in early Christianity. By rejecting Marcion's claim that the Hebrew Scriptures were not divine revelation, the church put itself in a secondary position with reference to Judaism. See Rémi Brague, *Eccentric Culture: A Theory of Western Civilization*, trans. Samuel Lester (South Bend, IN: St. Augustine Press, 2002), 57ff.

to throw out of balance. He soon found himself under siege by his own rebellious and outspoken flock in public dissent from the magisterium over birth control. He was lobbied by the Traditionalists who exploited his misgivings. In addition to the changes introduced into church life by Vatican II, there was unprecedented moral and cultural ferment. The falcon could not hear the falconer.

It was in this unstable world that Paul VI called and then presided over a world synod of bishops on evangelization for the express purpose of calming the storm and orienting attention away from ecclesiastical changes and toward evangelization. "On Evangelization in the Modern World" (*Evangelii Nuntiandi*), the relatively brief and schematic apostolic exhortation Pope Paul wrote based on that 1974 synod, was also the first universal mention by a pope of the phenomenon of secularism as a challenge in the post-conciliar period. In speeches Pope Paul delivered at the end of Vatican II and afterward he mentioned the challenge of secularism.

The technical formula, a "new evangelization" (*nueva evangelización*) did not come from the Holy See or from a pope but from a meeting of the Latin American Bishops Conference (CELAM) at Puebla, Mexico. With this formula, Puebla attempted to summarize the array of responses necessary to meet the challenges of the churches across all cultures in the southern hemisphere of the Americas. Latin American Catholicism, need I say, extends nine thousand miles from the border of the United States and Mexico to Tierra del Fuego at the southern tip of Argentina. It is still the largest bloc of Roman Catholics in the world whose *first* evangelization came in the fifteenth and sixteenth centuries by Spanish and Portuguese missionaries conveyed to Indian colonies by armadas and explorers in search of wealth and property. Widespread poverty, economic globalization, bishops too indentured to the upper classes, syncretistic religious cults mixed with Catholic rituals, and exported North American Pentecostal fundamentalism were just a few of the factors that led the church's pastors south of the border to call for this *new evangelization*.

It was John Paul II, however, who decided to turn this Latin American initiative into a motto for his own global apostolate. He invoked it first at the beginning of his pontificate in Poland (1979) and, a few years later, stressed it again on his apostolic visit to Port-au-Prince, Haiti (1983), where he spoke to the Latin American bishops themselves. Over and over, this extraordinary pope would refer to the new evangelization as the overarching ambition of the post-conciliar church. It became the preeminent inspiration for the broad cultural transformation he worked and prayed would happen at the end of the second millennium. John Paul II aligned himself closely with the dominant themes of the human person and modern culture in the Pastoral Constitution on the Church in the Modern World (*Gaudium et Spes*). The human person was his transcultural anthropological reference point in moral teaching. As a council participant, the former Cardinal Karol Wojtyla felt so strongly about the issues involved that he had submitted an alternative schema for *Gaudium et Spes*. Later, with Cardinal Joseph Ratzinger's help, John Paul II developed a syllabus of concepts for the new evangelization in his many speeches, addresses, and encyclicals in which secularism and other ideologies of the modern order played a prominent role. He put a juridical and catechetical stamp on the new evangelization in the *New Code of Canon Law* (1983) and in the encyclopedic *Catechism of the Catholic Church* (1994). By the turn of the millennium, the seventy-nine-year-old pontiff had produced a substantial magisterial library on the new evangelization in which the critique of secularized culture played a major part. U.S. bishops, especially the late Cardinal Francis George of Chicago, echoed the pope's concerns by making secularism in America a primary moral target of the new evangelization. Moral righteousness, however, was in for a shock.

When American Airlines Flight 11 struck the north tower of the World Trade Center at 8:45 on the morning of September 11, 2001, and eighteen minutes later United Flight 175 flew into the south tower, the rhetoric against secularism started to come apart. The final words on the hijacked jets carrying religious and secular passengers to their deaths were a Muslim religious acclamation, *Allah 'Akbar* (God is great). What exactly motivated those Islamic fundamentalists to do that? And, what made them hate secular America so much? Roger Scruton's opinion will surprise you:

> When Mohamed Atta flew American Airlines Flight 11 into the north tower of the World Trade Center on 11 September 2001 he was certainly expressing his resentment towards everything symbolized by that building: the triumph of secular materialism, the success and prosperity of America, the tyranny of high finance and the hubris of the modern city. But he was also expressing a grudge against architectural modernism, which he had already voiced in his Master's dissertation

for the university of Hamburg architecture school. The theme of that dissertation was the old city of Aleppo, damaged by Syrian President Hafez al-Assad in his merciless war of extermination against the Muslim Brotherhood, but damaged far more by the jerry-built skyscrapers that cancel the lines of the ancient streets, and rise high above the slim imploring fingers of the mosques. This junkyard modernism was, for Atta, a symbol of the impiety of the modern world, and of its brutal disregard for the Muslim city.[4]

The secular world, in the eyes of those religious terrorists, went beyond its moral faults. The secular order, for Atta and his fellow terrorists, made religion free and diminished it at the same time. When St. Patrick's Cathedral was built in 1815, its tower served in that context as a neo-Gothic symbol of the power of religious transcendence in Manhattan. Now the great cathedral is lost in a forest of steel and glass skyscrapers devoid of religious reference. An American Catholic tourist praying in the great church cannot comprehend Mohammed Atta's resentments. Osama Bin Laden weaponized one sect in Islam against the whole secular order of life.

The various ideologies criticized in the encyclicals of John Paul II, like materialism, consumerism, utilitarianism, scientism, and relativism, were working well in Manhattan. The *–ism* suffix tacked on to the secular carried little denotative value for most average Catholics. If they had known European religious history, they would have objected that the secular order came into existence in seventeenth-century Holland and England precisely to prevent what happened on 9/11—religiously motivated violence. The critique of the secular bandied about in sermons was shallow and moralistic. A more substantial account of its genesis was needed.

A second shock to anti-secular rhetoric in conservative Christianity, and for the church a far more serious one, came in January 2002. It was then that the *Boston Globe*'s "Spotlight" journalists began publishing stories (eventually six hundred articles) about the cardinal-archbishop of Boston having covered up the sexual abuse of children by Catholic priests. Catholic righteousness was forced to confront its own hypocrisies. Worse, the secular press discovered and reported on it. Secular

---

[4] Roger Scruton, *The Use of Pessimism* (New York: Oxford University Press, 2010), 144.

public institutions—the police and the courts—held the church accountable for crimes that bishops covered up. For twenty years prior to Boston, Catholic bishops and pastors had railed against the moral crimes of secularism and secular humanism. Now, it took secular institutions to bring Catholic bishops to justice, to defend the children bishops had sacrificed to preserve a false image. It was not long before stories of sexual abuse of minors and cover-ups in other countries came to light.

All of this came at the end of the second-longest pontificate in church history when John Paul II was disabled by Parkinson's disease. The church seemed at once shocked and paralyzed by all this. Responses adequate to the seriousness of the crimes were not forthcoming from the Vatican. The U.S. bishops, to their credit, attempted to respond in terms a secular society would understand—an independent extra-ecclesial investigation. As prefect of the Congregation for the Doctrine of the Faith, Cardinal Ratzinger had a role in handling clergy abuse cases in the United States for the Holy See. Without shortchanging his concerns about secular relativism, Ratzinger began to qualify the polarization between religion and the secular some of his statements could be taken to foment. He admitted to real pathologies in religion that needed the critique of reason. After his election as pope in 2005, Benedict XVI directed the Pontifical Council for Culture to open a new dialogue with the secular world. He published an apostolic exhortation on divine revelation in which he asserted that there were some "dark passages" in the Scriptures with no moral or religious relevance for us today. No fundamentalist could possibly admit anything like that. The pope was proposing a dialogical dimension of the new evangelization that would include the secular intelligentsia, the referees of public values in the secular order. Mere denunciation was never enough.

Benedict XVI went further. Prior to the 2012 synod of the new evangelization, he delivered a video message on March 25, 2011, from the Vatican to the forecourt of the Cathedral de Notre-Dame in Paris.[5] The gathering was part of a "Courtyard of the Gentiles" dialogue he had encouraged two years earlier. At Notre-Dame, Christians and secular nonbelievers came together in the city of the French *philosophes*

---

[5] Speech of Benedict XVI to the Courtyard of the Gentiles in Paris, March 25, 2011.

and the *lumières* in an atmosphere of openness and respect. The event was sponsored by the Vatican's Pontifical Council for Culture with the pope's blessing. In his brief video message, Benedict made six points that are important not only for the case I'm making here but for ordinary parish catechesis in the new evangelization as it relates to secularism. Some of those same mentalities represented at the 2011 Notre-Dame event are making intelligent parishioners wince at naïve attacks from the pulpit on the secular order. Pope Benedict underlined the following six points in his address:

1. There is an urgent need for a new encounter between believers and nonbelievers to make the whole world more free, just, peaceful, and happy than it is.

2. Everyone has a responsibility to build bridges between people of differing beliefs and convictions.

3. Reason in service to humanity must not be warped by narrow economic interests.

4. Religion cannot fear a secular outlook that is open, just, and respects consciences.

5. Fraternity is possible between people of opposing convictions without denying differences.

6. The symbol of a great Catholic cathedral that is still open at the center of the French Enlightenment in Paris is remarkable.

Think of this cathedral, the pope suggested, as a house of prayer where some address God by name and others sit in silence before an absent and nameless divinity. Whether we consider God to be a credible presence or an incredible intrusion on our humanity, the name cannot be banished from human discourse. The "Courtyard of the Gentiles" is a place within the schema of the new evangelization in a secular age. Parishes and dioceses should take up Benedict's challenges, now more than ever. The philosophical grounds for a new dialogue of faith and secular humanism had already been presented in the 1999 Gifford Lectures by Charles Taylor thoroughly worked out in *A Secular Age*. Many consider this book the most important philosophical work on religion and secularism in the past forty years.

In what would become the final major event of his seven-year pontificate, Benedict XVI presided over the Thirteenth General Assembly of the World Synod of Bishops on the New Evangelization for the Transmission of the Christian Faith (October 7–28, 2012). A few months later, the eighty-year-old pontiff resigned the office of the papacy. Writing an apostolic exhortation on the synod was left to his successor who took the name of Francis. As the former Cardinal Jorge Bergoglio of Buenos Aires, Argentina—this Jesuit pastor came from the culture where the *nueva evangelización* was first coined, largely in response to political and economic challenges in Latino societies and the failures of the hierarchy there to address them.

Francis's apostolic exhortation on the synod would alter evangelization rhetoric in one significant way. Even more than his predecessors, he would situate the secular challenges to the Gospel against the backdrop of the failures of individual Christians themselves and the resistance to necessary reform in the Vatican Curia. Coming in the aftermath of both the clergy abuse scandals and the disclosure of financial improprieties at the Vatican, the reform of some pastoral structures in the church became a major plank in the new evangelization for the pope. Some of his critics began to charge Francis with jeopardizing the dogmatic achievements of the previous two pontificates. Others claimed to detect the odor of Latino liberation theology in the pages of The Joy of the Gospel that deal with global capitalism's effects on the poor. One must give them this much. The pope's second encyclical, which dealt with our care for the environment of the natural world, *Laudato Si'*, will not boost oil stocks. Finally, a handful of the pope's more extreme critics took him to task for a footnote (no. 351) in the apostolic exhortation he wrote based on the world synod on marriage and the family, *Amoris Laetitia*. The footnote concerned the pastoral possibility of admitting divorced and remarried Catholics to reception of the Eucharist.[6]

In 2015, faith and secularism were again joined in another Courtyard of the Gentiles event (*Cortile dei gentili*) held in Rome. Captioned

---

[6] See Ross Douthat, *To Change the Church: Pope Francis and the Future of Catholicism* (New York: Simon & Shuster, 2018). Douthat is a *New York Times* conservative columnist and convert to Catholicism who argues that footnote 351 in *Amoris Laetitia* introduces an ambiguity that constitutes a breach in the church's teaching on the indissolubility of marriage, which has its foundation in the clear teaching of Jesus on divorce.

"The Piazza and the Temple—A Dialogue with Charles Taylor," Taylor delivered the keynote address. The meeting was sponsored by the Pontifical Council for Culture under the presidency of Cardinal Gianfranco Ravasi.[7] Concurrently, the Gregorian University held a conference about faith and secularism that featured Taylor in dialogue with philosophers and theologians from around the world.[8] The few pages on secularism in The Joy of the Gospel call for a historical and philosophical context to make sense of them. Charles Taylor has written a compelling and comprehensive narrative for it in *A Secular Age*.

## Stages in the New Evangelization: A Synopsis

I will go into the development of the new evangelization concept in a later chapter, but let me present a convenient outline of key stages in its evolution, starting with Vatican II and ending with The Joy of the Gospel. In broad strokes, let me briefly summarize the major stages along the way when the church took up the challenge of secularism in the context of the new evangelization.

*The Second Vatican Council did not use the word "secularism" in describing the modern world, but many of the cultural and moral issues treated in Gaudium et Spes relate to it.*

Vatican II offered a precise and extraordinarily sympathetic interpretation of modern atheism in the Pastoral Constitution on the Church in the Modern World (1965). It distinguished different types of atheism with the various motives inclining individuals to abandon belief in God. Words like "evangelization," "new evangelization,"

---

[7] See www.cultura.va. "The Piazza and the Temple—A Dialogue with Charles Taylor," March 6, 2015. See Charles Taylor, *A Secular Age* (Cambridge, MA: Harvard University Press, 2007). A helpful introduction to Taylor's book can be found in James K. A. Smith, *How (Not) to Be Secular: Reading Charles Taylor* (Grand Rapids, MI: Eerdmans, 2014). For a comprehensive background on Taylor's philosophical thought, see Ruth Abbey, *Charles Taylor* (Princeton, NJ: Princeton University Press, 2000) and *Charles Taylor*, ed. Ruth Abbey (Cambridge: Cambridge University Press, 2004), which includes an essay by William E. Connolly, "Catholicism and Philosophy: A Nontheistic Appreciation," 166–86.

[8] See *Renewing the Church in a Secular Age: Holistic Dialogue and Kenotic Vision*, ed. Charles Taylor, José Casanova, George F. McLean, and Joao J. Vila-Cha (Washington, DC: The Council for Research in Values and Philosophy, 2016).

and "secularism" were not yet in vogue in the 1960s. Some commentators still think the council misread modernity and underestimated its challenges for religious faith. *Gaudium et Spes* proposed a more pastoral and socially compelling vision of the human person as the basis for the church's philosophical and ethical positions. It installed a scripturally based philosophical anthropology of human beings as images of God, *imago dei*, at the center of theological ethics. Linking this to the rise of human rights and natural law theory remains a continuing task.

*Pope Paul VI in 1975 was the first to call for "evangelization" as a continuing renewal of the church's mission in the modern world, begun at Vatican II, and to focus that effort on the effects of secularism.*

The Second Vatican Council made "dialogue" a part of ecclesial mission in the modern world. By 1975, the accent shifted noticeably from dialogue to proclamation. Paul VI presided over a World Synod of Bishops on Evangelization in 1974 and the following year published "On Proclaiming the Gospel" (*Evangelii Nuntiandi*). In that seminal text for evangelization, the pope clarified its meaning, modernized for the perennial mission of the church and outfitted to modern mentalities. A major modern challenge facing belief and religious practice was identified as secularism. Beyond characterizing it as a militant form of atheism, the pope did not analyze the phenomenon in detail.

*The church's explicit summons to a new evangelization was announced in Latin America in 1979 with the Puebla Document of CELAM.*

The Latin American Bishops Conference (CELAM) was the first ecclesial assembly to call for a *nueva evangelización*—a "new evangelization." This was at CELAM's plenary meeting in 1979 in Puebla, Mexico. The issue of secularism in the European and American sense was less an issue for CELAM than syncretistic cults, fundamentalism, economics, and some episcopal distance from the masses. On the visit of John Paul II to Haiti in 1983, he quoted Puebla and again called for a new evangelization in celebration of the five hundredth anniversary of the first evangelization of the Caribbean in the fifteenth and sixteenth centuries. The pope envisioned it as a new ardor for living the faith and spreading it, as the use of new media for communicating it, and in the form of new expressions capable of conveying again the perennial vitality of the Christian message.

*The 1985 extraordinary synod in celebration of Vatican II was a subtle turning point in the Catholic Church's assessment of modernity.*

The Extraordinary Synod of Bishops in 1985 called by the pope to celebrate and interpret the significance of the Second Vatican Council was a significant turning point in the church's interpretation of modernity and the council. The growing moral dissent in Catholicism, the rise of Marxist forms of liberation theology, religious persecution in the Soviet Union, and religious indifference in secular societies added up, in the minds of synod fathers, to a unique post-conciliar challenge for proclaiming the Gospel. The goal of the synod was to unify Catholicism by stabilizing the conflict of interpretations over the meaning of Vatican II. Secularism was explicitly singled out in the synod's final report as a mentality inimical to faith. By 1993, when John Paul II promulgated I Will Give You Shepherds (*Pastores Dabo Vobis*) on the formation and continuing formation of priests, a more explicit countercultural view of secular modernity and the new evangelization was in play.

*The United States Conference of Catholic Bishops in the late 1980s chose the new evangelization as one of its top pastoral priorities.*

The first attempt by the United States bishops to translate the new evangelization for North America was done in the wake of the extraordinary synod's dark reassessment of modernity. The bishops understood the pastoral symptoms of modernity's erosion of religious vitality—decline in vocations, less frequent church attendance, and financial deficits. The moral issues associated with secularized societies like abortion became the focal point in the catechetical invigoration of pastoral life. The success of evangelical Protestantism led Catholic leaders to consider a corresponding "evangelical moment" in Catholic reform.

*Papal encyclicals between 1980 and 2012 clarified the cultural, moral, and theological challenges for faith associated with secularism. In 2010 Benedict XVI published an apostolic exhortation on divine revelation, The Word of God in the Life and Mission of the Church (Verbum Domini), which was a theological prelude to an encyclical he began drafting on faith.*

Many of the fourteen encyclicals of John Paul II called attention to the erosion of the moral underpinnings for Catholic doctrines about society, moral truth, the inviolability of human life, and just economics. That erosion was attributed to ideologies associated with a secular outlook on the world. The general impression, if one didn't reflect on the necessary emergence of a secular political order in European history, was to reduce the secular world to an overarching moral heresy with little redeeming value in it. In writing about the Word of God, Benedict XVI explicitly rejected what he called a "secularized hermeneutic" in biblical criticism which seemed to replace theological reflection with mere historical notes on an ancient religion.

*Benedict XVI formally established the Pontifical Council for the Promotion of the New Evangelization in 2010. He simultaneously encouraged the Pontifical Council for Culture to undertake a program of dialogue with the elite creators of culture, with secular humanists, and with atheists under the title "Courtyard of the Gentiles."*

By 2010, the theme of the new evangelization had matured beyond a slogan as bishops' conferences sought to implement programs carrying out its three main objectives—ardor, media, and expression. A Christocentric emphasis now took the place of the ecclesial reform preoccupations that had divided post-conciliar Catholicism. The primary goal of evangelization was that believers have a personal knowledge and encounter with the person of Jesus Christ as the only way to understand the doctrines and sacraments of the church. Meanwhile, the clergy sexual abuse crisis focused the secular world's attention on the responsible exercise of ecclesiastical authority in Catholicism, forcing the issue of ecclesial reform back onto the church's agenda. Benedict XVI established a new curial council—the Pontifical Council for the Promotion of the New Evangelization—to advance a better understanding of the church's evangelizing mission. A parallel initiative was soon under way in the Pontifical Council for Culture in spearheading dialogue with elite secular intelligentsia who had all but abandoned Christian faith and the practice of religion.

*Pope Benedict XVI presided over the Thirteenth Ordinary General Assembly of the Synod of Bishops on the theme of "The New Evangelization for the Transmission of the Christian Faith," October 7–28, 2012. In 2013, Pope Francis published his apostolic exhortation on the synod, entitled The Joy of the Gospel (Evangelii Gaudium).*

The election of a Latin American cardinal from Buenos Aries, Argentina, as pope in 2013 significantly altered the world's impression of Catholicism as an exclusively European form of Christianity. Pope Francis came from the hemisphere where the very idea of a *nueva evangelización* was first considered and undertaken. In the aftermath of clergy sexual abuse, the critique of secularism by the church began to feel hypocritical and hollow. Secular courts were bankrupting dioceses for tolerating the abuse of children by priests. Pope Francis lost no time in associating the Chair of Peter with a humane joy, divine mercy, and ecclesial reform. Later I will explain how "evangelical joy" can be more richly appreciated using the Homeric and Platonic image of *thymos* ("spiritedness" and "recognition") which has been retrieved in different contexts by Paul Ricoeur and Francis Fukuyama.[9] There is joy in being a missionary disciple because spirited agency is transformative and there is joy in mutual recognition that transcends human differences and becomes the basis for love. The pope has also highlighted mercy, just as John Paul II did, but Francis's approach has been reinforced theologically by the work of the German theologian Cardinal Walter Kasper.[10]

These are the major stages along the way through 2018. As further reforms are recommended to the pope by the Council of Cardinals (C9) to update those made in *Pastor Bonus* over twenty years ago, we can expect further clarifications of internal ecclesial structures in service to the new evangelization.

## Speaking Intelligently of the Secular Situation: Essential Concepts

In the following chapter, I will list the six pastoral crises affecting Catholicism in America. To provide a context for it, let me introduce here some of the concepts I will be building into the book's argument in chapters 6–8. What follows is a practical synopsis of the secular as related to the religious, including the ways it has come to be used,

---

[9] Paul Ricoeur, *Fallible Man*, trans. Charles A. Kelbley (Chicago: Henry Regnery Company, 1965), 161–202 on *thymos* as "Having, Power, Worth." Ricoeur finds in Plato's idea of *thymos* the ontological instability that gives rise to human fallibility. Also, Francis Fukuyama, *The End of History and the Last Man* (New York: The Free Press, 1992), "The Rise and Fall of *Thymos*," 181–91. Fukuyama argues for the importance of thymotic recognition in democratic liberal capitalism.

[10] Walter Kasper, *Mercy: The Essence of the Gospel and the Key to the Christian Life*, trans. William Madges (New York: Paulist Press, 2013).

often not without considerable misunderstanding, in the new evangelization. I will group my observations under three broad headings: the European Enlightenment and its effects on religious faith, the understanding of the differentiations and separations secularity introduced into civilized culture in the West, the problematic of the religious imagination in a technical age.

## The European and American Enlightenment

The eighteenth-century European Enlightenment is so important for the subject I am pursuing that without some understanding of its origins and effects it is virtually impossible to appreciate the challenges facing evangelization. Scaled down to its basic epistemic dimensions, the Enlightenment, as the elite understand it, withdrew human trust from the domain of religious interpretations and placed it entirely in the arms of the goddess reason. One of her arms was modern science; the other was the politics of limited government and human rights. Enlightenment thinking was expressed differently in the three different societies that embraced it first—France, Britain, and America.[11] All of them, however, shared this one basic conviction learned from the Treaty of Westphalia in 1648—a diverse society would require that all religious belief be subordinated to widely shared general principles of scientific and practical reason. Put in theological terms, reason and freedom, not revelation and religious authority, would guide public life.

Americans often misunderstand this radical shift in human sensibility. The reason is that they associate Puritan Christianity with the religious foundation of American political culture and not the real foundation in the separations crucial to a secular order: the separation of powers in government and the separation of the state from the church. Puritan divines were not the nation's founding fathers, but enlightened latitudinarian deists, like Jefferson and Franklin, were. These wise political visionaries, whatever their exegetical and theological limitations, put their political trust in constitutional law and

---

[11] Gertrude Himmelfarb, *The Roads to Modernity: The British, French, and American Enlightenments* (New York: Knopf, 2004). This approach demonstrates why the American approach to religious faith in a secular context is so different from the European versions of secularism, which have been the target of much of the church's critique.

rights. Ben Franklin's "kite" symbolized the Enlightenment's fascination with technical reason's capacity to generate progress to improve human physical and social conditions. Legislation and practical engineering replaced what such minds regarded as the pointless speculative arguments of religion, which inflamed dangerous passions in people. A constitutional republic without an established church would make freedom of all kinds, even the religious kind, possible with a state sheltered by a benevolent deity of your choosing.

### Religion without the State, Faith without a Sacred Canopy

The separation of powers in government (legislative, judiciary, and executive) and the disestablishment clause in the Constitution deprived Christianity of authoritative buttressing by the state. It would have to sail now on its own but sail freely without governmental indoctrination or interference. The image of a "sacred canopy" comes from the sociologist Peter Berger's discussion of secularization. The sacred had been the umbrella of transcendent religious meaning protecting human beings from the absurd in all its forms: the haphazard and inexplicable reality of evil, even when explained by causes that never fully explain it, from the magnitude of human suffering—especially of the innocent and martyrs—and, most of all, from death itself and nihilism. Once was when most people believed that Christian faith provided ready-made symbols for sheltering the soul from the absurd in truths like the will of God, grace, providence, and the afterlife. But historical sufferings on the scale we have known in the twentieth century defy explanations once based on the logic of theodicy. Indeed, the Holocaust and other modern genocides make the very attempt at theodicy seem a blasphemy itself. The secular world, according to Albert Camus, has replaced the Christian doctrine of God's grace and forgiveness with rights and laws that mete out justice. Justice is the best we can hope for in the absence of the sacred canopy and a transcendent court of appeal. If there is a religious language best suited to the scale of modern suffering, it is the ancient language of lamentation.

*The immanent frame and the transcendent frame.* This pair of terms is used by the philosopher Charles Taylor to structure a possible dialogue of worldviews between religion and secular humanism. It prevents participants from falling into convenient semantic traps set by each, on their own terms, for the other. An immanent framing of human worldly experience is possible, and today more plausible perhaps, for people despite whatever price in consolation they feel they must pay for taking down a sacred canopy. But make no mistake—experience does not frame itself as if its meaning could be directly deduced from facts. Meaning is "read into" things and persons precisely because people care about those things and persons, not because the things and persons themselves carry some objective patina of value anyone in his right mind can see. This is the illusion of scientific naturalism, which pervades our culture. Who would need advertising if the value of goods simply spoke for themselves? Meaning is not made up from whole cloth, but rather shaped through language, symbols, and images which convey more than what the naked eye can see. The transcendent framing of human experience inclines toward a sacramental interpretation of human life. Placing experience in a transcendent frame is not necessarily importing a mythical structure of interpretation on ordinary life. Only the rhetoric of religious interpretation and witness can convey and can serve as criterion for the plausibility of the transcendent frame. It is a framing of experience like all framings—secular-naturalistic, Marxist or capitalist, Buddhist or Muslim. Stigmatizing faith as an irrational imposition of an imaginary (unreal) frame on human experience is the jack-of-all-trades for default secularity. But every framing is a symbolic structure, in its political and economic expression often called an ideology, that serves to mobilize the social imaginary. The immanent and transcendent do not express two separate and entirely independent realms of experience, according to Taylor, as they do different interpretations of the one world we all share—two different horizons of meaning, two ways of interpreting the moral values of things, persons, and events.

*The sacred and the profane.* These classical terms serve to separate what deserves absolute respect from what does not. The purity laws in the book of Leviticus clearly demarcate those things considered to be sacred—that is, kept apart and preserved from ritual contamination—from the profane in Jewish life. In that worldview, certain physical acts and contacts, regardless of personal intention or inherent moral quality, render a person ritually unclean. Keeping kosher, removing one's shoes at the entrance to a mosque, keeping silence in the presence of the holy, blessing oneself with holy water, and bowing each symbolize in different ways the boundaries of the sacred-profane demarcation. The brilliant sociologist Erving Goffman applied the same binary terms to everyday actions considered to be defiling in some contexts (not removing one's hat in the presence of the queen, body odor in close contact, etc.). Some social philosophers agree that the sense of the sacred has migrated in modern culture from religion to secular human rights now considered so sacred they may not be contravened by any authority, religious or scientific.[12] That migration of the sacred into the secular helps to explain the social taboos and "political correctness" now associated with various racial, ethnic, sexual, and gender self-definitions, the last of which may lack any verifiable psychiatric medical basis other than a personal preference others must treat as inviolable. To violate someone's sense of the sacred, whether that be a traditional religious sacred like defiling the consecrated host or to violate a secularized sacred like the right to a personal self-definition, is tantamount to a profanation. The culture wars are largely contested on the battlefield of the sacred as different individuals in pluralistic situations define it.

*Politics, economics, and culture.* The three public spheres that envelop all human action and the purposes attached to them are political life, economic markets, and culture where values are inherited, developed, and sorted out. These spheres serve different human purposes and follow different principles. Religion, along with the arts, sciences, sports, entertainment, fashion, and mass media, belongs to the sphere of culture. The tendency in some totalitarian secular and religious systems of meaning is to think of all three as being one system. Marxist-Leninism is famous for proposing that. It was the dawning of secular consciousness in the seventeenth century that initially separated these fields from one another, the better for each to pursue without interference the legitimate autonomy it requires. The means and ends of these three spheres of action, according to Daniel Bell, are distinct and even antagonistic. If the state takes over the economy, as it does in communism, the necessary antagonism is eliminated just as when the economy takes over the culture, as can happen in some forms of capitalism. Politics concerns the right structures for citizen equality and participation; the techno-economic realm is

---

[12] Hans Joas, *The Sacredness of the Person: A New Genealogy of Human Rights*, trans. Alex Skinner (Washington, DC: Georgetown University Press, 2013).

driven purely by means-ends functions and efficiencies; and culture is the realm of human self-expression, self-realization, and the formation of values. Religion, in this schema, is a cultural not a political or economic institution. It provides a symbolic structure for human beings to make sense of their freedom and the values and goods worth pursuing in the other two realms. Religious freedom was born as a secular value to keep religion from interfering with political life. The church reads it as the freedom to preach the Gospel and bring its values to bear, appropriately, yet prophetically, without violence or ideology, on the political and economic spheres.

*Scientific versus cultural modernity.* In this book, I will explain two ideas of modernity that are often confused although they clearly are related. Scientific modernity is about progress in the techno-economic realm mentioned above. It is associated with mechanical, chemical, nuclear, and bio-tech engineering. Cultural modernity overlaps these technical developments with philosophical and moral legitimations that make them a part of the dialogue in culture about all values. Science certainly impacts this as we see from the ways in which evolutionary theory redefines the emergence of the human species in the incessant struggle of new life forms. But far more important for us today are Lockean ideas of individualism and Kantian views of individual autonomy, which legitimate for many the quest for personal authenticity and self-definition. The French poet Charles Baudelaire coined the world *modernité* to denote not so much technical progress as the right of the artist, and implicitly for everyone, to define their identity for themselves. Herein lies the birth of the existentialist value of personal authenticity. When culture changes, human beings begin seeing who they are and what they can be in new ways. While technological modernity enhanced the understanding and control of nature, it was cultural modernity, in the strict nineteenth-century sense that Baudelaire gave it, which constituted the birth of the modern self. That vision of the human self has more to do with personal freedom, lifestyle choices, and self-display than it does with the mere access to technical conveniences. "Lifestyle" itself is a metaphor for autonomy borrowed from the decorative side of life or a salon. Moderns can create a new "self" for themselves literally by adopting a new "style" of self- expression. "The clothes make the man" captures it perfectly, even though they don't.

*Steering systems and the human lifeworld.* The major institutions that direct modern life in its social configuration are the public steering systems of government and the economic sectors, including aspects of the cultural spheres that have fallen under market-oriented redefinition. These forces have exposed the far more fragile forms of what social phenomenology refers to as the "human lifeworld" to something the philosopher Jürgen Habermas calls "colonization." The lifeworld is that of face-to-face relationships and mutual conversation, the personal privacies of reflection and reading, and the natural ecology of family intimacies that are the right of spouses and their children. A market economy built on acquisitive values can't help but colonize such spheres where other more fragile values are preserved. In the lifeworld, the means are the ends—talk is an end-in-itself, not a means to manipulate people to buy something. Domestic life, play, and art belong in the lifeworld that is increasingly saturated with commercial interests. In the modern secular context, the home and the parish constitute two lifeworld realities where communication, celebration, and mutual care replace the commercialized values of the market. What has happened to poetry has happened to faith. Do we pay poets? The simplest sign of the colonization of the lifeworld by the system is when a family is eating out, or at home, with members texting someone outside the circle of conversation at table and feeling profoundly liberated from domestic boredom by this technology. These individuals are no less colonized than American Indians were as their life and land were taken away from them. But at least the Indians knew it. Reading is a refusal to be completely colonized by mass entertainment, and reading serious literature in actual books, not screen images, is the most radical of all refusals in a totalizing techno-economic culture.

*Critical reason, tradition, and religious language.* For all its greatness in advancing human civilization through political and instrumental reason, the Enlightenment turned its nose up at human traditions as carriers of symbolic meaning, the values of which are not easily recovered once those vehicles are set aside. Culture includes inherited traditions of meaning whose combined impact on human consciousness can be considered religious in the broad sense of a total world outlook, what Germans call a *Weltanschauung*. In truth, the Enlightenment's idea of reason was far too narrow.

Jürgen Habermas presents reason in much broader terms than the usual technical and the engineering sense. He points out three different interests—matters we care about as human beings—that cause reason to take one of three forms: rationalized control of physical nature, interpersonal communication, and the recourse to ideology critique for social emancipation. First, economics and technology use language for purposes of instrumental control and management. At the extreme, algorithms make decisions for us based on data we input. The quest for freedom makes reason have an emancipatory interest at the same time. Reason can create the algorithms that in turn deprive the subject of a sense of self-control and freedom. Second, the performance of reason in the clinical encounter of a troubled patient with a psychologist is emancipatory. It unmasks the unhealthy rationalizations and lies the patient tells himself that parade as reason. Third, reason can have a communicative interest that transcends the technical and self-critical interests. Because human beings are historical, they both live within and live off the values of their culture. But by the capacity for historical-communicative reason, human imagination can access values and sensibilities in other cultures through the exegesis of the documents of those cultures. Written texts allow us to communicate with the dead and make them, in some analogous way, our own contemporaries. Traditions are made of meanings buried in practices, customs, and ways of speaking that transcend the interests of technical control and critique based on suspicion.

There is no doubt that traditions can imprison human hope in memories from the past where horizons of freedom were far more limited. But traditions, properly received and interpreted, can also liberate imagination from present-day ideology. The purification of cultural traditions by reason goes hand in hand with the hermeneutical recovery of forgotten truths buried in the cultural soil of earlier times. The Romantic movement in the eighteenth and nineteenth centuries refused to abandon the wisdom and beauty found in older, simpler cultures for a technical salvation by novelties and gadgets alone.

Perhaps the most enduring contribution from the Romantic period for philosophy and theology was its exploration of human language and hermeneutical approaches to text-based truth and meaning. From Friedrich von Humboldt to F. D. E. Schleiermacher to Wilhelm Dilthey to Martin Heidegger, Ludwig Wittgenstein, and Paul Ricoeur, language, in all its breadth and versatility, has become the focus for philosophical reflection. Wittgenstein focused his genius on language-games; British ordinary language philosophy explored the use of "performative discourse" where words actually "do things" like judging, forgiving, and vowing. Ricoeur explored the semantic versatility in metaphor, symbol, and narrative discourse. Charles Taylor recently published *The Language Animal: The Full Shape of the Human Linguistic Capacity*. In Genesis, the first action of God is to speak: "Then God said, 'Let there be light'; and there was light" (Gen 1:3). The Gospel of John opens with a poetic prologue that starts, "In the beginning was the word" (John 1:1). From beginning to end, Christianity is all about language and about what its religious semantics do to enhance our spiritual, ethical, and social capacities.

Religious views of the world first came to expression in the language of myth and symbol. By the beginning of the Christian era, Jewish biblical hermeneutics had been wrestling with narrative, legal, and prophetic texts to extract livable, enduring meaning from this corpus of traditions. Christian theology soon attempted what many at that time considered an impossibility and some today regard as a mere re-mystification of myth, namely, to read the biblical canon through the lens of Hellenistic philosophy and allegorical hermeneutics. The Platonic metaphysics of ideas and the eternal forms would be succeeded in the Latin West by the Aristotelian-Thomistic synthesis of faith and reason. Today, this metaphysical discourse has become a specialty in a subdivision of philosophy and theology that has taken new analytic, social-pragmatic, and hermeneutical turns. In a pragmatic and secular age, such philosophical approaches hold greater promise for making sense of religious discourse than classical metaphysics seems to have. The literalism of the digital age is in dire need of rescue by metaphorical and narrative discourses. As a relative of poetic discourse, biblical language demands to be read out of the hermeneutic tradition begun by Jewish scribes, Greek allegorists, and modern literary and rhetorical criticism. In a digital age, where mathematics is the paradigm of measurement and truthful reference, religious discourse may seem fanciful and subjective. What can literature, much less poetics, tell political pragmatists about the nature of what's going on? Well, what did Lincoln's Gettysburg Address or second inaugural address do to a wounded nation? What about

King's "I Have a Dream" speech? Or, closer to the present post-truth era of presidential discourse, how about the kind of honesty there is in George Saunders's piece on "Little St. Don" in *The New Yorker* (July 2, 2018)?

Literature can provide an escape for secular naivete. Tom Wolfe's new journalism of the ironic, the bizarre short stories Flannery O'Connor wrote which one critic described as "the grotesque recovery of the holy,"[13] and the thoughtful essays of Marilynne Robinson in *The Death of Adam* concerning Darwinism and religious fundamentalism are creative efforts toward a second naivete of the secular. The poetry of religious texts—biblical narratives, psalms, prophetic oracles, parables, and prayers—are not mere sentiment but semantically rich discourses. The use of theological analogy can elevate the poetics of primary religious discourse into a form ordinary intelligence can consider not only plausible but challenging and revelatory. The analogical transfer from metaphor to concept enables theology to grow. What the poets of religion perceive is what all poets do—scattered fragments of a hidden ontology that suggest (only suggest) that common sense is set in a mysterious web of implied relationships no one may directly apprehend. This is "tacit knowledge" gained by those rare souls sensitive enough to what's happening in and around them that they become guides on the spiritual journey we are all part of.

*Secular State, Secularization, and Secularism.* Pope Paul VI was the first modern pope to begin emphasizing secularism as a cultural challenge to Christian belief. He was doing so already in his speech to the council fathers at the close of Vatican II. It gained still greater prominence in the pope's statement on evangelization in 1975, *Evangelii Nuntiandi.* The term is associated with a liberalized ethical humanism that has set God aside in search of greater human freedoms, especially in those areas that touch on the most sensitive life issues involved in sexuality, birth, and natural death.

The popes afterward have adopted this definition of secularism, which is accurate in many respects, but which can also be confusing to the faithful. The Catholic historian James Hitchcock published

---

[13] Preston Browning, "Flannery O'Connor and the Grotesque Recovery of the Holy," in *Adversity and Grace: Studies in Recent American Literature*, ed. Nathan Scott (Chicago: University of Chicago Press, 1968).

*What Is Secular Humanism? Why Humanism Became Secular and How It Is Changing Our World* in 1982, which gave a religiously traditionalist reading of the rise of secular humanism that he traces to a cast of characters, including novelists, economists, behaviorists, judges, and others, supplemented by a rogues' gallery of photos of some of them, among whom there are photos (Yes!) of the Lutheran exegete Rudolf Bultmann, Harvey Cox himself, and the Swiss Catholic theologian Hans Küng. Hitchcock is a capable polemicist and a trained but tendentious historian. I do not find this approach historically accurate or theologically persuasive as a read of secularization and secular humanism.

That is why I turn to other sources for interpreting the secular age. I do not doubt, however, that those who read the large drama of modernity as involving serious moral decline lack evidence for their positions. I have already noted the diverse apocalyptic that should give all cultural liberals and economic conservatives pause. The "signs of the times" can be read differently from different perspectives. The atheist Nietzsche, who told us what to expect as a down payment for a world without God, didn't offer consolations. Nor did Karl Jaspers or Hannah Arendt or Eugen Rosenstock-Huessy or the historian Eric Voegelin when they surveyed the modern world. Neither Kurt Anderson, an atheist, nor Rod Dreher, a Christian, find late modernity in America a satisfying place to be. Still, I find the narrative account of secularity that Charles Taylor offers, which others complement and critique, a more convincing way to unstack the evangelical deck against secularity as an interpretation of our situation in today's world.

The original meaning of the *secular* in Christianity was about things no better and no worse than ordinary matters of lay concern (family, labor, play) as distinguished from the *religious* lives of priests and nuns. Laity lived in the *secular* everyday world. The secular approach to social reality first came about by a series of strategic separations, such as the separation of church and state, or the separation of powers in government where the legislative, judicial, and executive functions were vested in different institutions governed by different interests. This is the birth of the *secular state*. When modernization accelerated in the nineteenth and twentieth centuries, one of its effects was called *secularization*. Urbanization, industrialization, and modernization in general were the combined social undertow taking religious outlooks on the world out to sea. *Secularism* and *secular humanism* represent the philosophical attempt to draw humanistic benefits from all of this, frosting it over as needed with deism, agnosticism, or atheism. But any humanism, atheistic or not, remains a possible dialogue partner with a Christian humanism born of the incarnation of God and our creation in the image of God (Gen 1:26-28; 5:1-3; 9:6). *A Secular Age* ends with Taylor's attempt to write a future prolegomenon or introduction to the way such a humanistic dialogue might proceed. The Vatican thinks it's worth serious consideration.

## Chapter 2

# The Pastoral Challenges and the Homily

The new evangelization is the daughter Vatican II gave birth to when Vatican II, as some saw it, seemed to land on a secular sandbar. Evangelization was first about reinvigorating the church grown a bit testy and argumentative within and about a world grown more religiously indifferent without. It was about redeeming the Pentecostal foundation of the church in "a new ardor, new methods of communicating the Gospel, and new expressions for doing so." This was some forty years ago. Where's the Spirit now and what's happened to it? My niece's bewilderment at her son's atheism begs for answers.

When bishops merge or close parishes, Catholics are routinely told they are doing so, not just for financial reasons, but to pull Catholics together for a new evangelization. When new pastors are assigned to those reconstituted parishes, they try pumping some life into them with a sermon or plan on the new evangelization. When the pope speaks of the new evangelization, he invites the whole church to undertake missionary discipleship in a spirit of joy. Some seminaries now market their programs as formation for the new evangelization. The Catholic book market is saturated with titles on it. Where do we start?

Depending on which pope a Catholic identifies with, if they identify with any, the thrust of the new evangelization is a little different. Pope John XXIII associated evangelization with ecclesial renewal, with letting new ideas into ancient traditions, opening the church's windows for some fresh air, pouring new wine into new wineskins. That was almost sixty years ago. His successor, Pope Paul VI, led the Second Vatican Council to its conclusion, only to be consumed with a host of problems at his doorstep afterward, which he saw as the rise of a new secularism that would make the church's renewal and mission even more difficult. With the fresh air John XXIII let into the church came the odor of the secular age. Maybe it was time to batten down the hatches. Pope John Paul II, who was elected in 1978, spoke and wrote more about the new evangelization until his death in 2005 than John XXIII, Paul VI, Benedict XVI, and Pope Francis combined. His emphases became its papal benchmark: stronger catechesis, clear moral teaching, greater ardor in ecclesial life, lack of an intimidation by secularism in defending the Gospel. At one point, John Paul suggested the world would end up secularizing the church herself. His successor in the papacy, the cardinal who had accompanied John Paul II from the start of his pontificate, was Cardinal Ratzinger, who took the name of Pope Benedict XVI. He brought theological and epistemological precision to the issues of truth and relativism in secular culture. His slogan "a dictatorship of relativism" helped to fuel a Catholic recrudescence of the culture wars. Yet, Pope Benedict also opened a new door of dialogue with the secular age. Then, without warning, he retired in 2013. Many speculate on what drove him to do that—turning eighty, the scandal of clergy sexual abuse, feeling boxed in by his own Curia, a lavender mafia within the Vatican.

A cardinal from Argentina succeeded the papal theologian from Germany. Pope Francis (formerly Cardinal Jorge Mario Bergoglio of Buenos Aires) shifted the rhetoric of the new evangelization to what struck some critics as rather sentimental themes of compassion, joy, and mercy, which seemed less tough on secularity than the rhetoric of his predecessors. Pope Francis started calling for further reforms in the church. He borrowed a phrase from his predecessors—"joyful missionary discipleship"—and wrapped it in a Latino edition of the new evangelization, where a critique of a liberal economic order played a much more significant role. Some who regard Paul VI and John Paul II and Benedict XVI as the paragons of new evangelization see Pope Francis's Latino edition as socialistic and perhaps doctrinally reckless.[1] Those who understood secularism in the light of abor-

---

[1] For a sampling of what writers on the new evangelization before Pope Francis wrote about it, see Stephen Boguslawski and Ralph Martin, eds., *The New Evangelization: Overcoming the Obstacles* (New York: Paulist Press, 2008); Avery Cardinal Dulles, *Evangelization for the Third Millennium* (New York: Paulist Press, 2009); Rino Fisichella, *The New Evangelization: Responding to the Challenge of Indifference*, trans. G. J. Woodall

tion and *Roe v. Wade* discovered it might also be about excessive greed on Wall Street and the superficial self of *Vanity Fair* and Madison Avenue. Could it be that the real estate tycoon and reality TV star elected president in 2016 embodied the worst of secularism more perfectly than his pro-choice opponent? Some Evangelicals and Roman Catholics didn't think so.

Immediately after the close of Vatican II, in the fall of 1965, Paul VI began to mention something called "secularism" in the majestic Basilica of St. Peter's. In Proclaiming the Gospel (*Evangelii Nuntiandi*, 1975), he made secularism one reason for a renewed evangelization. So, barely a decade after Vatican II, secularism had become a nagging problem. Why? One reason was that religious practice in Europe and other advanced societies was declining. Despite the council's reforms, many were yawning at religion. Convinced secular humanists regarded any religious belief—outdated or updated—as equally irrelevant to modern sensibility. If religion had any use at all in public life it was only as a lobby group or pawn for a political party. Foolish Christians fell for it. The world had moved on. Why even bother talking about religion anymore?

I will start with the local church before exploring in more depth what the new evangelization and secularization mean in broader terms.

## Signs of the Times in the Local Church

In the United States, a national pastoral plan for the new evangelization would not appear until the late 1980s, largely under the charismatic influence of the Paulist priest Father Alvin Illig (d. 1991). He had founded the National Catholic Evangelization Association in 1977 when the word "evangelization" still sounded strangely Protestant to Catholic ears. Already the symptoms of a growing disinterest in church in America had become undeniable.[2] In the years since,

---

(Herefordshire, UK: Gracewing Publishing, 2011); George Weigel, *Evangelical Catholicism: Deep Reform in the 21st-Century Church* (New York: Basic Books, 2013).

[2] See the USCCB Strategic Plan for the New Evangelization at http://usccb.org /beliefs-and-teachings/how-we-teach/evangelization/go-and-make-disciples/tenth _anniversaryedition.cfm. The foreword to the Tenth Anniversary Evangelization Program of the U.S. bishops was written by Bishop William Houck in 2002. It provides a summary of the conference's reflections on evangelization dating back to Paul VI

religious indifference has become culturally systemic. The following six signs of the times are what the new evangelization, whatever iteration of it you choose, is supposed to change.

1. *Declining numbers.* In recent years, the Catholic Church in the United States has been slowly but steadily hemorrhaging numbers of the faithful in church. Only the arrival of Latinos nationally disguises the depth of the domestic problem. In the 1970s alone, vocations to the priesthood were cut in half. Young people no longer displayed much interest in the convent or rectory. The religious right blamed this on Vatican II. Just as troubling, many laity began opting out of church attendance, once considered a mortal sin. The pews in some churches are now turning more silver than the senior celebrants presiding at the altars. Despite some remarkable counterexamples of religious enthusiasm, the Catholic Church has been struggling to fill its seminaries, grow its parishes, and maintain its many schools. What was causing this to happen? Everyone has a theory. Many said it was secularism.

2. *Staggering finances.* Church attendance, of course, affects the parish's bottom line. Without contributions, it cannot pay its bills; nor can the diocese support its many educational and charitable activities that go on at some remove from everyday parochial life. The deep pockets of Catholic philanthropy covered big-ticket items like (arch)diocesan campaigns, Catholic Charities, and popular and successful Catholic high schools and universities. But shrinking collections sounded a warning. Dioceses began bailing parishes out of deficits, then yoking two struggling ones together, before being forced to shutter a few and redraw parish boundaries. Without the contributed services of religious sisters and brothers, some parochial schools' tuitions became unaffordable for the poor they were designed to serve. Diocesan coffers were handcuffed to failing operations. An aging infrastructure of urban churches put additional strains on the

---

and running through John Paul II and the millennium. This serves as background for the publication of the 2013–2016 USCCB Strategic Plan for the New Evangelization, "Journey with Christ: Faith—Worship—Witness." The USCCB engagement with the effects of secularism on the practice of the faith dates to 1976, when religious education programs were developed for the "unchurched, fallen away Catholics, members of other churches, and Catholics themselves."

budget. The sprawling reach of the church's institutions could barely keep up with deferred maintenance. This could not last. We need numbers and we need money.

3. *Spiritual options.* Market economics means the customer decides, and more Catholics were deciding to switch parishes. Some did it for sheer convenience, like Mass schedules and parking. Others switched for better liturgy, preaching, and parish community. Those caught up in a liberal indifference began skipping a few Sundays here or there (it's no mortal sin, Father, right?). They kept their membership card by attending monthly or seasonally. Of course, unbeknownst to them, this was the well-trod path out of faith and into something else. The truly disaffected with the church abandoned worship entirely. Yet, all this was happening in Catholicism as evangelical congregations were renting warehouses for worship in strip malls, sweeping up de-churched seekers and searchers. Here the disaffected found a more contemporary feel, folksy music, a user-friendly approach, one high-tech mega service, even a coffee bar. Other searchers began meditating alone, doing yoga, or jogging. These rituals boosted mindfulness, health, and biochemistry at once. Some just flat out went secular and learned to like being away from the guilt and the boring clichés of homilies and sitting for an hour alongside strangers singing hymns you don't know or like. The market of meaning expanded into the religious market, and the Catholic enterprise was losing customers. Maybe the new evangelization was the answer? But how?

4. *Religious illiteracy.* The Pew surveys of religion say Americans for the most part believe in God, but the statistics don't tell us much about what belief in a deity means. The telling catechetical statistic was a growing religious illiteracy among Catholics themselves. That caught the attention of bishops who rested their hopes in the new evangelization on better catechesis and adult religious education. If church leaders—bishops, pastors, catechists, and others—were honest with themselves, they knew that most pre–Vatican II, Vatican II, and post–Vatican II Catholics not only never read the sixteen documents of Vatican II but also didn't read the Bible itself. One generation raised on the memorized answers in the Baltimore Catechism yielded to another raised on Montessori religion of games and balloons. In response to that, the Vatican produced the 803-page encyclopedic *Catechism of the Catholic Church*. This was now another piece of substantial

religious literature busy Catholics could ignore. Catholic lay *virtuosi* may read theology, spirituality, and Scripture, but the rank and file don't, never have. How do we pass on a faith as thick with religious symbolism, historical tradition, and metaphysical sophistication as Catholicism is in this culture? Modern popular culture is attached to the music, the image, the bullet-points, the slogans, not to the fine points of hermeneutics and dogma. Can the new evangelization do that?

5. *Moral and religious pluralism.* The Judeo-Christian ethic itself fell under attack with the social and moral tsunamis of the 1960s and 1970s. The noticeable moral shifts were largely on matters of sex. But the Vietnam War reinforced such moral ruptures with social and political ones. The meaning of what was good to do in private and what was right to do in government became controversial. Simple commandments children had memorized yielded to situation ethics and medical ethics and bioethics. American Christianity fractured along its moral axis and splintered twice along political lines. The Democratic Party, which supported the woman's right to choose, did not seem to have much interest in religion except as a lobby for Roe v. Wade, and the Republican Party, which claimed it stood up for the life of the unborn, marketed itself as the religious party. This political standoff has divided and dumbed down religion in America for forty years. The sociologist Robert Putnam speaks of American religion since the 1960s undergoing "one shock and two after-shocks."[3] The first shock was the right to abortion. The first aftershock was the pro-life religious alliance of conservative Evangelicals and Roman Catholics with the Republican Party in opposition to abortion. The second aftershock was the exodus of younger liberal-leaning Christians from what they regarded as an abortion-obsessed religion. In short, Christianity after Vatican II in America fused with partisan national politics. And it's been unable to free itself from that association or rise above it. The pews became not only gray but deeply partisan.

---

[3] Robert D. Putnam and David E. Campbell, with the assistance of Shaylyn Romney Garrett, *American Grace: How Religion Divides and Unites Us* (New York: Simon and Shuster, 2010), "Religiosity in America: Shock and Two Aftershocks," 91–133.

6. *Secularization and faith in a secular age.* In the space of twenty years, Vatican II Catholicism went from being the focus of intense curiosity in Catholic, ecumenical, and secular circles to being far less interesting just two decades later. Vatican II had come and gone, leaving lots of theological and moral partisanship in its wake. By the late 1970s, younger Catholics were entering mainstream professional culture, where someone's religious affiliation didn't count at all. The professoriate, the brokerage house, and the medical clinic didn't care if or where you went to church. Guilt and fear of eternal damnation, the psychic motives that got an older generation of Catholics to confession and communion, seemed implausible if not just neurotic. Practicing religion, for many, fell to third and fourth place behind busy careers and shopping and kids' soccer games. The 1970s was "The 'Me' Decade" Tom Wolfe wrote about. If the Spirit was moving at all, it was moving from religion to the authentic self or to civil rights for blacks and social rights for women and gays, all of whom found little theological sympathy with or ecclesial welcome in church. It was moving from sanctuaries into medical labs that might find a cancer cure and into marches and marathons raising money for breast cancer. It was moving into early warnings about the need for a limit to nuclear arms, a limit to spoliation of the environment. The bottom line is that religion—any religion at all, but especially those at odds with modern rights and emancipations in secular culture—went on the defensive. The new evangelization pitted itself against the secular humanism that powered these movements. In return, the movements declared religion itself irrelevant. In some elite circles, saying one was raised Catholic became tantamount to an admission of an intellectual deficiency or, worse, bigotry. The American pragmatist philosopher Richard Rorty once called all religion, not just the Catholic kind, a total "conversation-stopper."

In broad outline, these symptoms are what the new evangelization is supposed to address somehow and resolve. The positive developments since the council in pastoral life, theological reflection, liturgy, spirituality, social justice, lay leadership, and the role of women and youth, especially under the circumstances described above, have been extraordinary. The Vatican was not twiddling its thumbs. Its far-flung missionary efforts were bearing good fruit in Africa, South America, and Asia. But the way things stand now, as parishes are shuttered and schools close, the church's prospects in the United States seem to be getting worse. Without bishops of enormous vision and energies and local pastors with the same, how are we going to get things moving again? Then came the clergy abuse crisis and episcopal cover-ups of it. The church had created a self-inflicted wound which may take generations to heal.

## Diagnosing Secularity in Detail: Paul VI to Francis

Throughout the book, I will be treating pluralism and secularization in depth. Here, I only want to touch briefly on why the new evangelization, in some iterations of it, made secularism its major moral target. As I already indicated, this began with Paul VI as early as the closing address he gave at the end of Vatican II. The pope was left with the unenviable task of implementing the council's ambitious reform and renewal agenda. The traditionalist movement was already on record de-legitimizing the council and the popes who presided over it. Liberals were not allies either. They broke with Paul VI on birth control. As new ecumenical dialogues were getting under way, the pope was struggling to keep his own church together. Celibacy, theological feminism, liberation theology raised questions the council tabled or had not anticipated. Like all human institutions, the Vatican began to close ranks. It was in this embattled climate of internal dissent, partly on the progressive left and partly on the traditionalist right, and new social emancipation movements in culture, that Paul VI opened the subject of secularism. One paragraph only in *Evangelii Nuntiandi* in 1975 was devoted to it. But, it was a bellwether. In the rhetoric of some writers and preachers of the new evangelization, secularism is nothing but toxic.[4]

---

[4] See Scott Hahn, *Evangelizing Catholics: A Mission Manual for the New Evangelization* (Huntington, IN; Our Sunday Visitor, 2014): "The New Evangelization is more for the baptized than the unbaptized. It's for those who've been inadequately catechized but all too adequately secularized, and it's for those who've been de-Christianized in the very process of being sacramentalized" (13); and, "Today, however, when Catholics walk outside our homes and parishes into the culture at large, we feel the difference. It hits us in the face like a slap of ice-cold wind. The culture has turned toxic, and the gap between how the Church tells us to live and how the culture tells us to live has grown so wide, we can no longer bridge it" (44). The book is dedicated to Pope Francis but has nothing about The Joy of the Gospel in it.

A young Polish cardinal, who was present at Vatican II and personally submitted his own draft text for Schema 17 on the Pastoral Constitution on the Church in the Modern World, was elected pope in 1978. Cardinal Karol Wojtyla had lived under the two most oppressive totalitarian regimes of the twentieth century where human dignity, human rights, and religious freedom counted for absolutely nothing. Soviet Communism and German Nazism swallowed up religious people in a state-sponsored atheism. For John Paul II, the liberal order of the West, which on paper recognized human rights and religious freedom, was not immune to its own prejudices against religious faith. Its inclination was to reduce Christian faith and ethics to an anti-liberal ideology of the right. John Paul II set about challenging the dominant ideologies of modernity. The free human person created by God and redeemed by Christ became the premise of his ethics. In the inspiring homily he delivered upon being elected pope at the age of fifty-eight, the new pontiff implored believers and nonbelievers not to be afraid of Jesus Christ. Why choose the word "fear"? Perhaps because the modern world was searching for greater freedom and the church was trying to stand in its way. Perhaps because moderns have heard of the Crusades, the Inquisition, and the Wars of Religion which followed the Protestant Reformation. Perhaps because Christianity was not so much associated with Christ as it was with the church.

The Eastern European mind understood better than the liberal West what an ethically untrammeled ideology of progress, untethered from religious sources of truth and meaning, could make happen. The Soviet gulags and Nazi concentration camps were run by Christians as much as they were by revolutionary nihilists. So, the young pope had new reasons to warn the liberal and righteous West what a soft despotism relativism can be. He had read Nietzsche and seen it in action with his own eyes. The "last men" who yearn only for "a pitiful comfort" may not clearly see what's coming.

To bolster his political and cultural critique, John Paul II went about tightening up magisterial authority perceived as enfeebled by two decades of critical theological effluence. He was decidedly unfavorable to radical feminism and to liberal theologies flirting with Marxist doctrine. He reaffirmed the church's teaching on birth control within his theology of the body, constructed as a linkage for all life issues. He believed that the utilitarian pragmatic approach to moral values in secular culture—if it works for you and doesn't hurt anybody else, what's wrong with it—would lead humankind to choose ethical paths that would take them away from the truth about themselves as persons. In casting about for an image to express the ongoing tasks of ecclesial renewal and conversion to Christ, equipped ethically for cultural confrontation if necessary, the pope hit on an expression from Latin America.

In 1979, the Latin American bishops gathered for their CELAM conference meeting at Puebla, Mexico, where they issued a statement calling for a new evangelization (*nueva evangelización*). With this turn of phrase, John Paul II found the motto for his global mission. He acknowledged that each continent had distinct challenges and resources for evangelization. Accordingly, he linked evangelization to inculturation. Europe's challenges involved what was being called by the church the de-Christianization of the continent. French *laïcisme* and Soviet communism were behind it. North American challenges were different. These involved how best to engage the growing polarization in American Catholicism between Catholic liberals and conservatives with very little real estate in between. Latin America had clearly identified their challenges: Catholicism mixed with religious syncretism, a neo-fundamentalist and Pentecostal evangelicalism, and massive poverty abetted by anonymous forces of globalization.

In ordinary North American parochial church life, the six issues mentioned at the head of the chapter all came together. By 1992, the United States Conference of Catholic Bishops (USCCB) had issued its first new evangelization plan, "Go, and Make Disciples." It would later be superseded by another plan.

John Paul II, who drew inspiration for the new evangelization from *Evangelii Nuntiandi*, characterized it as a "new ardor, new expressions, and new methods" for transmitting the message and mission of the church.[5] His ardor was certainly not in doubt. The first Polish pope considered himself a global evangelist for Catholicism and human rights. Journalists covered him like a political celebrity. Intellectuals who opposed his strict personal moral doctrines nevertheless found his philosophical credentials and linguistic fluency impressive. The

[5] John Paul II Speeches in Nowa Huta, Poland (June 9, 1979) and Port-au-Prince, Haiti (March 24, 1983).

Vatican staged huge outdoor Masses and youth rallies where the pope could display that fluency as well as the full range of his personal charisma and intelligence. His vigor contrasted with the cassocked images of a curial gerontocracy. Most of all, in an age of ideological atheism, uncertain belief, or blasé indifference, his was the face of a firm believer, a fearless modern apostle for God, Jesus Christ, and the human person. Within a decade of assuming the papacy and standing up against the Soviet occupation of Poland, the Soviet Union folded like a deck of cards. Conservative and liberal Catholics at last had something they could agree on about John Paul II. He was changing the world.

In 1990, John Paul II published an encyclical letter dealing with mission and evangelization, *Redemptoris Missio* (On the Permanent Validity of the Church's Evangelizing Mission). The matter of *validity* was hardly theoretical. It signaled that no political regime or culture, illiberal or secular, would be allowed to silence the voice of religion in the public sphere when it came to morals and human rights. The encyclical distinguished three ways of seeing mission and evangelization according to the needs of different audiences: (a) the foreign missions were the oldest and traditional way of understanding mission in the sense of converting those who had never had the Gospel preached to them; (b) the ordinary, and increasingly necessary, expression of mission and evangelization took the form of catechesis (religious education) for practicing Catholics so that Christian conversion takes deeper roots in human life; (c) the third audience required a "new evangelization" or "re-evangelization" since many had become illiterate about faith or opted for secular existence apart from religious life. Today, some speak of them as the unchurched, the de-churched, and the religiously indifferent.

Clear-cut distinctions like these about audiences can be a little misleading. Many parishes have all three. The pastor's care of souls (*cura animarum*) embraces the invisible Buddhist and veiled Muslim soul at the supermarket, the comfortably secularized souls of those jogging past his church, the biblically challenged and theologically uneducated regular churchgoers greeting the pastor after Mass. In pluralistic, tolerant America, depending on where you look, the parish exists surrounded by foreign missions, catechetical reeducation, and a casual indifference to the whole project. Take your pick. Some indifferent Catholics are still in the pews, or at home while their parents and grandparents are there praying for them.

The United States Conference of Catholic Bishops based their national plan for the new evangelization on the papal interpretation of it by John Paul II. While the focus was largely on spiritual renewal and clarity in moral and doctrinal teaching, the specter of secularism was the paramount challenge. Meanwhile, sociologists were trying to figure out the paradox of an increasing secular relativism along with the recrudescence of fundamentalism here and abroad. Why were young Catholics dropping out of the faiths they were raised in? Why were others embracing evangelical Free Churches? What was behind the interest in New Age spiritualities and Eastern mysticism? Some seculars felt pulled toward spiritual experiences concurrently with a disinterest in institutional religion.[6]

This amalgamation of dwellers, seekers, and searchers makes many church leaders focus attention on catechesis and Catholic identity. Catholicism had always proved particularly attractive to disenchanted seculars and Protestants unhappy with liberal religion. Tradition had thickened the church's skin, made its moral fiber stubborn. Somewhat like Jewish identity, if you were Catholic you may not like everything about it, but you certainly knew who you were.

In his role as prefect of the church's doctrinal congregation, Cardinal Ratzinger toughened up the critique of secularism. He linked it to a soft moral relativism in values where privacy, preference, and tolerance kept any higher light from shining on conscience. Just before Cardinal Ratzinger was elected and took the name Pope Benedict XVI, he made his own position about relativism as clear as can be. In a homily delivered by him on the eve of the papal conclave, he warned the cardinal-electors of a growing "dictatorship of relativism" in culture. This was a metaphor but had the ring of a battle cry. It stuck in the minds of American Catholics upset about abortion and gay rights. Soft secular tolerance was not so tolerant after all. The dictatorial image caught on. It mobilized moral righteousness. Europe knew dictators, but what was so dictatorial about American relativism? The connotations of it pointed to the secular intelligentsia, the scientists, and secular referees of public values who were not above

---

[6] Robert Wuthnow, *Rediscovering the Sacred: Perspectives on Religion in Contemporary Society* (Grand Rapids, MI: Eerdmans, 1992).

disparaging religious moral convictions.[7] The phrase reinforced the feelings of political and moral resentment many Catholics and others felt in being overruled by Hollywood stars, liberal Democrats, and federal judges on abortion.

But few who relished their resentments against seculars knew about Cardinal Joseph Ratzinger's speech on religion and secular reason in Munich in 2004 where he admitted to pathologies in religion in need of purification by reason. He sat as a listener while the German secular social philosopher Jürgen Habermas chastised the "blinkered enlightenment" of secular reason and called for a post-secular society, open to both secular and religious citizens on equal terms. Even fewer may have known of the pastoral visit Pope Benedict made in 2010 to the Czech Republic, considered to be the most secular state in Europe. The welcome and respect he received as pope from these secular atheists astonished him. Impressions of secularism were changing at the highest levels. The "dictatorship of relativism," if and where it existed, was coming under fire by Habermas himself and being qualified by the Catholic cardinal who invented it.

Two years after the Habermas-Ratzinger colloquy at Munich, and now speaking as Pope Benedict, Joseph Ratzinger delivered a lecture at Regensburg University in Germany where he was once a professor. He titled it "Faith, Reason, and the University—Memories and Reflections." He spoke of religious violence as equally abhorrent to secular reason and religious belief. In his address, the pope allowed himself an imprudent illustration by quoting, and seeming to agree with, the words of a fourteenth-century Byzantine emperor about the sword being essential to Islam. Benedict XVI subsequently apologized for giving a misleading and damaging impression of Islam. Interreligious understanding and ecumenical amity were befuddled by it. The religious right wondered what the fuss was about after what happened on 9/11.

Later, I will mention some of the positive steps the pope took in opening a new dialogue with secular humanism. Suffice for now to say he also created a new Pontifical Council for the Promotion of the New Evangelization, appointed its first president, and personally presided over the 2012 World Synod on the New Evangelization for

---

[7] Hans Joas, *Faith as an Option: Possible Futures for Christianity*, trans. Alex Skinner (Stanford, CA: Stanford University Press, 2014), 135.

the Transmission of the Christian Faith. Prior to that, Pope Benedict had written an apostolic exhortation on divine revelation (*Verbum Domini*) as a preface to a planned encyclical letter on faith. The concluding years of a pontificate associated only with orthodox retrenchment and hostility toward secularism were in fact marked by a new initiative directed toward religious-secular dialogue.

Cardinal Jorge Bergoglio of Buenos Aires was elected to the papacy five months after the 2012 world synod of bishops on the new evangelization. Within six months, he produced his own apostolic exhortation on the new evangelization based on the 2012 synod entitled The Joy of the Gospel (*Evangelii Gaudium*, 2013). It integrates the two ecclesial-oriented constitutions of Vatican II—*Lumen Gentium* and *Gaudium et Spes*—with what his papal predecessors had written on the new evangelization and challenges of secularism. Additionally, Pope Francis drew on liberation themes from the Latino *nueva evangelización* as reflected in the CELAM document of Aparecida. That makes his approach to secularism somewhat different from the focus it often received in the American culture wars on the right. Pope Francis linked the new evangelization to the more neuralgic issues of curial and pastoral reform in Catholicism. He encouraged the church's pastors to test the human institutionalized arrangements in Catholicism against the demands of evangelical mission in a new world order. It wasn't a blank check, but it recognized the loss of credibility the church had suffered over the previous decade. The revelations of the summer of 2018 about Cardinal Theodore McCarrick and Pennsylvania created a catastrophic crisis for ecclesial trust.

In other chapters, I will explore papal teaching on the new evangelization and secularism more thoroughly. Let me now turn to the American context for the new evangelization.

## The American Context

Straight off, we must distinguish the American context of secularization from European de-Christianization. They are not the same. For one thing, in America, Catholics find themselves faced with multiple religious options. German citizens may check Lutheran or Roman Catholic or secular on their tax forms. Americans pay no taxes to any religion and have a thousand choices about how to be observant or indifferent. Religious groups pop up like mushrooms on this side of the Atlantic. Home-grown versions of it like Mormonism and Seventh-Day Adventists set up shop in an open religious marketplace with the Methodists, Episcopalians, and Greek Orthodox. So, disaffected Roman Catholics can choose to switch into a more liberal Episcopalian version as traditionalist Episcopalians look toward Rome. Some can explore charismatic and enthusiastic forms of religious observance, or just forget about religious practice until Christmas and Easter roll around.

There is room for taste in religiously observant America. Progressives offer readings of Vatican II that are more permissive and less condemnatory of the modern moral order. Traditionalists, and some conservatives, have disliked what the liturgical reforms took away. They have not forgotten the elevated cadences of Latin and Gregorian Chant at Sunday High Mass. In today's fast-paced, overstressed digital world, some Catholic worshipers afflicted with ADHD symptoms and addicted to text messaging reluctantly confess that only the silences and syncopated sounds of the Latin Mass calm them down and bring peace. Yoga does the same for secularized brokers on Wall Street. Certainly, there must be church order and liturgical directives, but to make a Procrustean bed out of them seems unwise when tradition itself offers so many alternatives.

In America, many unchurched are looking for spiritual reference points in life. It feels unserious to make up your own religion. So, people can choose nondenominational communities to bolster their spiritual hungers. Admission is free—just drop in. Such religion has lowered the dogmatic bar many notches. The sermons are often more relevant and down to earth. Pastoral leadership is usually managed professionally, in some instances by converted money managers and businesspeople. These types clearly understand what marketing a faith in the vast commodity culture of America demands. They have organized things well and know the members of their congregations care most about keeping their marriages and families intact. A "family-centered" congregation can be subdivided into workable "prayer-discussion" groups where more is asked for than weekend attendance and an offering that had been the norm in Catholic parishes. Preaching is not tethered to fixed lectionary cycles most Catholics might find bewildering. Sermons renamed as "messages" follow an advertised sequence of topical subjects matched to the social and existential syllabus of the average American household, to issues ordinary people worry and talk about. These congregations put the Gospel within reach.

Such entrepreneurial Christian communities have been at liberty to borrow and blend in comfortable Catholic or Baptist elements as they see fit. Is there some law against that? Liturgy became relaxed and Bible-centered. Americans instinctively take to that kind of religion. Catholic parish life seemed staid by comparison. Evangelical-style religion gave Catholics more choices. Worship there felt more like TV, which explains why televangelists were so successful, that is, until hypocrisy caught up with them as it is catching up to the bishops.

In this consumer-driven American context, the new evangelization was first launched as a catechetical renewal plan emphasizing a relationship with Jesus Christ.[8] It would be grounded in sound doctrinal catechesis. Unlike French *laïcisme*, American secularism was not saddled with memories of anti-clericalism, the state-sponsored religion and the union of throne and altar that made people hate religion as people loved to hate it in France. We can be thankful that clerical privileges and a cozy church-state relationship were not the reasons that gave rise to American secularism as they were for Parisians in 1789.

Religious freedom in America means all belief is optional: religious and non-religious options equally. It is ironic that the declaration on religious freedom at Vatican II was what French Catholic traditionalist bishops despised with all their hearts, yet it is now the document that conservative, centrist, and progressive bishops invoke constantly.

---

[8] The USCCB Strategic Plan approach was designed as a five-year plan for renewing the church and forming its members to be evangelizers. It is comprehensive, with all the marks of wide consultation and pastoral organization. The plan opened with the theme of faith (2012–2013) in seven points (pastoral outreach, education of priests, preaching, life issues, religious liberty, marriage, penance and reconciliation). The following years, 2014–2015, were dedicated to the theme of worship, also broken down into seven points (penance, Eucharist, youth, turning parishes into welcoming communities, formation of priests, strengthening marriage, and increasing Mass attendance). The next two years, 2016–2017, were focused on mission, where life issues would be stressed, training laity to be witnesses in "the public square," forming priests and laity as evangelizers and witnesses, supporting married couples, strengthening religious and consecrated life, and encouraging youth to consider a vocation to the priesthood and religious life. In speaking of the new evangelization, pluralism and secularism were neither mentioned nor analyzed.

If it stays neutral on worldviews, as it must, the secular state may be the best thing that ever happened to Catholicism as far as the new evangelization goes.

Which is only to say once again that religion in American society exists in a broad competitive marketplace of spiritual and moral ideas. The public sphere here is pluralistic, and pluralism automatically engenders a condition of contestability for any deep moral worldview. That goes with the territory. Pluralism also causes cognitive contamination, which unsettles belief from different sides and causes some to give it up and others to deepen convictions further.

The personal foundations of the new evangelization in the United States were presented as they were in evangelical Protestantism—having a "personal relationship" with Jesus Christ. This was unfamiliar turf for many Catholics except religious women and lay virtuosi. The ordinary guy thought of faith as just going to church. Let's not get crazy about this, huh!

When secularism was mentioned, it was mentioned usually because of abortion. On 9/11, Muslim religious fanatics attacked secular America as "The Great Satan," which, for all its moral problems, still felt quite congenial to Catholics. When clergy abuse came to light, secular journalists broke the story. When the bishops responded by calling for a full investigation of factors that contributed to it and promising complete transparency going forward, they hired seculars to help them on the National Review Board. A former chief of staff for a president (Leon Panetta), the psychiatrist Dr. Paul McHugh, forensic specialists, lawyers, human resource experts—some of whom no doubt even privately favored the right to abortion—contributed their skills to resolving the crisis.

Absolution, as sacramental theology in the church understands it, can be given by a priest only after a truthful confession, sincere contrition, penance, and a firm purpose of amendment are made. Some of the social penance for clergy abuse will unfortunately be imposed on a new generation of young clergy who had nothing to do with the crimes, on the good pastors struggling to prosper their pastoral responsibilities under a disgrace the effects of which still hang over them. In the summer of 2018, Pope Francis stripped retired Cardinal McCarrick (Archdiocese of Washington) of his title as cardinal for allegations the Archdiocese of New York found to be credible. On learning that McCarrick's behavior as bishop was widely rumored, some members of the National Review Board were rightly outraged at being taken in by McCarrick's word that the abuse was simply about "psychologically immature" seminarians. The bishops have a lot to answer for.[9]

## Returning to the Symptoms

This American scene for the new evangelization, as I described it above in six symptoms, is often blamed on the rise of secularism without much attention to the social exegesis of it. Much of the book later will be devoted to providing some background for that. I am setting aside the moral issues about which the church has spoken. It is the larger philosophical worldview of the secular that interests me. The fifth and sixth symptoms, on pluralization and secularization, will come up for closer examination further on. But let me frame the other four—numbers, finances, options, and literacy—in terms drawn from biblical foundations of the faith and the simple pragmatics of the secular that anyone can appreciate.

### *Numbers*

Jesus was concerned about numbers of people. Why else would he have been an itinerant missionary himself? John the Baptist had crowds coming to him at the Jordan. But Jesus, whom John said would baptize with the Holy Spirit, went on the road. Everywhere in the gospels there are crowds following him. Retreat masters may emphasize Jesus' moments of solitude, but he was anything but a monk. He was a missionary, and he chose missionaries to follow him in seeking and finding "the lost sheep of the house of Israel" (Matt 15:24). He elected twelve of those missionary disciples to be a symbolic core of a new and spiritually restored expression of the original Twelve Tribes of Israel—the pre-monarchical confederacy under the kingship of YHWH. Before Jesus went to his death, he ate a final meal, called the Last Supper, with the Twelve. The Sunday Eucharist is the weekly sacramental prolongation in the church of that paschal symbolism. Jesus is never depicted in the gospels, as far as I know,

---

[9] See Sohrab Ahmari, "How the Church Hoodwinked Its Anti-Abuse Experts," *Commentary Magazine*, July 30, 2018.

eating alone! Even the devil can't tempt him to do it. Following the death of Judas, the remaining eleven apostles elected a twelfth to reconstitute a number sacred to Jesus. When the Twelve died, the symbolism of a restored pre-monarchical Israel died with them. The mission to the Gentiles replaced the symbolism in Isaiah of the Gentiles streaming into Jerusalem in the end times. In the Christian mission, Jerusalem and the risen Christ stream out to the nations. Crowds matter in mission.

The pope's weekly blessing draws thousands every Sunday to the Piazza of St. Peter's. World Youth Days are essentially about generating a crowd, for crowds by their nature generate attention and interest. There were crowds at Pentecost. Crowds always matter. Bishops have good biblical reasons for merging parishes, if only to remove the impression few worshipers give of a religion dying in hospice. No one is happy when a parish is closed. But unless younger people are in church, merging many seniors together, no matter how large the retired crowd may be, will never generate the sense of a church on the move again as much as youth can. Nature is naturally creative and reproductive, even profligate in the boundless fertility it has. The church we call our Mother thinks of the baptismal font as a womb. Without new birth, there is no hope in future life.

### Finances

Jesus' itinerant ministry seems to have been financed by some of his disciples and benefactors. Judas kept the purse for the movement. An itinerant ministry was free to borrow a synagogue or private home or use the wilderness or a boat by the shoreline for preaching. There was no overhead, no mortgage. Jesus ran a low-maintenance ministry on the move, for mission is what was essential to his vision, not maintenance.

The "Jesus movement" as some call it was localized in Galilee and a few surrounding regions and dedicated to the "lost sheep of the house of Israel." Some estimate that the farthest he walked or rode in his ministry, barring his travel to Jerusalem, was barely twenty-five miles. This was a rural movement at the start, but when it spread into the Roman Empire, it demanded a more systemic approach to finances. Paul took up collections for the churches—meaning groups of Christians who still gathered in house churches for prayer, worship, and mutual help. He brought funds with him for the apostles in Jerusalem when he visited.

From its beginnings, the church depended on the wealthy to support its activities. A fascinating study of the financial support the very wealthiest Romans provided the church was published by the Princeton historian of late antique Roman Christianity, Peter Brown. St. Jerome got his famous library in Bethlehem underwritten by such individuals, often women. Some entrepreneurial pastors of parishes that lack many local resources manage to fund them with support from outside the parish among friends who are not members or neighbors but who believe in the pastor's enthusiasm and competency. Mission is expensive in religion just as good marketing is in business. Some parishes have adapted well to the new age of mass social media. Professional marketing is the one ministry many pastors need today in reaching seculars as much as they need able catechists, lectors, outreach ministers, and choirs.

## Options

Jewish Christianity is the name biblical scholars use for the nascent form of the Christian church in Jerusalem prior to the Gentile mission. This compound faith, which followed the Jewish ritual laws and at the same time celebrated Jesus as God's risen Messiah was the earliest form of Christianity we know. Judaism itself was pluralistic, with different parties and rabbis working from a similar corpus of sacred literature in an interpretative contest inherent to a text-based religion. There was no single way then or now of being Jewish. Competition in interpretation and mission may seem wrong and can be destructive, but it is the name of the deepest force in physical life and the driving spirit of economic culture to favor those who struggle to survive.

Competition serves higher values by promoting the victory of excellence in any human endeavor, whether that be athletics, business, or scientific research. All flourish under conditions of honest competition. This same law of secular life affects the church. Only the most competitive institutions with the most capable leadership and most involved laity will survive in a secular age. Parishes on the dole who lack the thymic passions necessary to move any worthwhile enterprise cannot be sustained indefinitely. Jesus himself told parables about buried treasures being repossessed and taken away from unprofitable stewards and given to those with more because they doubled their own winnings. "To those that have more, more will be given. To those that have less, even the little they have will be taken away" (see Matt 13:12).

Optional faith puts pressures on underperforming religious institutions. It is the responsibility of bishops and the seminaries they use to maximize the evangelizing skills of future priests. Pedestrian and secular as these may seem, these evangelizing skills include the ability to plan, research demographics, manage and oversee finances, raise funds, undertake campaigns, and market parishes that can deliver on what they promise. The special skills priests are supposed to have in biblical interpretation, theology, and sacramental ministry must never be shortchanged. These are the basis for the ministry of the Word.

## Illiteracy

Religious illiteracy is one of the most serious problems in a secular age. People who are competent professionals in the secular world find themselves like children when it comes to the history and meaning of the Bible and the church. They know next to nothing about the geography of Palestine, the stages in the expansion of the Christian mission in the West, not to mention the theologies of Augustine and Aquinas. The Reformation and Counter-Reformation periods from 1450 to 1950 are a closed book to most of them except what they might have picked up from college studies in European history.

*Social media and mass media.* The age of mass media and social media, of course, has changed everything about how we communicate with each other. It has also changed religion. Mass media technology is a major social condition indicative of post-industrial modernity. The faithful are entering church from the Tower of Babel. Listening to a homily today is not what it was with the great orators of the past. Could Bossuet or Newman hold the attention of a Sunday congregation now? The information superhighway is far more interesting than listening to a priest milk a bromide out of a biblical passage in his homily. Less well-known to parishioners is that busy priests have found it easier and more effective to parrot to their congregation online homilies they haven't composed themselves. Pulpit plagiarism is the next secret about priests to be unmasked by an astute Googler in the pews.

*Rhetorical commonplaces.* By a rhetorical commonplace I mean the handy stock of easy associations an audience will recognize in listening to a speaker. Judaism and Christianity are primarily textual and bookish religions. The liturgy begins with lectionary readings to establish the connections between the biblical sources and the contemporary message. The Sunday lectionary cycle is a liturgical abridgement of the whole Christian Bible, most of which is never read or commented on. The commonplaces of a mass media and consumerist culture lie elsewhere than Scripture.

*The laments of George Steiner.* Of all the challenges facing the proclamation of the Gospel in modern secular culture, one of the most intractable and daunting is rarely mentioned. Yet it has transformed the existential conditions for transmitting a biblical religion. This is the massive cultural shift away from the classical canon, in this case the canon of biblical reference and citation. Despite the achievements of critical exegesis and the availability of paperback Bibles and commentaries, the world of biblical allusion is almost unrecognizable for most Catholics. In the nineteenth century, Herman Melville knew his readers would get the allusion when he opened *Moby Dick* with the words, "Call me Ishmael." Today, the name demands a footnote. The full extent of this literary liability in modern culture for religion is hard to know. The irony is that secular critics would be the ones to get the point of this allusion. Many devout Catholics wouldn't. The following observation of the famed British literary critic George Steiner undoubtedly sounds snobbish to Americans, but it's hard to contest:

> Knowledge by heart of the "texts" has been done away with by the organized amnesia which now pervades schooling. The familiarity with scripture, the Book of Common Prayer, with the great current of liturgical allusion and ritual routine, which is presumptive in the speech and inference of English literature from Chaucer to Auden, is largely dissipated. Like the fabric of classical reference, citation, pastiche, parody, imitation within which English poetry developed from Caxton's Ovid to T. S. Eliot's *Sweeney Among the Nightingales*, biblical literacy is passing quickly into the deep-freeze of academicism. The "text" is receding from immediacy, from vital personal recognition

on stilts of foot-notes, ever more rudimentary, ever more unashamed in their conveyance of information which was once the alphabet of reading.[10]

To say the Bible is receding from immediacy and vital personal recognition in televised mass culture should worry us. The serious homilist works with stenciled cutouts of three-dimensional biblical narratives and characters. The allusive moral and metaphorical depths in Scripture which makes it so enduring are lost. Say what you want, but the biblical fundamentalists who come to their churches carrying dog-eared Bibles, glossed with sermon notes like medieval scholastics at *lectio*, are craving the feeling of recognition and personal application. Many Catholics listen respectfully to the Word of God at church but would never dream of opening a Bible at home afterward.

Add to that the speed of modern life, the fragmentation of attention by modern media, and the disappearance of rhetorical arts—all have radically altered the conditions for preaching in a secular age. More to the point, the times we live in pose a challenge that may also be a remedy. The *visual* and *musical* challenge. Again, I quote Steiner:

> Today's ideals of familial co-existence, of generational amity, of neighborliness are participatory, collective, non-dismissive. Music, performed or listened to, meets these social-emotive needs and aims as reading does not. The new humanistic literacies, where we can fairly make them out, are musical not textual. Eloquence is suspect, formal speech is palsied with lies, political, theological, moral, which it articulated and adorned. The honest man sings or mumbles.[11]

The new evangelization needs to take Steiner's point. Music is more crucial today as a vehicle for conveying the sentiments of faith than ever before. A fully ecumenical musical syllabus and aesthetic belongs alongside the lectionary, homily, canon prayers, eucharistic institution narrative, and communion. If the "joy of the Gospel" is one way to grasp the meaning of faith today, then nothing evokes such joy in a communal setting like music and song. One thinks immediately of

---

[10] George Steiner, *On Difficulty and Other Essays* (New York: Oxford University Press, 1978) 8–9.

[11] Ibid., 10.

great hymns of the past but also of chant (Gregorian and Taizé), Gospel hymns, Latino guitar. Music is also the voice of a religion. No one who has heard a Jewish cantor sing in Hebrew will soon forget it. Music bears the mystery of the invisible and intangible in ways that make it a perfect vehicle for immanent transcendence. Music in too many cases is pro forma hymn recitals without spirit or joy. You would not find yourself humming one on the way home. Better a soft piano piece by Mozart before Mass to settle nerves of the unsettled semi-secularized, stressed-out congregation than another announcement.

## Homiletic Evangelization

I opened the chapter enumerating six challenges facing the Catholic Church in the United States: declining numbers of clergy and the faithful, financial strains on diocesan mission and on parishes, new religious and secular options on Sunday morning, a growing illiteracy about religion, pluralism, and secularization. Much of the book concerns background for the final two challenges, so I won't go into them here. Since I have spent my entire priesthood serving in seminary formation, I want to offer some reflections at the end of this chapter on the role homiletics must play in the new evangelization and the preparation of future priests expected to lead it.[12]

From the very beginning, evangelization in its most specific meaning has been linked to preaching. With Pope Paul VI, the term "evangelization" was broadened to such an extent that the most obvious example of it—the homily—was somehow reduced to just one form

---

[12] "The Gift of the Priestly Vocation: *Ratio Fundamentalis Institutionis Sacerdotalis*," issued by the Congregation for the Clergy (2016), rightly places a major emphasis on the formation of a future priest as first a "missionary disciple." It says, "Formation is clearly missionary in character. Its goal is participation in the one mission entrusted by Christ to His Church, that is evangelization [*sic*], in all its forms." Along with pastoral charity, spiritual leadership, and sacramental ministry, there is no form of evangelization in the secular age that is more critical than priestly teaching, pastoral formation, and homiletics. Philosophical and theological studies in the seminary serve that ministry, or what is their purpose? That is why Pope Francis dedicated the whole third chapter of The Joy of the Gospel (110–75) to proclamation and homiletics! It is disappointing, then, to read in *Ratio* 177 an abbreviated treatment of homiletic formation in the seminary. The homily has come to be regarded by more educated laity as the rhetorical touchstone for the plausibility of the Christian faith in a secular age.

among many, lost, as it were, in a crowd of evangelizing activities. Second, the matter of secularism first came to the fore with Paul VI as the abortion debates were dominating American culture. What little was left in homiletic argumentation for the new evangelization ended up in moralizing against secularism and abortion.

It is unnecessary to say that Jesus of Nazareth was first and foremost a teacher. He refused other titles, but not the title *rabbi* (teacher). The Sermon on the Mount is normally included in anthologies of the greatest speeches ever delivered. St. Paul's oratorical skills by his own account did not match those of others (2 Cor 11). But if we take his letters as any indication, he was a master of rhetoric. In his Letter to the Romans, Paul links faith directly to preaching. "How are they to hear without someone to proclaim him? And how are they to proclaim him unless they are sent?" (Rom 10:14-15). Missionary discipleship begins from the pulpit even if it cannot end there.

On preaching and eloquence, it is worth pondering the significance of a story in Luke 1:5-23 about the Jewish priest Zechariah. Struck dumb by an angel for not believing that his wife Elizabeth would bear a son, he regains his voice after writing his son's name on a tablet, "His name is John." With those written words, Zechariah recovers more than his voice. Luke transforms this priest into a poet. The Canticle of Zechariah (Luke 1:68-79) is the prayer Catholic priests recite each morning at Morning Prayer. They are reenacting an event where faith is recovered in joy and bursts into speech. This is the very soul of preaching.

The Decree on the Ministry and Life of Priests (*Presbyterorum Ordinis*) placed a formidable responsibility for evangelization on the priest. The first of his ministries (*munera*) is, for that very reason, called the ministry of the Word. Preaching is the priest's first ministry and mission. In a famous passage from the book of Isaiah, an obscure figure called the Suffering Servant announces his mission as follows, "The LORD God has given me the tongue of a teacher, that I may know how to sustain the weary with a word" (Isa 50:4). Some who abandoned church attendance may have grown a bit tired of ordained preachers not so well-trained and the predictable clichés and bromides they call homilies. No need to blame them for falling asleep any more than the Suffering Servant blamed the wearied Jews of his day. When there is a priest or deacon or gifted homilist with a well-trained tongue and word to rouse them, many of the indifferent and unchurched might take a second look at religious observance. People are hungry for spiritual nourishment in a secular age, and the secular well is not exactly bubbling over with answers for them.

Paul VI first stressed the importance of preaching as part of evangelization in *Evangelii Nuntiandi* (1975), but it was lumped in with a whole array of evangelizing actions that contextualized preaching while simultaneously overshadowing its importance. Sunday churchgoers see things otherwise.

The ministry of the Word was underscored again in I Will Give You Shepherds (*Pastores Dabo Vobis*, 1992), but it was overshadowed by catechesis and human formation. In The Word of God in the Life and Mission of the Church (*Verbum Domini*, 2010), Benedict XVI set homiletics within a broader reflection on divine revelation and the new evangelization. His own paragraph on the homily was more disappointing papal boilerplate. To his credit, however, the pope ordered the preparation of a new Directory on Homiletics by the Congregation for Divine Worship and the Discipline of the Sacraments.[13] Two years later, the USCCB produced its exhortation on the Sunday homily, *Preaching the Mystery of Faith* (2012). The documentation is plentiful and often seems repetitiously predictable on the homily as a primary priestly instrument for the new evangelization.[14] But, sad to say, the rhetoric about the homily often feels like false advertising.

The Directory on Homiletics (2015) rehearsed all over again the reasons for the importance, nature, function, and context of the homily in the liturgy. It respectfully included what Pope Francis wrote about the homily in the third chapter of The Joy of the Gospel. In spelling out the four essential aspects of the homily as a liturgical genre—the place of the Scriptures in the liturgical celebration; the principles of sound biblical exegesis; the impact of Scripture and exegesis on the imagination and life of the preacher; and "the needs of those to whom the Church's preaching is directed, their culture, and circumstances, which also determine the form of the homily, so that its hearers might be more deeply converted to the Gospel"

---

[13] See www.vatican.va: Homiletic Directory and USCCB text *Preaching the Mystery of Faith: The Sunday Homily.*

[14] *To All the World: Preaching the New Evangelization,* ed. Michael E. Connors (Collegeville, MN: Liturgical Press, 2016).

(Homiletic Directory, 2)—it completely omitted extensive reflection on the fourth aspect. In my view, this is the crucial one for evangelization in a secular context. The philosophical hermeneutics of the secular age is what I mean.

The single most important thing about public rhetoric is the audience, just as it is in all evangelization. Figuring out the mentality of an audience is what enables a rhetorician to make a case that carries. Ask any defense attorney sketching a closing argument for the jury. The Directory claims that "the homily is a dimension of ministry that is especially variable both because of the cultural differences from one congregation to another and because of the gifts and limitations of the individual preacher" (Homiletic Directory, 3). The limitations can no longer be hidden.

Let me take a slightly different approach. Homiletics is a unique genre in public rhetoric. The reason for that is the linkage of four elements into an address: (1) an exegetical interpretation of God's Word in Scripture, (2) suitably contextualized in the great creedal tradition, (3) seamlessly integrated into a liturgical and sacramental context, while (4) proposing a contemporary and pastorally compelling argument for faith with undeniable cultural pertinence. There is no rhetorical analogue like it in ancient or modern culture. With the Sunday homily in a secular age, the contemporary plausibility of the Gospel itself is being put on trial.

Perhaps consistently high-quality homiletic rhetoric each Sunday, in the space of ten or fifteen minutes, can accomplish what the popes want regarding evangelization. Perhaps. But, if the reputation of Catholic homiletics can be trusted, homilies are anything but that. Pope Francis himself—in a lapse far too revealing and embarrassing—states: "We know that the faithful attach great importance to it [the homily], and that they and their ordained ministers suffer because of homilies: the laity from having to listen to them and the clergy from having to preach them! It is sad that this is the case" (The Joy of the Gospel 135). It is more than sad; it is a scandal to be told by the universal pastor that priests themselves don't like preaching.

The church has been encouraging the laity to start thinking of themselves as missionary disciples witnessing to the joy of the Gospel. If so, then the same church must start forming priests who are more rhetorically capable of motivating that joy. In the ordinary course of things, the Sunday liturgy is the place where it should happen.

An extraordinary story from the Gospel of Luke concerning Jesus' resurrection makes Jesus himself an exegete and homilist. In Luke 24, a fellow traveler joins two disciples, shorn of messianic hope by Jesus' crucifixion, making their way to Jerusalem. This unnamed stranger responds to their despair by interpreting those passages in the Jewish Scriptures that prophesied that the messiah had to suffer, die, and rise. No specific texts in the Hebrew Scriptures are cited in Luke, but the very appeal to proofs shows what the biblical scholar Barnabas Lindars once called "New Testament passion apologetic."[15] Early Christian evangelists selected citations from the Hebrew Scriptures to support their case for the necessity of Christ's death and resurrection in prophecy.

In the uncanny encounter the two disciples have with Jesus Christ, who comes incognito, Luke presents the Lord as a rabbi, a biblical exegete and a homilist at once. Enchanted, the two disciples persuade him to stay for supper, and he does. The nameless stranger now blesses and breaks the bread. After eating it, the eyes of the two disciples are opened. But Jesus is gone. The Emmaus story is a Liturgy of the Word and a Liturgy of the Eucharist in miniature. After the supper, the two disciples remark, "Were not our hearts burning within us while he was talking to us on the road, while he was opening the scriptures to us?" (Luke 24:32).

How can a priest-homilist-celebrant fail to see the point? After the supper, the discouraged disciples talked about what the homily of the stranger did to them. The ardor ("were not our hearts burning within us") that Paul VI and John Paul II asked for in the new evangelization is found right there.

It's been fifty years since the church began speaking of the first of the priest's ministries as the "ministry of the Word." It must be admitted, in all candor, that the church in America has yet to deliver on the promise such a prioritization suggested. For two generations, the sexual revolution, celibacy, and the vocation shortfall have led the church to put greater stress than ever on priestly identity in formation. Human formation and spiritual formation accordingly consumed more and more of formation time. The encyclopedic dogmatic tradition of Catholicism required that future priests master a comprehensive syllabus of theological subjects. Sound doctrine and solid

---

[15] See Barnabas Lindars, *New Testament Apologetic* (London: SCM Press, 1973).

exegesis are essential to the ministry. But, without the rhetorical skills needed in a secular age to deliver that, what is the point of a Master of Divinity degree? The rhetorical arts, including skills at forging arguments persuasive to secular mentalities, are what seminaries should be teaching. Lest we forget, the greatest theologian in Latin Christianity in the first millennium, St. Augustine of Hippo, was a trained rhetorician and teacher of rhetoric. Rhetoric is an authentic philosophical discipline dealing with all the arts involved in public persuasion.

In Place Saint-Sulpice in the Latin Quarter in Paris stands a monumental fountain-sculpture named Fontaine des Quatre Évêques (Fountain of the Four Bishops). All of those bishops were famous French preachers. Some Protestant traditions are renowned for preaching, like the Congregationalists, Anglicans, and Presbyterians. John Henry Newman held Oxford dons spellbound at Sunday Vespers. But I don't want to place all my evangelical eggs in this one basket. That's why I quoted George Steiner's observation about the modern age and its suspicion of formal rhetoric ("palsied with lies") and the preference for feeling and song ("the honest man sings or mumbles").

Some historians claim that J. S. Bach's hymns, far more than Lutheran sermons, saved the Lutherans from lay disinterest. There's more about church than the sermon certainly. Spiritual care, pastoral leadership, community spirit and outreach are as important as the homily and the eucharistic sacrament if one cares to speak of a successful parish. I don't want to overstate my case. But if the well-known success of the Baptists and the Evangelicals tells us anything about drawing many into their congregations, including ex-Catholics, we cannot underestimate the crucial importance of preaching either.

## Excursus: David Foster Wallace at Kenyon College

David Foster Wallace delivered the commencement address at Kenyon College in 2005, later published as *This Is Water: Some Thoughts, Delivered on a Significant Occasion, about Living a Compassionate Life*.[16]

---

[16] David Foster Wallace, *This Is Water: Some Thoughts; Delivered on a Significant Occasion, about Living a Compassionate Life* (New York: Little, Brown & Company, 2009). For similar commencement address homiletics to the secular academic public, see

Off-beat and humane, satirical yet serious, the talk made as good a case for compassion as one could make to an audience of intelligently secularized college undergrads and their families. The challenge he posed for himself was to cleverly upset the secular default setting in the minds and hearts of his listeners. In the talk, Wallace coined a neologism for secular selfishness—the "hard-wired solipsistic default setting" we all operate on.[17] The solipsistic default setting, however, could be reset, Wallace suggested, if I can see the world through someone else's eyes and put myself in their shoes for a minute. This is nothing dramatic or transcendental. I can just stand behind the lady in the supermarket check-out line who is holding me up but has three kids nagging at her as she fumbles in her purse for coupons and think that she has a much more difficult life than I do, and can't I give her a pass and not roll my eyes? After that, Wallace turned to spirituality. (The page numbers for the following quotations from the book are in parentheses.)

> In the day-to-day trenches of adult life, there is actually no such thing as atheism. There is no such thing as not worshipping. Everybody worships. The only choice we get is *what* to worship. And an outstanding reason for choosing some sort of god or spiritual-type thing to worship—be it J.C. or Allah, be it Yahweh or the Wiccan mother-goddess or the Four Noble Truths or some infrangible set of ethical principles—is that pretty much anything else you worship will eat you alive. (102)

> And the so-called "real world" will not discourage you from operating on your default settings, because the so-called "real world" of men and money and power hums along quite nicely on the fuel of fear and contempt and frustration and craving and the worship of self. (115)

> The really important kind of freedom involves attention, and awareness, and discipline, and effort, and being able truly to care about other people and to sacrifice for them, over and over, in myriad petty little unsexy ways, every day. (120)

------

George Saunders's witty address delivered May 11, 2013, at Syracuse University, *Congratulations, by the Way: Some Thoughts on Kindness* (New York: Random House, 2014). A faculty colleague of Saunders, Mary Karr, published her 2015 commencement address as *Now Go Out There (and Get Curious)* (New York: HarperCollins Publishers, 2015). The homily may be struggling at Sunday Mass, but it's alive and well at Syracuse University at commencement time.

[17] Wallace, *This Is Water*, 38.

The point is the same as Isaiah's about idols (Isa 45) and Augustine's reflections on self-love. It's not new, just newly stated rhetorically in a way that caught secularized graduates off-guard. Wallace himself was only a seeker and searcher. But he understood that the secular default setting would have people worshiping the wrong things most of the time and that the remedy for that had to be some "god or spiritual-type thing." He knew, having seen them up close and tried them, that many of the standard secular gods would, in time, eat these bright young men and women alive.

The new evangelization owes a similar rhetorical take on the Gospel to its searchers and seekers struggling to believe and to resist the little gods in the boutiques of modern culture.

## Chapter 3

# From Hugo Grotius to Bill Gates

Christian evangelization flows from the passionate belief in Jesus Christ. Without passion for Christ and the mission his Father gave him, believing in Jesus Christ amounts to little more than making gratuitous claims about a reality with little moral claim on us. The words of the creed dissolve into metaphysical gibberish. We join in a confession with little epistemic and moral weight. This is the liturgical path from meaningless religious talk into religious indifference. In this chapter, I want to get a handle on all that.

The secular age presents formidable challenges for evangelization as I've tried to show—the indifference to religion as such, the prejudice against religion as a myth whose metaphors and symbols have no scientific weight to back them up. The slippery slope out of religion starts with a simple befuddlement over its language. Like a tiller disconnected from a rudder, the metaphors and concepts of belief feel disconnected from the empirical spheres of common sense and science. In the end a person becomes what Max Weber once called being "religiously unmusical."[1] A fully indifferent secular mind would have a difficult time sympathizing (by the mightiest efforts at the willing suspension of disbelief) with the plight of a religious person suddenly overwhelmed with grief at having lost her faith in God. "Honey, what's to be sad about? Rejoice." If a writer was good enough—Flannery O'Connor or Marilynne Robinson, for example—maybe the nonbeliever could possibly imagine what struggling to believe and believing well might be like.

---

[1] See Jürgen Habermas's speech on the acceptance of the Frankfurt Book Prize, "Faith and Knowledge."

In this chapter, I attempt to tackle the issue of religious indifference as we know it today and how the new evangelization needs to address this issue. This larger question is far too ambitious for this book, so I must limit the discussion in such a way that the reader will see a mere handful of points that connect to the renewal of mission in the church, which is essentially what the new evangelization is all about. Turning religious indifference into missionary discipleship is the pastoral challenge of the new evangelization.

I begin this chapter summarizing some findings of the Pontifical Council for Culture about atheism and indifference. In later chapters, I will explain how an exegesis of modernity and secularity sheds further light on the social factors involved. When the experience of God wanes for lack of self-conscious cultivation in prayer, the idea of the divine becomes enfeebled. One becomes indifferent to religion by first being indifferent to the force of the idea of God in Christianity. In that case, the "Spirit" of God has departed from the ontological flesh of the language of God, so to speak. As I will try to show, Deism does exactly that. It not only does away with the Sacred Scriptures as a linguistic platform for faith, but it also empties the humanity of God in Christ. God is "Spirit," but for us to know the divine, God must take flesh in language and history.

In the modern age, the word "Spirit" (*Geist*) entered German idealism as the "Spirit of the World" (Hegel), which Marx reduced to materialistic economics. The immanent order of the world closed in upon itself. The master-idea of evolution simply transfers Marx's economic materialism to a more demonstrable biological version. The world is matter in dynamic motion. Where is the Spirit in this immanent battle of genes? In advanced democratic capitalism, Spirit moves to markets and rights. The Spirit which moves nations and individuals is always restless. That is its nature. I will offer some reflections at the end of this chapter on mission and Spirit in the church. Later, I will return to these themes when I write about the new evangelization in the "joy of the Gospel" and what some modern thinkers have made of the Homeric and Platonic notion of *thymos* ("spiritedness") in philosophy and politics. Simply put, without spiritedness and Spirit, nothing at all moves in matter or ideas. Spirit is the pneumatic element in religion. Religion without Spirit is a chassis without a transmission. You're not going anywhere!

With this chapter, and the two chapters following it, the beginner snowplowing on the novice slope of indifference and mission takes the chairlift to the intermediate runs, which require some parallel skiing.

Charles Taylor opens *A Secular Age* with a question of belief and nonbelief anyone can understand: "One way to put the question that I want to answer here is this: why was it virtually impossible not to believe in God in, say, 1500 in our Western society, while in 2000 many of us find this not only easy, but even inescapable?"[2] One might ask simply what happened in human religious consciousness and European culture between October 31, 1517, when a passionate young Augustinian monk named Martin Luther posted his ninety-five theses on the cathedral door at Wittenberg, Germany, and the causal stroll that Friedrich Nietzsche is said to have taken in Rapallo, Italy, in 1882 or 1883 when the expression "the death of God" first occurred to him. It takes a philosophical narrative like Taylor's to answer that question responsibly. Quoting metaphysical proofs or dogmas from a catechism won't get us far.

## Making Better Sense of Religious Indifference

It is well known that Vatican II addressed modern atheism as a challenge for contemporary faith in one of its most famous documents, the Pastoral Constitution on the Church in the Modern World (*Gaudium et Spes*, 1965). Less than a decade later, Paul VI added his own reflections to it when he mentioned secularism, practical atheism, and religious indifference. By the end of the twentieth century, the Pontifical Council for Culture had made progress getting at the cultural undertow pulling believers out of the faith. It highlighted seven shifts in culture that have taken place since Vatican II that established new conditions inclining the middle classes to abandon religious practice.

1. Unbelief is largely a Western phenomenon that globalization processes transfer to more traditional and intact religious cultures.

2. Militant atheisms once associated with totalitarian regimes are disappearing at the same time as the church is often under attack for its moral beliefs.

---

[2] Charles Taylor, *A Secular Age* (Cambridge, MA: Harvard University Press, 2007), 26.

3. The atheism of the intellectual elite is spreading to the middle classes more by changes in lifestyle than by philosophical conviction.

4. Ideological atheisms of the past have been replaced by practical atheisms of religious indifference. God no longer matters and is no longer missed.

5. Church attendance has fallen off by a "silent exodus" of individuals who continue to believe but do not belong to a church.

6. Despite the sociological expectation that science and technology would eradicate the religious instinct in human beings, that has not happened. There remains a desire for something more profound than material things.

7. In short, both modern forms of unbelief and traditional forms of religious belief have evolved under the influence of a generalized religiosity that is plastic and syncretistic. Dogmatic atheism and creedal Christianity are both set aside.

To call unbelief pragmatic means you don't have to think much about it. You don't need to read Nietzsche or Feuerbach or Marx or Freud. Pragmatic atheism needs no arguments. Scientific culture quietly de-legitimates religion as an endeavor worthy of serious consideration. It happens indiscriminately to Jewish, Christian, and Muslim convictions. This pragmatic de-legitimation gives us post-religious types: the secular Jew, the secular Christian, and the secular Muslim. Attachment of the human heart and soul to the words of YHWH, Christ, or Allah feels like handcuffs on enlightened freedom and reason to such people. What possible difference do such words make in pluralistic public life? Keep it to yourself, if you must believe. So why bother? No one really cares if you're bowing before a cross or have fallen on your knees. Religious indifference is becoming not just pandemic, but easy. The secular age does not require arguments against God and religion. A shrug of the shoulder is argument enough.

Vatican Council II distinguished two types of atheism: (1) a scientific atheism in which the idea of God no longer explains anything empirical in the world or how nature works and (2) a humanistic atheism where the idea of God gets seriously in the way of human freedom. So, the idea of God is either a "useless scientific hypothesis" we've all outgrown or an "imperious superego" we're glad to get rid of. The "new factors" that the Pontifical Council for Culture wanted to stress over this take on atheism included the following: (a) the breakdown of the normal means for transmitting the faith in the family and in Catholic education; (b) globalization, which almost exclusively transmits secular and consumerist values, moral relativism, and religious indifference; (c) a search for various religious experiences to compensate for a flat consumerist lifestyle; (d) the moral disorientation created by mass media; (e) the proliferation of spiritual sects and New Age movements in the form of experimental religion; and (f) the criticism of the church in some societies for making little economic or social difference in people's lives. The Pontifical Council for Culture states that "the problem is not that of secularization, understood as the legitimate autonomy of the temporal realm, but of secularism, 'a concept of the world according to which that latter is self-explanatory, without any need for recourse to God, who thus becomes superfluous and an encumbrance.'"[3] A transcendent orientation in life is abandoned for the pursuit of a realizable and modest worldly happiness. Secularism further clouds moral criteria in a tolerance indifferent to anything like moral truth. This is reflected above all in sexuality and life issues where ontological and moral norms yield to personal preferences. If the idea of an afterlife is not denied, it is not taken seriously because, frankly, it's felt as inconceivable to moderns for whom change and novelty are what we crave, not changeless contemplation. New religious sensibilities, if they have any interest in God at all, are inclined to depersonalize the deity into nature. And nature follows immanent evolutionary processes. Enjoy yourself. Life is short.

The Pontifical Council for Culture offered several proposals for dealing with this default indifference: greater dialogue with and about nonbelief, a renewed focus on the dignity of the human person, a presence of the church in society and public life, strengthening faith in the family, and religious education. It also encouraged the exploration of the resources of the arts for communicating the beauty of the Gospel message and stressed the importance of language in doing evangelization. Each of these proposals was explored further in subsequent plenary meetings of the Pontifical Council for Culture—in

---

[3] Pontifical Council for Culture, *Where Is Your God? Responding to the Challenge of Unbelief and Religious Indifference Today* 3: "Secularisation of Belief."

The Way of Beauty (2006) and in Language and Communication (2010). As if to confirm the importance of language for the new evangelization, Benedict XVI published The Word of God in the Life and Mission of the Church (*Verbum Domini*, 2010), which brought together a fresh reflection on the linguisticality of divine revelation and the Christian testimony and witness to God's Word called the missionary disciple in the new evangelization.

Thoughtful as these reflections are, they do not sufficiently bring out the historical turning points of religious indifference. To take just one example, the council's analysis of atheism does not explain what seventeenth-century religious violence in Europe contributed to the discrediting of religion as a basis for social co-existence. The first arguments for a non-religious, secular order arose not to disparage the ontology of religion but to secure social peace in Northern Europe, which was hopelessly torn apart by confessional conflicts. Inflamed religious passions served to de-legitimate it as a source of peace. Therefore, to understand the origins of modern religious indifference we must turn our attention to the circumstances of the Reformation and post-Reformation. When ecclesiastical real estate changed hands, economic and political passions amplified religious ones. Henry VIII confiscated over six hundred Catholic monasteries and bestowed them on faithful followers of the Anglican Church. A strong incentive to convert, no? A brilliant Dutch Calvinist named Hugo Grotius (1583–1645), whose role in the emergence of the secular order cannot be underestimated, was himself caught up in the wars of religion. Let me explain.

In Grotius's time, intense theological debates among Dutch Calvinists centered on the meaning of God's absolute sovereignty in human salvation, on predestination, and on the role human freedom could and could not play in the absolute divine order. Roman Catholics were also absorbed with similar theological disputes over human freedom and divine grace. Grotius belonged to the liberal camp of Calvinists (Arminian) who held that God, in his absolute divine sovereignty and by divine predestination, had bestowed on sinful human beings, as a sign and expression of his sovereignty, a degree of freedom in salvation. His arch-conservative Calvinist co-religionists found that totally unacceptable as an expression of predestination. Grotius was captured and imprisoned for his liberal theological views on predestination and human freedom, but managed to escape and avoid a worse fate by concealing himself in a trunk full of books.

Grotius was a brilliant jurist schooled in law, philosophy, and theology. He was a serious Calvinist.

In the early seventeenth century, then, Calvinist Protestantism was deeply embroiled in inner-confessional struggles over divine grace and human freedom. To cordon off society from a religion gone a bit haywire over this problem, Grotius wrote one of the first great modern tracts on war and peace as part of his new theory of natural law. In it, he inserted a Latin principle: *Etsi deus non daretur*, usually translated "As if God did not exist." This axiom implied that the credibility of certain church doctrines (including those he and his co-religionists were fighting over about predestination) was not strong enough to override a civil agnosticism in public life. *Etsi deus non daretur* was intended to safeguard social peace underpinned by a new formula for human social rights and confessional restraint. The meaning of *etsi deus non daretur* was not to dispute God's existence (it was a hypothetical, after all) but to substitute natural law for the impulses in religion that were rending the fabric of Dutch society.

After the religious wars ended in the mid-seventeenth century, no confessional code—even the rival theologies of predestination in Dutch Calvinism—could claim a right to order or pacify civic life. What Grotius had set out to do was to ground a more secure international social order in an idea of natural law understood as God's sovereign will inscribed in reason and human nature. This is a key piece in the intellectual puzzle of the birth of the secular order and what we have come to see as one consequence of it—the marginalization of religion and emergence of religious indifference.

Though religious conflicts continued, Grotius marked a sea change in social philosophy and law—the possibility of a civic society untethered to confessional convictions. In England, John Locke (1632–1704) later wrote the more famous *Letter concerning Toleration* (1689), which had a significant influence in America on the concept of disestablishment and religious freedom. The title of Locke's letter sounds more magnanimous than it was. Locke refused to extend toleration to atheists (who lacked the fear of God's judgment in them) or to Roman Catholics (for their religious allegiance to a foreign prince—the pope!). The deeper point I'm making, however, is that passionate religious partisanship in post-Reformation Europe led thinkers like Grotius and Locke to conceive a social order with a minimum of confessional buttressing. Europe, in short, already stood knocking at the door of the secular age in the early seventeenth century. If the secular option led, as it can and often does, to an erosion of belief, well, that was the price to be paid for a new social order built on toleration of differences. After Grotius and Locke, violence in the name of God would become politically illegal, morally unthinkable, and theologically unjustifiable. Violence in the name of God and religion is the one heresy any Catholic, Protestant, Jew, secularist, or atheist can condemn. Religious fundamentalism, as we have seen, is still prone to violence in the name of God and religion. Our Christian forebears in the sixteenth and seventeenth centuries were not so upset by it. The first thing to note about the rise of secularism is the social de-legitimation of religious violence in Hugo Grotius's *De iure belli ac pacis* (On the Law of War and Peace, 1625).

A second piece of the puzzle of religious indifference emerges later with the rise of Providential Deism—the natural religion of the Enlightenment. Deism attempted to square traditional Christian belief with the rising prestige of reason and science. Lord Herbert of Cherbury devised an abridged creed, a bowdlerized biblical faith with no need for a divine revelation. Reason itself was divine revelation. God or the Deity spoke not through prophets but through science now. Religious observance was not necessary, yet the vague sense of religion was preserved. Many of our nation's Founding Fathers held to this Deist theology of reason. Thomas Jefferson deleted from his New Testament all the passages concerning Jesus' miracles, which, as an enlightened believer, he considered offensive to reason.

In the early Enlightenment, if anything deserved the attribute "miracle" or "revelation" it was science itself. Alexander Pope caught it perfectly in the epitaph he penned for Sir Isaac Newton's grave in Westminster Abbey: "Nature and nature's laws lay hid by night, God said, 'Let Newton be,' and all was light." At the dawn of the Enlightenment, it is not the biblical prophet but Isaac Newton, the founder of modern physics, who brings true revelation. As Adam Gopnik smartly puts it in *The New Yorker*, "In most of the twentieth century, physics played the role of super-science, and physics is, by its nature, accommodating of God: the theories of physics are so cosmic that the language of physics can persist without actively insulting the language of faith. It's all big stuff way out there, or unbelievably tiny stuff, down there, and either way, it's strange and spooky. Einstein's

'God,' who does not play dice with the universe, is not really the theologian's God, but he is close enough to be tolerated."[4]

Because of *etsi deus non daretur* and the erosion of religious sensibilities, Deism has become the religion of the irreligious. Whether God exists or not, it doesn't really matter that much. In terms of physics, Pierre-Simon Laplace asserted that God is an unnecessary hypothesis. But, such blasé indifference to the biblical idea of God nevertheless created room for various Romantic spiritualities to flourish alongside traditional belief and atheism. Sunday morning joggers may not be saying the Apostles' Creed or hang a crucifix in the house, as their parents or grandparents once did. They may, however, have a print of "Desiderata" on the wall.

Max Ehrmann's 1927 prose poem "Desiderata" suits the sentimental side of religious indifference perfectly. I saw it taped to the ceiling of my Catholic dentist's office when he was filling a cavity. Any modern reader will immediately recognize the opening line of "Desiderata": "Go placidly amid the noise and haste, and remember what peace there may be in silence." The first line in "Desiderata" which sounds at all like a religious creed in a traditional sense tells us: "You are a child of the universe no less than the stars and the trees." It sounds consoling if you don't think about it too much, but for anyone schooled in biblical metaphors, being a "child of the universe" is pretty cold comfort. Piety survives as a romantic patina on blind cosmology. Finally, "Desiderata" offers us the most confident and tolerant theology anyone has ever conceived: "The universe is unfolding as it should. Therefore, be at peace with God, whatever you conceive Him to be." The revelation according to Max Ehrmann

---

[4] See Adam Gopnik, "Bigger Than Phil: When Did Faith Start to Fade," in *The New Yorker*, February 17 & 24, 2014: 111. This is a clever, literate, but not so magnanimous view of religious faith. The author piles the evidence of science on top of fundamentalist supernaturalism and miracles to make faith seem, well, hardly short of ridiculous. This is the elite version of the "subtraction narrative" of secularism that Taylor wants to supersede. The explanatory reductionism in science is no substitute for a philosophical and ethical outlook on human nature and its religious aspirations. Scientists routinely pronounce reductionist views of human nature with little attention to or respect for the humanistic traditions in religious faith or serious philosophy. See Edward O. Wilson, *The Meaning of Human Existence* (New York: Liveright Publishing, 2014). Steven Pinker, *Enlightenment Now: The Case for Reason, Science, Humanism, and Progress* (New York: Viking Press, 2018).

demands no exegesis, reflection, ecumenical or interfaith dialogue. Religion survives in a cocoon of pure sentimentality. Who needs this?

A third piece in the puzzle of indifference that enabled religion to survive in America, as it has, is denominational Protestantism. Unlike Europe, where Christians essentially had three choices—Roman Catholicism, Lutheranism, or Reformed Christianity (Calvinism)—the Anglo-Saxon expressions of faith spawned many options. Anglicanism fractured into the Puritans, British Baptists, and Methodists. American religiosity was in its heyday in the nineteenth century at the very moment German atheists like Karl Marx were dismantling the grounds of belief. The First Great Awakening, associated with the fire-and-brimstone sermons of Jonathan Edwards ("Sinners in the hands of an angry God"), was followed by the Second Great Awakening in the nineteenth century, associated with the rise of abolitionism alongside emerging religious groups like Jehovah's Witnesses, Seventh-Day Adventists, Mormons, European Catholic immigrants, and Jews. Denominational Protestantism, as much as the ideas of Grotius and Locke about disestablishment, fed and disciplined religious enthusiasm in our country. Optional belief has more outlets for religious instincts. Religion is not just permitted here but, until recently, has been socially encouraged. If denominational pluralism in Christianity seems weak by the standards of traditional Catholic dogma, it is strong on the side of opposing religious antagonism and ideal for cultivating spontaneous spiritual explorations or mere indifference, or becoming a teenage atheist.

Some, of course, will opt for agnosticism and atheism, which usually get most of the press when it comes to the secular age. But the larger story of religion in America, as I said above, is not the end of belief but the explosion of religious options in which some collapse and others are reinvented. Today, some secular agnostics agree that their form of nonbelief is as much a belief as religious belief is. The great nineteenth-century atheists were not so magnanimous. Ludwig Feuerbach, Karl Marx, Friedrich Nietzsche, and Sigmund Freud deconstructed religion into disguised sentiments. "Alienation," the "sigh of the oppressed," the "opium of the people," and the "future of an illusion" are familiar reductions of religion to something pitiful and unworthy for grown-ups. In his *Genealogy of Morals*, Nietzsche portrayed Christian morality as the exact inverse of itself. It was a slave morality driven unconsciously by a hatred for life and for others, the resentment of the weak against the strong. In these inverted herme-neutics of religious feelings, the atheist would find additional justi-fication for what he or she loathed—the dehumanization of natural instincts in some forms of traditional morality. It was Nietzsche, however, who pulled the rug from underneath the Victorian cultured despisers of religion when he asserted the "death of God" and the birth of a shallow humanism in search of "pitiable comforts." He is the true prophet of the twentieth century.

World War I (1914–1918), World War II (1939–1945), and the rise of totalitarianism in Russia and Germany shattered a lot of confi-dence, including the secular humanisms parading as worthy succes-sors of traditional faith. The wars shattered religious hubris at the same time. The opposing European armies were mostly armies of Christians, not militias of atheists. The bureaucrats managing com-munism and fascism once studied the catechism and made their first communions. Political ideologies like communism and fascism suc-ceeded religion and managed to re-absorb all its messianic fervor in the name of insane and hateful social utopias. The sheer magnitude of the suffering shamed Christian culture more than the wars of reli-gion shocked Grotius. After the Battle of the Somme and the Shoah, who needed prayers? What atheist still had the nerve to swoon over enlightened reason, which engineered the machinery of death and then sat down with a beer to listen like a Romantic to Beethoven? Violence and murder in the name of God, or in the name of man's freedom, or in the name of a messianism of progress is what we have now. Man, despite all the power at his disposal, could not be a re-placement for God. But, neither could an inhuman idea of God liber-ate the freedom of man for true flourishing in history.

In this light, the Jewish philosopher Martin Buber wrote that no name has borne a greater weight in history than the name of "God." The modern believer in God who knows something of the history of religious violence, the atheist who denies or mocks the idea of God in the name of man, the agnostic reluctant to declare or deny belief in either, the fallen-away practitioner of a faith who can no longer bring himself or herself to join a congregation of worshipers—all can identify with Buber's words. "God" is unlike any other name.

> None has become so soiled, so mutilated. . . . Generations of men
> have laid the burden of their anxious lives upon this word and weighed

it to the ground; it lies in the dust and bears their whole burden. The races of men with their religious factions have torn the word to pieces; they have killed for it and died for it, and it bears their fingermarks and their blood. . . . They draw caricatures and "God" underneath; they murder one another to say "in God's name." . . . We must esteem those who interdict it because they rebel against the injustice and wrong which are so readily referred to "God" for authorization.[5]

Vatican II suggested we at least esteem the search for God that ended some in an honest atheism and agnosticism. The new evangelization needs to take the same approach to secularization and secularism.

A year after Buber died, *Time Magazine* (April 8, 1966) put this question on a stark black and red cover, "IS GOD DEAD?" Vatican II had just concluded. *Time* and *The New Yorker* had been covering the obscure debates going on at St. Peter's for several years. It was big news. And, the idea of God's death was so implausible to average Americans at that time that former President Harry Truman, when asked about the cover story in *Time*, was forced to fake the usual condolences—"I'm always sorry to hear somebody is dead. It's a damn shame," he said. According to Daniel Bell, however, Nietzsche's declaration of "the death of God" was not provable at all if taken in the literal sense.[6] It had no denotative value. It was a form of religious pornography. Nietzsche was just stripping naked the hypocrisies of a sentimental religiosity that amounted to bad faith. God had been killed not by those attacking belief but by those who just pretended to believe. The once powerful idea of God that powered great religions had turned into sentimental origami and would fold once you figured out where the seams were. Nietzsche questioned a benign religious sentimentalism that carried no force with it. The serious forms of an early atheism that led Vatican II and Martin Buber to be so magnanimous in their estimation of its honesty have turned more cavalier. Today, many atheists just laugh at the whole idea of God.

---

[5] The original passage from Martin Buber appears in his book, *Meetings* (1973), 50–51. It is quoted in Walter Kasper, *The God of Jesus Christ* (New York: Crossroad Publishing Company, 1987), 3–4.

[6] Daniel Bell, "The Return of the Sacred? The Argument on the Future of Religion," *Bulletin of the American Academy of Arts and Sciences* 31, no. 6 (March 1978): 45.

David Foster Wallace wrote a review of Joseph Frank's biography of Dostoevsky, which many consider the most accomplished study of the great Russian novelist. In the review, Wallace wondered what a modern literary critic might make of the monologue in *The Idiot* where Dostoevsky has a character struggle with the idea of suicide as he is tortured by ideas of love and God:

> Can you imagine any of our major novelists allowing a character to say stuff like this (not, mind you, just as hypocritical bombast so that some ironic hero can stick a pin in it, but as part of a ten-page monologue by somebody trying to decide whether to commit suicide?). The reason you can't is the reason he wouldn't: such would be, by our lights, pretentious and overwrought and silly. The straight presentation of such a speech in a Serious Novel today would provoke not outrage or invective, but worse—one raised eyebrow and a very cool smile. Maybe, if the novelist was major, a dry bit of mockery in *The New Yorker*. The novelist would be (and this is our age's truest vision of hell) laughed out of town.[7]

Struggle with belief in God? You can't be serious? But, that's precisely what Bonhoeffer did at the end of his life. And, in a very telling way.

Waiting in his cell for execution at Flossenburg Prison in 1944, the Lutheran theologian Dietrich Bonhoeffer composed a few sentences on the new conditions facing Christian faith in the modern world. Who would expect that, at such a desperate hour, the words of Grotius—*Etsi deus non daretur*—would come to mind? Bonhoeffer translated its meaning as follows: "The God who lets us live in the world without the working hypothesis of God is the God before whom we stand continually. Before God and with God we live without God. God lets himself be pushed out of the world on to the cross. He is weak and powerless in the world, and that is precisely the way, the only way, in which he is with us and helps us."[8] A powerless God helps? How's that possible? Facing imminent execution by the Nazis, Grotius's maxim interprets the cross of Jesus Christ for Bonhoeffer. The principle intended to clear a space for secular toleration in

---

[7] David Foster Wallace, "Joseph Frank's Dostoevsky," in *Consider the Lobster and Other Essays* (New York: Little, Brown and Company, 2006), 273.

[8] Dietrich Bonhoeffer, *Letters and Papers from Prison*, ed. Eberhard Bethge (New York: Macmillan, 1967), 188.

seventeenth-century Holland boosted the courage of a condemned Christian theologian caught in a plot to assassinate Hitler. "Before God and with God we live without God": For Bonhoeffer this was not Christian atheism as some understood it, but a call to Christian responsibility for the world in faith when the scientific, social, and political order had changed. Biblical revelation had told Christians what God's will was. Miracles were and are always possible, but the Galilean miracle worker we call the Son of God hung alone on the cross without one.

Dietrich Bonhoeffer was executed at Flossenburg on April 9, 1945. Germany surrendered a month later, May 7, 1945. No one knows what Bonhoeffer might have written, had he survived, about meaningful God-talk, prayer, *etsi deus non daretur*, the theology of the cross, and God's willingness to be pushed out of the world so that men and women in the world would take greater responsibility for it. But he prayed in prison and found words of faith there to console his fellow prisoners in their anguish. If God was pushed out of the world by his own allowance, God was not pushed out of the language of courage, hope, love, and joy.

Two days after Bonhoeffer was hung, Elie Wiesel was liberated from the Buchenwald Concentration Camp (April 11, 1945). The archival photo of his young gaunt face staring from a bunk crammed with emaciated bodies is an icon. The opening words in his autobiography *Night* (1958)—"Never shall I forget . . ."—make the following anecdote astonishing. On a plane flight, Wiesel was once observed reciting prayers with a companion. Knowing his story, someone respectfully asked why he was praying at all. The Holocaust survivor replied: "If I have problems with God, why should I blame the sabbath?"[9] Very Jewish! Observance, even in the absence of the assurance of God, is necessary. Wiesel is like our modern Job addressing God in the whirlwind of chaotic political history. Refusing to be silent. Holding heaven and earth to account. Prayer after the Shoah, if one thinks twice about Bonhoeffer's cell and Wiesel, is more a protest than a piety. The moments when praise, gratitude, thanksgiving, contrition, and sorrow arrive in life, as they always do, require the words and gestures that lift up the heart whether in joy or anguish.

[9] Joseph Berger, "Elie Wiesel, Auschwitz Survivor and Nobel Prize Winner. Dies at 87," *New York Times*, July 2, 2016.

Religion is too filled up with petition. Lamentation is a noble psalm to say in the darkness: "Why, O Lord?" In a secular age, the new evangelization must begin with prayers uttered in absolute honesty about the stark realities of our human situation. If Elie Wiesel can recite sabbath prayers, having known the hell some men create for others, should we pusillanimous Christians and self-sufficient seculars not turn to invocation? The Psalms, Job, Ecclesiastes, and the Gospel of Jesus Christ have ways of speaking about the mystery of God, of the abandonment to suffering without an answer, and of hope that science and "Desiderata" know little or nothing about. God may feel dead to some, but the Word of God still speaks.

When Bill Gates was asked about his moral and religious beliefs, he struggled a bit to say what God meant to him.[10] He immediately said he didn't believe in myths to explain the world. Then, Gates went on to say that he participates in a Catholic parish with Melinda and the children because the moral beliefs in religion are, as he likes to put it, "super-important." Still, Bill Gates couldn't exactly say how God had anything to do with those "super-important" moral beliefs he wanted his children to have. Bill and Melinda Gates are often asked to explain the motives for their extraordinary philanthropy. They speak about those motives in the annual report of their foundation. Recently, they mentioned the example of their parents and Melinda's Catholic high school education in Texas where the stress was on Catholic social teaching. They spoke about the absurd inequity of human fates in the world beyond prosperous America and the ability their extraordinary wealth gives them to reverse nature's injustice with smart investments in health, clean water, education, and entrepreneurial social action.

Bill Gates is an outstanding modern example of technical brilliance and philanthropic benevolence. He may or may not pray, I don't know. But he and Melinda are certainly the answer to prayers. He somehow believes that being in church is an important way of keeping moral beliefs alive and working. My guess is that he sees good people there striving to be better people and hears words there that are essentially different words from how science and technology speak. The words he uses to explain his foundation's work are all

---

[10] Google "Bill Gates: The Rolling Stone Interview," by Jeff Goodell, March 13, 2014.

words in the lexicon of the Christian theology of grace—"gifts," "being gifted," "feeling blessed," and the "inequity" of human fates. These sound very religious to me. The God who allows himself to be pushed out of the world managed to leave a vocabulary behind whose potential for translation seems almost inexhaustible. That God has found a disciple in Bill Gates.

This brings me to the end of my historical reflections on religious indifference. The sources of it, as I have tried to show, are many. Violence perpetrated by believers in the name of God is one big reason for it. Hugo Grotius was among the first major Christian thinkers to imagine a political and civil society grounded in principles of natural law rather than confessional beliefs. John Locke developed the concept of religious toleration for multi-confessional societies. Denominational Protestantism generously enlarged the number of religious options in those societies. All of that played a role in the culture of religious indifference we see around us today.

Since I have brought up the matter of religious violence as one of the reasons for the rise of religious indifference, let me close this section with a few reflections about religion and violence. Critics of faith sometimes point to the ancient biblical sources for the divine justification for violence and holy war. The story of the sacrifice of Isaac by Abraham comes to mind (Gen 22). Understood in its first-millennium BCE context and with the help of rabbinic exegesis, the Bible itself offers two examples of cases where child sacrifice was at first accepted and then remarkably corrected.[11] The command of God to sacrifice Isaac is rescinded before the act. An ancient narrative way of doing what we call ethics tells a story which substitutes an animal for the sacrifice of the firstborn. In the Ancient Near East, people believed that by sacrificing the firstborn child, the divinity would bestow even more offspring and blessings. They overcame that cultural assumption, not with abstract moral principles, but with a narrative of substitution.

---

[11] See Jon D. Levenson, *The Death and Resurrection of the Beloved Son: The Transformation of Child Sacrifice in Judaism and Christianity* (New Haven, CT: Yale University Press, 1993). René Girard has written about the "scapegoat mechanism" by which people transfer the fear of evil and its expiation onto a victim—usually an outsider or deformed person. See René Girard, *Violence and the Sacred*, trans. Patrick Gregory (Baltimore, MD: Johns Hopkins University Press, 1977).

The second example of correction of child sacrifice is found in Ezekiel 20:25-26. In that text, the prophet hears God say something unheard of: "Moreover I gave them statutes that were not good and ordinances by which they could not live. I defiled them through their very gifts, in their offering up all their firstborn, in order that I might horrify them, so that they might know that I am the LORD."[12] Once again God corrects himself, but in this case justifies the outrage as a proof of divine power. The logic defies us because it is the religious logic of an ancient culture's imagination struggling with the progress of ethics. The death of Jesus by the will of his Father is not a justification for humans to kill one another but a revelation of the end of all scapegoating. No new sacrifices of blood are required to appease the Divine, only sacrifices of praise and forgiveness.

Sacrificial thinking can be profoundly dangerous. The Eucharist represents the sacramental transubstantiation of covenant sacrifice ("in my blood") as an un-bloody "sacrificial meal" of bread and wine which demands that nothing living be killed. The true Lamb of God died once for all. Don't kill. Eat and drink the transubstantiated body and blood of Christ in memory of the death of the Son of God which saves the rest of us from our sins and from having to kill anyone as a sacrifice to some deified human reality. The Eucharist is communion in the death of the divine martyr for truth and for mercy.

Violence that destroys lives can take many forms, as we know. The anonymous investment bankers who bundled junk mortgages together to make themselves wealthy brought about the collapse of the value of pension funds and a secure retirement for millions of Americans. I doubt any of those nameless gray flannel suits in BMWs lost much sleep about it or would know or recall Jesus' indictment in Mark 12:40 of the scribes who "devour widows' houses." These religious and religiously indifferent wealthy bankers ate and drank like the barbarians in Zbigniew Herbert's poem quoted below. One prominent theologian regards them as the late capitalist embodiment of Nietzsche's "last men."[13] Everything that Bill Gates is not.

It may surprise some to discover that Pope Francis alludes to the maxim of Hugo Grotius, *etsi deus non daretur*, in The Joy of the Gospel.

---

[12] For background, see Levenson, *The Death and Resurrection of the Beloved Son*, 5–7.

[13] See Miroslav Volf, *Flourishing: Why We Need Religion in a Globalized World* (New Haven, CT: Yale University Press, 2015), "Epilogue: God, Nihilism and Flourishing."

In speaking of the religiously indifferent and morally relativistic mind-set, the pope writes: "This practical relativism consists in acting *as if* God did not exist, making decisions *as if* the poor did not exist, setting goals *as if* others did not exist, working *as if* people who have not received the Gospel did not exist."[14] The fourfold repetition multiplies the force of a moral reminder. To live in the absence of the invisible God, the Totally Other, is often to make us indifferent to other realities, no less real than ourselves. *Etsi deus non daretur* is a two-edged sword.

*As You Like It* has a familiar saying: "All the world's a stage. And all the men and women merely players; They have their exits and their entrances" (act 2, scene 7). For the secular imagination, God was once a player. The substitution secularization narrative holds that with the arrival of new players—science and liberal freedom—an earlier player, God, took a bow and made an exit or, more accurately, was ushered off by the new stage manager as an embarrassment. Like Tolstoy's junior demon argued, things have gotten much better for us now that he is gone.

This is some of the context for the challenges atheism and religious indifference pose to religious faith today. A short prose-poem by the Polish poet Zbigniew Herbert captures the notion of an obsolete divinity in a post-religious age.

> First there was a god of night and tempest. A black idol without eyes, before whom they leaped, naked and smeared with blood. Later on, in the times of the republic, there were many gods with wives, children, creaking beds, and harmlessly exploding thunderbolts. At the end only superstitious neurotics carried in their pockets little statues of salt, representing the god of irony. There was no greater god at that time.
>
> Then came the barbarians. They too valued the little god of irony. They would crush it under their heels and add it to their dishes.[15]

The gods of night and tempest haunt the minds of religious fanatics. Zeus threw thunderbolts once, but now weather forecasters tell us where the lightning will be. Freud dispatched the god of neurotic

---

[14] Pope Francis, The Joy of the Gospel 80.
[15] Zbigniew Herbert, *The Collected Poems 1956–1998* (New York: HarperCollins Publishers, 2007), 180.

guilt. The barbarians then came—the "last men" of Nietzsche—seeking only a pitiable comfort. Free of myth and religious neuroses, they crushed the icons? Poetic license parading as theology? Well, just study twentieth-century European political history—the two World Wars, the genocides, the apartheids and enslavements—and ask yourself how well gods made in our own image have worked out. Some scholars say, after the death of God will come the death of humankind. That's entirely believable.

In Christianity, real faith is somewhat intermittent. It is born, becomes routinized by ritual, and often slips away or seems to lose the power it once had for us. Then, something happens, perhaps, that brings faith back to life in another way. At one moment, a cool disenchantment with religion feels liberating. Then, something uncanny happens—suffering, the birth of a child, an encounter with the mystery of existence in some way—that makes cool disenchantment seem shallow and unworthy. The human heart hungers for a plausible and believable Absolute, not for freedom from all belief or for wandering aimlessly among beliefs like a Don Juan of religious experience for its own sake. What William James described in *The Varieties of Religious Experience* is the human soul overpowered by the uncanniness of its capacity for evil or by a goodness it can't account for.

This is what happened to the Buddha, who, in a flash of insight, saw the hopeless futility of all craving. It is what overpowered Isaiah in the Jewish temple before the holy of holies. St. Augustine felt it probably when just beyond the walls of the garden where he sat holding a Bible, he perhaps heard a child sing a tune, *"Tolle lege, tolle lege"* ("Take and read, take and read"). He opened his Bible to a passage in St. Paul, and it changed his life. Transcendence over his own past by reading a biblical text. Augustine knew the feeling of transcendence again standing on a balcony at Ostia with his mother Monica sharing thoughts about spiritual ecstasy in God's presence shortly before she died (*Confessions*, book 9).

The idea of God in Christian theology has nothing to do with some transcendent Big Guy in the sky. The patriarchal image in cartoons with a long white beard is as childish as it is foolish. The most fundamental revelations of God in the Bible are just the sound of a Voice. YHWH speaks to Moses from the burning bush but cannot be seen. God speaks at Jesus' baptism in the Jordan River but without appearing. "This is my Son" tells the Christian where to look and whom to listen to and follow. God is a Voice in biblical revelation who creates

("God said let there be light . . ."), liberates slaves from bondage, leads them in the wilderness, gives them a teaching to guide them that they are to pass on. In the Christian revelation, the Son of God is Jesus Christ, who has given his disciples his word and a mission in the world. The final words of the risen Christ in the Gospel of Matthew are a commission to speak: "teaching them to obey everything that I have commanded you" (Matt 28:20).

There is much more that could be written about revelation. In concluding this section, though, let me highlight one factor that has a real bearing on the plausibility of a trinitarian theology of God. The trinitarian nature of the One God, though unprovable to reason and still obscure in New Testament revelation, means that the abstract concepts of "relationality" and "sociality" are the closest we can get to what God is like. The most powerful metaphor of "relationality" we know is Love. In a word, God is not like an individual human person, much less like three individual human persons, as many might imagine the Trinity to be. God is a communion, not a self as we are. That communion is what makes the brief credo of the divine in 1 John 4, "God is love," make sense. Self-giving Love is the basis for Divine Communion of Persons. God loves human beings and all creation because first God is Love—creative love, sustaining love, redeeming love, reconciling love. The "sociality" of the trinitarian God is what grounds the church's identity as a communion.

## Missionary Discipleship and the Christian God

The names of the Divine Persons are not three separate individuals. The closest word theology has for them is "person" because we associate love and freedom with that word. But, person is not a modern individual or self with a separate and distinct self-consciousness. That would transform the Christian Trinity into "tri-theism"—three gods in one. As the Great Doxology in the Mass expresses it, glory is given to the Father through, with, and in the Son in the unity of the Holy Spirit. The different prepositions tell us what we can know about the Trinity by telling us how to address the God of Jesus Christ.

The missionary disciple is a trinitarian disciple. Missionary discipleship turns revelation into autobiography. It is significant that Exodus 3:14-15 joins in the same passage God's self-revelation ("I Am Who Am") to the sending of Moses. As the revealed name, YHWH, is spoken, a correlative mission is attached to it. Indeed, the mission given Moses is part and parcel of the revelation. Andre LaCocque points out that Exodus 3 is both *theophanic* and *performative*.[16] The name YHWH is linked to the prophetic commission of Moses, who is also giver of the law to the Israelites. When God speaks, it is not for a private ecstasy or to share a metaphysical aporia about his being, but for a historical mission. The great prophets of Israel make that clear. Isaiah 55 compares the fruitfulness of the Word of God to rain and snow that water the fields for growth and harvest. Thymic passion inspired by the grace of the Holy Spirit makes missionary discipleship fruitful.

To understand mission in the historical Jesus, I turn to John Meier, who introduces what he calls the "Baptist Block" sayings of Jesus in Matthew 11.[17] Here John the Baptist inquires, "Are you the one who is to come, or are we to wait for another?" (11:3). Jesus lets his actions speak for him: "the blind receive their sight, the lame walk, the lepers are cleansed, the deaf hear, the dead are raised, and the poor have good news brought to them" (Matt 11:5). These force only one conclusion—the kingdom of God is already taking place and these events prove it. Meier adduces further sayings of the historical Jesus to show God's power and kingdom is already in process of being realized in some limited sense: "if it is by the Spirit of God that I cast out demons, then the kingdom of God has come to you" (Matt 12:28; see also Luke 11:20; Mark 3:2-27 and other exorcisms); "The kingdom of God is among you" (Luke 17:20-21) and "The kingdom of God has come near" (Mark 1:15); the beatitude on eyewitnesses to Jesus (Matt 13:16-17; Luke 10:23-24); and Jesus' rejection of fasting (Mark 2:18-20). The implication in all these passages is that the present time of Jesus' ministry is the time God has chosen to act and demonstrate divine power and grace.

Meier stresses that the kingdom of God is a "tensive symbol" in the usage of Jesus, not a clear concept, much less a full-blown theology or ideology. The seeming inconsistencies between the future

---

[16] Andre LaCocque, "The Revelation of Revelations," in Andre LaCocque and Paul Ricoeur, *Thinking Biblically: Exegetical and Hermeneutical Studies* (Chicago: University of Chicago Press, 1998), 316. LaCocque and Ricoeur take turns exegeting and interpreting eight passages from the Old Testament, demonstrating how to complement historical-critical, literary, and hermeneutical readings of texts.

[17] John Meier, *A Marginal Jew: Rethinking the Historical Jesus; Volume Two: Mentor, Message, and Miracles* (New York: Doubleday, 1994), 398ff.

kingdom and its present-tense realization in Jesus as well as its eternal character in God's will for creation cannot be harmonized. Jesus in his actions is like the prophet and dramaturge of the kingdom. The signs of it can be seen in what he did as much as in what he says; the dramatic intersection of words and deeds occurs in Jesus' exorcisms, miracles, and healings.[18]

These sayings indicate that the coming kingdom must be "the object of intense expectation and prayer on the part of Jesus' disciples," and in addition would "mean the reversal of all unjust oppression and suffering," the fulfillment of the Old Testament promises to "faithful Israelites," and "the joyful participation of believers (and even of some Gentiles!) in the heavenly banquet with Israel's patriarchs."[19] To share a banquet with the patriarchs obviously demands that the barrier of death has been transcended. As Meier puts it, "The symbol of the banquet is 'unpacked' with various images of consolation, the satisfaction of hunger, the inheritance of the land, the vision of God, the bestowal of mercy."[20] A missionary disciple who understands the historical Jesus will seek those human approximations that most closely resemble these eschatological images. As utopias function for the social and political imagination, the kingdom of God functions for the missionary disciple.

For missionary discipleship, one can draw this important conclusion: The disciple of the kingdom come, by faith and love, seeks to become a disciple of the kingdom here and now by the power of wisdom and love and joy in the resurrection of Christ

Again, we should recall, that Jesus barely traveled twenty-five miles during the years of his Galilean ministry and considered his divine mission as that of being sent to the "lost sheep of the house of Israel." He did not undertake a foreign mission and in fact some New Testament evidence suggests just the opposite. He declines to expel a demon from the daughter of a Canaanite woman in Matthew 15:21-28, saying, "It is not fair to take the children's food and throw it to the dogs." Like a good Jew, however, Jesus imagined that a fully restored Israel would draw the Gentiles into Jerusalem as we read in Isaiah 2:2; 66:12.

[18] Ibid., 451–54.
[19] Ibid., 349.
[20] Ibid., 349–50.

The full doctrine of Jesus' nature and mission only comes to expression in the gospels following his death and resurrection. Like the Exodus functioned for Israel, the Paschal Mystery of Jesus' death and resurrection functions for Christians. Death is an existential exodus from life; resurrection is the new life in God's kingdom. From Jesus' death and resurrection there follows another event of enormous significance for missionary discipleship: the outpouring of the Holy Spirit upon the church. From the resurrection experience, the full meaning of Christ on the cross comes to light.

## Missionary Discipleship in the Pentecostal Birthplace of the Church

After what seemed like the antithesis of a divine revelation in Jesus' abject crucifixion on the cross (when the Divine Voice heard at the baptism in the Jordan River says nothing) and because of the power of the resurrection experiences, the crucified and risen Messiah gives his disciples a mission. In Luke–Acts, the descent of the Holy Spirit on the apostolic community and the effects it has become the nucleus from which the whole idea of a prolongation of Jesus' mission is born. In short, two trinitarian events—the Christ-event and the Spirit-event together—bring about the mission of the church. In the Acts of the Apostles, the outpouring of the Holy Spirit on the apostolic community happens on the Jewish festival of Pentecost. The newly reconstituted Twelve receive the Holy Spirit in pneumatic fire. God breathes his Spirit onto them and into them. Acts 2 anticipates in a single event the entire mission of the church as sacrament, mission, proclamation, and evangelical re-translation of the revelation in Christ.

After two millennia, and despite many charismatic moments in church history, the doctrine of the Holy Spirit for most Catholics is obscure and irrelevant. Except for periodic outbursts of radical religious enthusiasm often accompanied by anti-institutional and anti-hierarchical impulses, the Holy Spirit means little to many who believe in Christ. What does the iconography of the Holy Spirit as a white dove, whose basis is in the baptism of Jesus, convey to ordinary believers? The baptismal "dove" is not a second incarnation of God. The language and symbolism of the Holy Spirit requires careful and deliberate rejuvenation in Christian catechesis.

The gift of tongues for a secular age may be considered tantamount to the capacity of Christians to translate the Gospel of Christ into new expressions that inspire and move those inclined to be religiously indifferent. Persuasively powerful language and witness can ignite healthy passion in a faith that has gone inert. Then the regular spiritual consumers of sacraments at church, the semi-believing pious bystanders to Christian mission might raise their hands to stand up and be counted as volunteers. Without passion and spiritedness in the new evangelization, all we will have will be diocesan plans for merging failing parish businesses.

Invisible Father, Voice of God, Spirit of God, Son of God—those images take us to the deepest levels of the new evangelization in the trinitarian mystery of God. No amount of spiritual enthusiasm or exegetical finesse can substitute for the unavoidable issue of the meaning of the word "God." Doctrines and prayers were volatile securities—and not very liquid. Some "cash out" for political and economic passions or for existential anomie and indifference.

Faith is "intermittent" in each Christian life.[21] At one moment we seemingly have more of it than is necessary, and other times not enough or none. Death may deprive us of the sense of a sacred canopy and easy consolations. But Rosenstock-Huessy claimed that the death and resurrection of Christ has communicated to the world the ground of a new belief which sees death as the beginning of life.

> The story of Christianity, both in the lives of individual Christians and in the life of humanity, is a perpetual reenactment of the death and resurrection of its Founder. Only by his great outcry, "My God my God, why has thou forsaken me?" did Jesus become our brother. All of us are bankrupt at times; by giving up the power of his spirit for this one moment he created his equality and unanimity with all men. . . . Faith cannot live unless it remains intermittent: that bitter truth admits death where it belongs in our belief, as a bringer of new life. So every Christian community or movement is the result of tears shed in common, of a bankruptcy faced in the fellowship of hearts that have survived defeat.[22]

---

[21] Eugen Rosenstock-Huessy, *The Christian Future: Or The Modern Mind Outrun* (New York: HarperTorchbooks, 1966), 89–91.

[22] Ibid., 90.

The resurrection experiences of the first witnesses give rise to contestable testimony. In some instances, not even Jesus' own disciples recognize their Master. This new Spiritual Incognito of the crucified Christ hides one revelation in another, like a Fabergé egg. In his resurrection appearances, Christ never assigns blame for his suffering nor gives grounds for apostolic recrimination. The wounds he displays to "Doubting Thomas" confirm his identity. But, in the resurrection, the wounds are healed. Like the scars on the foot of Odysseus, which the slave girl in the *Odyssey* of Homer observes as she bathes the feet of the long-lost hero, the wounds of Jesus allow Thomas to see and recognize who stands before him. Jesus does not demand penance from the disciples for abandoning him in his hour of need. Instead, in the Gospel of John he breathes the Spirit of forgiveness into them. The risen Christ brings *shalom* (peace) and mercy. To the demoralized disciples, the risen Christ is neither a simple reunion of friends nor a private consolation for each one. Encountering the risen Christ is a new bestowal of faith with a mission attached to it.

The gift of tongues for a secular age requires a contemporary translation of the Gospel of Christ that can move the apathetic disciple and the religiously indifferent. A passive faith soon becomes an unspoken and unspeakable faith. Thymic passion not fully engaged in the church goes seeking inspiration elsewhere. The same grace that transforms sinners can transform consumers of sacraments into stockholders in a mission and cause. Bystanders become disciples. Without *thymos* and "spiritedness" in parishioners, all you will have in the new evangelization are words.

Even during his earthly mission, Jesus said in Luke 12:49, "I came to bring fire to the earth, and how I wish it were already kindled!" In comparing his own prophetic mission of baptizing to that of the One Who Is to Come, John the Baptist declared, "I baptize you with water; but one who is more powerful than I is coming; I am not worthy to untie the thong of his sandals. He will baptize you with the Holy Spirit and fire" (Luke 3:16). This is what is needed in the new evangelization—the passion and fire of the Holy Spirit guided by the words and the redemptive witness of Jesus Christ.

*Chapter 4*

# The Long Nineteenth Century

The Christian conviction, founded on both covenants and on the explicit message of the risen Christ to his disciples in Matthew 28, is that the church will always be a missionary communion of faith. In breaking its ties with historical Judaism, the Christian church broke with a faith primarily built on blood, ethnicity, family, and national identity. That rupture in religious self-understanding carried the Gospel to the nations—the Gentiles. But, the Word of God needs a community to pass it on. The pious-sounding but innocuous idea of the deity in "Desiderata," emptied of personal voice, agency, and purpose, cannot move much in us. It bestows a cheap blessing. What does such a deity possibly mean without the testimony of spiritual encounters with God which we find in Scripture, without an assembly in which Scriptures are read and interpreted and celebrated with sacramental rituals, without the attempt to apply the truth in them to human life? The more impersonal the deity becomes, the more that witness and mission feel groundless and pointless. Christian trinitarian monotheism, without abandoning the name of YHWH in the first covenant, forms a new idea of God from the message and ministry of Jesus of Nazareth.

Familiar liturgical trinitarian prepositions such as "from the Father, with the Son, in the Holy Spirit" or "to the Father through the Son in the Holy Spirt" are the poetic syntax and grammar of a trinitarian God for Christians. The transcendent Father as creator becomes accessible to history, and to those making or suffering from it, only through the Divine Word given in the Holy Spirit. These religious metaphors are not mere arbitrary conjunctions but a differentiated experience of the tri-personal sociality of the One God. They must

105

hang together for someone to think and act like a Christian in any age, including the secular age. Christ's Father was not any deity. The Father sends the Son into the world on mission. Christ breathes the Holy Spirit into the church for mission as well.

Nothing sobers up bad religious ideas and passions like good religious history. And good history requires that the Catholic faith be understood against the larger canvas of social and political action. Many Catholics today lack any historical knowledge of the church in the modern age. Catholics raised on catechism teachings imagine faith largely in terms of what must be believed, a list of propositions in a creed. Unlike Jews, whose religious memories are powerfully linked to historical events, Catholics have little concrete notion of what their Catholicism meant to their ancestors in the faith. Catholics couldn't tell you how the Irish immigrants suffered from Nativism when they disembarked from Cork in New York City. All that some Catholics know about Catholic history are the Crusades and the Inquisition. Serious as these abuses of ecclesiastical power were, they don't gainsay the larger story of Christianity's contributions to Western civilization, philosophy, art, culture, and ethics. No small task of the new evangelization is to find a way to enlighten unenlightened Catholics about their own church history. I can only make some general points about it here relative to the case I'm making about the secular age.

In the next two chapters, I want to summarize what has happened in the history of the Catholic Church since 1800. The modern political and social world, as we know it today, started to take shape then in Europe. The historical prologue to Vatican II deserves the title of the "long nineteenth century" because it ran, in fact, 160 years from 1800 to 1965. Few Catholics realize the challenges that the European Enlightenment, together with German, French, and English Romanticism, had on their faith, not to mention the major political and technological changes in this whole period. Neither correct doctrine nor moral fervor in the new evangelization can exempt us from knowing something of the history of our church in this decisive historical period.[1] These major cultural changes, concurrent with the birth of

---

[1] A standard work on the Enlightenment is the trilogy by Peter Gay, professor of history at Yale University: *The Enlightenment: An Interpretation*, vol. 1: *The Rise of Modern Paganism* (New York: Simon & Shuster, 1966), and *The Enlightenment: An Interpretation,*

our country (1776) and the French Revolution (1789), upended the political premises of Christendom. It took a century and a half for the church to sort out the problems as well as the values in Enlightenment thought, to apply the historical reconstructive sciences to its own traditions, and to come to a new overall appreciation of what was involved for its mission in the democratic social conditions of the modern secular world. From the theological side, Vatican II harvested the best of the first millennium and modern biblical science for the faith. In the redefinition of the church's cultural mission, the council was a bolt out of the blue.

Essentially, Vatican II accepted the post-Christendom era as the socio-cultural condition for its modern mission. Preaching the Christian Gospel and spreading its message in culture would no longer be able to rely on political sponsors or on the hegemony of classical cultural canons of learning. In the modern world, the apologetics of religious faith would need to engage the social sciences and modern philosophies of critical reason in the light of history itself. The terms were set at Vatican II for the new evangelization as a new hermeneutic of divine revelation, the rebirth of evangelical rhetoric suitable for a rationalist and pragmatic age, and the persuasive force of the church's sacramental, personal, and institutional witness.

Some historians refer to the modern period, which reached a certain climax in the Enlightenment, as the birth of a second "Axial Age" in culture. The first Axial Age, *Aschenzeit* as the philosopher Karl Jaspers once called it, covered the five hundred years from 700 BCE to 200 BCE. During that period the mental universe of the ancient world turned over many times in the symbolisms and concepts associated with Confucianism, Buddhism, the biblical monotheism of Second Isaiah, and the philosophical systems of Plato and Aristotle. The "second Axial Age" began with the Enlightenment, which set new terms for rational discourse and political life. The terms of Christendom and a medieval hierarchical imaginary were set aside.

---

vol. 2: *The Science of Freedom* (New York: Simon & Shuster, 1969), and Peter Gay, *The Enlightenment: A Comprehensive Anthology* (New York: Simon and Shuster, 1973). A more popular introduction to the Enlightenment, with attention to the American context, can be found in Gertrude Himmelfarb, *The Roads to Modernity: The British, French, and American Enlightenments* (New York: Knopf, 2004).

I have titled this chapter using John O'Malley's apt characterization of the pre-conciliar church that preceded Vatican II as "The Long Nineteenth Century."[2] O'Malley's sweeping overview of this period is important for understanding the historical context for Vatican II and the new evangelization. The spectrum of philosophical and theological developments that took place in Protestant and Catholic Christianity during this period cannot possibly be treated in the space of this book, important as they are for understanding the nature of the secular age.[3] I will restrict myself only to a few lines in O'Malley's historical reconstruction of the church's first engagement with political and cultural modernity.

In 1784, the German philosopher Immanuel Kant published an important essay, "Answering the Question: What Is Enlightenment?" Kant represented the most sophisticated attempt to salvage something for religious faith from practical reason. It wasn't much. In 1799, a devout Protestant theologian, who had come under Kant's influence, named Friedrich Daniel Ernst Schleiermacher, tried to salvage more than Kant in *On Religion: Speeches to Its Cultured Despisers*. Modern evangelization has been a long footnote to these two texts in the awareness of a profound cultural transformation.

I have already mentioned the important exchange on faith and secular thought that took place in Munich in 2004 between then-Cardinal Joseph Ratzinger and the German philosopher Jürgen Habermas. When Ignatius Press published the papers delivered on that occasion by each of these distinguished representatives of different worldviews, it also chose to put a photo of them in intense

---

[2] John W. O'Malley, *What Happened at Vatican II* (Cambridge, MA: Harvard University Press, 2008), chap. 2: "The Long Nineteenth Century," 53–92. The chapter offers a comprehensive yet readable survey of developments in Catholic thought from the beginning of the nineteenth century through the Second Vatican Council. My approach follows O'Malley's account of the developments in Catholic doctrine from Leo XIII to John XXIII and Paul VI.

[3] For excellent introductions to theologians and theological movements in Catholicism and Protestantism since, see James C. Livingston, *Modern Christian Thought*, vol. 1: *The Enlightenment and the Nineteenth Century* (Upper Saddle River, NJ: Prentice-Hall, 1997) and James C. Livingston, Francis Schüssler Fiorenza, with Sarah Coakley and James H. Evans Jr., *Modern Christian Thought*, vol. 2: *The Twentieth Century* (Upper Saddle River, NJ: Prentice-Hall, 2000).

conversation on the cover.[4] It is inconceivable to imagine a similar dialogue in the early nineteenth century taking place between Immanuel Kant and Cardinal Barnaba Niccolo Maria Luigi Chiaramonte who became Pope Pius VII. In that difference lies the difference between 1800 and today.

## The Council of Trent to the Enlightenment

The Protestant Reformation didn't just divide European Christianity; it fractured it into multiple parts. Rome, the Evangelical Lutheran Church in Germany, the Anglican Church of England, the Reformed Church in Geneva and France, and the various other groups pluralized Christianity in ways it never had been before, even with late medieval reformers like John Wycliffe and Jan Hus. The Christian religion in Europe split along theological, nationalistic, and linguistic lines simultaneously, one cultural mitosis reinforcing the other. Protestantism nestled within the emerging European nationalisms. The Catholic Church inaugurated its own response, the Counter-Reformation, starting with the Council of Trent (1545–63).

Two aspects to the Counter-Reformation are relevant to the abbreviated story I'm telling here. The first was a mentality that put the church in a permanent defensive apologetic posture about the faith as modernity itself was being born. The mission of theological apologetics was to identify religious error, diagnose the reasons for it, and offer proofs from church teaching and Scripture that contradicted heresies. The second reaction to the Reformation was not defensive but positive and creative. The birth and renewal in this period of religious communities whose apostolates were educational, missionary, or contemplative also took place. A pragmatic apologetics of evangelical witness by these groups of men and women were influenced by but transcended the anti-Protestant apologetics of theology. Seminaries to form priests opened in Europe for the first time. Prior to that, one learned to be a priest as one learns a trade by being an apprentice at a cathedral. The Sulpicians established their first seminary in Paris in 1641 and then sailed to Montreal to establish another in 1657; finally, they were invited by Bishop John Carroll, a Jesuit and

---

[4] Jürgen Habermas and Joseph Ratzinger, *Dialectics of Secularization: On Reason and Religion*, ed. Florian Schuller, trans. Brian McNeil (San Francisco: Ignatius Press, 2006).

the first bishop of Baltimore, to establish a third in Maryland in 1791. Closely linked to reforms in priestly training were efforts to catechize and educate the young in the faith. There was high missionary energy released by the Reformation within the Catholic Church. The sacraments and devotional practices attached the lay faithful to a religion whose intellectual battles were beyond them. A powerful cultural current of general religiosity, Protestant and Catholic, ran across the continent. The Counter-Reformation had its share of Catholic genius. Pascal immediately comes to mind, with his scientific acumen in mathematics and physics as well as his classic, the *Pensées*. There was Malebranche too, a priest of the French Oratory and rationalist philosopher in the tradition of Descartes, who was also a Catholic.

What modernity likes to remember from this period, however, is the story of Galileo, whose heliocentric system contradicted the cosmic-theological tradition inherited from Ptolemy, which seemed to verify revelation in Psalm 113:3 "From the rising of the sun to its setting the name of the LORD is to be praised." Cardinal Roberto Bellarmine, who handled the case, urged Galileo to satisfy Rome's qualms by simply declaring that his findings were only a possible scientific theory. At his trial, so the story goes, in being forced to recant his own theory of the earth moving around the sun but refusing to do so, Galileo is supposed to have countered simply and candidly, "But it moves" (*E pur si muove*). He argued the true meaning of Psalm 113 could be squared with the findings of his telescope without sacrificing faith or science. The world would wait until Leo XIII before that principle enunciated by Galileo was stated by the highest religious authority.

For all their differences, the various fragmented parties in the Christian family of faiths spoke from a common spiritual lexicon even when the definitions and some of the grammar changed. Protestants might assert an absolute in "Scripture alone" (*sola scriptura*) while Catholic theologians countered with their "Sacred Scripture and tradition" (*sacra scriptura et traditio*), as Trent put it. Yes, Christianity was divided, but in a thousand subtle ways it remained one thing, bound together by a single religious language. With the Enlightenment, the vocabulary and the grammar of truth changed radically.

The Enlightenment's dictionary drew only on the grammars of freedom and reason, not the Bible or the sacraments. The continental language of intellectual culture began changing from words in Latin, French, and German on "faith"—*credo, foi*, and *glaube*—to "reason"—*raison* and *vernunft*. The French celebrated the French Revolution with a new political trinity of values: *liberté, égalité, fraternité* (liberty, equality, fraternity). This was a discourse far removed, or so it seemed then, from redemption and justification. Public intellectual arguments about truth shifted from scriptural interpretation to physical science, from doctrinal truth to social freedom, from religious authority to popular sovereignty. Even the Enlightenment's idea of how reason worked and what it was had little in common with scholasticism's understanding of *ratio* and Luther's pessimism about it. A dialogue between the Christian faith and the early Enlightenment became all but impossible. In the mind of the church, every important theological question had been asked, and all had been adequately and substantially answered in its dogmatic teaching. The Enlightenment idea of truth was opposed to tradition. It was based on science alone and practical reason. Cultural tradition was not highly prized as a vehicle for truth, and the religious version of tradition was least prized of all. In that respect, the French *philosophes* saw in religious tradition only the darkened dogmatisms of the unenlightened mind. In his novel *Candide*, Voltaire ridiculed Leibniz's theodicy written to explain the tragedy of an earthquake in Portugal. The Lisbon Earthquake in 1755 posed a shock to theological confidence similar to the scandal of the Holocaust for us today. Voltaire's satire on theodicy meant one thing for the church, but liberal democratic politics meant quite another.

Concurrent with the antiseptic and critical rationalism of the political Enlightenment was the Romantic movement, then in full swing in Europe as well. Quite different from the *philosophes*, it was inclined to glorify the past, celebrate feeling, explore aesthetic sensibility, and even revive the taste for medievalism. The major English representatives of Romanticism are poets like William Wordsworth; Samuel Taylor Coleridge, who was on opium while composing *Kubla Khan*; and the mystic William Blake, whose poem "And did those feet in ancient time," composed in opposition to the soot of the Industrial revolution in England, became the basis for the stirring British hymn "Jerusalem," recognizable by many from the movie *Chariots of Fire*. Romanticism was a celebration of feeling and the irrational which held secrets reason knew nothing of.

It takes an unforeseen event sometimes to topple a view of the world. In 1804, Pius VII traveled to Paris fully intending to place a crown on the head of the new emperor, Napoleon Bonaparte, in Notre-Dame Cathedral. A thing unimaginable to the pope happened in that famous sanctuary. Before Pius VII could reach for the imperial crown, Napoleon seized it himself! And then placed it on his own head. The scene is memorialized in the monumental oil portrait by Jacques-Louis David, *The Coronation of Napoleon*, painted in 1807 and now hanging in the Louvre.[5] The insult to religion was epochal. Enlightened monarchs no longer desired, nor would they countenance, ecclesiastical authority presuming to add its own sacral legitimacy and blessing to civil authority. Minerva's owl had taken flight as the sun was setting on Christendom in Europe.

## The Long Nineteenth Century in the Church

John O'Malley begins his narrative of modern Catholicism with the "beleaguered papacies" of Gregory XVI (1831–1846) and Pius IX (1846–1878).[6] What overwhelmed these pontiffs was insurgent Italian nationalism more than strict theological debates. Districts in Italy demanded that the church transfer its vast properties, known as the Papal States, to lay or secular hands. Napoleon had captured these territories earlier, but the Congress of Vienna (1815) returned them to the pope. Even devout Italian Catholics had lost any taste for clerical landlords or Vatican militias prowling about. A secular understanding of lay political life was blowing in the wind. In France, this spirit was called *laïcisme*, the forerunner of and synonym for secular society.

That background is necessary for understanding the encyclical *Mirari Vos* (1832) written by Gregory XVI. It asserts the pope's principled opposition based on history and law to any suggestion of attempts to remove any of the Papal States from control by the pope. O'Malley writes, "For the popes, the struggle to maintain the States became a major focus in the struggle against 'the modern world' and

---

[5] The size of the canvas testifies as much to Napoleon's ego as to the epochal nature of what took place. The painting is 33 feet x 20 feet. Jacques-Louis David had also painted a very warm portrait of a very human Pope Pius VII in 1805 in appreciation for his journey to Paris for the coronation at which he sat respectfully while the political universe turned on its axis.

[6] O'Malley, *What Happened at Vatican II*, 57–61.

all that it stood for."[7] Pope Gregory's encyclical made the Papal States a symbol of his defiance of a modern liberal order and the occasion for attacking emerging political convictions concerning freedom of conscience, freedom of speech, and freedom of the press. In the nineteenth century, these and many other matters fell under cover of a single heresy—liberalism. Movements were labelled as such for heralding social and personal freedoms that broke with church control and doctrine. The idea of religious liberty was condemned by the church for placing personal liberty ahead of revealed truth. It is no surprise that the Declaration on Religious Freedom (*Dignitatis Humanae*), approved by Vatican II in 1965, was regarded by Catholic traditionalist bishops at the council as a complete betrayal of the nineteenth-century popes.

Pius IX (1846–1878) attempted to strengthen the barricades of doctrine even further against all forms of religious and political liberalism. This pope expanded Gregory's proscribed propositions to eighty in his inventory of heresies, known as the *Syllabus of Errors* (1864). One anathematized proposition asserted that the church did not have the right to be the only religion permitted by the state. In the pope's eyes, not only was an established religion the ideal, but the state's proper role in the political order was to be the guardian of faith and morals as those were taught by the church. As in the medieval context of the Holy Roman Empire, the state was the good *secular arm* established by God to safeguard the *spiritual mission* of the church. This was the very soul of Christendom. And that soul was leaving the body of modern political life.

The distance separating such church-state theories as those above from our U.S. Constitution and the teaching of Vatican II on the church's role in the modern world is enormous. To read the *Syllabus of Errors* alongside the Decree on Ecumenism and the Declaration on Religious Freedom from Vatican II gives some idea of the distance the church has traveled in bringing its mission into proper theological alignment with political and social modernity. The traditionalist bishops at Vatican II, or, as they were known then, the International Group of Fathers, were convinced that these conciliar documents had sacrificed Gregory XVI and Pius IX to a twentieth-century version of

---

[7] Ibid., 75.

liberalism and to the secular Enlightenment of which it was the source.

Father John Courtney Murray, SJ, wrote a defense of conscience that became the theological cornerstone of the Declaration on Religious Freedom. As Genesis taught, human beings, he argued, were created in the image of God and, despite sin, never lost that image or the freedom of conscience that went with it. The theological tradition and *Gaudium et Spes* recognize that sin and its effects took away the grace given human beings at creation, but the remaining propensity to do evil could not be used to deny religious freedom even if it embraced error. The *imago Dei* remained and gave all human beings an inherent and inviolable dignity. That is what grounds the church's arguments against capital punishment and torture. Utility does not trump inviolability. A new pastoral chapter was beginning to be written in the church on human freedom. It would be no easy chapter to write. "Freedom in the Church" was the dangerous and intentionally provocative title of Hans Küng's celebrated 1963 lecture tour in the United States. Freedom, on the eve of Vatican II, was still a suspect concept for theology because of the liberalism condemned by the nineteenth-century popes.

Pius IX called the First Vatican Council in 1869 for the express purpose of defining divine revelation, faith, and papal authority against the rationalism and fideism of the period.[8] The council rejected fideism as a blind faith in divine revelation that we now associate with fundamentalism but that originally found philosophical justification in Kant. The council also took aim at rationalism as a reductive philosophy of reason with no theoretical room for faith or revelation. With fideism and rationalism, the two great cultural titans of the nineteenth century, Enlightenment reason and Romantic feeling, clashed head on. Modern consciousness, as Charles Taylor explains, is still cross-pressured by currents of thought arising from these two formidable sources. It is unlikely that it will pass soon. Steven Pinker and Kurt Anderson will push our rationalist buttons

---

[8] *Decrees of the Ecumenical Councils*, vol. 2 (Trent to Vatican II), English ed. Norman P. Tanner (Washington, DC: Georgetown University Press, 1990), "Vatican Council I," 801–16. The original Latin decrees of Vatican I are followed by Tanner's English translation. The entire doctrinal teaching of Vatican I amounts to only eight pages of text in Tanner.

while occasionally a movie, play, liturgy, or poem will touch a sensibility in us that refuses the reductive explanation.

Splitting the difference between these two modes of modernity, the church at Vatican I offered a presentation of revelation and faith that made generous room for reason as the council understood it in the light of the great medieval theological syntheses along with an authoritarian notion of revelation that inclined one to see faith as mere submission. In opposition to nineteenth-century rationalism—a more important challenge for religion in a scientific age than fideism was—Vatican I proposed what approximated a propositional and authoritarian concept of revelation.[9] The *intellectus fidei* praised by St. Augustine and St. Thomas was overshadowed by a view of faith too close to a *sacrificium intellectus* in response to the threat of an aggressive rationalism.

The nineteenth-century ecclesiastical-political struggles of the papacy with an emergent secular order associated with liberalism narrowed religious faith to little more than submissive obedience. Vatican I, at the urging of Pius IX, was held to strengthen religious certainty in the face of a skeptical rationalism and an intuitive romanticism. To reassure the faithful of truth, the dogma of papal infallibility was defined in *Pastor Aeternus*. Shortly after that, war broke out in Italy and the council was suspended, never to be resumed on its own ecclesial and theological terms. It left in its wake a staunch sense of Catholic opposition to modernity.

## Beyond the Impasse

The Second Vatican Council was held almost a century after Vatican I.[10] In all, it approved and promulgated sixteen substantial documents that included texts on religious freedom, ecumenism, and relations with the Jews, as well as its most important constitutions on liturgy, the church, divine revelation, and the modern world. It is quite astonishing that Vatican I and Vatican II both, and less than

---

[9] See Paul Ricoeur, "Toward a Hermeneutic of the Idea of Revelation," *Harvard Theological Review* 70, nos. 1–2 (January–April 1977): 1–37. Ricoeur's argument seeks to transcend an unprofitable and sterile antagonism of religious faith and critical reason using a hermeneutic reading of biblical genres and a philosophy of testimony.

[10] *Decrees of the Ecumenical Councils*, vol. 2, "Vatican II," 816–1135.

ninety-five years apart, approved major dogmatic definitions of the very same subject—divine revelation. Noteworthy as well is the fact that Vatican II resumed and revised the engagement with modernity suspended in a kind of doctrinal limbo by the *Syllabus of Errors.*

Regarding the idea of revelation, *Dei Filius* (1869) at Vatican I was little more than a one-paragraph conciliar rehash of what the standard theological manuals presented on the subject after Trent. On the other hand, *Dei Verbum* (1965) at Vatican II treated revelation in more biblical, historical, personal, and literary terms and in five substantial chapters. The nine decades separating the two councils, unbeknownst to most Catholics, proved to be one of the most productive periods since the Reformation regarding the textual and hermeneutical rethinking of divine revelation, a dogma that divided Catholics from Protestants and from modern science all at once. If revelation was the major impasse for the Enlightenment mind and if the nineteenth-century popes, as I have indicated, set themselves against religious freedom, the new teaching on economic justice begun by Pope Leo XIII began the process of transforming the papacy from a reactionary to a prophetic religious institution.

No liberal by any measure, Leo XIII inaugurated the transformation of the church into a constructive moral conscience in the face of modern social challenges. His pontificate opened three paths forward for the beleaguered nineteenth-century church. First, his encyclical *Aeterni Patris* is responsible for the revival of the philosophy and theology of St. Thomas. Baroque versions of it were no more than adaptations of Thomas's thought, but neo-Thomism would return to the sources of the Angelic Doctor in his own writings. Neo-Thomism influenced Karol Wojtyla (John Paul II) through the Lublin School of Thomism in Poland. Vatican II emphasized the human person as the philosophical touchstone for Catholic moral teaching because of neo-Thomism and modern French personalist philosophy. We can thank Leo XIII for paving the way for that.

The second path that took the church out of the nineteenth-century impasse for which Pope Leo was responsible is his support for modern biblical studies. In 1893, Leo published *Providentissimus Deus* on the use of scientific methods in studying Sacred Scripture. Overly cautious by modern standards, yet appropriately suspicious of nineteenth-century higher criticism, this text did not hesitate to admit what fundamentalists consistently deny, namely, that the scientific notions assumed by biblical authors were not obligatory in the modern context. The theory of evolution that booby-trapped Protestant fundamentalism in a desperate and hopeless creation science was thankfully avoided. Toward the end of his papacy, Leo XIII established the Pontifical Biblical Commission (PBC) to advise his successors about biblical questions. In 1964, an important intervention by the PBC on the nature of Gospel historicity preserved the language that assured passage of the Constitution on Divine Revelation (*Dei Verbum*). In 1993, the PBC published one of the most important documents on exegetical and interpretative biblical methods ever to appear in print: *The Interpretation of the Bible in the Church*.[11] This was approved by then-Cardinal Joseph Ratzinger.

A third route taken by Leo XIII was the publication of the social encyclical *Rerum Novarum* (1891). This was the first modern papal encyclical on labor and economics. While explicitly rejecting communism, Leo XIII grasped equally well that industrial markets required a social ethic founded on workers' rights and adequate to new economic realities. *Rerum Novarum* (New Matters) set the stage for a series of papal social encyclicals over the next century on such diverse subjects as war, peace, justice, life, economics, and the environment. Pius XI later wrote *Quadragesimo Anno* on economics. John XXIII issued *Pacem in Terris* on war and peace. John Paul II's encyclical *Sollicitudo Socialis* dealt with social change. The most recent expression of social papal encyclical teaching is *Laudato Si'* by Pope Francis on the environment. Leo XIII helped chart a new role for the church in the post-revolutionary moral order—as prophet for a humanizing social order. This moral battlefield is littered with ideological landmines. If encyclicals are not usually infallible, they are nevertheless reliable diagnostics of some of the deepest moral issues in the modern world. With the pontificate of Leo XIII the church began slowly to pivot away from the closed world of *Mirari Vos* and medieval Christendom to the human person as the church's primary reference point in its teaching concerning politics, economics, and ethics. Many Catholic religious congregations were founded in the seventeenth, eighteenth, and nineteenth centuries to assist the sick, the poor, and the illiterate and uneducated girls in society. The Industrial Revolution of the nineteenth century created a new class of impoverished city workers whose children were factory employees themselves,

---

[11] Pontifical Biblical Commission, *The Interpretation of the Bible in the Church*, 1993, www.vatican.va: Pontifical Biblical Commission.

homeless and illiterate. Congregations of women like the School Sisters of Notre Dame on the continent and the Sisters of Mercy in Ireland led the way in addressing some of these problems. In retrospect, political and economic modernization began to cast the church out of power as a political force while stimulating in its best souls a more prophetic mission of responding to modernity's excesses. Those excesses were already leaving young human capital as "roadkill" under the advancing juggernaut of urbanization and industrialization. Modernity creates new problems which challenge the church to invent new solutions founded on its beliefs and mission.

In other areas of its life, the church was unable at the turn of the twentieth century to offer a theological synthesis equal to the slowly accumulating body of relevant biblical, historical, and theological knowledge. Its intellectual spheres were sophisticated, but all but incomprehensible to an emerging pragmatic human consciousness. An impressive scholastic synthesis left little room for integrating insights arising from the reconstructive social sciences. Despite *Providentissimus Deus*, exegetical methods were immature by contemporary standards. Those Catholic intellectuals who later became known as Modernists were proposing perspectives that could not reasonably be squared with the church's teaching on revelation and Scripture at Vatican I. In 1907, Pius X issued a double-barreled anathematization of the biblical and dogmatic errors of Modernism in *Pascendi Dominici Gregis* and *Lamentabili*. These papal texts identified the roots of a Modernist hyper-heresy—more precisely, "the synthesis of all heresies," as the indictment of it written for the pope by Father Umberto Benigni would have it.[12] After *Pascendi*, "Modernism," like its political predecessor "Liberalism," was equivalent to "anti-Catholic." Ordained deacons in the Catholic Church were required to swear an "Oath against Modernism."

Looking back over church history since Trent, even a critic of the Catholic Church would concede that Counter-Reformation Catholicism was a formidable religious world of pastoral mission and religious enthusiasm. It had achieved remarkable results in evangelization in parochial growth, priestly vocations, new religious orders, and Catholic education. The church in America built a pastoral infrastruc-

---

[12] Encyclical of St. Pope Pius X, *Pascendi Dominici Gregis* (September 8, 1907), 39.

ture capable of integrating new immigrants into society without sacrificing their own languages, customs, and cultural sensibilities. In the late nineteenth century, Father Michael McGivney founded the Knights of Columbus as an insurance agency to assist Irish widows in Connecticut. The Counter-Reformation was more than a fortress apologetics. Religious sisters and brothers played a major role in it. The church was very much in the world compensating as it could for modernity's worst effects, especially on children and the poor. The popes began canonizing simple religious men and women as saints— St. John Vianney for priests and St. Theresa of Lisieux for contemplatives whose vocations stood at the antipodes from the world of enlightened elites.

The paradox is that the Enlightenment and Romanticism did leave some very important effects in theology. Despite the early opposition to historical-critical methods of biblical interpretation, their application to less neuralgic areas were proving to be valuable. Nineteenth-century Romantic interest in classics led Prosper Gueranger and the monks at Solesmes to revive Gregorian chant. One way to offset a robust scientific rationalism in culture was with the splendor and simplicity of medieval chant. Likewise, in the theological field known as patristics (the study of church fathers from the second to the seventh centuries), Jacques-Paul Migne published the monumental (383 volumes in all) *Patrologia Latina* and *Patrologia Graeca* on primary Christian sources from antiquity, much of which was unavailable, if not unknown, to scholastic theology. These texts swung the theological door open to the theologies of the first millennium later eclipsed by the great Thomistic synthesis of the thirteenth century.[13] The *ressourcement* approach to theology and doctrine employed at Vatican II, and, by no less than Joseph Ratzinger himself, was a direct byproduct of this retrieval of patristic traditions in the church.

Thus, historical criticism and editing of ancient theological sources for tradition was playing a quiet but significant role in preparing for the conciliar decisions made at Vatican II. To take one small example that affected Catholic devotional life, Jesuit scholars (Bollandists) totally altered the approach to religious hagiography. The ancient Roman Martyrology and lives of saints had always abounded in pious

---

[13] O'Malley, *What Happened at Vatican II*, 71–76.

legends until the arrival of critical manuscript history allowed scholars to identify later redactions. This corresponded to the philological methods that were being applied to the Old Testament by Catholic biblical scholars, which demonstrated that a second-millennium BC figure like Moses could not have possibly authored the Pentateuch which pious tradition referred to as "The Five Books of Moses." The Tübingen School of theology in Germany and the British Oxford Movement had already adjusted theological scholarship to the fact of doctrinal development in Christian tradition.

Such incremental steps of historical scholarship as the ones I've mentioned had an indirect effect on preparing the path toward the conciliar renewal at Vatican II. A deep respect for tradition does not rule out the application of the historical reconstructive sciences to it. What was quietly taking place in the remote theological libraries of major universities and monasteries made possible a textual archeology of the Catholic tradition in all its scope. Vatican II, in that respect, was no infatuation with the Enlightenment and liberal Protestantism, as traditionalists held, nor was it a simple footnote to Trent and Vatican I. It was the recovery of the "unremembered past" of the great Catholic tradition of two millennia as an awakening in the Catholic world of the richness of the past. The challenge was how to blaze a trail forward armed with this new and old wisdom. In this context, it is worth noting what Rémi Brague, a French medieval expert in Judaism and Islam, asserted about the church and Marcion. He called the church's condemnation of Marcion the most significant hermeneutical decision of early Christianity. Marcion refused to accept the Jewish Scriptures as divine revelation. The church turned them into its Old Testament and considers them the Word of God no less than the New Testament.[14] Preservation of religious history in all its strange diversity is the first task of historical-theological consciousness. The long nineteenth century and the progress in historical-critical scholarship allowed Vatican II to withdraw the deposit of faith in many of its forgotten sources.

But the road forward from Leo XIII to John XXIII was not smooth. In the 1940s, French patristic scholars like Jean Daniélou, SJ, and Henri de Lubac, SJ, who were exporting insights from Origen and

---

[14] Rémi Brague, *Eccentric Culture: A Theory of Western Civilization*, trans. Samuel Lester (South Bend, IN: St. Augustine's Press, 2002), 55ff.

Augustine for theological purposes, drew the suspicious attention of Dominican Thomists René Labourdette, OP, and Reginald Garrigou-Lagrange, OP, who characterized their Jesuit colleagues as advocating *la nouvelle théologie*. To say "new" then was tantamount to a charge of Modernism. Soon, Pius XII warned of "new" theological methods in his encyclical *Humani Generis* (1950). American Jesuit John Courtney Murray was forbidden by his superiors in the early 1950s to publish his ideas on religious freedom.

## The Breakthrough of Religious Freedom

The case of American Jesuit John Courtney Murray is particularly instructive for understanding the new evangelization in secular modernity. The focus of his scholarship was the American constitutional disestablishment of religion along with the equally important constitutional principle of the freedom to practice religion as a basic right protected by law. Murray considered the teaching of the nineteenth-century popes on religious liberty as only the "received opinion" on the subject, not defined teaching. Texts like *Mirari Vos*, however, were accepted by many as "official teaching," so in the early 1950s, despite what the U.S. Constitution said about the matter, a Catholic approach to religious freedom was theologically off limits. Shortly before Vatican II, in 1960, when Murray was allowed by his superiors to publish *We Hold These Truths: Catholic Reflections on the American Proposition*, the intellectual climate in the church about religious freedom was changing. The "American Proposition," of course, was the separation of church and state and religious freedom. Murray's case proved convincing to the council fathers. After some years of intense debate, Vatican II approved one of its most far-reaching documents for the church in the secular age: the Declaration on Religious Freedom (*Dignitatis Humanae*). It has since become a cornerstone of the Catholic Church's engagement with the realities of ecumenism, religious pluralism, and anti-religious secularism.

With such watershed documents as the new teaching on religious freedom, Vatican II radically changed the apologetic theological culture of the church and the terms of its mission in secular society. The Declaration on Religious Freedom (*Dignitatis Humanae*) joined four other conciliar documents in shifting the axis in ecclesial mission and vision for a secular age: the Dogmatic Constitution on the Church

(*Lumen Gentium*), the Decree on Ecumenism (*Unitatis Redintegratio*), the Declaration of the Relation of the Church to Non-Christian Religions (*Nostra Aetate*), and the Pastoral Constitution on the Church in the Modern World (*Gaudium et Spes*). These provided key concepts which began the process of integrating teachings on the collegiality of bishops with those on papal authority, ecumenical dialogue with Trent, religious freedom with the concordat traditions of state and church, religious pluralism and Judaism with salvation in Christ, and the engagement of the church's divine mission with modern culture. In each of these instances, earlier doctrinal formulations once thought cast in stone were caught in the very process of developing, as we say today, in *real time*.

Bringing mission and evangelization up to date fell to the bishops in the council's final session, but the theme had already been introduced in other Vatican documents. In 1965, the bishops finally promulgated the Decree on the Church's Missionary Activity (*Ad Gentes*). Like many other texts at the council, this document had a rocky drafting history. It began as a mere sketch of doctrinal principles covering mission before evolving into a theological debate about what "mission" truly involved in the mid-twentieth century.[15] Some council fathers regarded mission as little more than "foreign missions" the way the Congregation for the Propagation of the Faith had always taught. Others favored a new definition of mission along the lines of what Paul VI and John Paul II would later call evangelization and the new evangelization. The bishops, however, were eager to bring Vatican II to a close after four years of debates. Debating the meaning of mission was the last thing they wanted.

The Decree on the Church's Missionary Activity did have the distinct advantage of the overall conciliar context behind it. The Constitution on the Church, the Decree on Ecumenism, the Declaration on Religious Freedom, the Declaration on the Relation of the Church to Non-Christian Religions, and the Pastoral Constitution on the Church in the Modern World provided much of that. The opening chapter of *Ad Gentes* spelled out doctrinal principles for the church's missionary identity framed in a trinitarian theology and written by Joseph Ratzinger at the suggestion of his own archbishop, Cardinal

---

[15] See Edward P. Hahnenberg, *A Concise Guide to the Documents of Vatican II* (Cincinnati, OH: St. Anthony Messenger Press, 2007), 133–40.

Frings of Munich.[16] Drafters of *Ad Gentes* were not unaware of the secularization of Europe. But a new kind of mission of the church to seculars in its own European backyard was not enough to defeat the dominant "foreign missions" mentality of the Congregation for the Propagation of the Faith. In the end, its preference was for a traditional definition of mission.[17] With that decision, Vatican II effectively "kicked the can" of evangelization down the road until Paul VI revived it himself a decade later in the synod he called in 1974 on evangelization.

A small minority of bishops at the council gave voice to their disagreement on some of Vatican II's overall shifts in theological and pastoral emphasis. Traditionalist fathers claimed that on crucial points—liturgy, religious freedom, and ecumenism—Vatican II had altered if not reversed papal teachings of the seventeenth, eighteenth, and nineteenth centuries. These conciliar documents, in their eyes, amounted to a blatant sacrifice of the doctrinal substance of Catholic teaching. For them, sacred papal tradition was being bled out on the various altars of modernity. The divided assessment of the modern world after Vatican II replayed the nineteenth-century cultural drama of Enlightenment reason and cultural Romanticism. The usual political categories to describe that drama (progressives and conservatives) don't mean much apart from the nineteenth century and some of the events mentioned above. To understand the issues demands a brief consideration of the five conciliar texts that, even at the time of the council, aroused the greatest controversy.[18]

All commentators on Vatican II are unanimous that the most contentious debates involved the five documents mentioned earlier: The Constitution on Divine Revelation, the Decree on Ecumenism, the Declaration on the Relation of the Church to Non-Christian Religions,

---

[16] *Commentary on the Documents of Vatican II*, ed. Herbert Vorgrimler, vol. 4 (New York: Herder and Herder, 1969), 98–99.

[17] Hahnenberg, *A Concise Guide*, 133–34.

[18] John O'Malley, *What Happened at Vatican II*, narrates the political drama that unfolded outside the limelight between nineteenth-century Catholicism and theological developments based on Scripture and tradition. Vatican II didn't settle all of this. More detailed analyses of the struggle between progressives and traditionalists since Vatican II may be found in the major commentaries on the council and in more popular treatments. See Paulist Press's series, Rediscovering Vatican II and especially Massimo Faggioli, *Vatican II: The Battle for Meaning* (New York: Paulist Press, 2012).

the Declaration on Religious Freedom, and, most important for this book, the Pastoral Constitution on the Church in the Modern World (in draft forms also known as Schema 13 and Schema 17). Its willing sense of engagement with modernity, without at all overlooking the many crises taking place in modern culture, reflected nothing of the suspicion and hostility of the church in the nineteenth and early twentieth centuries.

The *aggiornamento* envisioned by John XXIII involved asking the assembled bishops at Vatican II to take a fresh look at church tradition in the light of the Gospel of Christ and the Christian experience of two millennia, and to inform that assessment with the help of critical history and the human sciences. One such tradition was the Latin liturgy, which many considered so sacrosanct it could never be changed. But the vernacular translation was approved to make worship more comprehensible precisely for the sake of evangelization. What was lost in translation were the Latinized cadences and sounds that conveyed something of the transcendent mystery of faith. What would happen to Judaism without the sounds of Hebrew? An American Catholic liturgical aesthetic must necessarily accommodate English comprehension, but at the same time not forget the *Kyrie Eleison* (Greek), the *Agnus Dei* (Latin), and *Maranatha* (Aramaic) as well as the native languages of new immigrants (*Pan de vida*). The more languages, the better to escape the routinization, occasional banality, and isolation that is still so present in American worship.

More neuralgic semantics of faith surfaced later. Divine revelation at Vatican II was understood as inflected by history and literary forms. Understanding the Scriptures demanded an exegetical awareness of the events and circumstances out of which those memorable passages arose. The collegiality of bishops at Vatican II struck traditionalists as an ecclesial millstone around the neck of papal infallibility, which had, in fact, been defined collegially by bishops at Vatican I. Dialogue with the Orthodox Communion, Anglicanism, and Protestantism was long overdue. It had become impossible with mass communications to ignore the great monotheisms of Judaism and Islam and the more exotic beliefs of India, Asia, Africa, and Pacific Oceania. Religious pluralism was everywhere that Christianity was.

Despite all of that, the most troubling doctrinal change for traditionalist bishops was, as I mentioned above, in the Declaration on Religious Freedom. Intentionally or not, it jeopardized the truth of such fundamental matters as revelation, salvation in Christ, and the necessity of baptism. Personal conscience had become the wild card in the battle for religious truth. Vatican II put all this in jeopardy as far as circumspect archconservatives were concerned. The irenic engagement with modernity, as the Pastoral Constitution on the Church in the Modern World (*Gaudium et Spes*) presented it, however, aroused the most serious theological partisanship among many of the council fathers. Because this is the subject of this book, I want to end this chapter explaining the reason why. In many ways, the Pastoral Constitution on the Church in the Modern World is what launched evangelization into new socio-theological waters by calling for a new diagnostic of the signs of the times.

What makes this text different is that, for the first time in church history, sociological perspectives had been introduced into a conciliar document. The popes, it is true, had drawn on philosophy and historical events in composing their encyclical letters, but a conciliar document was a different matter. Employing socio-cultural exegesis in a conciliar genre was a magisterial novelty. A rupture in theological judgment had taken place for traditionalists by introducing contingent guesses about culture into a document of faith. Traditionalists who took the *Syllabus of Errors* and *Mirari Vos* as the final word on modernity objected to the changes at Vatican II. After Vatican I defined papal infallibility, any papal utterance seemed bathed in the light of the irreformable. For those traditionalists who refused the legitimacy of doctrinal development, it was impossible to reconcile the stark differences between the dicta of Pope Gregory and Pius IX and the documents of Vatican II.

The underlying issue at the heart of Vatican II was and remains the legitimacy of doctrinal development on major points of doctrine in Christian tradition. No consensus existed then nor is there one today in the church on the subject. The historical research I mentioned above revealed seams in the great tradition which time and the loss of memory had papered over. That fact was undeniable. Development was even present in the New Testament, as indicated by the exegetical reconstruction of the different titles for Christ (rabbi, messiah, son of God, son of man, prophet like Jeremiah, logos of the Father). Such biblical reconstructions of early faith trajectories were gradually transforming the idea of the church in the New Testament. The historic evidence of Christian anti-Semitism had become undeniable. The

Second Temple context of the ministry of Jesus of Nazareth as a first-century Jew slowly led the church toward a new theological relationship with the Jewish religion. In all these ways, received teachings by the church, once assumed to be Gospel-truth, were undergoing major development.

The nineteenth- and twentieth-century objections to religious freedom never counted much for American Catholics. The practical legal wisdom of the disestablishment clause in a Protestant culture made eminent sense. Not so with French traditionalists like Archbishop Lefebvre. Even though Vatican II did not base its teaching about religious freedom on the philosophy of John Locke or on constitutional law, the inviolable sanctuary of human conscience allowed it to cut the Gordian Knot sealed in church-state concordats privileging the Catholic religion. The truth of the Gospel was never denied, but the pseudo-principle that "error has no rights" was just a category mistake. Only human beings have rights, not abstractions like truth. State-enforced belief was becoming not just unenforceable but implausible as well.

Finally, the conclusion of the church was that the modern world, marked as it was by enormous progress in some spheres of human life and profound social and moral dislocation in others, was still open for evangelization. But, that had to be done on new terms of rational persuasion, ecumenical dialogue, cooperation, and when necessary moral resistance. All of this involved a revision in ecclesial perspective and temper that could not possibly be absorbed in a few years or, as we now realize, even in three generations.

### *Gaudium et Spes* **and the Modern World**

Any discussion of modernity in the new evangelization must take its point of departure from the Pastoral Constitution on the Church in the Modern World. Thanks to the sustained and controversial attention it received at Vatican II, this document offers the broadest framework for evangelization of any conciliar document except *Lumen Gentium*. Council teachings on ecumenism, non-Christian religions, religious freedom, and missionary activity specify the means for the larger evangelical aspirations and inculturation found in the pages of *Gaudium et Spes*.

I have already mentioned that the genre of this conciliar text was unprecedented. It wove doctrinal teachings together with contingent pastoral issues. It's a fact that, prior to Vatican II, no ecumenical council had ever enjoyed such a sociological vantage point as this council did on its own ambient culture. The Council of Trent, for all its accomplishments, had nothing approaching a historical and social hermeneutic for fifteenth- and sixteenth-century European culture the way Vatican Council II had on the nineteenth and twentieth centuries. While *Gaudium et Spes* differs in many respects from papal encyclical letters, encyclicals are its nearest magisterial analogue. Such occasional letters apply classical doctrinal truths to cultural moral problems—timely and prudent applications of Catholic teaching to pressing social issues.

To evangelize the modern world, the church first had to take it seriously on its own terms and offer the world a plausible phenomenological portrait of itself. Part 1 of *Gaudium et Spes* (GS) does precisely that. In doing so, the human person became the reference point, the criterion, and litmus test for all cultural, social, and technical progress. The document contains the statement authorizing the application of social hermeneutics to the cultural situations in which we find ourselves as a church: "the church carries the responsibility of reading the signs of the times and of interpreting them in the light of the Gospel" (GS 4). A responsible and suitable hermeneutic of social action must be joined to a theological hermeneutic of the Gospel acceptable to the Magisterium to do this successfully.

Part 2 of the document focuses on some urgent issues calling for a response from the church in the light of its teaching. These include Marriage and the Family (GS 47–52), the Development of Culture (GS 53–62), Economic and Social Life (GS 63–72), the Political Community (GS 73–76), and Peace and the Community of Nations (GS 77–90). In the eyes of Vatican II, the human person is inextricably caught up in the social and moral webbing that, like a second nature, inclines toward a default moral outlook. The legitimate autonomy which the economic, social, and political spheres of human action enjoy does not absolve them from facing the moral judgment that the church has in virtue of the mission it received from Christ. The Pontifical Council for the New Evangelization quoted extensively from *Gaudium et Spes* for its *Enchiridion* of texts given to the synod fathers in advance of the 2012 synod.

The signs of the times as the Catholic Church read them in 1965 are in many respects the same ones that envelop secular social life today. In that regard, modernity hasn't so much changed as accelerated in many directions, most especially through modern social communications technologies and new ideologies. There is mounting statistical evidence that modernity is having trouble finding a way to balance its programmatic dismantling of older cultures with a respect for the abiding truths in them.

The emancipatory interests of reason (more freedoms) can now be situated better in face of the hermeneutical interests of cultural traditions (cultural and religious memory). A longer and more detailed history of modernity than what was sketched out at Vatican II enables us to track the sources of our modern secular self-understanding, the gradual emergence of a new social imaginary in Europe, and the specific malaises of modernity that cry out for better explanations and responses in political and cultural life. *Gaudium et Spes* is at once a cry of distress, a motive of hope, and a summons to mission that seems to imply further interpretations of modernity, which is precisely what the conclusion of the document explicitly calls for. The task of understanding our modernity and our secularity remain an ongoing project for the church, its pastors, and its laity. In that respect, the comprehensive interpretation of our secular age is the opening and closing chapter in the new evangelization.

William Connolly's refusal of the name "secularist" for his thinking, and his frank admission that secularism as a matter of fact is itself a belief system, creates new conditions for religious and secular dialogue.[19] The new evangelization should not caricature secularist nonbelief but afford it all the dignity that religious belief wishes to receive in return. With secularists, Christians also hold a respect for human rights, legal guarantees for justice, the assistance of humanitarian aid for victims, and freedom of religion along with many other values.

This distinction between the independent realms of church and society, however, does not warrant making religion private, as if it constituted a mere cult and an individual moral code with no relevance to secular social platforms and practices in culture. The social dimension of the Gospel is an intrinsic consequence of its commitment to redeeming human beings and humanizing culture. The healings of Jesus clearly manifest the will of God regarding human

---

[19] William E. Connelly, *Why I Am Not a Secularist* (Minneapolis: University of Minnesota Press, 1999).

suffering. Never does Christ suggest the lame or blind should consider their state to be God's will. Matthew 25 envisions Christ the Judge administering only an ethical test at the Last Judgment—did you feed the hungry, clothe the naked, welcome the stranger, care for the sick, and visit the imprisoned? Neither the just nor the unjust, in this eschatological parable the great Michelangelo painted on the front wall of the Sistine Chapel, recognized the figure of Christ in his chosen social incognito. Nothing paralyzes biblical religion more than reducing it to a cult.

*Gaudium et Spes* is the point of departure for the church's renewed engagement with secularism and unbelief as part of its mission in the new evangelization. Persuading other people can happen only with dialogue that makes a plausible case for a Christian humanism based on the Gospel of Christ. Humanism is the first chapter in an evangelization based on the Incarnation of God in Christ. Overlapping interests between secularity and Christian faith are possible on that basis. The dialogue between secular culture and faith is, for many in the church, an uncomfortable conversation they are having with themselves and their kids.

The "long nineteenth century" in Catholicism ended in one sense at Vatican II. But, the council opened a new chapter of debate over its meaning and over the meaning of the evolving modern world which had become more secular. The council's work on mission and evangelization was subsequently transferred to fourteen world synods of bishops, to papal exhortations on those synods, and to encyclical letters of the popes themselves. It's that story I want to tell in chapter 5.

*Chapter 5*

# Mission to the Courtyard of the Gentiles

Following the Second Vatican Council, the immediate task was to implement its doctrinal teaching and the reforms it authorized. All things considered, the transition to a vernacular liturgy was managed well and has won the wager of better comprehension of sacramental liturgy as full and active lay participation. At the same time, no one should deny that the vernacular also affected the distinctive structure, sound, and cadence of post-Tridentine religious experience. How could it be otherwise? The carry-over in the depths of unconscious attachment from a faith full of medieval echoes to a vernacular liturgy had to undergo some loss.

Ecumenical dialogue was generally welcomed but proved to be extraordinarily technical and remote from parish life. The breakthrough in Catholic-Jewish relations had enormous theological consequences for exposing anti-Semitism in a post-Holocaust age, but the Palestinian question and the State of Israel stood then and still does in the way of more cordial relations. *Nostra Aetate* verified at last the permanent validity of God's covenant with the Jews as well as the truth, goodness, and beauty that was present in other world religions. But then theologians started to ask about the importance of baptism as the sacrament for salvation. The very thought of the Catholic Church endorsing religious freedom was pure heresy to traditionalists.

Such developments as these were deeply destabilizing for a religious institution that had hung so much of its identity on unchanging and unchangeable traditions. There was no accepted theological theory about the development of doctrine, which would have allowed many Catholics to make better sense of the grounds on which the council based its teaching and reforms.

Lacking a hermeneutical understanding of Catholicism as an historical tradition of faith, all these developments were lumped together in popular media and religious consciousness. The bishops, they said, were changing Catholicism and modernizing it. Those most closely involved with conciliar renewal never saw it that way at all. For them, patristic and biblical sources, more ancient in Christianity than Trent, belonged to the "unremembered past" of the church, and it was that past which brought the reforms about. Nevertheless, there was no denying that novel ideas had broken through the Tridentine bastions as well. It is a mistake to think of Vatican II as completely continuous with the earlier church teaching and past practice despite the evident ruptures with it. Critical consciousness cannot abide papered-over harmonizing in exegesis or ecclesiology.

American Jesuit John Courtney Murray became the council's lead expert on religious freedom. Before the promulgation of the Declaration on Religious Freedom, church-state relations were customarily seen in the context of *Mirari Vos* and the *Syllabus of Errors*. Error, these teachings said, had no rights. In Protestant states, the church demanded the right to practice. In Catholic states, it denied that right, or found ways of discouraging it, for Protestants. With the text on religious freedom, certainly in the mind of Catholic traditionalists, the European Enlightenment had slipped through the gates of Vatican City. Some traditionalist critics of the council maintained that, at Vatican II, it was as if Diderot himself were rolled into St. Peter's in a Trojan horse. The council was nothing more than a rationalist betrayal of the faith. The rhetoric of the "long nineteenth century" was hidden but, on the margins, it was alive and well.

While some describe Vatican II as a pastoral council, that judgment misses what the traditionalists intuitively felt about the reforms: the council was essentially a matter of changing earlier church teaching widely regarded as definitive. John Courtney Murray, to his credit, claimed that the *development of doctrine* was in fact the "issue under the issues" at Vatican II.[1] The theological principles that might make

---

[1] John O'Malley, *What Happened at Vatican II* (Cambridge, MA: Harvard University Press, 2008), 39, n. 52, explains that John Courtney Murray in 1965 noted that the development of doctrine at Vatican II was "*the* issue under all issues."

some coherent sense of development were formulated in the nineteenth century by John Henry Newman in his *An Essay on the Development of Doctrine* and later by Maurice Blondel. Doctrinal development is continuous with the tradition in some organic way, but it does not take place in an intellectual vacuum either. Development cannot be reduced to a slogan like "catching up to the times," whatever that means. "Reading the signs of the times and interpreting them" is quite different. Jesus gave us the closest thing to an evangelical axiom for development when he said: "Therefore every scribe who has been trained for the kingdom of heaven is like the master of a household who brings out of his treasure what is new and what is old" (Matt 13:52). There were new things at Vatican II. That was undeniable. Only further development would indicate whether it was treasure or not.

## The Development of Doctrine in Service to Ecclesial Mission

Let me recall several new developments in doctrine at the Second Vatican Council. The Dogmatic Constitution on the Church (*Lumen Gentium*) introduced transformational scriptural and trinitarian metaphors for the church's identity. This set aside the canonical-juridical approach to ecclesiology that had prevailed since the Middle Ages. There's development. The Dogmatic Constitution on Divine Revelation (*Dei Verbum*) developed the doctrine of Vatican I on revelation by employing trinitarian, personalist, historical, and literary critical concepts. The Pastoral Constitution on the Church in the Modern World (*Gaudium et Spes*) moved the church from a bastion mentality after the Reformation and Enlightenment to one of dialogical engagement with modernity. Finally, The Declaration on Religious Freedom (*Dignitatis Humanae*) undercut the theological logic of political Christendom and an arrogant religious absolutism in the church. The emerging centrality in theology and philosophy of the dignity of the human person became one basis for religious freedom. In these four major Vatican II documents, doctrinal development was undeniable.

Doctrinal development at Vatican II was not limited, however, to these major texts. The teaching of the Decree on Ecumenism (*Unitatis Redintegratio*) and the Declaration on the Relation of the Church to Non-Christian Religions (*Nostra Aetate*) abandoned the apologetic rhetoric of condemnation in exchange for a rhetoric of recognition and dialogue. The chapter on the Jews in that latter text condemned anti-Semitism in all its forms. The Decree on the Church's Missionary Activity (*Ad Gentes*) was limited in its vision to "foreign missions," but its missionary boilerplate was prefaced by trinitarian principles written by a young *peritus* (expert) of Cardinal Frings—Father Joseph Ratzinger. The divine foundations for mission are based on the trinitarian mystery of God I stressed in chapter 3.

While the Second Vatican Council never reflected on the theological principles for doctrinal development, or even employed the expression "new evangelization," its thrust for renewal was powered by the development of the concept of ecclesial mission in the world.

## The Chrysalis of the New Evangelization

In 1974, Paul VI called a world synod of bishops to discuss the new challenges facing the church in the aftermath of the 1960s. It was apparent that *Ad Gentes* was insufficient as a framework for the new work of post-conciliar evangelization.

The distinguished Swiss Protestant theologian Karl Barth had already criticized Vatican II for seeming to prefer the concept of *dialogue with* the world to the mandate of proclamation of the Gospel *to the world*. Preaching the Gospel of Christ, he insisted, was the church's essential and first mission.[2] In Barth's opinion, dialogue was certainly necessary but always theologically subordinate to proclamation and evangelization. Dialogue is in service to the mission, not in place of it.

In the apostolic exhortation that followed the 1974 World Synod on Evangelization, Paul VI succinctly summarized the purpose of Vatican II: "to make the Church of the twentieth century ever better fitted for proclaiming the Gospel to the people of the twentieth century."[3] There was Barth's whole point. Resourcing and refreshing the great tradition of Christianity; delving more deeply into the Scriptures with the aid of modern exegesis; attending to the evangelical wisdom

---

[2] Karl Barth, *Ad Limina Apostolorum: An Appraisal of Vatican II*, trans. Keith R. Crim (Richmond, VA: John Knox Press, 1968), 27: "Is it so certain that dialogue with the world is to be placed ahead of proclamation to the world?" Barth's influence has extended to some Catholic thinkers like Hans Urs von Balthasar who shifted in his assessment of Vatican II.

[3] Paul VI, Apostolic Exhortation, *Evangelii Nuntiandi* (1975), www.vatican.va: Paul VI.

in other Christian traditions; grasping Christianity's roots in Judaism, which was a living world religion in its own right—all these challenges the council set for itself were meant to outfit Catholicism for a constructive engagement with modernity by proclaiming the Gospel more effectively.

Dialogue, however, is no less demanding than proclamation. It requires a deep knowledge of the Catholic tradition so ecumenical interlocutors have confidence they're communicating with a faithful representative of another faith. Dialogues among those who don't know their own traditions are pointless.[4] For the church of 1965, dialogue involved engaging ecumenical pluralism—the Eastern Catholic Churches (united to Rome but different from it in many ways), the Orthodox Communion of Patriarchates, the Anglican Communion, and Protestant ecclesial communities. The diameter of that ecumenical circle must be widened to include the various groups within the world of Judaism, Islam, and other world religions. The widest circle of ecumenical conversation is with the sciences, the arts, and those spiritual seekers and nonbelievers I wrote about earlier. This modern ecumenical and interreligious world is also a secular world. The Word of God in the Life and Mission of the Church (*Verbum Domini*) and The Joy of the Gospel (*Evangelii Gaudium*) make that all too apparent.

A decade of ecumenical dialogue after the council could not possibly erase three hundred years of antagonism and suspicion. But it was a start. Much has been accomplished at the top tier of theological dialogues, but the popular ecumenical fervor of the late 1960s and 1970s has passed. Dialogue is a demanding and long path to a truth that may not have found perfect expression yet in the words of either interlocutor. The new evangelization, as John Paul II asserted, needs "new expressions." If these are also to be better expressions, they will take time and patience.

Paul VI (1963–1978) presided over the final sessions of Vatican II and the early years of post-conciliar renewal. These were years of considerable ecclesial turmoil made more difficult by social tsunamis

---

[4] Cardinal Walter Kasper, *Harvesting the Fruits: Aspects of Christian Faith in Ecumenical Dialogue* (New York: Continuum Press, 2009). See also, Cardinal Walter Kasper, *A Handbook of Spiritual Ecumenism* (Hyde Park, NY: New City Press, 2007) for practical suggestions to incorporate an ecumenical awareness into Catholic parish life.

in American culture. The Holy Father attempted to contain the schismatic impulses that seemed to be metastasizing within the church while advancing the reforms mandated by the council. The centripetal religious forces liberated by the renewal threatened to overwhelm him.

### The 1974 Synod on Evangelization

Paul VI wrote the first apostolic exhortation on evangelization, *Evangelii Nuntiandi* (EN), in 1975. It is relatively brief—only eighty-two succinct paragraphs with no chapters or major headings to guide the reader through it. All the same, it is an extraordinary text and an excellent introduction to why evangelization has become so important. Every pope since has drawn inspiration from it. Until the encyclical on mission *Redemptoris Missio* (1990) by John Paul II and The Joy of the Gospel (2013) by Francis there was no church document on evangelization more important than *Evangelii Nuntiandi*.

The social and ecclesial traumas after the 1960s overshadowed the pope's presentation and argument. He sees a church too unsure of its recent universal ecumenical self-expression to convince anyone about the truth of the faith. The hope was that his statement on evangelization would spark a renewal of fervor after recent controversies have cooled off (EN 80). Despite that hope, the text conveys more worry than confidence. Only those who came through this exceptional period, followed its great progress and were engaged in its debates, and saw how the partisan struggles wore the spirit down in some or challenged others can fully appreciate the pope's misgivings.

Paul VI was especially concerned about theologies that threatened to separate God and Christ from the church and its sacramental life. *Evangelii Nuntiandi* reads, in that respect, like a first draft of the new evangelization in the shadow of ecclesial indifference and discord. A divided church could not evangelize the modern world. The rise of indifferentism in religious matters, where personal belief is disconnected from the traditions of the church, indeed from the Gospel itself, troubled the pope greatly.

*Evangelii Nuntiandi* opens by affirming the "central axis" of evangelization in terms of a double "fidelity"—fidelity to the intact Gospel message itself communicated in a vital way and in fidelity "to the people to whom we must transmit it." Then the pope poses three essential questions. First, something has obviously happened to the "hidden energy of the Good News" that the church saw present at Vatican II. What are the reasons for the lack of enthusiasm about the church's mission? Second, the modern situation in culture and humanity may be so unique as to be beyond reach by the "evangelical force" of the Gospel. Finally, the church needs to explore new methods and means for evangelizing late modernity.

The key paragraphs on secularism and atheism follow the pope's acknowledgment of a "split" between the Christian faith and modern culture (EN 20). It is from this text that John Paul II will draw his many appeals to inculturation and the transformation of the culture by the Gospel. Humanization drawing reasons from the Gospel can affect social, economic, and political structures. This is a broader moral framework than that of the culture wars. The Christian humanism of the first chapter of *Gaudium et Spes* is evident here.

On the specific matter of secularism, the document mentions the "drama of atheistic humanism," about which Father Henri de Lubac had written in the 1940s. Unlike the more generous treatment given to atheism in *Gaudium et Spes*, Paul VI is more severe. The document distinguishes an ideology of secularism from the other secularizing factors of modern societies brought about by urbanization and industrialization.

Secular atheism itself is distinguished from earlier atheisms that Christian metaphysics sought to refute. It is less philosophical than pragmatic. Many no longer argue against God; they don't care about God. Those weak in faith and religiously indifferent are swept up in it. At the same time, these same people feel spiritually starved by the flattened-out worldview of secularism. *Evangelii Nuntiandi* regards the key elements of evangelization as summarized in three Vatican II documents—*Lumen Gentium*, *Gaudium et Spes*, and *Ad Gentes*.

The very idea of evangelization is multiplex. It is "a complex process made up of varied elements: the renewal of humanity, witness, explicit proclamation, inner adherence, entry into the community, acceptance of signs, apostolic initiative. These elements . . . must always be seen in relationship." Therefore, in its fullest sense, evangelization is a comprehensive theological category for mission and ecclesial existence that can't be limited to preaching and catechesis (EN 24).

Anticipating, as it were, the approach taken by Pope Francis in The Joy of the Gospel, Paul VI touches on the political, social, and economic issues, especially as they impact the Developing World. These challenges stand in the way of God's will as expressed in the Gospel. Echoing the global testimony of bishops, the pope says, "The Church, as the bishops repeated, has the duty to proclaim the liberation of millions of human beings, many of whom are her own children—the duty of assisting the birth of this liberation, of giving witness to it, of ensuring that it is complete. This is not foreign to evangelization" (EN 30). But these are precisely the matters that cut across the political divisions in the United States and elsewhere. Without them, the new evangelization cannot fulfill its mission. The dangers of privatizing faith, making its language purely devotional and sentimental, deprives the Gospel of public reasons capable of influencing and transforming a society.

This papal text is foundational for the new evangelization. It seeks to implement the overall vision of Vatican II. Yet it places a stronger accent on mission and proclamation than the council stressed. It also anticipates the coming challenges of secularism for religious faith and ecclesial mission. A secular humanism, more confident of its agnosticism than some Catholics seemed to be of their belief, was spreading. Privatized religion, even in the vernacular, would be no match for secular nerve and aplomb.

## Puebla to Poland to Port-au-Prince

The expression "new evangelization" (*nueva evangelización*) was first used in 1979 at the meeting in Puebla, Mexico, of the Council of Latin American bishops (CELAM). Building on *Evangelii Nuntiandi*, the Latin American bishops tried to identify the diverse cultural, social, economic, and religious issues impeding the proclamation of the Gospel in their own hemisphere. That hemisphere, lest we forget, stretches across many societies from the Rio Grande River, Mexico, and the Caribbean to the tip of Argentina and Tierra del Fuego. The meeting was a response to the concerns Paul VI had raised in *Evangelii Nuntiandi* about liberation theology, popular religiosity, and base communities (*communidas de base*). Despite linguistic similarities, the Latino hemisphere is enormously diverse in history, culture, and the resources available for addressing human and ecclesiastical problems. But there is no doubt that the matter of economic and political factors played a huge role in the new evangelization for the Central and South American bishops. The core theological principle of liberation theology—the "preferential option for the poor"—provided the new evangelization in its Latin setting with a decidedly economic and social accent. American evangelicals and evangelically influenced Catholics focused almost exclusively on abortion.

The expression *nueva evangelización* got the attention of the Vatican. John Paul II adopted it first (1979) in Poland at an address he delivered at Nowa Huta, the poster-child city of Polish Communist ideology. He took up the same Spanish term again in his address to CELAM at Port-au-Prince, Haiti, on March 9, 1983. On that occasion, John Paul II reaffirmed Paul VI. Speaking to the bishops in Spanish, he defined the new evangelization as being new in its ardor, in its methods, in its expression.[5]

*New ardor, new expressions, and new methods* were a bit abstract then and, in some respects, still are, certainly in the minds of some pastors and many lay Catholics. Vatican II had already used new expressions for the faith. What newer ones did the pope have in mind? Throughout his papacy, John Paul II would associate himself constantly with the new evangelization in encyclical letters, speeches, and global travels. He earnestly prayed that the upcoming millennium would be the fulfillment of what Vatican II proposed for the renewal of the church, for the ecumenical and interreligious situation of Christianity, and for culture at large. In his mind, an impediment to that was the prolonged theological standoff and conflict of interpretations about Vatican II. This post-conciliar division of interpretation posed enormous problems in the pope's mind for a unified and impassioned ecclesial mission. With the help of then-Cardinal Joseph Ratzinger, John Paul II set about closing off a twenty-year theological dispute in the church over the meaning of Vatican II.

Before that, John Paul II instituted the Pontifical Council for Culture (1982) whose purpose it was to relate the church to the vast sphere of human culture—intellectual currents, sciences, and the arts.[6] Evangelization, as Paul VI had made clear, always complemented mission with inculturation. This was integral to the vision

---

[5] John Paul II, Speech, Port-au-Prince, Haiti, March 9, 1983, www.vatican.va: John Paul II, Speeches, March, 1983. "La conmemoración del medio milenio de evangelización tendrá su significación plena si es un compromiso vuestro como obispos, junto con vuestro presbiterio y fieles; compromiso, no de re-evangelización, pero sí de una evangelización nueva. Nueva en su ardor, en sus métodos, en su expresión."

[6] John Paul II, *Pastor Bonus*, May 20, 1982.

of *Gaudium et Spes*, with which John Paul II aligned his whole pontificate. Ten years later, the pope moved the Pontifical Council for Dialogue with Non-Believers under the direction of the Pontifical Council for Culture. This would become the umbrella dicastery (office in the Curia) for religious pluralism and secularism.[7]

Since 1999, eight plenary sessions have been held by the Pontifical Council for Culture, starting toward the end of the pontificate of John Paul II with a New Christian Humanism (1999). Under Pope Benedict, the Pontifical Council for Culture has addressed Atheism and Indifference (2004), Beauty (2006), and Secularism and Secularity (2008). It was clear that the new evangelization had to take account of the cultural causes of religious indifference as well as the continuing appeal of beauty to the human soul and other social realities that evoke, compromise, or choke off the sense of transcendence. In this respect, John Paul II made clear from the beginning of the new evangelization that the reality of God could no longer be simply assumed or regarded in Catholicism as a settled metaphysical issue. It is an issue that had moved from piety and philosophy to human cultural experience. The privatization of belief in God and the cultural insignificance of the Christian religion was where the conversation was headed.

## A Dark Modernity: Secularism and Indifference

A decade after *Evangelii Nuntiandi*, John Paul II called an extraordinary synod to celebrate the twentieth anniversary of the close of Vatican II.[8] The event was more than celebratory; it was political in the strategic sense of trying to settle the theological debate over the authentic and authoritative meaning of Vatican II.[9] In the synod's final report, evangelization is recognized as the primary mission of

[7] John Paul II, *Inde A Pontificatus*, March 25, 1993.

[8] Second Extraordinary Synod, "The Church, in the Word of God, Celebrates the Mysteries of Christ for the Salvation of the World," Final Report, November 24 to December 8, 1985.

[9] See Massimo Faggioli, *Vatican II: The Battle for Meaning* (New York: Paulist Press, 2012); Richard R. Gaillardetz, *An Unfinished Council: Vatican II, Pope Francis, and the Renewal of Catholicism* (Collegeville, MN: Liturgical Press, 2015); Ormond Rush, *Still Interpreting Vatican II: Some Hermeneutical Principles* (New York: Paulist Press, 2004). The Paulist Press series *Rediscovering Vatican II* provides an excellent explanation of the background debates and texts of Vatican II.

the church in the Holy Spirit. A separate paragraph is devoted to evangelization as the *first duty* of all Christians, not only of bishops, priests, and deacons. The word now comes to mean far more than "mission" previously did in the minds of Catholics where it denoted conversion subcontracted to ordained religious missionaries whom lay Catholics funded with contributions on mission Sundays. Now it meant this: "the self-evangelization of the baptized and in a certain sense, of deacons, priests, and bishops." These themes would be reworked by the church in various ways until Pope Francis consolidated them in The Joy of the Gospel, where all Christians, probably much to their surprise, are declared to be "missionary disciples."

A marked shift in the assessment of the world as a field for missionary activity now begins to take place. In the sixth part of the synod's final report, "The Mission of the Church in the World," the document asserts that "the signs of the times" have become more serious in 1985 than they were when Vatican II concluded in 1965. Violence and socio-economic problems had moved to the forefront of global consciousness. This text trims back the optimism of Vatican II with a sober "realism" based on a theology of the cross. It warns of a "false aggiornamento" that tends to an "accommodation" with secular society that may even lead to a "secularization of the Church." The report stresses that inculturation does not mean an "external adaptation" of the church to a culture but a "transformation of authentic cultural values" by the Gospel. It balances the authentic value of dialogue with non-Christian religions as well as nonbelievers by asserting a centrifugal effort to precipitate a deeper Catholic identity. Since the social world is constantly in flux, a continuous reading of the "signs of the times" is always required in the church.

In this redaction of the problem of modernity, the challenges of secularism and secularization have grown far more threatening to the church than they were just a decade earlier in *Evangelii Nuntiandi*. The extraordinary synod threw the weight of the synod and the papacy of John Paul II against the secular world and progressive theology. At the same time as the pope wanted to represent a Christian humanism to modernity, he would present himself as a "sign of contradiction" to much of it.

In subsequent encyclicals, *Veritatis Splendor* and *Fides et Ratio*, John Paul II would press his case against such intellectual currents as relativism and positivism inimical to a Catholic vision of moral truth and reason. The onset of the coming third millennium breathed a second wind into the pope whose personal biography had been overshadowed by German fascism and Eastern European communism. Against these he proposed a humanism based on Jesus Christ.

John Paul II contributed further specificity to the new evangelization in three other ways. In 1992, he wrote an apostolic exhortation based on a synod on the priesthood titled *Pastores Dabo Vobis* (I Will Give You Shepherds). In the sections of that exhortation that dealt with culture, the darkened horizons of the secular world raised in the extraordinary synod overshadowed priestly ministry too.[10] In many respects this text was a breakthrough in terms of clarifying how the priest is configured to Christ, how the integral linkage of word and sacrament come together, and how the priest's role primarily is as a pastor and shepherd. But, where *Gaudium et Spes* presented a neutral phenomenology of modernity, *Pastores Dabo Vobis* divides up the positive factors in modernity favorable to religion and sorts out the negative ones as if one has little or nothing to do with the other. Many of the issues the pope would touch on in his encyclicals on moral truth and reason, he expresses here. This sentence captures much of it: "Furthermore, despite the fall of the ideologies which had made materialism a dogma and the refusal of religion a program, there is spreading in every part of the world a sort of practical and existential atheism which coincides with a secularist outlook on life and human destiny."[11] This will lead many younger priests to think preaching the new evangelization largely amounts to attacking secularism. The stress on the priest's ontological "configuration to Christ" will conceal within it a mistaken incentive to a recrudescence of clericalism.

John Paul II issued the encyclical letter *Redemptoris Missio* (1990) to explain mission more fully than *Evangelii Nuntiandi* or *Ad Gentes* had. This encyclical introduced a distinction in possible audiences for mission.

---

[10] John Paul II, I Will Give You Shepherds (*Pastores Dabo Vobis*), March 25, 1992. See especially chapter 1, "Chosen from Among Men: The Challenges Facing Priestly Formation at the Conclusion of the Second Millennium," 5–10.

[11] Ibid., 7.

The fact that there is a diversity of activities *in the Church's one mission* is not intrinsic to that mission, but arises from the variety of circumstances in which that mission is carried out. Looking at today's world from the viewpoint of evangelization, we can distinguish *three situations*.

First, there is the situation which the Church's missionary activity addresses: peoples, groups, and socio-cultural contexts in which Christ and his Gospel are not known, or which lack Christian communities sufficiently mature to be able to incarnate the faith in their own environment and proclaim it to other groups. This is mission *ad gentes* in the proper sense of the term.

Secondly, there are Christian communities with adequate and solid ecclesial structures. They are fervent in their faith and in Christian living. They bear witness to the Gospel in their surroundings and have a sense of commitment to the universal mission. In these communities the Church carries out her activity and pastoral care.

Thirdly, there is an intermediate situation, particularly in countries with ancient Christian roots, and occasionally in the younger Churches as well, where entire groups of the baptized have lost a living sense of the faith, or even no longer consider themselves members of the Church, and live a life far removed from Christ and his Gospel. In this case what is needed is a "new evangelization" or a "re-evangelization."[12]

Only in the case of the third audience, does John Paul II speak properly of a "new evangelization" or a "re-evangelization." Clearly the assumptions that different people hold about religion determine the expressions and means one uses to reach them. For many pastors, the new evangelization was interpreted as a fuller catechesis and an inoculation against moral relativism. The second and third audiences are conflated. But important differences in mentality and reception are lost by doing that.

The normative catechetical text for the new evangelization, envisioned as a re-catechesis of lapsed Catholics, was the *Catechism of the Catholic Church* (1994).This is an encyclopedic summary of all church teaching up to, including, and following the Second Vatican Council. Strangely, however, the *Catechism*, despite its breadth, does not treat the new evangelization as such even while summarizing mission as expressed in *Ad Gentes* and *Redemptoris Missio*. Nor does the *Catechism*

---

[12] John Paul II, *Redemptoris Missio*, 33.

address secularism or secularization in its sections dealing with atheism and agnosticism (2123–28), as one might expect. Religious liberty is clearly presented based on *Dignitatis Humanae*, yet without any hint that this is a major development of doctrine from the papal teaching found in *Mirari Vos* and the *Syllabus of Errors*. Micro-ruptures in recent papal traditions tend to be papered over.

With the *Catechism of the Catholic Church*, *Redemptoris Missio*, and *Pastores Dabo Vobis*, the major intellectual, catechetical, and pastoral pieces were thought to be in place for the new evangelization—(1) a comprehensive summary of Christian doctrine reinforced with encyclical letters clarifying major moral questions, (2) followed by an updated statement on mission, and (3) the renewal of the sacramental identity and pastoral ministry of the priest. The pope also issued various documents relevant to the meaning of the millennium and, on the eve of it, rejoiced in the achievement of the first doctrinal ecumenical agreement in five hundred years between the Catholic Church and the Lutheran World Federation.[13] Everything was positioned for the transformation the Holy Father had prayed for in the new millennium.

No one could have predicted what happened next. Nineteen Islamic jihadists attacked America on September 11, 2001. The confidence of the West in the immediate post-Soviet era ended. A new adversary—smaller, religiously fanatical, from the Islamic world—appeared. This act of religiously motivated terror was followed in a few months by the exhaustive "Spotlight" coverage (six hundred separate articles) of clerical sexual abuse of children reported in the *Boston Globe*. These two different events altered the cultural reception of the church's one-sided critique of secularism the popes had given since Paul VI. A religious war had begun against secular America fueled by an extremist Islamic theology (Saudi Arabian Wahhabism). The nation then went to war in Iraq ("Shock and Awe"), the consequences of which still spread across the Middle East, Europe, and America.

---

[13] *Joint Declaration on the Doctrine of Justification*, Lutheran-Catholic Dialogue, Augsburg, Germany, 1999. Approved by the Congregation for the Doctrine of the Faith and signed by Cardinal Edward Cassidy and Bishop Walter Kasper. In 2006, the World Methodist Council formally associated itself with this important ecumenical declaration.

Some historians claim the twentieth century began not on January 1, 1900, but on June 28, 1914, in Sarajevo with the outbreak of the First World War. The young and traumatized twenty-first century—for religion at least—effectively began on September 11, 2001, in New York and, for Catholicism, on January 6, 2002, with the revelations of clerical abuse of children reported in the *Boston Globe*. The new evangelization forced upon the church the task of rethinking secularism and again undertaking the necessary but difficult discernment of reform. The process of rethinking secularism in philosophical culture had already begun with the Gifford Lectures Charles Taylor delivered on the subject in 1999. In 2015, he was invited to deliver a major address at a Courtyard of the Gentiles event in Rome.

## The Courtyard of the Gentiles

One source of the Courtyard of the Gentiles concept I will treat here can already be found in *Redemptoris Missio* by John Paul II, where he invokes the related idea of the "New Areopagi" in modern culture. This expression, unfamiliar to many Catholics, refers to St. Paul's sermon at the Greek Areopagus in Athens (Acts 17) where he makes mention of seeing an altar in the city bearing the inscription "To an unknown god." Paul proceeds to compliment the Athenians on their natural religiosity before preaching on the God of revelation.

The election of Benedict XVI in 2005 was not altogether surprising in light of all this. Many cardinal-electors regarded the challenges facing the church and the new evangelization as primarily moral and doctrinal. The situation demanded a theological intelligence equal to the challenges of secular thought. Many bishops and priests believed a firm grasp of the most controversial issues and a correspondingly deep sense of the doctrinal tradition were needed in the Chair of Peter.

Following the death of John Paul II on April 2, 2005, and his funeral, Cardinal Ratzinger opened the papal conclave liturgy (*Pro Eligendo Romano Pontifice*) with a homily, partly based on Ephesians 4:14.[14] In that homily, Ratzinger warned about a "dictatorship of rela-

---

[14] See "Cardinal Ratzinger's Homily in Mass Before Conclave," in https://zenit .org/articles/cardinal-ratzinger-s-homily-in-mass-before-conclave/. The lectionary texts for the Mass were Isaiah 61:1-3a, 6a, 8b-9; Ephesians 4:11-16; John 15:9-17. Referring to Ephesians 4:14, "tossed to and fro and carried about by every wind of doctrine,"

tivism." With that phrase, the future pope reignited the resentments many Catholics harbored about secularism. But too much had been written in sociology and philosophy about secularization and secularism to compress it into a dictatorship of one thing or another. Benedict XVI came to understand that as time went on, and before retiring as pope he opened a new dialogue with secular thought. The remote origins of that gesture, as I have pointed out earlier, can be found in 2004 when, still a cardinal, he shared a podium in Munich on the topic of secularization and religion with the agnostic social philosopher Jürgen Habermas.

Cardinal Ratzinger's post-conciliar career and theological contributions had been focused less on the larger ambitions of the new evangelization than on the re-catechization of Catholics themselves. The *Catechism of the Catholic Church* was his greatest theological achievement as prefect of the Congregation for the Doctrine of the Faith. The *Catechism* itself was not presented as evidence of any doctrinal development in the church whatsoever. Recent developments on the theology of the church, divine revelation, ecumenism, and religious freedom were harmlessly harmonized with the great tradition. Benedict XVI, for all his theological erudition, was succeeding a global personality who had left his spiritual footprint on every continent managing, if not always by argument certainly by personal conviction and charisma, to reinvigorate a sense of Catholic identity and missionary zeal. A catechetical renewal could not equal that.

For a whole generation, Cardinal Ratzinger had been the church's lead critic of secularism. Strange, though, how events and invitations can alter thinking and perceptions. In 2004, Ratzinger accepted an invitation to speak on religious faith in a secular age. Jürgen Habermas, one of the world's most prominent secular thinkers, addressed the same topic. This was a colloquy, not a debate.[15] The *Dialectics of Secularization: On Reason and Religion* reveals how these two major

---

Ratzinger asks rhetorically: "How many winds of doctrine have we known in these last decades, how many ideological currents, how many fashions of thought? The small boat of thought of many Christians has often remained agitated by the waves, tossed from one extreme to the other: from Marxism to liberalism, to libertinism; from collectivism to radical individualism; from atheism to a vague religious mysticism; from agnosticism to syncretism, etc."

[15] Joseph Cardinal Ratzinger and Jürgen Habermas, *Dialectics of Secularisation: On Reason and Religion*, ed. Florian Schuller, trans. Brian McNeil (San Francisco: Ignatius Press, 2006).

intellectuals—one a cardinal, the other an agnostic social philosopher—approached the pre-political foundations of the liberal secular order. Posing the question in those terms means this: Does the secular state, from its own intellectual and constitutional resources, have the moral grounds for generating and regenerating what it considers sacred—human equality, human rights, and freedom? Ratzinger, for his part, said no, it does not, but he conceded that reason could purify toxic ideas within religion such as violence and hatred. This was an important concession. Habermas also admitted candidly that liberal society could not regenerate from political principles alone the moral outlooks and motives needed to sustain its own basic commitments. Habermas even suggested that society needs to move to a post-secular stage if by secular one means the hegemony of one worldview. A humble agnosticism and a magnanimous Catholicism met face to face in Munich in a productive exchange that holds promise for evangelization in a secular age. Catholicism was moving the dialogue forward between faith and secular thought, and the future Pope Benedict himself was doing it.

Associated as he had been with doctrinal truth, many were surprised that Benedict's first encyclical letter as pope was on the virtue of love, *Deus Caritas Est*. Another encyclical followed on the virtue of hope, and a draft was later written before he retired for an encyclical on faith. As much as Ratzinger was influenced by St. Augustine, surely the saint's *Enchiridion on Faith, Hope, and Love* was on the pope's mind. Perhaps writing about these supernatural virtues revealed his instinct that, having mapped the boundaries of Catholic doctrine, it was time to move the conversation to a more spiritual level. *Deus Caritas Est* sounded a note that was as Franciscan as it was Johannine. This is where Christians and secular humanists can talk of God—the meaning and motives for human love and hope. Perhaps in the motives for joy as well.

The issue of secularism can be approached from political, theological, and moral perspectives. Theologically, the pope regards it as a practical atheism in which talk about God cannot count as an example of or basis for reasonable discourse. In the moral spheres, on the other hand, the pope saw secularism as a brazen attempt to silence religious voices in public life by declaring them irrational or bigoted. In such societies, only those religious values are considered rational that align perfectly with secular values. An inclusive moral pluralism and a magnanimous secularism were both required for a productive and rational exchange.

In 2009, Benedict XVI delivered a major address to the Pontifical Council for Culture, whose plenary assembly was titled "The Church and the Challenge of Secularization."[16] I will quote the pope's concluding address in full here because it summarizes very well the concerns that the church has about cultural secularization after Vatican II and that renders Catholic belief today more problematic for many. I will emphasize in the pope's speech those expressions important for observations I've already made about religious indifference and for my argument going forward.

> I congratulate you on your work and on the theme chosen for this Assembly: "The Church and the challenge of secularization." This is a fundamental issue for the future of humanity and of the Church. Secularization that often turns into secularism, abandoning the positive acceptance of secularity, harshly tries the Christian life of the faithful and Pastors alike, and during your Assembly you have additionally interpreted and transformed it into a providential challenge in order to propose convincing answers to the questions and hopes of man, our contemporary.
>
> I thank Archbishop Gianfranco Ravasi, who has been President of the Dicastery for only a few months, for his cordial words on your behalf illustrating the pattern of your work. I am also grateful to all of you for your commitment to ensuring that *the Church enters into dialogue with the cultural movements of our age* and that the Holy See's interest

---

[16] See www.cultura.va: Plenary Assembly, "The Church and the Challenge of Secularization," March 6–8, 2008, www.vatican.va: Benedict XVI. Pope Benedict's address to U.S. bishops on their "Ad Limina" visit (January 19, 2012) drew attention to the connections between a "reductive secularism" and a "radical secularism" and the American tradition of religious freedom with obvious reference to moral issues in health care: "In light of these considerations, it is imperative that the entire Catholic community in the United States come to realize the grave threats to the Church's public moral witness presented by radical secularism which finds increasing expressions in the political and cultural spheres. . . . Of particular concern are certain attempts being made to limit that most cherished of American freedoms, the freedom of religion. Many of you have pointed out that concerted efforts have been made to deny the right of conscientious objection on the part of Catholic individuals and institutions with regard to cooperation in intrinsically evil practices. Others have spoken to me of a worrying tendency to reduce religious freedom to mere freedom of worship without guarantees of respect for freedom of conscience."

for the vast and varied world of culture may be increasingly known. Today more than ever, in fact, reciprocal intercultural openness is a privileged terrain for dialogue between men and women involved in the search for authentic humanism, over and above differences that separate them. Secularization, which presents itself in cultures by *imposing a world and humanity without reference to Transcendence,* is invading every aspect of daily life and developing a mentality in which God is effectively absent, wholly or partially, from human life and awareness. This secularization is not only an external threat to believers, but has been manifest for some time in the heart of the Church herself. It profoundly distorts the Christian faith from within, and consequently, the lifestyle and daily behaviour of believers. They live in the world and are often marked, if not conditioned, by the cultural imagery that impresses contradictory and impelling models regarding *the practical denial of God*: there is no longer any need for God, to think of him or to return to him. Furthermore, the prevalent hedonistic and consumeristic mindset fosters in the faithful and in Pastors a tendency to superficiality and selfishness that is harmful to ecclesial life.

The "death of God" proclaimed by many intellectuals in recent decades is giving way to a barren *cult of the individual*. In this cultural context there is a risk of drifting into spiritual atrophy and emptiness of heart, sometimes characterized by surrogate forms of religious affiliation and vague spiritualism. It is proving more urgent than ever to react to this tendency by means of an appeal to the lofty values of existence that give life meaning and can soothe the restlessness of the human heart in search of happiness: the dignity of the human person and his or her freedom, equality among all men and women, the meaning of life and death and of what awaits us after the end of our earthly existence. In this perspective my Predecessor, the Servant of God John Paul II, aware of the radical and rapid changes in society, constantly recalled the urgent need to come to terms with human beings in the sphere of culture in order to pass on to them the Gospel Message. For this very reason he established the Pontifical Council for Culture in order to give a new impetus to the Church's action by introducing the Gospel to the plurality of cultures in the various parts of the world (cf. Letter to Cardinal Agostino Casaroli, 20 May 1982; *L'Osservatore Romano* English edition [ORE], 28 June, pp. 7, 20). The intellectual sensitivity and pastoral charity of Pope John Paul II encouraged him to highlight the fact that *the Industrial Revolution and scientific discoveries made it possible to answer questions that formerly were partially answered only by religion*. The result was that contemporary man often had the impression that he no longer needs anyone in order to understand, explain and dominate the universe; he feels the centre of everything, the measure of everything.

More recently, through new information technologies, globalization has often also resulted in disseminating in all cultures many of the materialistic and individualistic elements of the West. *The formula* "Etsi Deus non daretur" *is increasingly becoming a way of living* that originates in a sort of "arrogance" of reason—a reality nonetheless created and loved by God—that deems itself self-sufficient and closes itself to contemplation and the quest for a superior Truth. The light of reason, exalted but in fact impoverished by the Enlightenment, has radically replaced the light of faith, the light of God (cf. Benedict XVI, Address, La Sapienza University, 17 January 2008). Thus, in this context the Church has great challenges with which to deal. The commitment of the Pontifical Council for Culture to a fruitful dialogue between science and faith is therefore especially important. This comparison has been long awaited by the Church but also by the scientific community, and I encourage you to persevere in it. Through it, faith implies reason and perfection, and reason, enlightened by faith, finds the strength to rise to the knowledge of God and spiritual realities. In this sense seculari-zation does not foster the ultimate goal of science which is at the service of man, "*imago Dei.*" May this dialogue continue in the distinction of the specific characteristics of science and faith. Indeed, each has its own methods, contexts and subjects of research, its own aims and limitations, and must respect and recognize the other's legitimate possibility of exercising autonomy in accordance with its own prin-ciples (cf. *Gaudium et Spes*, n. 36); both are called to serve man and humanity, encouraging the integral development and growth of each one and all.

I above all exhort Pastors of God's flock to a tireless and generous mission in order to confront with Gospel proclamation and witness, in the arena of dialogue and the encounter with cultures, the disturbing phenomenon of secularization that enfeebles the person and hinders him in his innate longing for the whole Truth. Thus, may Christ's dis-ciples, thanks to the service carried out particularly by your Dicastery, continue to proclaim Christ in the heart of cultures, because he is the light that illumines reason, man and the world. We also set before us the warning addressed to the angel of the Church in Ephesus: "I know your works, your toil and your patient endurance. . . . But I have this against you, that you have abandoned the love you had at first" (*Rv* 2: 2, 4). Let us make our own the cry of the Spirit and of the Church: "Come!" (*Rv* 22: 17), and let our hearts be pervaded by the Lord's response: "Surely, I am coming soon" (*Rv* 22: 20). He is our hope, the light for our way, our strength to proclaim salvation with apostolic courage, reaching to the heart of all cultures. May God help you in carrying out your arduous but exalting mission![17]

These words of Benedict XVI following the plenary assembly on secularization highlight secularization as a cultural process that science effectively promotes with the effect that God is deemed disposable with no loss to human self-understanding and cultural values.

The final years of Benedict XVI's papacy before his retirement involved further actions related to the engagement of the new evangelization with secularization. On December 21, 2009, the pope delivered his Christmas address to the Roman Curia in which he employed an image for evangelization he had not used previously. It came in the wake of the pope's pastoral visit to the Czech Republic, where he encountered among secular atheists an openness and humanity that personally affected him. That experience persuaded Benedict that secularism could be more than just a denial of God. Secularists he met saw their secularism as another humanism parallel to and different from the humanism of *Gaudium et Spes*. Both humanisms had to be put in touch with each other. Moral salvos from a distance could not achieve that. The Scriptures offered some promising images for a religious-secular encounter. Again, I quote Pope Benedict at length (the italics are mine).

> Finally, I would like once again to express my joy and gratitude for my Visit to the Czech Republic. *Prior to this Journey I had always been told that it was a country with a majority of agnostics and atheists*, in which Christians are now only a minority. *All the more joyful was my surprise at seeing myself surrounded everywhere by great cordiality and friendliness, that the important liturgies were celebrated in a joyful atmosphere of faith; that in the setting of the University and the world of culture my words were attentively listened to; and that the state authorities treated me with great courtesy and did their utmost to contribute to the success of the visit.* I could now be tempted to say something about the beauty of the country and the magnificent testimonies of Christian culture which only make this beauty perfect. But I consider most important the fact that *we, as believers, must have at heart even those people who consider themselves agnostics or atheists.* When we speak of a new evangelization these people are

[17] Address of His Holiness Benedict XVI to Participants in the Plenary Assembly of the Pontifical Council for Culture, March 8, 2008, www.vatican.va: Benedict XVI.

perhaps taken aback. *They do not want to see themselves as an object of mission or to give up their freedom of thought and will. Yet the question of God remains present even for them,* even if they cannot believe in the concrete nature of his concern for us. In Paris, I spoke of the quest for God as the fundamental reason why Western monasticism, and with it, Western culture, came into being. As the first step of evangelization we must seek to keep this quest alive; *we must be concerned that human beings do not set aside the question of God, but rather see it as an essential question for their lives.* We must make sure that they are open to this question and to the yearning concealed within it. Here I think naturally of the words which Jesus quoted from the Prophet Isaiah, namely that the Temple must be a house of prayer for all the nations (cf. Is 56: 7; Mk 11: 17). *Jesus was thinking of the so-called "Court of the Gentiles"* which he cleared of extraneous affairs so that it could be a free space for the Gentiles who wished to pray there to the one God, even if they could not take part in the mystery for whose service the inner part of the Temple was reserved. A place of prayer for all the peoples by this he was thinking of people who know God, so to speak, only from afar; who are dissatisfied with their own gods, rites and myths; who desire the Pure and the Great, even if God remains for them the "unknown God" (cf. Acts 17: 23). They had to pray to the unknown God, yet in this way they were somehow in touch with the true God, albeit amid all kinds of obscurity. *I think that today too the Church should open a sort of "Court of the Gentiles" in which people might in some way latch on to God, without knowing him and before gaining access to his mystery, at whose service the inner life of the Church stands.* Today, in addition to interreligious dialogue, there should be a dialogue with those to whom religion is something foreign, to whom God is unknown and who nevertheless do not want to be left merely Godless, but rather to draw near to him, albeit as the Unknown.[18]

This is an extraordinary speech—so sympathetic to the search of many secular people for truth and a fuller sense of humanity. The tone of hostile diagnosis and moral indictment is absent. The initiative taken by the Pontifical Council for Culture based on this speech is called "The Courtyard of the Gentiles" (*Cortile dei Gentili*). The image recalled the outer courtyard in Herod's temple where Jews and Gentiles assembled to interact based on common interests.

---

[18] Address of His Holiness Benedict XVI to the Members of the Roman Curia, December 21, 2009.

This sacred interface of biblical religion and Greco-Roman paganism was reinforced as well by the memory of St. Paul's famous speech at the Greek Areopagus in Acts 17. Paul told his audience that the "Unknown God" inscribed on the altar of a pagan temple was what he was prepared to preach to them. Benedict himself suggested the church needed to create its own "Court of the Gentiles." How could that take place? The Pontifical Council for Culture took up his suggestion under the presidency of Cardinal Gianfranco Ravasi.

The first event in a whole series of planned encounters in the Courtyard of the Gentiles took place on February 12, 2011, in Bologna, Italy, which "considers itself at the crossroads of Catholic and secularist cultures."[19] In 2012, another Courtyard of the Gentiles event took place in Paris in front of Notre-Dame—in Paris, the church's "eldest daughter" and the very epicenter of Enlightenment *laïcisme*. Other Courtyards of the Gentiles have since been held under the auspices of bishops, academic institutions, and the high patronage of the Pontifical Council for Culture. The unrelenting critique of secularism, however, which was inculcated in the new evangelization over the course of two papacies and in America by Cardinal Francis George of Chicago, would be difficult to overcome.

The Pontifical Council for Culture has now become the lead agent in the Catholic Church for the engagement with culture, more particularly with religious pluralism, indifferentism, agnosticism, atheism, and secularism. The Courtyard aims to bring together serious thinkers to discuss common themes where religious and non-religious humanisms can learn from each other in the hope of finding greater understanding and bases for common action. The Courtyard's objectives are stated in its literature on the Vatican website (www.cultura .va) as follows: "Find a synthesis and a precursory and profound dialogue between the spirit of enlightenment, secularism and faith. Recognize the genuine achievements of the age of enlightenment. The presence of secularity does not imply a separation or opposition between culture and faith. Here there is an anomaly that must be overcome. What is needed is to find a path of dialogue, to integrate faith and modern rationality in a unified anthropological vision."

---

[19] Alessandra Nucci, "The Courtyard of the Gentiles," in *The Catholic World Report*, May 13, 2011.

Recognizing the "genuine achievements of the age of enlightenment" gets at the heart of the matter.

In his second gesture to promote the new evangelization, Benedict XVI appointed Archbishop Rino Fisichella as first president of a new curial office, the Pontifical Council for the Promotion of the New Evangelization, in 2010. Fisichella is a specialist in foundational theology, and his appointment signaled a stress on fundamental articles of faith in the new evangelization, such as the nature of God, divine revelation, Jesus Christ, and the church. The new evangelization needed "new expressions" for these, as John Paul II had said. In the address Benedict delivered to the plenary session of this dicastery, he reiterated the connections between secularization and the new evangelization. The Czech experience notwithstanding, the pope's concern for the effects of secularization on the faithful remained firm.

> When, on 28 June of last year, at the First Vespers of the Solemnity of Sts Peter and Paul, I announced that I wished to institute a Dicastery for the promotion of the New Evangelization, I opened the way for a reflection to begin on a subject I had pondered over for a long time: the need to offer a specific response to a moment of crisis in Christian life which is occurring in many countries, especially those of ancient Christian tradition. Today, with this meeting, I note with pleasure that the new Pontifical Council has become a reality. I thank Archbishop Salvatore Fisichella for the words which he addressed to me, introducing me to the work of your first Plenary Assembly. I extend my cordial greetings to all of you with my encouragement for the contribution that you will make to the work of the new Dicastery, especially in view of the Thirteenth Ordinary General Assembly of the Synod of Bishops which, in October 2012, will address the theme: *The New Evangelization for the Transmission of the Christian Faith.*
>
> The term, "new evangelization" recalls the need for a renewed manner of proclamation, especially for those who live in a context, like the one today, in which the development of secularization has had a heavy impact, even in traditionally Christian countries. The Gospel is the ever new proclamation of the salvation worked by Christ which makes humanity participate in the mystery of God and in his life of love and opens it to a future of strong, sure hope. Highlighting that at this moment in history, the Church is called to carry out a *new* evangelization, means intensifying her missionary action so that it fully corresponds to the Lord's mandate. The Second Vatican Council recalled that "The groups among whom the Church operates are utterly changed so that

an entirely new situation arises" (Decree *Ad Gentes*, n. 6). The farsighted Fathers of the Council saw the cultural changes that were on the horizon and which today are easily verifiable. It is precisely these changes which have created unexpected conditions for believers and require special attention in proclaiming the Gospel, for giving an account of our faith in situations which are different from the past. The current crisis brings with it traces of the exclusion of God from people's lives, from a generalized indifference towards the Christian faith to an attempt to marginalize it from public life. In the past decades, it was still possible to find a general Christian sensibility which unified the common experience of entire generations raised in the shadow of the faith which had shaped culture. Today, unfortunately, we are witnessing a drama of fragmentation which no longer acknowledges a unifying reference point; moreover, it often occurs that people wish to belong to the Church, but they are strongly shaped by a vision of life which is in contrast with the faith.[20]

Finally, in the fall of 2012, Pope Benedict presided over the world synod he had called to take up again the question of the new evangelization. An earlier synod devoted to clarifying the meaning of the Word of God gave Pope Benedict an opportunity to explain again what the church meant by revelation. He did that in his apostolic exhortation *Verbum Domini*. The Catholic idea of revelation is not a form of fundamentalism with which it is easily confused. The autonomous human quest for truth and meaning meets in free encounter the religious language of divine address in Scripture and Christ. The dialogue of reason and sacred texts mediated by biblical and theological hermeneutics is unavoidable in a secular age.

In part 3 of *Verbum Domini*, the pope inserted paragraphs on the new evangelization in relation to Christians who are "baptized but insufficiently evangelized" where they are "losing their identity under the influence of a secularized culture."[21] In the same text, however, he admitted the presence of "dark passages" in the revealed Scriptures, especially those making God order or condone human

---

[20] Address of His Holiness Benedict XVI to Participants in the Plenary Assembly of the Pontifical Council for Promoting the New Evangelization, May 30, 2011.

[21] Benedict XVI, Apostolic Exhortation, *Verbum Domini*, September 30, 2010, 96. Ratzinger has often raised questions about positivistic abuses of the historical-critical method in theology and the complete autonomy of reason. In *Verbum Domini*, he alludes to both tendencies.

violence.[22] The christological moral axiom of the love and forgiveness of enemies is the filter through which one must run biblical passages to the contrary. No text is revelation for Christians unless it passes that crucial test.

## 2012 World Synod on the New Evangelization

Pope Benedict XVI retired as pope on February 28, 2013. The task of summarizing the synod's discussion on the new evangelization fell to his successor, Pope Francis, the former cardinal-archbishop of Buenos Aries, elected March 13, 2013. He wrote and promulgated *Evangelii Gaudium* (The Joy of the Gospel, 2013) the following fall. The text communicated an undeniable evangelical fervor and ardor which both Paul VI and John Paul II had wanted the church to recover. And it gathered together in several chapters a summary of what Benedict XVI, above all, had criticized about secular culture. In a later chapter, I will take up the analysis and critique of secularism and the overall approach to the new evangelization in The Joy of the Gospel in some detail.

One thing, however, is clear about it. Secularism was parsed more carefully in The Joy of the Gospel than before. September 11, 2001, was a shock to the Westphalian system where religious violence in the name of God had become unthinkable. Clergy sexual abuse of minors was mortifying for the Catholic Church which had closed in on itself in certain ways to preserve its identity. Two generations of criticizing the secular world by the church made the hierarchical hypocrisy of it all the more insulting to seculars and lay Catholics alike.

Without abandoning the philosophical and moral critiques of relativism and secularism, the second synod on evangelization uncovered

---

[22] Ibid. Benedict XVI also recognized the Bible itself can be a carrier of ideas that are not revelation in the proper sense. In para. 42, he wrote of "dark" passages of the Bible "suited to the cultural and moral level of distant times." The pope's recognition of moral evolution in human history cannot be restricted only to the pre-Christian ages. Charles Taylor's *Sources of the Self: The Making of the Modern Identity* argues for the developing human awareness in values and hyper-goods. Hans Joas notes that the church on its own was not able to deduce the modern concept of human rights from its meditations on human creation in the image of God. It took the secular Enlightenment to enable it to do that.

more links in it to religious indifference in the modern economic order than previously and far more reasons for internal reform in the church. Global economics and commodity-based views of human life can and do corrupt morals. The market collapse in 2008 was all the evidence anyone needed. Hierarchical secrecy and arrogance can and do cause great harm to the faith. Both modernity and secularity demand much more philosophical, theological, and ecclesial exegesis than we have had.

In an even larger sense, what the Protestant Reformation was for late medieval Catholicism, secularism is today for the whole universe of religious belief—an optional worldview previously not even considered a possibility. The question is whether this new option—the option of choosing to follow a religious faith or none—can stimulate in modern Catholicism something the Reformation did for late medieval Catholicism in the new sixteenth-century spiritual movements, associated largely with the Jesuits and contemplative communities. On the other hand, a counter-secular reaction, as we see it today in some parts of Islam and the church, will not favor the creation of new Catholic evangelical options in a secular age. It will just pour more fuel on a culture war.

The next three chapters will be on philosophical modernity, secularization, and Charles Taylor's major work, *A Secular Age*. They will likely be challenging for readers unfamiliar with sociology and philosophy. I wrote them in the conviction that the ongoing reform of the church needed after clergy abuse can be matched by an ongoing reassessment of the modern secular order as well. I believe that with Charles Taylor's massive study, *A Secular Age*, the church has an ally in the task of "reading the signs of the times" and "interpreting them in the light of the Gospel."

# Chapter 6

# The Malaises of Modernity

What does modernity itself mean? What kind of moral conflicts underlie the three malaises Charles Taylor writes about? How does our modernity affect the traditional mission of the church? These are a few of the questions I want to treat in this chapter. Beneath the many theological, biblical, and pastoral issues of Vatican II, the basic question was the meaning of our modernity. The Pastoral Constitution on the Church in the Modern World (*Gaudium et Spes*) sought to address these issues in summing up the astonishing mélange of progress, moral ambiguity, and conflict of values in the modern age.

The next three chapters of this book constitute the sociological and philosophical framework for the case I'm making about the secular age as the social context for the new evangelization. In the three previous chapters, I offered in broad strokes a historical and ecclesial context for what follows. In the following three chapters, I will shift gears from the history of Vatican II and the new evangelization to social philosophy, first, on the meaning of modernity and secularization, followed by a chapter offering an in-depth reading of *A Secular Age* by Canadian philosopher Charles Taylor. It is not an exaggeration to say that these three topics define the historical context of the church's mission today as much as the Hellenistic Age defined the cultural context for the apostolic mission of St. Paul to the Gentiles.

Some would say the modern world, as distinguished from the medieval world, began around the late fourteenth and early fifteenth centuries in Europe. A chief philosophical marker of it was the birth of a philosophical school of thought we call nominalism. This approach, associated with the name of William of Ockham, abandoned an ontology of stable "universals," "essences," and "substances" found in Platonic and Aristotelian thought. In place of them, it turned to empirical particulars. Universals enjoyed no ontological status; they were merely "names" (hence, nominalism). Essences become no more than names applied arbitrarily to particular objects in the world. The eternal verities slipped from the heavens into a changeable order of temporal signification. For nominalist philosophy the omnipotent will of God was the ground for truth and worldly order, not the essences and natures divine intelligence had created.

William of Ockham's nominalist thought had an influence on German theologian Gabriel Biel, whose ideas of human freedom and divine grace struck an Augustinian doctoral student in theology by the name of Martin Luther as heretical. Luther would write that Biel's idea of the role of will in human salvation was destroying the whole idea of grace in the church. Biel used the Latin phrase *facere quod in se est* (to do everything one could) to indicate what God looked for from humans deserving of salvation. Christians at the time were haunted by threats of divine punishment and eternal damnation. But, how could anyone know he or she had "done everything one could" to deserve salvation? This anxiety deeply affected Luther personally and, as he finally came to see, precipitated the practice of works of righteousness in the form of fasting, pilgrimages, and amassing indulgences.[1] Philosophical and theological voluntarism was the order of the day. The idea of will—the sovereign divine will and the human will struggling for eternal salvation—captivated the religious imagination. In short, the modern human individual first came into existence with Ockham, Biel, and Luther. Rod Dreher makes much of the influence of nominalist thought in his critique of the modern age. Gabriel Biel wrote the first modern philosophy of economy and currency. Prices, he wrote, were determined by the costs of production, the scarcity of products, and human needs (*Treatise on the power and utility of moneys*).

Of course, the emergence of new techniques in engineering, banking, and commerce dovetailed perfectly with the emphasis on will-

---

[1] See Heiko Oberman, *The Harvest of Mediaeval Theology: Gabriel Biel and Late Mediaeval Nominalism* (Cambridge, MA: Harvard University Press, 1963). Biel was responsible for a theological axiom intended to relieve the late medieval believer's anxiety over eternal damnation. Theological nominalism was built on a voluntarist idea of God who would not, by his own will, deny sufficient grace for salvation to someone who, in good faith, did everything they possibly could (*facere quod in se est*). This teaching was regarded by Martin Luther as the downfall of the church in a Pelagian idea of works instead of grace.

power in philosophy and religion. The debates in Calvinism between strict Calvinists and Remonstrant Calvinists, like Hugo Grotius, whose importance in the story of religious indifference I mentioned earlier, belong to the same culture. Descartes's discovery of a new kind of mental subjectivity in his maxim "Cogito, ergo sum" ("I think, therefore I am") occurs a short time later. Portraits of individuals by painters begin to look like actual people. The individual human subject much like we know it today was in the process of coming into existence. The fifteenth and sixteenth centuries are the philosophical and social birthplace of the modern age.

Factors like those mentioned above destabilized the premodern hierarchical symbolism on which church life and theology depended. The Constantinian order of things eventually gave way to religious and philosophical pluralism and the politics of popular sovereignty—the will of the people. This sea change in human self-consciousness could not help but affect religion. Even more than reason as such, the drive of the human will to alter nature for its own use would become modernity's hallmark. We are not done understanding the sources, effects, bewildering metamorphoses, and limits of this epochal transformation.

In 1989, Charles Taylor published a philosophical genealogy of the modern sense of selfhood—*Sources of the Self: The Making of the Modern Identity*. His sweeping philosophical narrative told the story of how human self-understanding evolved from Plato's world of forms through Augustine's discovery of interiority to Descartes's *Cogito, ergo sum* to John Locke's new political individual to Charles Baudelaire and Nietzsche to modern expressive individualism. Taylor reached a wider audience speaking about modernity on the Canadian Broadcasting Company (CBC) in the early 1990s, explaining what he meant by the "malaise of modernity" as a struggle among different kinds of goods we cannot absolutely deny, yet cannot seem to reconcile with each other. His fair-minded moral balance sheet of gains and losses in modernity were like inverted images of each other. Every gain in individual authenticity brought with it a loss of larger social goods and meaning; each step forward in the instrumental control of nature obscured larger embodied human purposes; and the dream of untrammeled freedom wound up trapped in a rationalized bureaucracy of its own making—a "soft despotism" of algorithms and bureaucratic procedures that put freedom in an "iron cage." Together with his later work on the secular age, *Sources of the Self* reads like our philosophical autobiography.

I have already indicated how Vatican II offered its own view of the modern age in *Gaudium et Spes*. That important document told Catholics to scrutinize "signs of the times." But no one has found the elusive Rosetta Stone to decipher them all.

## Vatican II and the Conflict of Meaning

The new evangelization is part and parcel of a fifty-year debate on the meaning of Vatican II.[2] In 1959, when the council was called, no one could have possibly foreseen what would happen a decade later. Three political assassinations; the struggle for civil rights; the Vietnam War; campus rebellions compounded by the emerging youth culture's antinomian distrust of institutions, authority, and tradition would spin ecclesial change in a social vortex. The individual game-changer, as all now realize, was the sexual revolution built on the principle of personal authenticity. In a decade, the *Zeitgeist* of the comfortable postwar 1950s vanished. No one was prepared for the cultural tsunami ahead. The post-conciliar period was the beginning of the end of an astonishingly robust parochial Catholic grammar school system in America. Nothing can duplicate the celibate feminine capital that made parish schools social slingshots for poor immigrants into the American middle class. What happened to Catholic schools without the dedicated skills and economies nuns brought to them is now affecting parish life.

Progressives blamed Vatican II for not changing enough and more. Liberal *Schadenfreude* for the church's compounded demographic and financial troubles today is an unworthy trump card, but it often takes suffering to turn people's minds around. To think that the church got what it deserved in terms of inner conflict over the past half century for not delivering on hopes it aroused has some plausibility. There is truth in the contention that the post-conciliar popes put more em-

---

[2] The best introduction to the history of the conflict of interpretations of Vatican II in the interest of overcoming sterile polarities can be found in Massimo Faggioli, *Vatican II: The Battle for Meaning* (New York: Paulist Press, 2012). See also Richard R. Gaillardetz, *An Unfinished Council: Vatican II, Pope Francis, and the Renewal of Catholicism* (Collegeville, MN: Liturgical Press, 2015).

phasis on centralized consolidation after Vatican II than they did on further changes to the culture of the institution. The council sowed the wind, and the popes who came after it were trying to tame the whirlwind. John Paul II had focused the new evangelization on inculturation—missionary faith transforming the ambient culture surrounding it. What a shock it was in 2002 to learn that the ecclesial culture itself needed transformation. The clergy abuse crisis revealed, among many other things, that the hierarchical structure of power in the church created the conditions for it.

Culture was a major factor in the council's own debates on modernity. Emancipation from cultural traditions in the pursuit of a rationalized approach to human social life is at the heart of the Enlightenment. Romanticisms of various kinds inevitably rise up alongside excessive rationalization. From one point of view, religion is a form of cultural romanticism—the love of symbolisms that seem archaic and yet obscure to reason, the power of oceanic feelings, and the sense of being overpowered by something greater and higher in beauty and art. John Paul II established the Pontifical Council for Culture (PCC) at the very beginning of his pontificate, sensing that the question of cultural change and rationalist transformation was at the heart of modernity and therefore inculturation had to be central to the new evangelization. The International Theological Commission published Faith and Inculturation (1988) building on *Gaudium et Spes*. A decade after that, PCC issued Towards a Pastoral Approach to Culture, which begins by quoting Paul VI: "The split between the Gospel and culture is without doubt the drama of our time, just as it was of other times. Therefore, every effort must be made to ensure a full evangelization of culture, or more correctly of cultures. They must be regenerated by an encounter with the Gospel. But this encounter will not take place if the Gospel is not proclaimed" (*Evangelii Nuntiandi*, 18–20). In order to do this, it is necessary to proclaim the Gospel in the language and culture of men."[3] This precedes an inventory by PCC of challenges facing faith in secular culture.[4]

---

[3] Pontifical Council for Culture, "Towards a Pastoral Approach to Culture," 1999, 4.

[4] Ibid., 23. This paragraph summarizes the challenges for Christian inculturation in secularized cultures.

"Culture" is not an easy term to define. It has one meaning in cultural anthropology and another in aesthetics where it refers to norms of artistic excellence. The church understands culture more broadly as a unique human configuration of the collective expression of moral and religious values in different societies. In common usage, culture has come to mean a lifestyle—a self-consciously chosen identity or manner of self-presentation in everyday life. The metaphor of a lifestyle draws upon the figure of décor in which it extends its application from furnishings to clothing to overall appearance to social and moral values. The richer an individual is, the more lifestyle choices he or she will have. Peasants may have a limited supply of lifestyle choices when it comes to economic opportunity and at the same time be the bearers of a rich and forgotten cultural tradition. Tolstoy dressed like one. The philosopher Martin Heidegger liked to wear lederhosen.

In the broadest sense, then, culture is a symbolic language of values. Culture therefore furnishes an individual with the material ingredients of a livable philosophy of life. When the church speaks of the new evangelization as inculturation, this is what it is talking about—a livable authentic Christian faith in a particular culture.[5]

Traditional cultures existing for centuries in the same marinade enjoy the sense of depth in a single symbolic universe of meaning but allow little scope for independence and diversity. Modern culture, on the other hand, is far more pluralistic and urbane. In the West, mass culture is largely determined by the economic and commercial spheres of life where material symbols of meaning can be bought, worn, and displayed. But the meaning of such symbols can change over time. Consider James Dean who wore denim jeans in the movie *Rebel without a Cause*. In that context, jeans represented an antibourgeois philosophy of life. In modern *haute couture*, on the other hand, their meaning reverts to elite fashion.

In a commercial market, culture can change the meaning of clothing, and religion, too, can be subsumed into style. Belief can be treated in modernity as another commodity. It can be produced and marketed

---

[5] See the Consortium of Humanities Centers and Institutes (CHCI) membership list by countries and states. Boston College, University of Virginia, and the Rutgers Center for Cultural Analysis (1986) seek to foster interdisciplinary scholarship in the human, natural, and social sciences.

for religious consumers by distributors we call churches and clergy, with accoutrements such as distinctive clothing. The local parish from the perspective of modern economic culture is in the religion-production business. People shop for a faith in modernity. Their parents inherited one. This pluralistic cultural condition has radically changed the nature of ecclesial mission and the transmission of a religious tradition in late modernity.

*Gaudium et Spes* 40–45 and 53–62 took up the whole question of modern culture. It affirmed the church's legitimate role as a leavening agent in culture—enhancing what is good in it by reference to God and Christ. The church is autonomous in its own sphere and its role in relation to culture is only to offer principles from revelation to humanize it according to the Gospel, not to dominate or colonize it. The church understands its cultural role today as that of an educator of human values in private and public life.

No other Western institution has such a long and diverse cultural experience as the Christian church. Its Scriptures are saturated in Hebraic and Greco-Roman culture. Two millennia have seen the Gospel go to every human culture, survive in it, and, in many instances, completely transform it. Christianity is a cultural palimpsest, a page of text overwritten with other texts from the Hebrew Scriptures and philosophical images from Plato and Aristotle. In the artistic spheres of culture, the Christian faith was embodied in the *terza rima* of the *Divine Comedy*, in the sculpture of Ghiberti's bronze bas-relief "Gates of Paradise" opposite the entrance to the Duomo and beneath Brunelleschi's magnificent dome, and in the San Marco Museo with the fresco of the "Annunciation" by Fra Angelico on the wall at the top of a staircase. Christianity is a textual and cultural mosaic in its own way, rich and much more human than dogma alone might tell us. A catechism tells someone very little about all that.

## Faith and Culture:
## A Theological Intermezzo

H. Richard Niebuhr, a church historian at Yale, once surveyed the conflicts that trailed the enculturating process in Christianity from its beginnings until the modern period. *Christ and Culture* picked out some of the most revealing and decisive moments when Christianity radically separated itself from, fell under the spell of, or synthesized itself successfully with an ambient cultural matrix.[6] He constructed a typology in which a limited menu of options faces the church in every culture situation.

Option 1 is "Christ *against* Culture," where the church resisted a dominant cultural situation and refused to be dominated by its values. The moral norm, in that case, is open resistance or strategic withdrawal. Option 2 is "Christ *of* Culture," where some Christians see good reasons to adjust religious practices and teachings to the prevailing or emerging matrix of human values. The resistant-martyr culture of early Roman Christianity was succeeded by the civic *Christianus* type—a good Roman and a Christian both. In European history, this option will take various other forms of cultural accommodation. Option 3 is "Christ *above* Culture." This is that rare instance when the church neither withdraws from nor takes the path of easy accommodation with but can work out a productive synthesis of authentic Gospel values and culture. According to Niebuhr, this search for an intelligent equilibrium between culture and Christianity has historically found expression in the work of St. Augustine, St. Thomas, and Martin Luther. Each of the three types of Christ and Culture imposes on the Christian moral imagination different risks and benefits. Let me briefly analyze these ideal-types further.

*The Christian option for resistance.* For the first three hundred years of Christianity, the church was a total outsider to imperial Roman culture. The mission theology in the Pastoral Epistles in the New Testament, along with passages in the Gospel and Epistles of John, bring that out. The book of Revelation portrays it in dramatically symbolic forms with dragons attacking the church. Persecutions of Christians as an outlawed sect made the first option of "Christ *against* Culture" the earliest, most radical church-culture paradigm we have. It prolongs the spirit of biblical prophecy into church history. The Jewish linguist Noam Chomsky once noted that the prophets (*navi*) of Israel were the original dissident intellectuals.[7] They attacked power with truth. By that norm, Jesus himself was a dissident intellectual-rabbi and eventually a martyr "crucified under Pontius

[6] H. Richard Niebuhr, *Christ and Culture*, 50th ann. ed. (New York: Harper & Row, 2001).

[7] Q&A: Noam Chomsky, "Noam Chomsky Interviewed by David Samuels," A New Read on Jewish Life, November 12, 2010, www.chomsky.info.

Pilate." The image of the Gospel has always been in the sign of the cross. Resistance by open critique, by alternative lifestyle, or by withdrawal into the desert or monastery remains Christianity's oldest cultural option. No theology that lacks some degree of evangelical resistance to something in a prevailing ambient culture (in the world or in the church as a human institution) is worth much. Liberation theologies as well as reactionary withdrawal positions follow the same logic. They differ on where the truly objectionable issue lies.

*The Christian option for accommodation.* With the conversion of Emperor Constantine in 325, a persecuted religious sect became the official religion of the Roman Empire. The seeds were scattered in Christianity from that time forward for a Christ *of* culture option represented by Christendom. The blood that martyrs shed in the Colosseum would still be revered as the true "seed of the Church," but the warm welcome bishops received in the imperial basilica of Theodosius was hard to turn down. The paradigm of imperial Christendom would prevail in the church's cultural imagination for well over a millennium and lingers somewhere in the shadows of contemporary resentments.

When Catholic throne and altar model of public life finally collapsed with the Enlightenment, liberal Protestantism adopted the option of accommodation in modern culture. The kingdom of God wore a mantel of progress and humanitarian benevolence. The "already" and the "not-yet" of the eschatological kingdom Jesus preached was making its appearance in the advances of social justice and secular modernization. How could Christian faith be true to its birthplace on Calvary, much less to the non-progressive moral radicalism of Jesus while accommodating itself to modern liberal culture? Liberal Protestantism would transform the Gospel into social ethics and interior sentiments. The scandal the Gospel posed to Enlightenment modernity could be removed by removing all evidence of miracles which Thomas Jefferson did in his personal translation of the New Testament. Exorcise the primitive imagination of possessions, exorcisms, and miracles, and make Jesus sound like a rationalist or, later, a social reformer.

*The Christian option for transformation.* St. Augustine's *City of God* differed from the strategy of imperial accommodation. He saw divine grace and love reforming and transforming both the church and the culture. The Catholic Church could not turn itself into a sect even if sectarians like the Montanists and the Donatists regularly split off from it or as Puritans would later do from Anglicans. But neither could the church merge its identity and value system into the imperial order. Christianity was to remain a sign of the kingdom of God, not an acolyte to the prevailing civil power. St. Thomas Aquinas developed an extraordinary synthesis of theology and philosophy to raise the eyes of cultural Christendom above itself to the mystery of God at work in cosmos and spirit. Martin Luther proposed a paradoxical two-kingdoms theory of church and society where the Lord had apportioned different tasks to each sphere. The moral realism of Reinhold Niebuhr was a modern version of it. Don't expect the state to be holy; it is enough if it aims to do the possible and the just.

*Christ and Culture* thoughtfully surveyed two millennia of church history, extracting example after example of the difficult choices that faced evangelization through the centuries. Of course, things are never so simple as ideal-types make them out to be. Modern culture is so vastly different from previous cultural heritages that one honestly must wonder how to apply such typologies today. The judgment on modernity varies with its moral metamorphoses and with intuitive ecclesial tendencies partially authorized by different biblical texts and the theological trajectories they set in motion. When the church is reduced to a sociological category in a secular culture, when religious affiliation becomes a commercial transaction backed by different private lifestyles, economic ideologies, or class affiliations, we know something of the neat paradigms in Niebuhr have collapsed on us.

## The Presence of the Church and Culture Change

In 1991, James Davison Hunter wrote the book that became the sociological poster-child for the modern crisis of Christ and culture—*The Culture Wars: The Struggle to Define America.*[8] Taking up where

---

[8] My focus, however, is on James Davison Hunter, *To Change the World: The Irony, Tragedy, and Possibility of Christianity in the Late Modern World* (Oxford: Oxford University Press, 2010). Also see James Davison Hunter and Alan Wolfe, *Is There a Culture War? A Dialogue on Values and American Public Life* (Washington, DC: Brookings Institution Press, 2006).

Niebuhr's typology left off, Hunter surveyed the ideological conflicts cutting across modern American culture, which divided Christian culture warriors from their liberal co-religionists and secular humanists. This war of words and protest marches was waged from entrenched positions angling for more control of Congress and the courts. *Roe v. Wade* set it off on the political right as Jim Crow laws once had done for the political left.

In Hunter's telling (unfortunately, he didn't go into detail about Catholicism), the culture wars split Protestant fundamentalists from Protestant liberals, both of whom were parade examples, in their way, of Niebuhr's second type—cultural accommodation. The religious right attacked the permissive society while endorsing economic liberalism in the Republican platform. The religious left defended the interests of greater equality and social justice while leaving the right to abortion and sexual lifestyles a private matter. Private property rights went up against private sexuality rights. Opposite versions of a laissez-faire ethical liberalism divided Protestant Christianity. It ruptured much of Catholicism along with it.

As the director of the Institute for Advanced Studies in Culture at the University of Virginia, Hunter examined the intellectual assumptions about culture change at work in the right-left culture wars. The real issue at stake was the nature of something as amorphous as culture itself and what changing something that complex and differentiated would involve. Hunter concluded that the culture wars, oddly enough, were badly informed about the thing they called "culture" and what it would take on their part to change it. In his book *To Change the World: The Irony, Tragedy, and Possibility of Christianity in the Late Modern World* (2010), Hunter developed a global approach to culture in America and the inertial forces that make change, in the short run, unlikely. His arguments amount to a sociological textbook for and against cultural change in the new evangelization.

First, Hunter carefully defines culture, which many of the culture warriors do not. Seven propositions capture a global picture of what's involved in culture:

1. Culture is a normative system of truth claims and moral obligations of which people are hardly even aware.

2. Culture is deeply embedded in a history and for that reason not easily changed.

3. Culture is made up of ideas and institutions and individuals who develop culture, but the institutional repositories outweigh the individuals.

4. Culture is a "symbolic capital," which some people and groups have more of than others.

5. This symbolic cultural capital is produced at the center and consumed at the periphery of the culture.

6. Culture certainly has its geniuses, but institutional networks are what make it work.

7. Culture is distributed through many fields of human action and it is not entirely coherent.

Add all this up, and one quickly realizes that there's much more involved than one sees at first sight.[9] Evangelical mission must be based on a realistic assessment of ecclesial capacity.

If the seven points above tell us how cultural inertia operates, the following four points capture how it might change:

1. Cultures change from the top down and very rarely from the bottom up.

2. Cultural change is often generated by elites, but not necessarily those figures who rule the center of a culture at any time.

3. Cultures change when the elites outside the center and the big institutions holding the greatest cultural capital team up.

4. Cultures change, but vested interests mean there will be a fight.

Cultural change is driven by elites who have accumulated more cultural capital (i.e., influence) than others. The self-interest and institutional inertia involved make changing culture extremely difficult. Every pastor who tries changing Mass schedules knows that. Sexual harassment in the entertainment and media cultures started collapsing because cultural capital in mass media shifted from men to women. Customs and systems reinforce the status quo. In that respect, power and who has more of it at any given moment are major factors. Evangelical culture warriors accordingly turn to politics.

[9] Hunter, *To Change the World*, 32–47.

I think Hunter's analysis of culture and culture change is helpful for the new evangelization. It's sobering. His diagnoses of the challenges involved in the new evangelization as inculturation are balanced. They are not loaded in favor of religious enthusiasts or skeptics. Instead of a war, Hunter offers Christians disturbed by the drift of pluralistic culture away from stronger moral positions regarding justice and human rights his favorite image of Christians being a "faithful presence" in pluralistic culture instead of a belligerent religious quasi-state.

It is certain that cultural change is far more apoplectic than it is rational and organic. Discourse ethics has its limits. Usually conflict and unexpected suffering bring change in human life. The elite producers of what we call culture are for the most part now secular producers. The great New England universities of Harvard and Yale were founded and led by faithful believers, but no longer are. Their divinity schools are a bow to tradition, not to philosophy. The cultural capital some Christians still wish they had is held by others now. The church can persuade only by public witness underwritten by plausible arguments and by maintaining a robust internal community life that exists on the periphery of the high culture and mass culture. Some degree of resistance and some attempts at synthesis of Christ and secular culture seem to make sense. A total accommodationist approach to secular culture for Christianity would seem to make religion pointless. Should the church allow itself to become the choir singing at political conventions? Is this honest?

What Hunter's analysis makes abundantly clear is just how radically different modern secular culture is from traditional culture. The evangelization of the Slavs by St. Cyril and St. Methodius is extraordinary by any measure. Translating the Greek gospels for Slavic peoples by creating the Cyrillic alphabet—that's a kind of inculturation that still astonishes historians. But can that be a prototype for meeting our challenges of inculturation?[10] More sobering is the

[10] Rino Fisichella, *The New Evangelization: Responding to the Challenge of Indifference* (Leominister, Herefordshire, UK: Gracewing Press, 2011), 32–35. The evangelization of earlier cultures, which Fisichella rightly notes, like that of Sts. Cyril and Methodius, while extraordinary by any measure, is a world away from the modern situation. The secularization of Christianity itself, along with many Christian values, into the liberal democratic order has no previous parallel in history.

unsuccessful attempt at evangelization by Matteo Ricci, SJ, in China.[11] In Martin Scorsese's movie *Silence*, based on Shusaku Endo's novel, the Japanese leader in the Shimabara Rebellion against the Togugawa shogun explains to a young Jesuit missionary that the Japanese culture will transform the missionary himself as a swamp digests plant material.[12] The novel tells the story of Jesuit missionaries who apostatized on mission in Japan.

Secular culture has already digested what it believes is salvageable in the Christian Gospel for a culture of justice, rights, and charitable benevolence. In certain respects, mission today has more in common with that Japanese narrative than it does with what St. Cyril and St. Methodius accomplished for Slavonic literature. American Protestant, Deist, and secular political culture has digested what they consider viable from the Gospel in modernity. That includes rights, freedoms, philanthropic benevolence, an elite cosmopolitan indifference to religion together with periodic resurgences and awakenings of religious feelings branching in multiple directions. Culture is no longer a melting pot. It's not a war either, and Christians should be loath to use such a term as "culture war" for anything like evangelization.

## The Meanings of Modernity

Historians and social philosophers for two hundred years have been trying to parse the logics (the plural is intentional) in modernity. Since the beginning of the twentieth century, Max Weber, Talcott Parsons, Eric Voegelin, Karl Jaspers, Jürgen Habermas, Peter Berger, John Milbank, Robert Bellah, and Daniel Bell have proposed interpretations of it.[13] Because the subject of modernity is so complex,

---

[11] Charles Taylor, "A Catholic Modernity?," in *A Catholic Modernity? Charles Taylor's Marianist Award Lecture*, with Responses by William M. Shea, Rosemary Luling Haughton, George Marsden, Jean Bethge Elshtain (New York: Oxford University Press, 1999), 64.

[12] Martin Scorsese has dramatized Endo's novel in his movie *Silence* (2016). The director had also written an introduction to a recent edition of *Silence* about Catholicism's encounter with Japanese cultural resistance.

[13] The philosophical analysis of modernity has become a central theme in contemporary thought. See Jürgen Habermas, *The Philosophical Discourse of Modernity: Twelve Lectures*, trans. Frederick Lawrence (Cambridge: MIT Press, 1987); *Religion and Ratio-*

I have chosen to focus only on some telling points from a few thinkers: Paul Ricoeur, Daniel Bell, and Charles Taylor. They will help me clarify for the purposes of this book how to understand modernity and the modern identity.

In one of his final philosophical studies, called *Memory, History, Forgetting*, Paul Ricoeur traces the different meanings modernity has as part of a "semantics of historical concepts."[14] Historians invent concepts to label different periods of history based on documentary evidence of changes in social ways of life and mentalities. Terms like "ancient," "Hellenistic," "medieval," "modern" and "post-modern" convey the evidence of a significant historical change even when those experiencing it were or are unaware it is taking place. The word "modern" began its semantic journey in the fifteenth-century Renaissance with evidence of new inventions. Technical improvements would henceforth be one of its key trademarks. With that technical denotation, "modern" generated its own antonyms. "Medieval" did not mean an age with its own satisfying if limited lifeworld but it implied the "premodern condition of lack." Cultural patrimonies and traditional customs could then be characterized as "anti-modern." Tradition slowly collapses into something like cultural "decrepitude."[15] The term "modern" suggests something more than just technical progress. It connotes a cultural superiority and moral privilege.[16]

The second stage in the lexical transformation of the word modern comes in the eighteenth- and nineteenth-century Romantic Period in Europe. To be truly modern, in the Romantic era, was to turn back to the classical past whose superior moral stature overshadows the

---

*nality: Essays on Reason, God, and Modernity*, ed. Eduardo Mendieta (Cambridge, MA: MIT Press, 2002); Gertrude Himmelfarb, *The Roads to Modernity: The British, French, and American Enlightenments* (New York: Knopf, 2004); Charles Taylor, *Sources of the Self: The Making of Modern Identity* (Cambridge, MA: Harvard University Press, 1989); and Charles Taylor, *The Malaise of Modernity* (Concord, Ontario: Anansi Press Limited, 1991).

[14] Paul Ricoeur, *Memory, History, Forgetting*, trans. Kathleen Blamey and David Pellauer (Chicago: University of Chicago Press, 2004), 294. "The semantics of historical concepts will serve to bring to our attention the dream of self-sufficiency expressed by the formula 'history itself' (*Geschichte selber*) claimed by the authors concerned" (305ff.).

[15] Ibid., 307.

[16] Ibid., 308–11.

present. It was in the classic that we find superior excellences and paradigmatic forms—the *Iliad* of Homer, Plato's *Dialogues*, and the speeches of Cicero. Being modern in the Romantic sense meant knowing how to read the classics in Latin or Greek. Ricoeur writes, "Modernity has gone a long way in defining itself in opposition to itself."[17]

The third stage in the lexical evolution of the modern comes with the European Enlightenment. Here modern coincides with reason. By the late eighteenth century, a "philosophical chronology" comes into existence whose name is the "age of reason," which succeeds and replaces an earlier "age of faith."[18] This chronological replacement theory of faith by reason is what sheds light on the nineteenth- and twentieth-century ecclesiastical conflicts I explained earlier in the book.

The fourth stage in the semantics of modern, according to Ricoeur, arrives with the nineteenth-century French poet Charles Baudelaire (1821–1867). To him, we owe the creation of the neologism *modernité* (modernity). *Modernité*, as opposed to the word "modern" by itself, designates the birthplace of a new human sensibility, a truly novel sense of "historical self-consciousness."[19] The essence of it is the psychological celebration of diversity for itself.[20]

These four lexical shifts in the semantics of the modern from technical mastery to romantic excellence to reason cut away from faith to cultural *modernité* are important sources for appreciating the assumptions supporters and critics of religious faith fail to understand. With *modernité* especially, both the Greek classic and critical reason lose their authority. Culture is opened to a radically new set of values signifying an "evolution of mores, ideas, practices, feelings" thought to be not only superior but irrevocable.[21]

The fifth stage in this etymological biography of the modern comes with "postmodernity." This signifies the rebellion of freedom against all language-based oppositions which are seen as only masks for power. Jean-Francois Lyotard sees in postmodernity "the powerless-

---

[17] Ibid., 308.
[18] Ibid., 309.
[19] Ibid., 310.
[20] Ibid., 311.
[21] Ibid.

ness of the desire for consensus to arbitrate the debates."[22] The very structures of language as a symbolic mediation of reality begin to collapse. If we cannot reasonably discuss values and debate them, dialogue is pointless. Postmodernity is a symbol of a despair over meaning and truth. Ratzinger was not being reactionary when he called for the recovery of the normative idea of truth. If we abandon the search for it in some magnanimous recherché relativism, what will we have gained?

The word "modern" as we use it in ordinary language reflects the technological side of it more than anything. But, the historical etymology Ricoeur gives advises us that the significance of modern and modernity are anything but obvious. From Ricoeur's semantic history of the word, I now turn to Daniel Bell's sociological reconstruction of modernity and its effect on the sacred.

Over the course of his career, Daniel Bell wrote extensively on ideologies, political economics, and technology.[23] His views on the cultural contradictions of capitalism are well known. Simplified to their essence, they argue that once an ethic of personal gratification was substituted for the original Calvinist ethic that both powered and restrained capitalism, capitalism was caught in a cultural contradiction. The old Protestant ethic lost its appeal. Everything people envy and despise about Wall Street hedge-fund managers with no moral compass except success and hedonic enjoyment results from this.

In Bell's philosophically tinged sociology, culture stands for "the modalities of response by sentient men to the core questions that

---

[22] Ibid., 313.

[23] Daniel Bell (1919–2011) was a sociologist and major neo-conservative Jewish intellectual who taught at the University of Chicago, Columbia University, and Harvard University. In 1980, he published a collection of seventeen lengthy essays in *The Winding Passage: Essays and Sociological Journeys 1960–1980* (Cambridge: Abt Associates, 1980). In that collection is the essay he wrote on religion and cultural modernity: "The Return of the Sacred? The Argument on the Future of Religion," 324–354. Bell delivered this paper for the Hobhouse Memorial Lecture (1977) at the London School of Economics. It was intended to be the programmatic essay for a book he planned to write but never did. Bell's more celebrated works include *The Coming of Post-Industrial Society: A Venture in Social Forecasting* (1973), *The Cultural Contradictions of Capitalism* (1976), and *The End of Ideology: On the Exhaustion of Political Ideas in the Fifties* (1960). Bell received the Tocqueville Award from the French government in 1995.

confront all human groups in the consciousness of existence—how one meets death, the meaning of tragedy, the nature of obligation, the character of love—these *recurrent* questions which are, I believe, cultural universals, to be found in all societies where men have become conscious of the finiteness of existence."[24] Culture in this broad sense deals with anthropological constants.

Times change, but the existential constants remain. "Culture, thus, is always a *ricorso*," Bell says. "Men may expand their technical powers. . . . There may be progress in the instrumental realms. But the existential questions remain."[25] We understand a culture by how it answers such fundamental existential dilemmas as birth, death, and love. Religion, in Bell's view, is a set of symbolic answers to these questions, answers clarified and carried forward by a specific tradition. But translating a religious tradition as history itself requires is no simple matter. Bell puts it this way: "Translation cannot reproduce the 'color' of culture—the exact syntax, the resourcefulness of its phonology, the particular metaphors, or the structure of associations and juxtapositions that the original tongue provides. What it can render is its significant meanings."[26] With this distinction between the translation of meaning and the untranslatable color and syntax of an original tongue, the whole post-conciliar struggle in Catholicism for deep continuity and creative renewal finds a more accurate expression. Translation by its very nature brings some loss with it. Not translating at all paralyzes a religious tradition by preserving it in amber. Paul Ricoeur's philosophy of translation makes this linguistic art, practiced by skilled diplomats and spies, a paradigm of historical consciousness.[27]

Against a prevailing totalizing understanding of culture and society, Bell argued for a disjunctive understanding in which politics, economics, and culture are driven by different processes and norms that are often quite antagonistic to one another.[28] Modern society, as Bell sees it, is not a system but a struggle between and among systems.

---

[24] Bell, "The Return of the Sacred?," 333.

[25] Ibid.

[26] Ibid.

[27] See Paul Ricoeur, *On Translation*, trans Eileen Brennan (New York: Routledge, 2006).

[28] Bell, "The Return of the Sacred?," 329.

Looking at contemporary society, I would say that there is a radical antagonism between the norms and structures of the techno-economic realm (whose axial principle is functional rationality and efficiency, and whose structure is bureaucratic); the polity (whose axial principle, in Western democratic societies, is equality, and whose structures are those of representation or participation); and the culture (whose ruling principle is that of self-realization, and, in its extremes, self-gratification). It is the tensions between the norms of these three realms—efficiency and bureaucracy, equality and rights, self-fulfillment and the desire for novelty—that form the contradictions of the modern world, contradictions that are enhanced under capitalism, since the techno-economic realm is geared to promote not economic necessities but the cultural wants of a hedonistic world.[29]

In short, when capitalist economics separated from Calvin's ethic of self-restraint and fused with a *modernité* as Baudelaire and others presented it, culture changed radically. The plasticity of desire rules.

Bell emphasizes what I have stressed, namely, that the *secularization* that results from the political *separation* of state and religion differs from cultural *secularization*. The usual interpretation of secularization mixes up social processes with cultural changes that are "not congruent with each other."[30] As an alternative, Bell proposes two distinct processes at work in modern societies.

There is, thus, a double process at work. One is secularization, the differentiation of institutional authority in the world, which is reinforced by the processes of rationalization. The second, in the realm of beliefs and culture, is disenchantment, or what I would prefer to call, for the parallelism of the term, profanation. Thus, the sacred and the secular become my pair terms for the processes at work within institutions and social systems, the sacred and the profane for the processes within culture.[31]

The choice of terms is significant. The *sacred* and the *profane* have traditionally defined a religious view of life. In that schema, to violate the sacred is not to secularize it but, much worse, to profane it. José Casanova argues that this classic religious binary (sacred-profane)

---

[29] Ibid., 329–30.
[30] Ibid., 331.
[31] Ibid., 332.

has migrated almost entirely from religion to the sacral nation-state and human rights.[32] The issue of transgender redefinitions then becomes a new expression of the *sacred*. Meanwhile a French journal of opinion can *profane* a religion because religion has slipped many notches in the estimation of modern life. Biblical prophets like Isaiah satirized the idols of neighboring paganisms to mock the pseudo-sacred in them.

Because culture is a *ricorso*, that is, a perennial reworking of symbolisms that identify and respond to the human predicament, culture presumably forgets, abandons, and destroys older symbolisms in the process of creating new ones. The destruction and creation of religious heritages in a society was the mission God gave the young prophet Jeremiah. "Now I have put my words in your mouth. See, today I appoint you over nations and over kingdoms, to pluck up and to pull down, to destroy and to overthrow, to build and to plant" (Jer 1:9-10). The emergence of a new concept of the sacred often entails pulling another one down. The Reformation saw its mission that way. The secular state did as well. Now, a metastasis of new human rights challenges the morally sacred in traditional faith.

Charles Baudelaire plays the same role in Bell's narrative of modernity as he does in Ricoeur's. *Modernité* by its nature rejects limits. On the contrary, it draws its breath from the experience of excess and transgression. For Bell, economics detached from the Protestant ethic made a devil's pact with cultural *modernité*. What is different now for capitalist economics from a pre-Baudelaire era is that experience itself has become detached from reason as much as from revelation. The moral norms are gone, or simply replaced by a spare pragmatic utility. The modern individual exists in a culture of the "unrestrained" self.[33] With the abandonment of religious belief in elite cultures, Bell says, it fell to the expressive arts to manage the pre-rational impulses of human nature.[34]

Nihilism is the result of Nietzsche's declaration, "God is dead." But building a bridge over the void is not easy when it comes to

---

[32] José Casanova, "The Secular, Secularizations, Secularism," in *Rethinking Secularism*, ed. Craig Calhoun, Mark Juergensmeyer, and Jonathan Van Antwerpen (New York: Oxford University Press, 2011), 65.

[33] Bell, "The Return of the Sacred?," 334–35.

[34] Ibid., 335.

materialisms, political ideologies, raw experience, or technology. For Bell, it was inevitable that alternative religions would arise after the death of God. Marxism and Fascism in politics, existential angst or polite civil religions without any eschatology, much less moral bite, and the deification of the expressive arts where impulses are given free rein in the cult of the kinky—all these have become an option with the failure of traditional religion to capture the moral imagination.

A decade before the Berlin Wall came down, Bell asserted that the deep impulses behind Marxism were effectively "exhausted."[35] Civil religion is essentially banal, but it allows secularized bourgeois to feel pious. The postwar existential self in revolt is now a mere trope and wearisome to boot. Technology enchants, of course, but people have become wary of its ethically unhinged and destructive potentials.

The conclusion I draw from Bell's analysis for the argument about the church in the modern age is a hopeful one. Religion, despite being out of fashion, will never be replaced by materialism, by the arts, by political ideology, or by the anomic cynical self. When it comes to the deepest questions, all answers count as beliefs and all ultimate beliefs in some sense are quasi-religious ones. When the false alternatives to religion play themselves out, a search for more humanizing values begins.

A sign that the culture of transgressive excess is in trouble began dawning on some observers of the larger social scene as early as the 1970s. Almost out of nowhere the word "limits" began to appear. This was an odd rhetoric in a culture enthralled by all kinds of excess, held in rapture to a Nietzschean vision of going "beyond" everything. We started hearing calls for a limit to nuclear proliferation, a limit to the destruction of nonhuman species, and a limit to torture in the name of human rights. Though it was difficult to determine where to draw the line in such things, it was increasingly evident that a line must be drawn. Now, Americans are debating new limits to firearms, to sexual harassment, and to the cyber-culture itself in Facebook, which has been wiping out the concept of privacy in the public pursuit of a hyper-connectivity.

---

[35] Ibid., 344–45.

But how does religion figure in all this? The religious substitutes had proven to be empty, but sociology also predicted the end of religion in secularization theory. Bell observes, "Almost every Enlightened thinker expected religion to disappear in the twentieth century."[36] For the cultural vanguard, religion is from the "'childhood' of the human race,"[37] when human beings resorted to superstitions and myths lacking a solid scientific understanding of nature and society. This is still the prevailing attitude. The periodic battles of fundamentalist belief with science from the seventeenth to the nineteenth centuries only reinforced it.

Forty years ago, when Daniel Bell published his essay "The Return of the Sacred," he saw three possible ways religious sensibilities would rebound in the wake of the exhausted substitutes for religious faith in cultural *modernité*.[38] The first way would take the form of a recrudescence of moralistic religion—a "scourging" fundamentalism he called it. The culture wars in America and Islamic Wahhabism proved him correct. The recent resurgence of xenophobic forms of nationalism in America caught many by surprise. This tribalism is the political form of a fundamentalism whose political sacred is the preservation and superiority of the white race.

The second kind of religious resurgence, according to Bell, would likely come in the form of a renaissance in traditional historical religions like Judaism and Christianity, where ideas of redemption and reconciliation dominate the imagination. Ecumenic faiths situate the modern self—a victim of *anomie*—within the symbolic nets that biblical metaphors of transcendence provide. Redemptive religiosity must be hermeneutical if it is to transcend fundamentalism on the one hand but not collapse into reason alone on the other. The scriptural foundations and traditions of historical religions abound with wise commentary, revitalized community, philosophical reflection, and respect for humanizing values.

The third way in which religion might return as an option in the aftermath of *modernité*, in Bell's judgment, would be in the rise of mysticism. While gnostic New Age versions will probably fade in time, ancient mysticisms in the East and West with deeper roots in sacred scriptures, in nature's rhythms, and in psychic archetypes

---

[36] Ibid., 326.
[37] Ibid.
[38] Ibid., 348–51.

would not lose their appeal. The flat florescent worldview of a technical rationality has produced a strange yearning in us for depth. A certain animal mysticism in alliance with science is what powers the ecological movement.

Bell's essay on secularization-profanation, on the rise and fall of *modernité*, and on the "return of the sacred" offers the new evangelization necessary perspective when it comes to secularism. His hunch about the three forms of religious revival in modern mass culture have their Roman Catholic equivalents. One is the path of resistance that lies in Rod Dreher's Benedictine withdrawal from secular culture. It is romantic, meant for the few, and perhaps impossible, but it can still fuel inner ecclesial renewal if it doesn't turn so morally sour on secularism that it is blind to its benefits. Another path might go through Eastern Orthodoxy and evangelical models of parish life exploring the aesthetics of sacramental and rhetorical alternatives to the dominant cultural ethos. Still another might be found in the contemplative search for inner depth and peace with the natural world and its creative rhythms. The *ricorso* in culture applies to religious culture too. An ecumenical Catholicism already exists in the patriarchates, in different dioceses, and in the experimental forms of Catholicity.

Much of Charles Taylor's philosophical work, as I will show later, has been devoted to clarifying the nature of modernity and the emergence of our modern sense of selfhood. He has rewound the implicit conflicts and tensions in our modern consciousnesses from Nietzsche and Baudelaire to Kant and Voltaire to John Locke and René Descartes back to Plato by way of St. Augustine. Taylor offers a richer palate of colors than Bell's stark portrait of *modernité* provides. In *Sources of the Self: The Making of the Modern Identity*, Taylor reaches the sober conclusion we all intuitively grasp no matter where we stand as far as religion goes: modernity is conflicted to its core.[39] The sources for our moral identity are multiple. *Sources of the Self* is a ponderous, highly literate piece of modern social and moral philosophy. Because the book is so important in understanding Taylor's view of modernity and secularity, I will try to summarize its relevance for evangelization. It takes Taylor 601 pages in five large sections to explore the sources of moral conflict in us. Let me unpack what they say.

---

[39] Charles Taylor, *Sources of the Self: The Making of the Modern Identity* (Cambridge, MA: Harvard University Press, 1989).

In the opening section, "Identity and the Good," Taylor sets out his overarching moral theory. The sense of self correlates with some concept of what the true good is. By the word "good," he means the "inescapable frameworks" that define the "moral space" in which people live.[40] This is where Taylor offers what has come to be known as a neo-Aristotelian view of ethics—recognizing what it is *good for us to be* not merely *right for us to do*. The ideas of justice and *agape* in the biblical tradition constitute the hyper-goods of such a moral space.

With the second section of the book, "Inwardness," Taylor means to unravel the Platonic and Augustinian sources for the search in modernity for interior authenticity. In such philosophical classics, moderns find justification and early echoes of their sensibilities. In Augustine, those echoes come in his reflections on the self's interior resemblance to the Trinity itself. But the rhetoric of inwardness moves on from theology in philosophical history. It keeps metastasizing in unforeseen directions. Descartes marks another discovery of inwardness with the *Cogito, ergo sum*—"I think, therefore I am." In time, inwardness becomes the subjective mind (without physical extension) that thinks, calculates, and controls extended objects in space. The human body itself, strange to say, is demoted by the thinking self to the rank of all physical objects. Plato's contemplation of the good has passed through Augustine's confessions to Descartes's "thinking thing"—the *Cogito*. With John Locke, inwardness turns into what Taylor calls the "punctual self." The mind is nothing but a blank slate (*tabula rasa*) on which sensuous impressions are written.

"Inwardness" in its more emotive meaning rebounds in the European Romantic period (the late eighteenth and nineteenth centuries) in someone like Rousseau, who claims everyone has his or her own unique inner truth. Thus, a major source of what we think of as the modern self is the reworking of a theme that began with Plato and traveled from Greece to Rome to France by subterranean philosophical channels until it reached your teenager's acute and often painful sense of uniqueness. Here is a feeling that no modern person can entirely rid oneself of and that takes incessant expressivist and narcissistic detours in culture.

One of the most important sources of the modern self is found in section 3 of Taylor's book, "The Affirmation of Ordinary Life." Hier-

---

[40] Ibid., 3–25.

archical and aristocratic moral ideals originally conceived in Greek culture gradually changed places with newly discovered values in the everyday existence of men and women. A remarkable chapter in the affirmation of the ordinary is titled by Taylor "God Loveth Adverbs," which turns out to be the title of a Puritan sermon by the preacher William Perkins: "God loveth adverbs; and cares not how good, but how well."[41] With this anti-hierarchical affirmation of the worthiness of the ordinary, Puritan spirituality undercut a moral hierarchy of values established in ancient Greek society and medieval Christianity. In Perkins's estimation, to perform a humble trade and carry it out *well* ranks higher, in the eyes of God, than social position. Thus, the sacrifices in good marriage and the dignity of common labor come to outrank the monk on his knees, the nun with her beads. To set ideals like celibacy above family refuses to acknowledge God's own wisdom in creation and procreation. In the seventeenth and eighteenth centuries, rationalized forms of Christianity will appeal to a providential natural order that completes the affirmation of ordinary life over against the religious supernatural. It is here that Taylor locates "the culture of modernity."

In his fourth section on the different sources playing themselves out in the modern sense of selfhood we encounter "The Voice of Nature." This is where older theistic images for human identity began to be replaced by other sources—chiefly by reason and the natural world. Taylor puts it like this: "Deism appears as the first step on the road which next led to the unbelieving Enlightenment of figures like Helvetius, Bentham, Holbach, and Condorcet. And beyond them the road seems to lead to modern secular culture."[42] This part of the book shows how older Christianized sources of behavior reflected in love and *agape* morphed into a secular humanism once they could be reclaimed as the equivalent of altruism and ordinary benevolence. Thus, begins *the reinterpretation of Christianity* for immanent secular purposes. The secular is not always the outright rejection of religion. The modern self, with its openness to charitable benevolence in a figure like Bill Gates, is in many ways a secularized version of earlier Christian ideals. The values originally embedded in scriptural revelation are cut loose from a religious narrative. One can be religious without religion.

---

[41] Ibid., 211–33.
[42] Ibid., 308–9.

The fifth and final section of *Sources of the Self* is called "Subtler Languages," where two of the most influential strands of the modern self, the very DNA of our received moral identity—the un-synthesized and undeniable values of the Enlightenment and the Romantic movement—enter the drama. Reason here gained the status of a divine gift. So, in following the reasonable course as they understood it, human beings were, in a sense, following the will of God. The absolute faith moderns put in calculation has its roots there.

But, calculative reason also lacks something. We are creatures with inexplicable feelings that also inform us about ourselves from the inside and incline us toward what is true, good, and pleasing. The arts, historical memories, the wilderness by itself constitute the moral universe of modernity, not only mathematics and science. The ecological movement is charged with romantic intuitions as much as it is with climate science in contesting the rationalized calculus of oil profits.

With the three great strands of Providential Deism, the Enlightenment, and the Romantic movement, the moral genome of the modern self is complete. Yet, they conflict the modern self which from another point of view is their offspring and beneficiary. Modern identity, for Charles Taylor, is essentially agonistic. This unreconciled condition of modernity cannot help but influence religion.

In my opinion, to adequately understand what the new evangelization demands in the modern age is to see it against the backdrop of Taylor's narrative of selfhood. In his review of *Sources of the Self*, Paul Ricoeur summarized the book's argument as follows: "Taylor proposes an interesting interpretation of secularization that does not reduce, for him, to the progress of the sciences and the development of a commercial economy but that consists in the birth of new alternatives on the most radical plane of moral sources."[43] That in turn leads Ricoeur to assert that the fundamental importance of Taylor's philosophical narrative of the modern self might be put as follows: "What is perhaps most striking about the portrait he paints of the modern self is its conflicts, considered to be just as strong between disengaged reason and the creativity of nature as between the two

---

[43] Paul Ricoeur, *Reflections on the Just*, trans. David Pellauer (Chicago: University of Chicago Press, 2007), "The Fundamental and the Historical: Notes on Charles Taylor's *Sources of the Self*," 177.

branches of modernity and the unexhausted heritage of Hellenism and Judeo-Christianity."[44]

The post-religious "Nones" who are not in the pews are just as conflicted in their own ways as those coming to church. The religious-self and the secular-self both suffer from inner conflicts in a conflicted modern culture. The new evangelization will be stronger for not ignoring the common ground between them, which Charles Taylor has sketched for us in *Sources of the Self*. The history of pre-conciliar and post-conciliar Catholicism I traced out earlier represents in many ways what Ricoeur says about Taylor's judgment on the conflicts of modernity.

## Conclusion: The Malaises of Modernity

I want to conclude this chapter with some remarks taken from Taylor's Massey Lectures first delivered on CBC radio in 1991. The lectures were first published in Canada as *The Malaise of Modernity* and later by Harvard University Press as *The Ethics of Authenticity*.[45] The second title does better justice to Taylor's goal of carefully extracting an important modern moral source called "authenticity" from its more debased forms. This moral source, which I explained above about "inwardness," is important. Authenticity as a genuine and genuinely ancient moral source of the self needs to be distinguished from the forms of modern individualism and subjectivism. The authentic self cannot detach itself from goods and hyper-goods. We all exist with others who in various ways bestow meaning on us as individuals. Human meaning is intersubjective meaning, even if the self must authentically put his or her own signature on it. Religion cannot survive as a moral source if believers do not own its vision in a more personal and emotional way. That is the crucial truth that the modern self brings to catechesis and the new evangelization.

The second moral source of the self that goes off the rails in modernity, even as it bestows enormous benefits, is our absolute trust in reason to handle and resolve all human problems. A completely rationalized approach to life excludes too much of the pre-rational in us. At the limit, rationalization gone haywire makes men and

---

[44] Ibid.

[45] Charles Taylor, *The Malaise of Modernity* (Concord, Ontario: Anansi Press, 1991).

women feel like prisoners of systems and anonymous bureaucracies. Reason anticipates outcomes but can never control all the factors. It tends to disenchant the world in the process of managing it. Technology as a total philosophical worldview tends toward becoming Dr. Frankenstein's monster which finally terrifies its creator who is no longer capable of managing it. Already scientists are predicting that artificial intelligence (AI), for all its promise, has the potential of turning human beings into slaves of machines. Stanley Kubrick's movie *2001: A Space Odyssey* introduced moviegoers to the paranoid spaceship computer named HAL. Without HAL, you die in space; with HAL, you are its slave.

Taylor's third moral source of meaning is found in community and nation. We belong to something larger than ourselves, which matters—families, churches, local and national communities. But the ethos of individualism and the immense impersonal systems of modern life make it easy to withdraw from them into ourselves. We celebrate freedom, but at the same time feel, despite everything to the contrary, not free at all. The powerful "steering systems" of rationalized culture come to dominate and colonize the fragile ecosystems of the human lifeworld.[46]

*The Malaise of Modernity* offers a busy pastor a simple profile of our modern conflicts of meaning without the usual moral indictment of modernity. Taylor sums the malaises up as follows: "These, then, are the three malaises about modernity that I want to deal with in this book. The first fear is about what we might call loss of meaning, the fading of moral horizons. The second concerns the eclipse of ends, in face of rampant instrumental reason. And the third is about a loss of freedom."[47]

But some people don't see things that way at all. They love individualism for its independence and self-actualizing potential. In their view, we should be pushing it more, not hemming individualism and individual choice in with old-fashioned traditions and culture. Nor do they see technology as some potential enemy of the individual

---

[46] For a clear introduction to the social thought of Jürgen Habermas, see James Gordon Finlayson, *Habermas: A Very Short Introduction* (New York: Oxford University Press, 2005). See Habermas's "social ontology" on "the human lifeworld vs. the system" on pp. 51–61.

[47] Taylor, *The Malaise of Modernity*, 10.

self but a liberation from nature's constraints and dangers. The postmoderns want to release human freedom from moral and institutional limitations. For them, the codes of speech are oppressive and must be thrown off.

From Paul Ricoeur, Daniel Bell, and Charles Taylor, I draw these conclusions. Modernity is far from the simple concept and identity we like to imagine it is. It keeps shifting in meaning. Latent within our modernity are deep conflicts about the good, about truth, and about human freedom and religion which remain unreconciled. Judeo-Christianity will survive the exhausted substitutes for it in political ideologies and the unrestrained self. The language of "limits" will continue to gnaw away at the hedonistic excess in Modernist culture. The modern self will continue to search for some new language of authentic transcendence. The ecological consciousness is a harbinger of things to come.

In the next chapter, I turn to the historical semantics of the secular in secularization, secularism, and the secular state.

# Chapter 7

# *Omnia Saecula Saeculorum*

In certain ways, the modern world and the secular order overlap. Economic and industrial modernization brought secularization in its wake. I already singled out for special mention Daniel Bell's reading of cultural modernity, political secularization, and the profanation of the sacred in the last chapter. I complemented Bell with Charles Taylor's malaises of modernity—the expressive forms of individualism that obscure the common good, the technological revolution that overwhelms more fragile human values, and the rationalized systems that colonize the human lifeworld. The modern self is conflicted because the values of the modern world conflict with each another.

In this chapter, I tackle the meaning of the secular order itself. The Latin title, *Omnia Saecula Saeculorum*, means "forever and ever." The Mass of the Roman Rite in Latin concluded the eucharistic canon with this expression. It is a deep Christian conviction about Christ expressed as doxology in praise of the Trinity without end. *Saecula* was a liturgical word as part of a doxology before it became the symbol of unfaith.

## The Semantics of the Secular

The semantics of historical and cultural concepts take time. Pierre Manent explains how the secular order emerged in Europe thanks to six distinct separations:[1] (1) the economic separation of the profes-

---

[1] Pierre Manent, *A World Beyond Politics? A Defense of the Nation-State*, trans. Marc LePain (Princeton, NJ: Princeton University Press, 2006). Manent derives the modern

sions (the division of labor); (2) the separation of executive, judicial, and legislative powers in government; (3) the separation of the state from the church; (4) the separation of free civil society from the state; (5) the separation of the represented (the people) and their representatives in parliaments; and, finally, (6) the separation of scientific facts from ethical values.[2] All of these separations resulted in what we call the secular order. In sum, they constitute what Charles Taylor calls the modern moral order. José Casanova traces the different meanings of the secular, secularization, and secularism.[3]

The Pontifical Council for Culture (PCC) holds that Christians today live in a "new age in human history" where cultural diversity and religious pluralism set the context for religious experience. An epochal shift has taken place *from religion-based to secular-based cultures.* "Born in countries with a long Christian tradition, this secularized culture, with its values of solidarity, generous dedication to others, freedom, justice, equality between men and women, an open mind, a spirit of dialogue and sensitivity to ecological issues, still bears the imprint of these fundamentally Christian values which have imbued culture over the centuries and of which secularization itself brought the fruits to civilization and nourished philosophical reflection."[4] Here is the palimpsest image I mentioned earlier—a Christian cultural text overwritten and partially borrowed by a secular one. The PCC then notes an emergent danger: "the loss of respect for the person and the spread of a kind of anthropological nihilism."[5] A displacement of traditional values is seen as having enormous cultural consequences in "the reductive effects of the secularism that spread through western Europe towards the end of the 1960s are at

---

liberal order from six distinct but related separations in human consciousness. The separation of the political authority from civil society is what distinguished totalitarian from liberal regimes. Liberal regimes affirm the legitimacy of individual opinions and self-identities in their citizens. The work of Marcel Gauchet on religion and secularization is central to Manent's argument in the chapter, "The Theologico-Political Vector."

[2] Manent, *A World*, 13.

[3] José Casanova, "The Secular, Secularizations, and Secularism," in *Rethinking Secularism*, ed. Craig Calhoun, Mark Juergensmeyer, and Jonathan Van Antwerpen (Oxford: Oxford University Press, 2011), 54–74.

[4] Pontifical Council for Culture, "Towards a Pastoral Approach to Culture," 23.

[5] Ibid.

present contributing to the destructuring [*sic*] of culture in Central and Eastern Europe."[6] The secular order is a tangled skein of different religious traditions, moral values, humanizing and dehumanizing potentials all interwoven in an open public sphere of options. At this point in the chapter, let me offer some remarks on the common semantics of the secular as that word appears in ordinary discourse. I will begin with the philosophical use of "secular" and work my way back to the neutral sociological term, "secularization."

*Secular humanism* is a philosophy of life. Some forms of it support moral qualities many religious people regard as highly admirable and noble—philanthropic generosity; improved medical care, education, and housing for the underprivileged in society; relieving suffering; and the pursuit of ordinary undisturbed happiness. Secular humanism often aims to liberalize moral and social conventions, especially in sexuality and marriage, which have been traditionally supported by religious belief. This humanism is well-suited to a liberal economic order of private choice and belief. Individuals are left free to choose how they want to live.

Choosing how to live life includes believing what life is all about. Non-religious belief is another kind of *belief*. As William Connolly points out: "The dispute (which does not always have to take the form of an 'antagonism') is not exactly between 'belief and unbelief,' with the implication that one side is filled with belief and the other has a vacancy where belief might have been."[7] Humanism is as much a form of belief as religious belief is. Its worldview exceeds in crucial respects the weight of its own evidence as all belief must. Connolly says all belief in modernity is "contestable belief." Secular humanism, despite being marketed as an obvious choice for how to live based on science, is very contestable.

The concept of a *secular state* was created in the seventeenth century for one major reason—to pacify a hundred years of religious wars between and among Catholics and Protestants following the Protestant Reformation. The secular state replaced a theocratic political order where a religion takes the form of a quasi-state. When the power to punish (Inquisition) and to make war (Crusades) were removed from ecclesiastical control, the secular political order came into existence. Some regard the secular political order as having saved

[6] Ibid.
[7] William Connolly, *Pluralism* (Durham, NC: Duke University Press, 2005), 46.

Christianity from destructive theocratic impulses. Francis Fukuyama asserts that, with the Protestant Reformation, Christianity literally secularized itself.[8] Marcel Gauchet makes the same point.[9] The French and American political revolutions, in very different ways, sealed the fate of a confessional political state. The book of Leviticus or the Quran, if interpreted in fundamentalist terms, would regard a secular state as an apostasy from God's will. The Christian church once harbored such ideas. In secular politics, legislation and the constitutional arguments to support it must be based on public reasons, not on documents of faith. Churches, synagogues, and mosques lack legal, punitive, political, or military authority in the secular order.

Thus, in the ongoing moral debates about secularity, Catholics need to be clear on this. The secular state, for all its problems, in principle rescued Christianity from non-evangelical politicized ambitions. Despite its problems, and using Joseph Ratzinger's own words, the secular order was a "purification" of religion by reason.[10] Secular states may not impose worldviews on religious citizens who have a right to hold their own beliefs or on non-religious citizens as well who have a right to their nonbelief. Charles Taylor and Paul Ricoeur speak of an *open secular* state that reasonably accommodates differences in worldviews.

*Secular civil society* refers to the free, open, and pluralistic public sphere of opinion formation about values. This is the social space religious organizations operate in. They are value-laden communities that recharge moral and religious beliefs for those who freely choose to associate with them. But other institutions also play important roles in value formation. Educational institutions, the free press, journals of serious opinion (religious and secular) enjoy and must enjoy freedom of expression in the contest of ideas and values in modern secular culture. The secular state should declare itself neutral on ultimate worldviews, leaving its citizens a maximum reasonable freedom to form their own consciences and live according to the dictates of their own beliefs and values.

[8] Francis Fukuyama, *The End of History and the Last Man* (New York: The Free Press, 1992), 216.

[9] Marcel Gauchet as quoted by Pierre Manent and Charles Taylor.

[10] Joseph Ratzinger, "That Which Holds the World Together: The Pre-political Moral Foundations of a Free State," in Joseph Cardinal Ratzinger and Jürgen Habermas, *Dialectics of Secularization: On Reason and Religion*, ed. Florian Schuller, trans. Brian McNeil (San Francisco: Ignatius Press, 2006).

When most of civil society was de facto Christian and religious in America, public values reflected that cultural consensus. As culture has changed, and as the leading referees of ideas and values in culture have become more independent of religious worldviews and convictions, many religious citizens regard themselves as victimized by a secular hegemony in politics and culture. The "dictatorship" of relativism is one way, and perhaps not the best way, to account for the shift in the public spheres of human value formation from religious institutions to institutions in modern society that subscribe to some version of secular humanism.

*Secularization* is a sociological term about the effect that modernization processes of various kinds, urbanization and industrialization at the start, had on religious consciousness. As modernization shifted further to a post-industrial communication-oriented society, the open public sphere became more susceptible to colonization by ideologies with more cultural capital than religious worldviews had. The kind of secularization that comes from modernizing technologies is automatic and unintentional. Working on an assembly line dramatically increases worker productivity and overall raises income levels, but it brings with it less connection with nature and natural symbols of transcendence. The Amish farmer feels more connected to a world ploughing his farm at dawn with a team of horses than the coal miner does to the same world in West Virginia. The sun that rises in Lancaster County, Pennsylvania, does not rise in the same way in a steel mill. Natural religious sensibilities are more difficult to sustain in certain settings unless they are intentionally cultivated. Formalized worship allows for the cultivation of humane religious sensibilities in a secularized environment that tends to neutralize the sense of transcendence. Something similar happens in the theater and the concert hall which intentionally and institutionally cultivate aesthetic sensibilities in pragmatic commercialized culture. Churches, synagogues, and mosques do the same thing for religious sensibilities overpowered and worn thin in ordinary life by processes of secularization.

The First Amendment to the U.S. Constitution defines what a secular state is in the disestablishment clause. But modernizing processes like urbanization, technology, the comprehensive financial and industrial sectors, modern communications, and entertainment are far more crucial for the secularization of consciousness than constitutional law is. The commercial and cultural spheres of life in modern society are de-coupled from religious and moral influence. Religious practice is turned into a pious enclave while political life tends to become almost religiously fanatical in partisan politics. In the view of economics, the local parish is another commercial enterprise specializing in the distribution of a religious product to consumers who feel they need it. The biblical sabbath once preserved in "blue laws" slowly morphs into the secular weekend. Despite these diverse effects of secularization, religion in America remains more alive, diverse, and entrepreneurial than anywhere in Europe.

Any parish priest today knows what celebrating a liturgy is for those who can still grasp the meaningfulness of sacramental symbolism. He also knows what celebrating family baptisms, marriages, and funerals for those estranged from religion feels like. It's become another language. Max Weber originally described the religiously estranged secular as "religiously unmusical." Priests can expect there will be more mourners at funeral liturgies who are attending in polite disbelief bordering on incomprehension about the afterlife. Memorial celebrations of life's past achievements match the immanent sensibility of a secular age better than rhetorical exuberance or anxiety over fates in the afterlife.

The *secular state, secular civil society,* and *secularization* make conditions favorable in modernity for the spread of philosophical *secularism* and *secular humanism.* Secularism still runs the gamut from militantly atheistic versions to philosophically agnostic positions to what I would call magnanimous ecumenical secularists like William Connolly.[11] A secularism intolerant of religious faith in public life will inevitably overplay its hand. Figures like Paul Ricoeur, Jürgen Habermas, and Charles Taylor, along with William Connolly among others, are calling for a post-secular approach to the public sphere because of its legitimate multicultural diversity in humane worldviews.

## Three Waves of Secularization

The "linear" or "religious-replacement" model of secularization and secularism that once held sway in sociology is increasingly being challenged. Religion seems to have the plasticity capable of returning in culture after suffering a defeat. Hans Joas uses the example of the

---

[11] See William E. Connolly, *Why I Am Not a Secularist* (Minneapolis: University of Minnesota Press, 1999), "The Conceits of Secularism," 19–46.

Pantheon in Paris to show that. The Pantheon was originally built as a church (Sainte-Geneviève) before transitioning to a secular monument to the *philosophes* (Voltaire, Rousseau, etc.). Then it became a church again until 1871, when the wooden cross was sawed off and the building became the secular Pantheon to the "immortals," but now with a new stone cross at the pinnacle. The story of the Pantheon is an architectural parable of what Joas means by "waves of secularization" and the resistance of the sacred.

> In the words of the British historian Owen Chadwick, to whom I owe
> this story, this building "became a sign of de-Christianizing revolution,
> national virtues instead of old virtues, La France instead of Sainte-
> Geneviève; and because it became a sign, it was buffeted to and fro in
> accordance with the see-saw of party politics, holy and secular, until
> at last, like so much of Western Europe, it lay almost secularized, but
> with the not so old stone cross still there to make a memory and a
> blessing, the past of Europe still speaking to the present, and keeping
> guard over men once thought to be the vilest enemies of the cross, but
> now seen to have fought for freedom and for truths that were neces-
> sary to the human spirit.[12]

Joas concludes that "secularization in Europe was never a linear, continuous, uniform process. Instead we are dealing with a highly conflictual, heterogeneous, contingent history."[13] Secularization is often followed by instances of "religious revitalization." These religious "counter-movements" to secularization can take very different forms, as they do in Catholic traditionalism, the modernization of doctrine, and new ways of organizing religious life. In modern European history, instances of secularization began in 1791 and lasted only a decade, until 1803. Then a second wave began in the nineteenth-century processes of industrialization and urbanization. Finally, Joas suggests that a third wave began in 1969 and ended in 1973. This wave crested as the Protestant evangelical movement and the Catholic new evangelization were just beginning.

This narrative of "waves" puts thinking about secularism in a historical perspective. It challenges what Joas calls the "myth of the anti-religious French Revolution." Early meetings of the revolutionar-

---

[12] Hans Joas, *Faith as an Option: Possible Futures for Christianity* (Stanford, CA: Stanford University Press, 2014), 38.

[13] Ibid.

ies concluded, he notes, with the recitation of the *Te Deum*.[14] Things changed, of course. The Revolution soon turned into the first attempt since the early Roman Empire to crush Christianity. But, Joas counters with the crucially important qualification that "what prompted this escalation of the revolutionary process in an anti-Christian direction was not the religious but the economic and political role of the church."[15] He goes on to say, "One of the tragic results of this spiral of hostility was papal condemnation of the Revolution and the principles it proclaimed, including human rights, as blasphemous, heretical, and schismatic."[16] The papal support for the monarchy, at the very moment that this contingent political institution had lost popular support, brought the church into disrepute. The condemnation of democracy and religious freedom by the nineteenth-century popes and their preoccupation with the preservation of the Papal States cost the church dearly.

The second wave of nineteenth-century secularization came about in part by the institutional vacuum of the church in the new urban environments where rural populations were settling in vast numbers in Paris, Berlin, or London. Peasants dressed in shabby clothes were ashamed to attend Mass in magnificent cathedrals. Catholic peasants and the new bourgeois drifted away from religious practice because the new urban centers lacked the institutional supports in religion there to care for them. The demographic crisis of the urban poor in cities compounded the political crisis of religious freedom for the church. That's another dimension of secularization.

The third wave of secularization, in the view of Joas, occurred both in Europe and America from 1969 to 1973. In those four years it had to do with the rise of "expressivist" views of life in which the body suddenly played a much larger role in human self-realization.[17] Eastern religions, like Hinduism, were more open to the erotic dimension than Christianity, which saw the new spiritual and secular experiments with sexuality as simply pagan. This led many young people

---

[14] Ibid., 42–43.

[15] Ibid., 43.

[16] Ibid.

[17] Robert Bellah, Richard Madsen, William M. Sullivan, Ann Swidler, and Steven M. Tipton, *Habits of the Heart: Individualism and Commitment in American Life* (Oakland, CA: University of California Press, 2007).

to reject religion and enter new cults or choose nothing at all. Others in that cohort became more puritanical and hyper-religious.

Joas agrees with Charles Taylor that we need a new theory of modernity and secularization that sees the secular order not as a total replacement for religion but as one that continues along with religion and is even able to draw on religious intuitions. The secularization processes did not happen all by themselves or, as some traditionalist polemicists claim, from a conspiracy of secular humanists and religious liberals against ordinary Christian decency. Joas writes:

> Leading Catholic thinkers of the twentieth century such as Max Scheler and key figures of Protestantism such as H. Richard Niebuhr and, taking things to the outer limits, Dietrich Bonhoeffer, already recognized that the history of secularization has always been a history of the guilt of Christians and their refusal to take responsibility. Scheler, for example, responded to the previously inconceivable bloodletting of World War I with the insight that Christians could not simultaneously declare Europe deeply Christian while at the same time denying their responsibility for the war.[18]

Secularism in the new evangelization demands a political and philosophical dictionary to make the proper distinctions for the faithful. The Latin word for "secular" is *saeculum*. To complete this semantic genealogy of the secular, let me add remarks about the antiquity of the word "secular" within the Christian faith.

## *Per Omnia Saecula Saeculorum*

The Canon of the Mass in English concludes with a beautiful doxology: "Through him, and with him, and in him, / O God, almighty Father, / in the unity of the Holy Spirit, / all glory and honor is yours, / for ever and ever." In Latin, "for ever and ever" is *per omnia saecula saeculorum*. The repetition of *saeculum* takes the ear and eye back to Roman antiquity and Latin Christianity. *Saeculum* is much older than its English cognates.

In classical Latin, the word *saeculum* referred to time immemorial. It meant one hundred years, which explains the etymology of the

---

[18] Joas, *Faith as an Option*, 48–49.

French *siècle* and Spanish *siglo*.[19] The Romans celebrated *ludi saeculares* (the secular games) just once a century. No one who saw them once lived long enough to see them again. In the Latin Mass, the repetition of *saecula saeculorum* in the Great Doxology expressed human history and hope in the longest timeframes humans can imagine. "Forever and ever" (*per omnia saecula saeculorum*) is a long, long time.

The word *saeculum* appears on our currency in the Great Seal of the United States, *Novus Ordo Seclorum* [*sic*], to represent the significance of the American Revolution and the Declaration of Independence. Astronomy describes certain stellar movements as *secular motions*, and economics has long-term *secular trends*. How is it, though, that a word that meant a century in Latin can mean what it does today?

St. Augustine employed the word *saeculum* in its hundred-year temporal meaning. He divided time into *sacred* time, which ran from the creation (Genesis) to the coming of Jesus Christ, and *secular* time, which succeeded the resurrection. The birth of Christ (incarnation) was the summit of sacred time. Following Jesus' death and resurrection, the church awaited the end of time when Christ would return in glory (the Parousia). For the mature Augustine, the *saeculum* was the *meantime* of empire and daily life between biblical sacred time and the end of time. There's more to the story, however.

As a young bishop, Augustine understood secular time, *saeculum*, in a different way because of the Christian empire. The church went from being a cult persecuted by different Roman emperors, to a faith legitimated by the conversion of the emperor Constantine in 313 AD. Christianity became the official religion of the empire. When Theodosius I was emperor, the church had enjoyed fifty years of imperial legitimation and support. In 393, the emperor Theodosius terminated the Olympic games traditionally held in honor of Zeus and the gods. The games were only resumed in France in 1896. By then, all that remained of devotion to the Greek gods stood on pedestals in the Louvre!

Its status as the official imperial cult changed Christianity in many ways. Roman imperial culture and architecture became its aesthetic. More to the point, the neutral *saeculum* between resurrection and

---

[19] Rémi Braque, "The Impossibility of Secular Society: Without a Transcendent Horizon, Society Cannot Endure" *First Things* (October 2013).

Parousia turned into a "holy Roman empire." To some early Christian bishops like Eusebius of Caesarea (260–340), the Christian empire of Constantine fulfilled New Testament prophecies about Christ filling the universe that "God may be all in all" (1 Cor 15:28). The early rhetoric of Augustine reflected his own enthusiasm for Theodosian Christianity. The imperial order was bending the knee before Jesus Christ. God the Father seemed to be subjecting the principalities of the age—the pinnacle of the *saeculum*—to his Son.

After the invasion of Rome by the barbarians in 410, Augustine was at work in North Africa marshaling his arguments for the *City of God*. One task was to counter the view of Roman aristocrats who charged the Christians with responsibility for Rome's collapse because they refused to petition the gods for protection or take up arms. Augustine responded by calling attention to "the internal contradictions in Roman religion, statecraft, and political theory."[20] To do that, he needed an irrefutable logic, knowledge of Roman cults, and familiarity with classical authors. Pagans came to hear him preach. Augustine was the fifth-century equivalent of a public intellectual. He founded a monastery, but his thinking had nothing cloistered about it.

In *City of God*, Augustine reversed his position on Theodosian Christianity as a reinstitution of sacred time. The "city of God," as Augustine meant it, was not identical with the church in secular time. The heavenly city was present wherever the love of God and neighbor was present in the secular. The church gave sacramental expression to the city of God but was not identical with it. Grace transcended ecclesial frontiers. The *saeculum* could manifest it in its own way.

Robert Markus defends the opinion that what we call the secular world was regarded by Augustine in a positive light for its contributions to knowledge, culture, and security. He calls Augustine "the outstanding critic of the ideology of the Christian Empire as it had developed by the end of the fourth century and in the time of the Theodosian emperors."[21] The secular sphere of life was different from

---

[20] Sabine MacCormack, "Classical Influences on Augustine," in *Augustine Through the Ages: An Encyclopedia*, ed. Allan D. Fitzgerald (Grand Rapids, MI: Eerdmans, 1999), 209.

[21] Robert A. Markus, *Christianity and the Secular* (Notre Dame, IN: University of Notre Dame Press, 2006), 10.

the profane, which could exist within it. " 'Secular' does not have a radical opposition to the sacred; it is more neutral, capable of being accepted or adapted: the domain of the religious—though not moral—*adiaphora*. It will be the shared overlap between insider and outsider groups, the sphere in which they can have a common interest and which—from the Christian point of view—need not be repudiated or excluded."[22] It is, we might say, an Augustinian "courtyard of the Gentiles" for late antique Roman Christianity.

The Holy Roman Empire was called holy for a reason. It was a Christianized imperium. Power slipped back and forth between church and empire, as the Investiture Controversy would show. *Saeculum* stood for the indefinite ages—usually a millennium—before Christ's Parousia. But it was also a Christian *saeculum* with a clergy it called *clericus saecularis*. A secular priest lived and ministered in the world like diocesan priests do today. The secular became part and parcel of a Christian canonical vocabulary.

To sum up, by the medieval period, *saeculum* connoted a century, ordinary time, Christian history until Christ's Parousia, a liturgical doxology of grace in epochal temporality, or even a class of clergy without a community rule of life. When church property was sold and returned to everyday use, it was said to be *secularized*. Secular then meant ordinary, not anti-religious. When ecclesiastical properties were forcibly seized and transferred to political authority at the time of the Reformation, secular took on another meaning that required a new word. Secularized monasteries were then profaned. A new chapter in the semantics of the secular opens with the expropriation of church monasteries in England by Henry VIII. The anti-clericalism of the French Enlightenment will go much further.

## The Scientific Alternative for the Sacred Canopy

The beginnings of modern cosmology with Copernicus, Kepler, and Galileo had as much to do with establishing new conditions for contesting religious belief as did the seventeenth-century secular state and nineteenth-century secularization. The universe, as we know it from Galileo's time forward, is radically different from how ancients and medievals imagined it. Measured in light years, secular

[22] Ibid., 5–6.

stellar movements and magnitudes dwarf a century, much less a single human lifetime. In some sense, it strikes people as presumptuous to think human life even matters. Later, with Darwin, biological evolution reduces human significance a second time beneath the weight of billions of years of cosmology. In the book of Genesis, Adam and Eve are created in the image of God—innocent and then fallen, yet in another way like titanic figures whose disobedience casts a fateful shadow of guilt and fallibility across human history. With Darwin, the titans are diminished to the status of higher hominids, the species homo and Homo sapiens. As a higher life form, individual men and women are seen as hosts for genes on a planet of a small star in the corner of the Milky Way which itself is a minor galaxy under the influence of some massive black hole.

The psalmist could ask God, "What are human beings that you are mindful of them, / mortals that you care for them?" (Ps 8:4). Still, he had no idea of the diminution of existential stature modern science demands human consciousness accept. The Copernican revolution changed human self-understanding in many ways. Only by bracketing cosmology and astrophysics, the protoplasmic backstory of life on earth, and the Neanderthals and ancient civilizations come and gone can moderns take ourselves with biblical seriousness. Narcissism seems less a fault than a solace for a creature lost in time and space. Impersonal providence cares for and keeps track of nothing. Desiderata tries to redeem human yearning for divine care by calling man or woman "a child of the universe."

The impact of cosmology and evolution on the biblical imagination changes when we turn our attention to history and ethics. Human beings have no choice but to choose and choose wisely how to manage events and configure them into a coherent narrative endowed with existential meaning. Augustine wrote the first and greatest Christian theology of history in his *City of God*. Its plotlines were drawn from the symbolisms of Genesis and Apocalypse: the eschatology of the kingdom of God, the Parousia of the second coming of Christ, and the final resurrection at the end of time.

The modern secular imaginary of historical meaning operates without that eschatology. Yet it is still haunted by the threat of an environmental, nuclear, biochemical, and social disaster. Until the eighteenth century, the sense of purpose in human history derived from the Augustinian-biblical narrative of temporality, the *saeculum* until the Second Coming of Christ and the Apocalypse. This is no longer the case. Human hope today is centered, not on the return of Jesus Christ, but on short-term progress in politics, economics, and well-being.

By a secular imaginary of time and history, I mean one in which the flux of life is grounded, not in biblical eschatology, but in physics, life sciences, economics, technology, and politics. Critical history of human civilizations with no theological intent is how most people—except some fundamentalists—now imagine time. It has been neutered of any plausible religious significance that the course of events had for biblical prophets. With them, a theodicy of divine blessings and punishments hung like a sacred canopy over military victories and defeats. Secular history is the default narrative of the modern imagination. What remains of a Christian teleological vision is existentially squeezed onto the moment of death—one's personal exit from life and time to eternity or oblivion. What was once seen as a providential history of temporality embracing all events, even into the nineteenth century, has all but disappeared. At Mass, we pray "Christ will come again," but nobody asks where or when. With the decline of belief in anything approaching a Christian eschatology of human time, is it any surprise that the faith turns inward for consolation, or is simply abandoned?

## The Axial Age

The German psychiatrist and philosopher Karl Jaspers called the period 700 BCE to 200 BCE the "Axial Age" (*Aschsenzeit*). Something like a global mutation in human thought seems to have occurred during this timeframe. In China, the *Analects* of Confucius were written around the same time as the Buddha achieved enlightenment in India. In Greece, philosophy broke free of myths into dialectical reason in the *Dialogues* of Plato and Aristotle's philosophical treatises. In the very same epoch, the Jewish prophets Isaiah, Jeremiah, and Ezekiel appeared. Though these were all different, what they had in common was that a fragmented mythical vision of reality was passing into the unified field of reason and monotheistic thought.[23] More remarkable yet, the concepts and arguments forged in the Axial Age still move and persuade moderns. People still read Confucius, the

---

[23] Robert N. Bellah, *Religion in Human Evolution: From the Paleolithic to the Axial Age* (Cambridge, MA: Belknap Press of Harvard University Press, 2011).

biblical prophets, and the Greek philosophers and find relevance and truth in them. We are their contemporaries and they are ours.

Some believe the last three centuries in modern history constitute a second Axial Age. The center of gravity in human imagination has shifted away from philosophy and religion to science, economics, and politics. By whatever name we call the present age—modern or post-modern, secular or post-secular—there is a sense of having entered a new stage in historical existence.

The Second Vatican Council was called because the church sensed this was happening. The post-conciliar period of the new evangelization clearly wants to swing secularized imagination of Christians in the direction of a moral and religious interpretation of history centered on the figure of Christ, on truth, on mercy, and on joy. Charles Taylor contrasts what he calls the "hierarchical imaginary" with the "modern moral imaginary."[24] In the hierarchical imaginary, the heavens and the church herself were preloaded with surplus meaning which spills over onto the world from above. The church was responsible for nourishing the spiritual life of society on earth and for providing the means to salvation. Mundane matters fell to the so-called secular arm and temporal powers divinely ordained to assist the church by providing security and safeguarding orthodoxy and orthopraxis. When the Dominican inquisitors found Joan of Arc—the French peasant girl who dressed like a soldier and rode on horseback like a man and could not answer catechism questions—guilty of heresy, it was the secular arm that carried out her execution. The smoke that suffocated her did not make inquisitors cough then as much as the memory of it inflames our secularized conscience. The management of violent impulses in religion and outside religion is one of the greatest challenges a religious and post-religious culture must address.

The hierarchical imaginary can be described, as Arthur Lovejoy did, in terms of a "great chain of being."[25] The whole of reality, from the lowest to the highest—the spiritual, ecclesiastical, political, social, and biological spheres together—all mirrored one another in a universe literally saturated with spiritual meaning. The angels were

---

[24] Charles Taylor, *Modern Social Imaginaries* (Durham: Duke University Press, 2004) 3–22.

[25] Arthur O. Lovejoy, *The Great Chain of Being: A Study of the History of Ideas* (Cambridge: Harvard University Press, 1976).

ranked in a celestial hierarchy of nine choirs, which in turn reflected the nine planets which analogously paralleled nine separate vocations in the church. Creation was one echo chamber of resemblances from the angelic to the ecclesial to the human to the animal world. The mystical writer Dionysius the Pseudo-Areopagite made all reality mystical.[26] Such artificial resemblances fail us in the age of science and the double helix. Not only have facts been separated from values in a secular age but poetry has been separated from the ontology of human life.

Today, a religiously neutral secular state presents no religious problems for American Catholics. It may and does, however, raise ethical concerns of various kinds. The separation of church and state is constitutionally axiomatic. Disestablishment is based on the First Article of the Bill of Rights. New England Puritans certainly didn't see religion that way, nor did Anglican colonists in Jamestown where established churches were the norm. Maryland was the first of the colonies to incorporate the Lockean principle of religious toleration in its legislation. The U.S. Constitution turned colonial established-church models of Christianity on their heads by excluding any political establishment of a faith. The moral ethos of America, apart from creed and worship, was widely held even if slavery and other matters were considered acceptable.

Denominational Christianity was generally regarded by Enlightenment thinkers, who personally had little use for it, as a bulwark against the amoral impulses in the lower classes. Religion in optional denominational form served a worthy social purpose for enlightened deists. It kept the lower classes in line with religious fears and hopes. In time, that too would change.

The nineteenth century proved a turning point in this overlapping consensus between the country's political geniuses and the lower classes. European intellectuals began attacking religion openly as anti-rational and anti-liberal. The great atheists worked up theories of religion that reduced it to unworthy, if not inhuman, sentiments. After them, Max Weber forecast that something as unremarkable as modernization would bring disenchantment with it. Secularization became the synonym for this monopolization of meaning by science

---

[26] See *The Mystical Theology and the Celestial Hierarchies of Dionysius the Areopagite,* trans. Editors of The Shrine of Wisdom and Poem by St. John of the Cross (Surrey, England: The Shrine of Wisdom, 1965).

and technology. Who needs gods anymore? If the First Axial Age brought civilization out of the mythical into the rational and mono-theistic understanding of reality, the Second Axial Age aimed to slough off faith entirely.

## From Secularization to Pluralization Theory: Peter Berger

Peter Berger's early sociological work was on religion and secu-larization. He developed his approaches in *The Sacred Canopy: Elements of a Sociological Theory of Religion.*[27] The "sacred canopy" is a symbolic umbrella sheltering human meaning from life's absurdities, especially from death. "The power of religion depends, in the last resort, upon the credibility of the banners it puts in the hands of men as they stand before death, or more accurately, as they walk, inevi-tably, toward it."[28] The traditional name for it was "theodicy," literally, justifying the ways of God in the undeniable experience of evil in the world. But the appeal to God's justice to explain suffering and the hope for eschatological justice in the afterlife does not "serve any longer to assuage most men's anguish."[29] A divine will is no longer able to explain, much less legitimate, the arbitrariness of human fate. Albert Camus observed that in the modern world grace was replaced by justice.[30] Old Testament prophecy, in Berger's reading, shattered the natural paganisms by appealing to YHWH as a Voice above and apart from nature. The pantheons were secularized. In his view, the Protestant emphasis on the Word of God effected something analo-gous for the Catholic sacramental imagination. It is curious that the Israelites never built a shrine on Mount Sinai where the Law was given to Moses. God's throne was in heaven, not on a mountain, much less on the "Golden Bull" of the pagan divinity Baal. The pro-phetic imagination tends to privilege ethics over liturgy. God says in Hosea 6:6, "I desire steadfast love and not sacrifice." Jesus quotes Hosea in Matthew 9:13. Berger just says that for Israel God is "im-

---

[27] Peter Berger, *The Sacred Canopy: Elements of a Sociological Theory of Religion* (New York: Anchor Books, 1990). This was originally published in 1967.

[28] Ibid., 51.

[29] Ibid., 54.

[30] Ibid., 55.

mune to magical manipulation."[31] The divine transcends nature and Israel itself. Jesus and his mission transcends the church even in its legitimate self-understanding as the Body of Christ.

Despite the effects of secularization on religion, it is no juggernaut. Religion will rebound in some fashion. Berger's *A Rumor of Angels* argued against secularization as a fate for moderns by pointing to resurgent religious revivals and movements in the modern world.[32] It was naïve of secularists to imagine religious faith would just vanish even if social circumstances made belief more difficult.

Some critics saw religious revivals as no more than a late recrudescence of magical thinking. Others read them differently as evidence of a lack in secular consciousness itself. Jürgen Habermas went so far as to write that in the secular approach to all of reality, "something is missing."[33] Along the same lines, Daniel Bell predicted the "return of the sacred" after the dalliance with nihilisms and the false substitutes for religion, like nationalism, aesthetics, consumption, and the unrestrained self, were exhausted.

I have already explained why toleration of religious pluralism was essential for a civil secular order. Religious beliefs were private beliefs. Brackets were put around the desire to force them on others. Different faiths could exist side by side as private options in the name of civil harmony. But, in the beginning, religious doctrines were largely shored up by a common moral creed. Today, that is gone. In secular society, people not only disagree on religious worldviews but also on how to live and what is good to do. For that reason, Peter Berger has argued that pluralization theory is needed to supplement the secular state and secularization in explaining the cognitive conditions imposed on faith in the modern world.[34]

Pluralism in society engenders what Berger calls "cognitive contamination." We saw that six separations altogether created the secular order. But moral and religious pluralism makes the ideal of separation impossible. The pluralistic-ecumenic age brings religious

---

[31] Ibid., 56.

[32] Peter Berger, *A Rumor of Angels: Modern Society and the Rediscovery of the Supernatural* (Garden City, NY: Anchor Books, 1970).

[33] Jürgen Habermas, *An Awareness of What Is Missing: Faith and Reason in a Post-Secular Age*, trans. Ciaran Cronin (Cambridge: Polity Press, 2010).

[34] Peter Berger, *A Far Glory: The Quest for Faith in an Age of Credulity* (New York: The Free Press, 1992), 37–46.

toleration and the possibility of mutual interaction among people of different beliefs. This creates new conditions for doubt.[35] Strong belief is still possible for religious people in pluralistic society, but it is less easy in the context of "cognitive contamination." People begin to ask themselves: How can my belief be right if other good people find it unpersuasive and even mistaken?

The diversity of religious and moral outlooks in secular modernity fragilizes strong belief. Two possible ways to reinforce it are to withdraw from too much pluralism into a community of like-minded people (the "intentional communities" of Rod Dreher) or to push back against pluralism in a moral crusade. The religious ghetto of an Amish-style existence and the moral crusade of the culture war seem the only possible options for faith in response to pluralism and cognitive contamination. In a nutshell, that restates the crisis of faith in terms of pluralization theory. Catholic faith exists today in a new cognitive situation caused by religious and moral pluralism. The new evangelization needs to explain to people why believing today has become so difficult. That is why so many searching people today wander between a disappointing relativism and an impossible fundamentalism in belief.

No matter how people choose to deal with it, religious symbolism commits someone—whether Catholic, Protestant, Jew, Muslim, or Hindu—to a certain interpretation of Daniel Bell's "ricorso" of unavoidable questions: What is the nature of love, character, and obligation? The answers will differ as they must, but the questions are constant. Pluralism means that Catholics will live in a continuous ecumenical state of cognitive contamination. The new evangelization must acknowledge that and equip believers to manage it intelligently. Catechesis today is catechesis for coping well with pluralism and its effects.

In saying this, I must assume the average parish contains many in the pews coping privately, almost secretly, with a degree of cognitive contamination. They may not name it as such, but their pastors need to address it. Some attend Mass having surrendered traditional beliefs that don't make sense to them anymore. If they're in church, it's for other reasons—maybe for a spouse and kids.

---

[35] Berger, *A Far Glory*, "Secularization and Pluralism," 25–46.

If the pastor could see some ghostly hypertext written above the heads of those in his congregation with the beliefs of their close friends and coworkers, and what their regular diet of TV, internet searching and serious reading are, where they turn for news and thoughtful commentary on it, then he could get some idea of the actual amount of cognitive contamination at work in his parish. The Joy of the Gospel (24) asks evangelizers to "take on the smell of the sheep" meaning that preachers and teachers of the faith need to identify with the struggles parishioners are having believing in the face of cognitive contamination and cognitive dissonance in a pluralistic society.

In modern pluralistic secularity, religious traditions necessarily become more fragile. This fragility is caused by the incapacity of social institutions like churches to pass on moral heritages other than liberty and equality.[36] Some wish to silence religious convictions of moral goodness at odds with secular rights. As American pluralism grows with the arrival of other religions on our shores, American secularism as the default non-religious belief will be forced to adjust its assumptions. Optional belief is more powerful than ideology.

Is Daniel Bell on to something when he predicts the exhaustion of religious substitutes in modernity?[37] If so, many Catholics have not yet caught on. Is Peter Berger right that cognitive contamination as much as poor catechesis makes belief harder today?[38] Probably, but the lack of any apologetics for ecclesial faith that makes sense to secularized Catholics is hard to come by. Is James Davison Hunter on target, that changing modern culture is a "bridge too far" for the churches but that "faithful presence" of Christians in small communities of faith will make a difference, however negligible it might seem in the short run?[39] Successful parishes make one think so.

---

[36] Francis Fukuyama, *Trust: The Social Virtues and the Creation of Prosperity* (New York: The Free Press, 1995). He returns here to the quest for recognition (*thymos*), which Fukuyama treated extensively in *The End of History and the Last Man*. He regards recognition and worth as "one of the chief motors of the entire human historical process" (7).

[37] Daniel Bell, "The Return of the Sacred? The Argument on the Future of Religion," in *The Winding Passage: Essays and Sociological Journeys 1960–1980* (Cambridge: Abt Associates, 1980), 344.

[38] Berger, *A Far Glory*, Part 1: "The Social Context of Belief."

[39] James Davison Hunter, Essay 1: "Christianity and World-Changing," in *To Change the World: The Irony, Tragedy, and Possibility of Christianity in the Late Modern World* (Oxford: Oxford University Press, 2010).

Secularism is searching for something. In part 3 of *A Secular Age*, Charles Taylor speaks of the "Nova Effect" in which modernity exploded in different directions—into atheistic and religious and pagan forms. Daniel Bell said modern men and women worship the god of experience in whatever overpowering form it takes for them— political, economic, aesthetic, or religious.[40] Extraordinary beauty is not unlike the *mysterium tremendum et fascinans*, the overpowering encounter with the sacred. In a way, this is the ecstatic rendezvous point for secular experience and religious experience. Beauty is one of those meeting places. The church now speaks of an "apologetics of beauty" (*via pulchritudinis*). Pope Francis recommends it as a mode of evangelization in The Joy of the Gospel (167).

The secular order is not one-dimensional. The "conflicts of modernity" (Taylor) conflict us all—religious and secular alike.[41] Technical rationality enchants for a while before yielding to the latest innovation. A great religious tradition demands fidelity to understand what it means. Syncretism is not the answer. On the other hand, an ecumenical religious sensibility may draw more from the treasure house of the kingdom of heaven about God's mysterious ways than we think possible.

## Seculars Searching for the Holy

Increasingly, it seems that secular agnostics want to make a case for their nonbelief as something rediscovered to enrich human existence. Freedom from religion equals saving one's authentic humanity. In different ways, a non-religious spirituality attuned to nature and the human psyche wants to substitute itself for a passive and empty agnosticism. One example is Stephen Greenblatt's *The Swerve: How the World Became Modern*.[42] The popular book by Hubert Dreyfus and

---

[40] Bell, "The Return of the Sacred?," 334.

[41] Charles Taylor, Conclusion: "The Conflicts of Modernity," in *Sources of the Self: The Making of the Modern Identity* (Cambridge, MA: Harvard University Press, 1989).

[42] Stephen Greenblatt, *The Swerve: How the World Became Modern* (New York: W.W. Norton & Company, 2011). Compare two very different reviews of Greenblatt's thesis. A scathing one by Jim Hinch, "Why Greenblatt Is Wrong—and Why It Matters," in *Los Angeles Times*, December 1, 2012, and a very approving review by Dwight Garner, "An Unearthed Treasure That Changed Things," in *The New York Times*, September 27, 2011. Good history has a way of embarrassing a superficial apologetics of the secular too.

Sean Dorrance Kelly, *All Things Shining: Reading the Western Classics to Find Meaning in a Secular Age*, is another. It aims to rescue secularism from its nihilistic impulses by exploring Homer's polytheistic "shining world of the gods."[43] "Godlike Achilles" and Helen "shining among goddesses" evoke the sacred. Dreyfus and Kelly search in paganism for a rhetoric to enhance post-religious secularism with a made-up fake polytheism. The final words of the final chapter conclude its philosophical brief on secularity: "This contemporary Polytheistic world will be a wonderful world of sacred shining things."[44] How can philosophers be so sure about that? Have they read modern history? The hunger in the young for something that feels religious, despite the indifference to the local parish, is what inspires such a book. We are mistaken to condemn such searching. These are the modern relatives of the Athenians who listened to St. Paul speak at the Areopagus in Athens. This searching, and the "shining things" which are supposed to substitute for historical Christianity, is what the Courtyard of the Gentiles needs to understand.

Modernity is complex and conflicted, and it conflicts us accordingly, even if we are religious. The secular order of existence liberated Christianity from posing as a quasi-state and its temptations to religious violence in the name of God and the church. But it also emptied out our sanctuaries in the search for something else that feels religious in some way. Daniel Bell in the late 1970s predicted the exhaustion of substitute religions and a "return of the sacred."[45] Charles Taylor offers a reasonable hope for a new evangelization set into the conditions of a secular age. That's what I turn to next.

---

[43] Hubert Dreyfus and Sean Dorrance Kelly, *All Things Shining: Reading the Western Classics to Find Meaning in a Secular Age* (New York: Free Press, 2011). See the critical reviews of it by David Mikics, "All Whooshed Up," in *New Republic*, March 29, 2011; and Garry Wills, "Superficial & Sublime?," in *The New York Review of Books*, April 7, 2011.

[44] Dreyfus and Kelly, *All Things Shining*, 223.

[45] Bell, "The Return of the Sacred?," 349–54.

# Chapter 8

# The Secular Age

Throughout the book I have referred to the work of Charles Taylor on the modern self and the secular age. In my view, his approach provides a narrative key to unlock many of the issues the new evangelization seeks to address. The "moral space" for making sense of human purposes in a secular age is reduced by the secular imaginary to the immanent frame.

In this chapter, I focus on the nature of the secular age as Taylor understands it. To set his narrative apart from other interpretations of the secular, Taylor composed a new philosophical vocabulary for it. This more neutral phenomenology of the secular opens a space for productive exchange of views between religious and secular worldviews. To get a clear idea of what Taylor is driving at, go online and read the op-ed piece the *New York Times* columnist, David Brooks, wrote on *A Secular Age.*[1] In *How (Not) to Be Secular*, James K. A. Smith breaks down Taylor's philosophical jargon for novices. It includes a handy glossary of terms and neologisms. Future priests need to read what Taylor has written. They won't relish the reading assignments, however. His book *Sources of the Self: The Making of the Modern Identity* (1989), with index, runs to 601 pages. It took Taylor all of 874 pages to finish *A Secular Age* (2007). Doubtless, more introductions will

---

[1] See James K. A Smith, *How (Not) to Be Secular: Reading Charles Taylor* (Grand Rapids, MI: Eerdmans, 2014). In under 150 pages, this book is the best primer out there for pastors and laity eager for an idea of Taylor's reading of the secular age and the implications it holds for faith and religious life. For a quick overview of *A Secular Age* itself, see the Op-Ed "book report" that the conservative political columnist David Brooks wrote, "The Secular Society," in *The New York Times* (July 8, 2013).

appear showing Taylor's importance, not only for philosophical and political issues, but for the dialogue between belief and nonbelief parents and pastors need to have with the next generation.[2] Both *Sources of the Self* and *A Secular Age* have earned Taylor's work a major place in epistemology, moral theory, and political philosophy. A substantial body of secondary literature on his thinking has already appeared.[3]

Most philosophers teach in and write for the academy. The guild's discourse is inbred, obscure, and fragmented into various schools of thought (analytic philosophy, metaphysics, pragmatists, and Marxists, etc.). On the specific matter of religious outlooks, many philosophers are skeptics, agnostics, and atheists. A handful of prominent philosophers such as William James, G. E. M. Anscombe, Paul Ricoeur, Alasdair MacIntyre, and Charles Taylor take religion seriously. Like those named above, Taylor is one of a rare breed of contemporary philosopher who qualifies as a "public intellectual." His early involvement in Canadian politics sensitized him to the social repercussions of philosophical, moral, and religious ideas. America, too, has its public intellectuals like John Rawls, Susan Sontag, Michael Sandel, Gertrude Himmelfarb, Francis Fukuyama, and Michael Walzer. In France, one thinks of Emmanuel Levinas and Jacques Derrida. For many years, Jürgen Habermas in Germany was considered its leading public philosopher. John Milbank fills out the category for England. The ideas these thinkers write about are the current questions under debate in public life. They left the ivory tower. *A Secular Age* puts philosophy out in the street. Taylor writes philosophy like French

---

[2] The best philosophical introductions to Charles Taylor's thought can be found in Ruth Abbey, *Charles Taylor* (Princeton, NJ: Princeton University Press, 2000) and the collection of essays by Ruth Abbey, ed., *Charles Taylor* (New York: Cambridge University Press, 2004).

[3] *Social Research* 76, no. 4 (Winter 2009): "The Religious Secular Divide: The U.S. Case." *Modern Theology* 26, no. 3 (July 2010): "Symposium: Charles Taylor: *A Secular Age.*" *New Blackfriars* 91, no. 1036 (November 2010): "Symposium on Charles Taylor with His Responses." Carlos Colorado and Justin D. Klassen, eds., *Aspiring to Fullness in a Secular Age: Essays on Religion and Theology in the Work of Charles Taylor* (Notre Dame, IN: University of Notre Dame Press, 2014). Christopher Garbowski, Jan Hudzik, and Jan Klos, *Charles Taylor's Vision of Modernity: Reconstructions and Interpretation* (Newcastle upon Tyne: Cambridge Scholars Publishers, 2009). *The Taylor Effect: Responding to A Secular Age*, ed. Ian Leask with Eoin Cassidy (Newcastle upon Tyne: Cambridge Scholars Publishers, 2010).

and Russian novelists once wrote about life—in long narratives saturated with fascinating details and sudden revelations. The payoff only comes from a reader's patience.

## Who Is Charles Taylor?

Charles Taylor (b. 1931) put himself on the professorial track in philosophy as a young Rhodes Scholar at Oxford after finishing an undergraduate degree at McGill in Montreal.[4] At Oxford University, he received a doctorate in philosophy directed by Isaiah Berlin and G. E. M. Anscombe, the renowned expert in analytic philosophy and ethics. He returned to his alma mater in Montreal but soon found himself taken with Canadian politics, running four times for the House of Commons, once losing to Pierre Trudeau who eventually became prime minister. That experience gave him a taste for the practical moral issues in political debates. His roots growing up in Francophone Quebec drove the conflicts between culture and freedom home to him in a personal way.

Subsequent academic appointments took Taylor from McGill and the University of Montreal (1961) to the University of California, Berkeley (1974) before returning to Oxford (1976), where he was appointed to the academic chair once held by Berlin. Taylor has held distinguished lectureships at Queens University in Ontario (1980), the Centre for Developing Societies in New Delhi (1981), the Institute for Advanced Studies at Princeton (1981–1982), the University of Frankfurt (1984 and 1996), the Hebrew University in Jerusalem (1985), Stanford University (1992), and Yale University (1998). In 1998, he was named professor emeritus at McGill. In 2002, he went to Northwestern University as professor of law and philosophy. For purposes of the new evangelization it is important to add that in 2015 Charles Taylor delivered an address at the Vatican for a Courtyard of the Gentiles event, "The Piazza and the Temple." The church was beginning to recognize his importance on the issue of secularism and the

---

[4] See en.m.wikipedia.org: Charles Taylor (Philosopher). Further internet sources can be found on the websites for Taylor's Gifford Lectures (1999), the 2007 Templeton Prize (www.templeton.org), 2008 Kyoto Prize, 2015 John W. Kluge Prize awarded by the Library of Congress, and the 2016 Berggruen Prize. Some of these prizes carry an honorarium of one million dollars.

new evangelization. Cardinal Ravasi, prefect of the Pontifical Council for Culture, was a participant.

Such academic and cultural settings enriched Taylor's understanding of diversity around the globe. Raised in a bilingual and ecumenical home in Quebec, his upbringing prepared his appreciation for multiculturalism, mutual recognition across differences in worldviews, and the preservation of historic identities. And preserving a historical religious identity is crucial to all evangelization as much as expanding its range of influence and reforming its internal vigor. Taylor is a practicing Roman Catholic.

For his many contributions to contemporary intellectual life, Taylor has been honored as a Companion of the Order of Canada (1995) and Grand Officer of the Order of Quebec (2000). He delivered the distinguished Gifford Lectures at Edinburgh in 1999, which later became the basis for *A Secular Age* and for several smaller monographs.[5] In 2007, he was awarded the prestigious (and lucrative!) Templeton Prize for his contributions to philosophy, religion, and spirituality. For similar reasons, he became the recipient of the Kyoto Prize (the Japanese Nobel in the humanities), the John W. Kluge Prize of the Library of Congress, and the million-dollar Berggruen Prize. *Sources of the Self: The Making of the Modern Identity* (1989), *Modern Social Imaginaries* (2004), and *A Secular Age* (2007) constitute Taylor's overall assessment of our contemporary human condition.

No sooner had *A Secular Age* appeared than it became the subject of immediate philosophical and sociological discussion.[6] His philosophical reconstruction of secularity had an impact on theology as well.[7] Those who judged Taylor to be cutting off too much of the

---

[5] Charles Taylor, *Modern Social Imaginaries* (Durham, NC: Duke University Press, 2004) covers the same ground as chapter 4 in *A Secular Age* while chapter 8 builds on Taylor's earlier publication of the same title, *The Malaise of Modernity* (Concord, Ontario: Anansi Press Limited, 1991).

[6] William A. Barbieri Jr., ed., *At the Limits of the Secular: Reflections on Faith and Public Life* (Grand Rapids, MI: Eerdmans, 2014). Michael Warner, Jonathan VanAntwerpen, and Craig Calhoun, eds., *Varieties of Secularism in a Secular Age* (Cambridge, MA: Harvard University Press, 2010).

[7] Charles Taylor's work has helped to advance this recognition. In recent years, events sponsored by the Pontifical Council for Culture and the Courtyard of the Gentiles justify Taylor's significance as the church seeks to reach out to secular intellectuals and artists. His is now a marquee name when it comes to the question of secularization and religious faith. The issue of the meaning of secularization for faith,

supernatural cloth of belief chastised him for shortchanging Christianity in relation to the secular worldview. The positive critics led one to write an introduction to Taylor as a "survival manual" for those who still want to believe in our secularized situation.[8]

Taylor develops his thesis about secularity in five parts of *A Secular Age*, some of which constitute a book themselves. *A Secular Age* opens with the question every serious thinking Catholic is asking: Why is it so much harder to believe in God and in religion generally today than it was to believe five hundred years ago? Perhaps a brief look at what Taylor says can put that question into perspective. To do that, I'll try to summarize each of the five parts of Taylor's narrative of the secular age.

## How Does Charles Taylor Make His Case for a Secular Age?

Part 1 in *A Secular Age* is titled "The Work of Reform." A crucial concept in Taylor's approach—the evolution of what he calls "the modern moral order"—is the subject of this first section. By "reform," he means the continuous transformation of social frameworks and horizons that first got underway in Europe in the late Middle Ages. This process of transformative reform in horizons crossed its first frontier with thinkers like Hugo Grotius and John Locke, who devised concepts to preserve social order and peace following the breakdown of a unified Christian civilization. Unorthodox as they might have

---

which many in the social sciences and religion had taken for granted, has become one of those questions most alive now in scholarly research cutting across the humanities and social sciences. In 2011, the Institute for Advanced Studies in Culture at the University of Virginia held a conference titled "Secularism in the Late Modern Age: Between New Atheisms and Religious Fundamentalism" (January 28–29, 2011). The Council for Research in Values and Philosophy had sponsored a conversation in 2009 between Charles Taylor and Francis Cardinal George at the Catholic University of America on the topic of "Faith in a Secular Age" (November 19, 2009). The goal of the conversation was to stimulate further research on culture and religion worldwide. In the summer of 2016, the former students of Joseph Ratzinger, who have met with him since 1978 to discuss their mentor's approaches to theology in the context of current questions, gathered at Castel Gandolfo (Benedict XVI remained in seclusion at the Vatican) to consider the topic, "The Question of God in the Context of Secularization." The French medieval historian, Rémi Braque, delivered a paper.

[8] Smith, *How (Not) to Be Secular*, ix.

been in their beliefs by Catholic standards, both thinkers worked out concepts for safeguarding social harmony when confessional diversities after the Reformation, for obvious reasons, were no longer capable of doing so. This constituted the birthplace of the modern secular order within a religiously diversified Christian culture. The secular concept effectively terminated the ideal of the church herself serving as a "quasi-state." This is what started to change what Taylor calls the "conditions" for belief.

Part 2, "The Turning Point," tells us why something more was necessary to give full shape to the secular order than the ideas forged by Grotius and Locke in the seventeenth century. It also required that Protestantism diversify in new directions beyond the originating ideas of Luther, Calvin, and the other early sixteenth-century reformers like Ulrich Zwingli and John Knox. One path for Protestant reform was a diverse denominational Protestantism, but another was in Providential Deism. In this form of belief, the biblical God is reoutfitted as the creator of a cosmic order in the universe and the universal moral sense in human beings. Deist belief was powered by religious capital borrowed from historical Christianity, like the doctrine of creation. But it reworked that idea in such a way as to make the notion of redemption all but unnecessary. Gradually, then, the awe bound to the concept of biblical creator God began dissolving into an awesome Impersonal Order. What led to the admiration for impersonal order was not atheism, as we know it, but a spiritual admiration for the creator's genius to have made natural things as they were: not only to form the world but to plant moral instincts in the human heart, to arrange things so that social harmony among people was possible. The admiration for rational and moral order in the world was the feeling that sustained the religiosity of Deism. If the founding fathers of the United States could be said to follow a religious belief and have a religious sensibility at all, it was this. Grotius and Locke and latitudinarian Protestantism and Deism altogether, not scientific atheism, brought us to the secular age.

Part 3 of *A Secular Age* explains "The Nova Effect" in Taylor's philosophical chronology of the secular as it relates to religious belief. As it turns out, especially for the American context, this is a crucial development. Providential Deism did not put an end to religious exploration in culture as many still suppose. Post-Protestant Deism literally mushroomed in many different directions. The default linear narrative taught in high schools and colleges about scientific reason replacing religious belief and rendering it unbelievable is not historical at all. Both religious belief and secular unbelief germinated and flowered in many new ways after 1800. Late twentieth-century expressive individualism will be one of those flowers. By that point in Taylor's chronology of the secular, the religious aspects of the Nova Effect become largely disconnected from religious institutions while retaining its patina of spirituality. The liturgical and moral traditions of the churches can then be sloughed off or retained as needed.

The concept of the Nova Effect in the secular age allows Taylor to work out a complex and subtle genealogy of belief and unbelief. Each is unstable and potentially metastatic. Unlike Catholicism, Protestantism, and even Providential Deism, atheism will have nothing to do with dressing up religion as reasonable, much less holding fast to its confessional symbols. According to Taylor, the case atheism makes against all forms of religious belief, even the accommodated deistic types, eventually comes down to the following. The formal accusation, the secular indictment against religion, can be summarized as follows:

1. It offends against reason (harboring a role for mystery, proposing paradoxical notions, such as the God-man).

2. It is authoritarian (that is, it offends both freedom *and* reason).

3. It poses impossible problems of theodicy. Or it tries to avoid them; being often pusillanimous in proposing to compensate for the most terrible events in history in a future life; or else bowdlerizing in covering up how terrible these events are.

4. It threatens the order of mutual benefit:
    i. In mortifying the self: it inveighs against the body, sensual satisfaction, etc.
    ii. In mortifying others: in the ordinary case, as well, by its condemnation of the body and sensual satisfaction, but rising to an extreme in actual persecution (Calas case).
    iii. In threatening legitimate authority in societies dedicated to furthering the order of mutual benefit.[9]

___

[9] Taylor, *A Secular Age*, 305.

This is the atheist brief in a nutshell. The Deists, stuck with their anonymous deity of grandiose order and purpose, are put out of business along with Catholics. Religious belief comes to be replaced by a new atheistic humanism that considers all faith in something or someone higher than the human to be dishonest and unworthy of humanity's own dignity. The indictment atheists made against religious theodicy as a way of making sense of all human suffering has held up. But the escape into a secular humanism has not, or not completely.

In an important subsection of the Nova Effect which Taylor entitles "The Dark Abyss of Time," he shows how modern cosmology and evolutionary theory, together with the new social order, help to bring about a new "cosmic imaginary." The inconceivable magnitudes of time and space reduce the significance of human existence. Yet the same cosmos which diminishes human stature is incredibly beautiful in its very ignorance of us. This gives rise to a paradoxical spiritual effect. Atheism manages to morph into a cosmic mysticism as easily as it does into a secular humanism or an aggressive anti-religious program. Cosmology stimulates an Orphic poetics that can be grafted onto a blind materialism. The magnitudes of space are magnificent even if they reduce human life to an accident, much less deserving of a god's attention. Out of this paradoxical experience an atheist spirituality with roots in the nineteenth-century Romantic movement can come to life. A lyric poetry of blind nature, even more beautiful than order, arises to replace an older sense of the sacred. The Nova Effect has brought about a metaphysical search without the necessity of settling on an answer. Here's how Taylor puts it:

> Thus the salient feature of the modern cosmic imaginary is not that it has fostered materialism, or enabled people to recover a spiritual outlook beyond materialism, to return as it were to religion, though it has done both of these things. But the most important fact about it which is relevant to our enquiry here is that it has opened a space in which people can wander between and around all these options without having to land clearly and definitively in any one. In the wars between belief and unbelief, this can be seen as a kind of no-man's land; except that it has got wide enough to take on the character rather of a neutral zone, where one can escape the war altogether. Indeed, this is part of

the reason why the war is constantly running out of steam in modern civilization, in spite of the efforts of zealous minorities.[10]

The Nova Effect is the metaphysical real estate the American Nones live on. Peter Berger's description of modern believers and unbelievers in the Nova dispensation is that they hold their convictions "until further notice."[11] Hans Joas calls it "faith as an option."[12]

From this point forward, unbelief is powered by an exclusive humanism joined to a scientific explanation of nature supplemented, when necessary, by an Orphic poetry of the sublime unconscious cosmos. It would seem from this that science and cosmic spirituality can coexist peacefully on such terms. But mystical unbelief is as restless as religion. The divinely ordered conception of a moral structure in human nature that Providential Deism created starts coming apart in political revolutions. That polite version of Enlightenment humanism gets mocked by the radicals as a sellout. At the other end, Modernist poetics with Baudelaire starts exploring a demonic version of inverted-transcendence "from nether regions" of the psyche, far beneath the elevated and intoxicating lyricisms of Rilke. Between political revolutionaries and Modernist poetics, the Enlightenment domestication of religious intuitions goes awry. Nothing remains stable in Taylor's dialectics of belief and unbelief in the Nova Effect.

Part 4 of *A Secular Age* is called "Narratives of Secularization." In his introduction to the book, Taylor had distinguished three ways of seeing secularization. The first, until now, has served as the gold standard for it—the political narrative. Secular states are not religious states; they do not sponsor a religious doctrine nor take sides in religious disputes. Nor do secular states argue about public policy in terms of religious proofs or biblical texts. Secular states don't legitimate themselves or their laws on religious grounds. In that respect, certainly, America is a secular state. The references made to God in our founding documents are sentiments, not constitutional principles anyone can appeal to. Culture warriors fighting for monuments of

---

[10] Ibid., 351.

[11] Peter Berger, *A Far Glory: The Quest for Faith in an Age of Credulity* (New York: The Free Press, 1992), 68.

[12] Hans Joas, *Faith as an Option: Possible Futures for Christianity* (Stanford: Stanford University Press, 2014).

the Ten Commandments always miss this point. In an earlier section of the book, I explained the birth of the secular with Christian political theorists like Grotius and Locke as a form of rescue from religious fanaticisms and violence. If a secular state can be bad in many ways, a religious state in fact can be far worse. No one wants tribal religious conflict. All the same, a new political tribalism in secular America seems the closest a modern state can come to that in drawing down so much moral passion, intense hatreds, and outrage. The irrational impulses the Enlightenment once accused religion of harboring are now turning up in secular politics in the United States.

The second narrative of secularization is the scientific explanation of it. In this account, it was modern science, not the political state, that brought secularization into existence. The explanatory power of scientific reason is credited with driving out the dark age of religious belief, as if no serious scientist could possibly be religious. Taylor calls this the "subtraction" narrative of secularization. Subtract religion from the cultural equation and one is automatically left with a remainder we call science. But, if the Nova Effect has taught us anything, it is that things didn't develop that way at all. The substitution narrative is a pure bowdlerization of the facts of history. The subtraction narrative of secularization is what Taylor's philosophical phenomenology of secular consciousness seeks to replace. The truth is that religious developments in Western history paved the way for secularity by inspiring new moral sources for religious and secular humanisms. This leads Taylor to argue that the secular order changed the "conditions of belief" but not the possibility or the power of religious belief as such. Disenchantments with belief and periodic reenchantments go hand in hand. William James's classic, *The Varieties of Religious Experience*, in its own way, supports some of the claims of Taylor's Nova Effect.

As Taylor reads the secular story so far, the new moral order that arose in the eighteenth century gave rise to different religious responses. Setting aside the reactions of Baroque Catholicism, Providential Design made possible two future moves for belief. One was to baptize the new liberal order as being, in effect, the will of God for human beings. The free market was said to be guided by the mysterious workings of an "Invisible Hand." In secular democracy, the *vox populi* was understood as being, in fact, the *vox dei*. The second move away from Deism for Taylor took the path of denominational Christianity.

Here we see Christianity mobilize itself on its own terms without harboring the dream of a political authority as a bulwark for faith as in Catholic traditionalism. Denominational Protestantism plays off the new secular order differently—partly baptizing progress as divinely willed and partly deploying the full resources of freedom of choice in the religious spheres of life. In some branches of nineteenth-century Christianity, churches evolve into voluntary denominations. Anglicanism gives rise to Methodism. Churches exist for the members and by the will of the members. Such churches do not see themselves as divinely established but as religious membership organizations.

In their own way, Taylor claims, the new denominations replicate, in the religious sphere, the emerging moral order of mutual support and benevolence in civic life. Catholicism, by contrast, was still wedded in its vision to a descending hierarchical-Platonic order. The church was not a membership organization but a divinely established institution within which the individual believer found salvation. The American denominational imaginary was unavailable in Europe, where secularization first established itself without voluntary religious alternatives to compete with it.[13] Denominational Christianity in America tended to be socially progressive as well as optional. It often led the way in social moral reform in early opposition to slavery. On that score, at least, denominational religion was far ahead of the thinking of Thomas Jefferson.

Yet, this gradual unfolding dialectic of belief moves on. As the evidence mounts of technological advancement and social planning, some religious assumptions in denominationalism about human powerlessness and need for grace begin to seem less necessary.[14] In America, Taylor says, the two ideal types of mobilization—the civil society and denominational Christianity—came together. "The Republic secures the freedom of the churches; and the churches sustain the Godly ethos which the Republic requires."[15] When much later the cultural covenant between the liberal state and churchly virtue was sundered, Daniel Bell's contentions about the "cultural contradictions of capitalism" become apparent.[16] The antibourgeois ethos

---

[13] Taylor, *A Secular Age*, 450.

[14] Ibid., 452.

[15] Ibid., 453.

[16] Daniel Bell, *The Cultural Contradictions of Capitalism* (New York: Basic Books, 1976).

of the unstrained modern self pulls against the pessimism and grace in Calvinism that powered the capitalist spirit Max Weber had written about.[17] In this sense, two moves that seem so far apart, like Catholic Christendom and denominational Protestantism, become cousins. Taylor writes: "It is absolutely essential to much Christian apologetics from the French Revolution onwards, that the Christian faith is essential to the maintenance of civilizational order, whether this is defined in terms of the Modern Moral Order, or in terms of the earlier hierarchical complementarity."[18] Bell simplifies the logic. Take away ethical motives for sacrifice, motives religion has traditionally supplied, and then acquisitiveness itself will degenerate into an unabashed selfishness. The dialectic of secularization in Ratzinger and Habermas is that the secular moral order somehow needs "something like" religious intuitions and motives to power higher values against its worst inclinations. It's difficult to put that "something" into doctrinal terms, but it can be felt socially in communities inspired by public service and religious *agape*. Whether secular communities of deep moral intuition can supplant religious ones is yet to prove possible in a secular order of individualism. President Donald Trump claimed he did not even understand what George H. W. Bush meant by a "thousand points of light."

This is to say that Weber's thesis concerning a Calvinist ethic and Durkheim's thesis about a synthesis of culture and religion is confirmed. It is confirmed differently in an old Catholic version of throne and altar and in Protestant denominational-patriotic forms. This explains the continuing relevance of religion to civic life in secular America that it does not have in secular Europe. There was no Inquisition, Crusaders, or Pope Pius VII summoned to bless a presidential election in America.

In short, Taylor does not buy the linear accounts of secularization. He admits, of course, that modernization, urbanization, social pluralism, and scientific progress all changed the shape of the mental landscape. He sums it up:

> Positively, my aim is to suggest, in place of the supposed uniform and
> unilinear effects of modernity on religious belief and practice, another

---

[17] Max Weber, *The Protestant Ethic and the Spirit of Capitalism*, trans. Talcott Parsons (London: G. Allen & Unwin, 1930).

[18] Taylor, *A Secular Age*, 456.

model, in which these changes do, indeed, frequently destabilize older forms, but where what follows depends heavily on what alternatives are available or can be invented out of the repertory of the populations concerned. In some cases, this turns out to be new religious forms. The pattern of modern religious life under "secularization" is one of destabilization and recomposition, a process which can be repeated many times.[19]

This is another way of thinking about what has been and is continuing to take place in Catholicism under the auspices of the new evangelization.

Using the nineteenth-century parish situation in Catholic France as the main reference point, *A Secular Age* argues that reforming zealotry by clergy tried separating normative Catholic doctrine from French folk religion and festivals and that, in addition, the state itself also bore down on them. Considering his reform and mobilization thesis, Taylor calls the whole effort of centralized consolidation under Pius IX a "mission impossible" as compared with the denominationalism that kept religion vital in America.[20] Centralization through strong institutions are not without value in business, politics, or religion, but they can work at cross-purposes to local creativity in all three spheres. The parish, as Pope Francis insists, is crucial to the evangelizing flexibility of the diocesan local church. The utmost pastoral freedom possible in canon law ought to be extended to local pastoral imagination.

In America, the different Protestant and immigrant Roman Catholic mobilization efforts reached down into the middle and lower classes where spiritual life, moral self-discipline, patriotism, and a consolidated sense of being together convinced them that the modern moral order would collapse without them. "One nation under God" was more than an empty political piety. Catholic sanctuaries displayed the Vatican flag and Old Glory together. It was unremarkable.

Such patriotic religiosity lasted until roughly 1960, when it began coming apart. What Taylor calls "The Age of Authenticity" was being born. He already treated this theme in *Sources of the Self* and in his monograph *The Malaise of Modernity*, based on his radio lectures in

---

[19] Ibid., 461.
[20] Ibid., 465.

Canada. But his treatment here is different. In a secular age, any religious belief if taken seriously needs to be "owned" in a personal way by the one who subscribes to it. It must feel authentic as an expression of a person's inner self-identity. The issue of individualism usually presented as the bane of a communal religiosity has finally arrived. In a secular age, people think of religious belief as serving one's already-chosen self-definition. It is not supposed to challenge it.

Individualism has taken many forms since John Locke first gave it philosophical and political articulation. One form is an "expressive individualism" dear to artists and poets. The age of mobilization brings expressive individualism to religious life. One chooses the religion one wants and that suits one's authentic sense of self. The sexual revolution is part of expressive individualism and emblematic of the youth culture of the 1960s, which also included utopian aspirations for social equality and interracial community. The ideal of personal authenticity linked to expressive individualism embedded itself deeply into the general culture. Like any value, the new value of individual authenticity can be trivialized.

One of the trivial forms was characterized as the "higher selfishness" of IT culture in David Brooks's *BoBos in Paradise*.[21] A bohemian and a bourgeois set of different values (the *BoBos*) mingled together. Another version of this phenomenon of blending opposites in culture is the "Crunchy Cons" Rod Dreher writes about who eat yogurt and granola between visits to brokerage houses.[22] Taylor points out how expressivist authenticity has trivialized the abortion debate in the slogan of "choice." Can this term associated with a consumer lifestyle, and without any context or qualification much less moral distinctions, manage the differences between jeans, vacations, careers, and unborn fetuses? Hardly. But it embodies self-expressivist autonomy, so how can one say they're against "choice." The banners of pro-life protagonists accordingly say, "Choose Life." Choice is what the age of authenticity instinctively understands.

[21] David Brooks, *BoBos in Paradise: The New Upper Class and How They Got There* (New York: Simon & Schuster, 2001).

[22] Rod Dreher, *Crunchy Cons: How Birkenstocked Burkeans, Gun-Loving Organic Gardeners, Evangelical Free-Range Farmers, Hip Homeschooling Mamas, Right-Wing Nature Lovers, and Their Diverse Tribe of Countercultural Conservatives Plan to Save America (or at Least the Republican Party)* (New York: Crown Forum, 2006).

The two different choruses cheering or bemoaning the age of authenticity, in Taylor's view, only keep the conversation dumbed down. There is no returning to the 1950s family as represented in comedies of that era where women prepared supper dressed in high heels and passengers boarded planes wearing suits and hats as if they were attending a concert. But much has also been lost in the liberation that hasn't yet been recovered, if it ever can be. Secular moral space in the meantime has created other options.

Taylor understands the moral revolution starting in the 1960s as the discovery of the new sense of sacredness along with the moral relativism criticized by the church and many commentators. Hans Joas and José Casanova agree that the traditional religious concept of the sacred has migrated in secular culture to human rights.[23] The defense of human rights is felt in a secular culture and religious one as well as a sacral action. Authenticity changes the notion of what religion is supposed to feel like. "Where before there was lots of passionate belief, and the life and death issues were doctrinal; now there comes to be a widespread feeling that the very point of religion is being lost in the cool distance of even impeccable intellectual orthodoxy. One can only connect with God through passion."[24] A catechetical faith will never be enough alone to power missionary discipleship.

J. S. Mill caught the early spirit of this strain of modernity when he wrote: "Pagan self-assertion is better than Christian self-denial."[25] It spoke to the sense that one owes it to oneself to transgress the rules and that's what made the sexual revolution different from plain old hedonism. Feminism's embrace of sexual equality puts college men and women on equal footing for such obligatory transgression. No one is hurt when both are equal in asserting their right for pleasure. Birth control liberates women from fear of pregnancy, so they can explore their own sexual needs like men always did. The old gender breakwater is breached by new values of equality and personal au-

---

[23] See José Casanova, "The Secular, Secularizations, Secularisms," in *Rethinking Secularism*, ed. Craig Calhoun, Mark Juergensmeyer, and Jonathan Van Antwerpen (Oxford: Oxford University Press, 2011), 65–66. Hans Joas, *Faith as an Option: Possible Futures for Christianity* (Stanford: Stanford University Press, 2014), 46–47.

[24] Taylor, *A Secular Age*, 488.

[25] Quoted in Ibid., 492.

thenticity, but even that was still held hostage to the sexual economics of power—that is, until the emergence in 2018 of the "Me Too" movement's revelations of sexual harassment by powerful men in Hollywood and journalism.

In responding to this shift in cultural self-understanding built on a new idea of authenticity, Taylor thinks Christianity retooled a puritanical ethic of sexual self-denial and abstinence. The unintended effect of that was to associate religion again with the repression of what many people had come to regard as normal instincts. The sacrament of confession eventually suffers a decline. People dislike a prurient clergy prying into their private lives. In the end, sexuality itself is all but de-ethicized as it is more and more medicalized as reproductive health. Thus, authenticity creates new values and trivializes them at once.

In short, Taylor claims that different kinds of values were linked together in the sexual revolution: the body is good as are its natural feelings, including sex, which should be expressed as long as men and women are equal partners in pleasure; the most liberating forms of sexual experience are most likely those that are still forbidden by society; and then personal identity becomes almost totally bound up with sexuality. LBGT morphs into LGBTQ and so on to include more sexual diversities deserving equal rights and respect.

Taylor wisely points out that there are many stumbling blocks along this path of diversified sexual identities: first, human sexual life is so much more complicated than the mutual satisfaction theory of sexual expression recognizes; second, transgressive sexual experience is not only deeply unstable as such but ends up trumping true intimacy between equals; third, annihilating all gender differences is probably impossible. Sexual utopias as much as political utopias backfire in strange ways. Transgenderism cannot be settled rationally if sexual self-definition is sacred. If insurance companies begin to deny coverage for gender reassignment procedures, on grounds that medical and psychiatric evidence in individual cases is lacking, the current political favor for this may suffer de-legitimation especially as regards children.

"Religion Today" concludes Taylor's chapter on narratives of secularization following his discussions of the "Age of Mobilization" to the "Age of Authenticity." What has the cultural search for authenticity done to Roman Catholicism and to Protestant denominationalism according to Taylor? How is the religious instinct and spiritual quest in human beings to be understood today? The short answer is that something called spirituality has emerged as the alternative to institutional religion. In the age of authenticity, religion as seculars saw from the outside and as youth saw it from within was largely about forbidden acts especially in the area of sexuality. Moreover, the formal structures of religious authority turn spiritual searchers off. The catechism provides the orthodox answer to every question, so to speak, in advance. Searchers, on the other hand, want to feel the questions and relish the freedom of possible responses. Religious searchers will not find the truth they say they desire, church authorities might say, but only what appeals to them at any given moment. In the modern context, others will emphasize how the quest for personal authenticity actually trivializes spirituality. Daniel Bell captures it by arguing that seekers of religious experience move on incessantly to a "new nostrum."[26]

Taylor holds there's a vast middle space between seriously belonging to a church with a religious tradition and indulging in frivolous spiritual fads. Practices, not catechesis and theological doctrine as such, will offer both searchers and dwellers alternative paths to satisfy longings for depth—pilgrimages, retreats, social outreach, protest movements, contemplation, visits to places like Lourdes or Rome, prayer groups, etc. The desire for experiences that feel spiritual and authentic can lead to worse things than drifting aimlessly along. People can settle on dangerous paths. Remember Jonestown in 1978, known first as the Peoples Temple Agricultural Project, which ended in a mass "revolutionary" suicide in Guyana. There are, however, healthy forms of searching encouraged by the church in its World Youth Days and papal visitations where huge crowds of dwellers and searchers assemble. Others may seek spiritual peace in solitary ways: following the Camino de Santiago in Spain or hiking the arduous seven-hundred-mile Shikoku pilgrimage to eighty-eight temples in Japan in search of Buddhist enlightenment. Social philosophers look for terminology to describe these phenomena, like believing without belonging or a "diffusive Christianity."[27]

---

[26] Daniel Bell, "The Return of the Sacred? The Argument on the Future of Religion," in *The Winding Passage: Essays and Sociological Journeys 1960–1980* (Cambridge: Abt Associates, 1980), 348.

[27] Taylor, *A Secular Age*, 518–19.

Secularization theory can explain something of the decline in traditional belief and practice better than it can the disenchantments with the secular order that make religious experiences attractive. It was Pope Benedict who extended an invitation to agnostic and atheist seculars to come sit in Notre-Dame Cathedral in Paris before what they hold as an absent and nameless divinity. Pope Francis wants the church doors left open for the seeker in search of spiritual respite. These can seem romantic and unrealistic sentiments in a world as violent as ours, but they are dim recognitions of the need to look at evangelization in new ways.

John Wolffe wrote this about secularization in Great Britain, which could just as easily apply to many Catholic parishes today:

> A vague non-doctrinal kind of belief: God exists; Christ was a good man and an example to be followed; people should lead decent lives on charitable terms with their neighbours, and those who do so will go to Heaven when they die. Those who suffer in this world will receive compensation in the next. The churches were regarded with apathy rather than hostility: their social activities made some contribution to the community. Sunday School was felt to provide a necessary part of the upbringing of children, and the rites of passage required formal religious sanction. Association was maintained by attendance at certain annual and seasonal festivals, but weekly participation in worship was felt to be unnecessary and excessive. Women and children were more likely than men to be regularly involved, but this did not imply that adult males were hostile; merely—it was surmised—that they tended to see themselves as the main breadwinners, and felt that women should therefore represent the family's interest in the religious arena. The emphasis was on the practical and communal rather than on the theological and the individual.[28]

Grace Davie's term for this phenomenon is "vicarious religion."[29] Religion is something your mom and dad valued and perhaps still value, and one day you might possibly have need of it when you're at the end of your rope, when planning a marriage or a funeral. Possibly, but not always. Entrepreneur "providers" of "religious-like" services at funeral parlors or wedding chapels show what happens to religion in commercial cultures. You buy it when you need it.

[28] Ibid., 519.
[29] Ibid., 522.

America, as many surveys have shown, is the one Atlantic culture that stands as an exception to the general rule of secularization theory, namely, that modernization by itself leads to the decline and disappearance of religion. It's not enough to say America is a culture of immigrants and therefore different from European society. The real factor is that American churches are perfectly equipped for "the age of mobilization" with denominationalism anchored to civic patriotism. In addition, religious freedom and the separation of church and state removed the thorn of privilege and power that haunted European Christendom. Religion remains a choice you made in American Protestantism. Increasingly that is the case for Catholics as well. Finally, the expansive ecumenical context in America provided more options for those interested in religion—traditional churches, nondenominational communities, sects, world religions, and new cults (the list goes on)—so it has been perfectly positioned for the age of authenticity.[30] Such religious diversity and options have not been the experience in Europe, at least until now with Islam. "Even French atheists," Taylor observes, "are a trifle horrified when religion doesn't take the standard Catholic form that they love to hate."[31]

Though he is not entirely satisfied with this way of explaining the continuing force of religion in American life, Taylor does believe that when religion is seen, not only as antiscientific and premodern, but also as "the enemy of authenticity," some powerful cards are stacked against it.[32] Pope Francis is appealing as a religious figure because he seems humanly authentic in his spirituality of poverty and simplicity and compassion for others. He was the unknown cardinal from Buenos Aires at the 2013 papal conclave who paid his own hotel bill.

"Narratives of Secularization" sets the table for the concepts Taylor introduces in *A Secular Age*, part 5, "Conditions of Belief." The secular age is about new conditions for religious belief that are different from the conditions which made it plausible for others in the Hellenistic period, in European medieval cultures, and after the Renaissance. Not the beliefs as such, but the social and cultural conditions that make their presentation seem plausible or implausible for people

[30] Ibid., 527.
[31] Ibid., 529.
[32] Ibid., 530.

whose default epistemology is scientific and whose sense of identity is linked to authenticity is what's changed. This is the crux of secularization. The ideal of authentic belief is hardly new. Luther made it central to his idea of faith in Christianity in 1517. Secularity has pushed Christianity further toward authentic belief.

From the secular side, people report vague feelings of emptiness which incline them to seek relief in some way. Daniel Bell describes the disillusionment of cults to satisfy this search for fullness: "But the deception—and the undoing—of such experience—however 'sincere' and anguished like so many 'enthusiastic' quests—occurs because the search rests basically on some idea of a *magical* moment, and on the power of magic. Like some headache remedy, it gives you fast, fast, fast belief, if not relief. And it is no accident that the half-life of these movements is so short and that the heteroclites move on ceaselessly, to a new nostrum."[33]

Secularization can take the searchers for spiritual fullness in other directions as well, like being super fit and healthy, saving whales, building wells in Africa, attempting extraordinarily dangerous adventures in the wild, practicing medicine at the site of Ebola outbreaks. Such secular pursuits go beyond the "pitiful comforts" Nietzsche scorned in bourgeois culture. There is an aristocratic dimension in these thymotic approaches to life that transcends the satisfaction of simple instincts. If non-religious secularism admires anything, it admires excellence—prowess in athletics, artistic brilliance, inventors and explorers, entrepreneurs, philanthropic generosity. This is what figures like Warren Buffett and Bill Gates admire—the transcendence of the ordinary, of a self-satisfied individualism. Successful professional athletes in America today routinely establish foundations to fund hospitals and schools for children. The secular age is not the age of abortionists only but of spiritual humanists of this sort.

The final part of *A Secular Age* is a diagnosis of the state of living in a secular world where the question of human flourishing remains very much alive. The conflicted conditions of human existence are "cross-pressured" by the religious and secular humanisms at once. Human experience is far too uncanny and paradoxical for either the

---

[33] Bell, "The Return of the Sacred?," 348.

religious or secular worldview to grant the other position no grounds for its case. Cross-pressured positions are inherently unstable. A person can be tipped from one stance to the other depending on how a life unfolds. Both options tug at the secular self and the believer. Neither position has an open-and-shut case.

In a chapter called "The Unquiet Frontiers of Modernity," Taylor resumes the discussion of our conflicted modernity and self-identity from the final pages of *Sources of the Self*. To shed some light on the "cross-pressured" and "unquiet" human condition in late modernity, he turns to conversion stories. In the 1999 Gifford Lectures which he delivered in Edinburgh, Scotland, Taylor discussed William James's *Varieties of Religious Experience*, yet did not include that discussion in the book he wrote on those lectures, *A Secular Age*. He published them later in a small monograph, *Varieties of Religion Today*. He concludes that small book asking if William James was correct in thinking that religious experience would permanently float between and among spiritual options in what sociologists call a "post-Durkheimian" world where religion is "unhooked" from culture. "Many people will find their spiritual home in churches, for instance, including the Catholic church. In a post-Durkheimian world, this allegiance will be unhooked from that to a sacralized society (paleo style) or some national identity (neo style); but it will still be a collective connection."[34] The conditions for belief have changed.

Taylor, then, notes something that traditional and conservative Catholics make about the seekers, searchers, and drifters in the world of religious experience, but upends it. "Doesn't every dispensation have its own favored forms of deviation? If ours tends to multiply somewhat shallow and undemanding spiritual options, we shouldn't forget the spiritual costs of various kinds of forced conformity: hypocrisy, spiritual stultification, inner revolt against the Gospel, the confusion of faith and power, and even worse. Even if we had a choice, I'm not sure we wouldn't be wiser to stick with the present dispensation."[35] The present dispensation, of course, is the secular age.

---

[34] Charles Taylor, *Varieties of Religion Today: William James Revisited* (Cambridge, MA: Harvard University Press, 2003), 112.
[35] Ibid., 114.

The shift in human consciousness that marks the secular age tips interpretation toward what Taylor calls "the immanent frame." This option did not exist five hundred years ago. The immanent frame is what science, technology, and commerce, among other human pursuits, must take for granted. These inform us about the reality of the world that is "out there" as an objective fact independent of human preferences and desires. In the immanent frame, the goal of thinking and action is to have whatever representations of reality we carry in our heads correspond exactly and mathematically to what's out there. Inside our heads, so the theory goes, the brain is building a map of reality that should be made to correspond as closely as possible to the objective realities that are independent of desire. So, science, mathematics, technology, money, and hospital MRIs inform us what's out there as a fact. This is the real world of facts. Religious interpretations of reality, as far as the immanent frame is concerned, do not reflect realities that exist "out there." The best that can be said of them is such religious discourses bring consolations; the worst is that they deal in illusions or convey a purely imaginative construct that cannot be made to match the facts. What Taylor wants his readers to understand is that religious maps of reality are not like the maps the sciences use. More than that, the epistemology of the sciences fails to understand how the human being actually builds a meaningful world for herself or himself.

Taylor's argument here hinges on assessing a set of epistemological presuppositions in the sciences which ignore the undeniable fact that even the objective world that is "out there" is one human beings impart meaning to because something in that world matters to them. An oil man naturally sees oil and profits beneath the arctic tundra. The environmentalist sees wilderness and unspoiled beauty. Which is more important to us? The human mind interprets the meaning of facts. Travel and multicultural experiences are realities that tell us how differently objective facts can be weighed in different cultures. Being born is a fact, but the meaning of our natality goes far beyond the objective physiology of obstetrics.

This commonsense but naive epistemology of the mind as a map of objective facts makes atheism feel like the only coherent position since God is not an empirical fact alongside other facts in the world. But, that doesn't make the idea and experience of the divine an illusion. But if human boundary experiences of uncanny paradox can tip some people toward religious belief and others to a rejection of it in secular belief, there is more going on with atheism than scientific objectivity. Taylor explains how modern atheism ironically began to present itself not just as the no-nonsense objective take on reality, but as something morally courageous, even heroic. Nonbelief starts to strike some people as a very brave and honest way to live by letting go of what seems like make-believe crutches in the acceptance of a godless world, yet with great passion to make things better, knowing full well there's nothing beyond awaiting us after death. In this perspective, religious individuals are not only in denial about objective reality, they are afraid and unheroic. So, it's not just cosmology and evolutionary theory that propel some people out of religious faith. It's the feeling that atheism takes far more guts and nerve than belief.

As Taylor understands it, our condition in the secular age about the possibility of belief comes down to three factors that come together in a fourth: (1) believing is intellectually dishonest; (2) once religion started to wane, humanism had a chance to flourish independently on its own; (3) people needed God when they couldn't explain how things really worked; and (4) science and technology have pulled the rug out from underneath the explanations of religion.[36] An exclusive humanism buys into all four of these arguments. But the more religion still survives in advanced scientific cultures, the less the arguments sound completely persuasive. Maybe something else might be going on.

At this point, Taylor argues that an exclusive or secular humanism can take very different forms based on some of these same atheistic principles. Alongside the positivist atheism born of progress in scientific understanding there is the atheism of someone like Jean-Paul Sartre, fascinated with communism, and the more stoical atheism of Albert Camus. The atheism of Nietzsche creates a chasm in meaning described as nihilism, which only the blind will to power in human beings is capable of bridging. The elite and civilized atheistic humanism that was supposed to issue from the end of religion easily turns to a darker barbarism by the very same logic. It makes no more sense to assume that a passionate secularism is invariably humane, moral, and ecumenical than to assume, in every case, that religious belief is

---

[36] Taylor, *A Secular Age*, 573–74.

such. All humanisms have the capacity to turn narrow, hateful, xeno-phobic, and racial. Eugenics saw itself as a humanism.

On the other hand, honesty demands that people of faith admit that the reasons humanists adduce for renouncing religion have a certain plausibility to them. Perhaps they're right that religious faith is an illusion. After all, the trope of a brutally honest and heroic athe-ism has secured its status in the secular social imaginary. Religion can then be considered by some of the public as a stage in human evolution we have slowly left behind. But, if the evidence of history and politics matter, aren't secular humanists forced to contend with a struggle interior to different humanisms which is forced to appeal to values which transcend facts? Taylor thinks an exclusive secular humanism cannot provide the objective grounds for the values it admires. Nihilism must be considered a perfectly honest consequence of a humanism that is forced to deny *a priori* that there is any possi-bility of a transcendent grounding for certain values. Taylor bases his case on Isaiah Berlin's practical arguments about values carried by long traditions which allow developments, of course, without on that account collapsing into a pure relativism.

All along, Taylor is trying to move the argument between belief and nonbelief from mere "spins" on immanent or transcendent worldviews, which apodictically claim there's no sense to the other position, toward transparent interpretations or what he calls "takes" on life's meaning and the grounds for it. The "open spaces," as he calls them, between these two interpretations of ultimate reality make the "two takes" on life's deep meaning possible, somewhat plausible yet always to some degree contestable. Taylor's concept of the "open space" of world horizon interpretation comes from William James, who refers to objective experiences that can tip people toward belief or away from it.[37] Taylor rejects "closed world structures" where an exclusive humanism can nest rather arrogantly in favor of a mag-nanimous agnosticism, which more closely fits the ambiguous char-acter of the open spaces all people in a secular age inhabit. In three subsequent chapters, Taylor examines the "cross-pressures" that cannot be forced into stock atheist or religious narratives.

Much of his treatment of religious dilemmas hinges on what to make of another humanist argument that religious belief can place

[37] See William James, *The Varieties of Religious Experience* (Harmondsworth: Penguin, 1982).

impossible demands on human beings to rise above themselves. The price for this, the humanist argues, is to deny or even mutilate normal bodily impulses. The history of the Christian approach to human sexuality in hyper-Augustinian pessimism is an example. A mutilation of erotic impulse doesn't necessarily cease with quests for sexual perfection because darker regions of sacrifice and violence seem to lodge themselves in the same irrational registers. Sexuality remains altogether ambiguous in this respect which accounts for the fact that the liberated search for sexual expression beyond norms easily brings violence in its train.

On the matter of sexuality often seen as religion's Achilles heel when it comes to exclusive humanism, Taylor holds that the irrational links between human desire and violence are far from well understood. Only a deeper and more comprehensive humanism that seeks the sources of violence in human nature as such, not in religion necessarily, will take us closer to the truth. Laying the problem of violence in human nature at the doorstep of religion is essentially dishonest. The scapegoat mechanism of Rene Girard's anthropology of violence teaches us that.[38]

For Taylor, the process of reform in Christianity, one decisive strand of which was the Protestant Reformation, is the main plot "of which 'secularization' is only an offshoot."[39] Protestant churches in America diversified into denominational movements, such as happened with American Methodism. Such religious enthusiasm continued through the mid-twentieth century, when religious belief seriously began declining in Europe while in America it managed to hold its own. With the dawning of the 1960s, the search for authenticity has stalled out religious progress in the mainstream churches.

To make his larger case about religious options in a secular age, Taylor tries redefining what is meant by religion. If it is meant to be the twentieth-century equivalent of thirteenth-century Catholicism with a lively belief in supernatural happenings as manifested in miracles, then there is no doubt that religion has declined in the secular age. But perhaps religion is more than beliefs in the miraculous and closer to "a wide range of spiritual and semi-spiritual beliefs; or if you cast your net even wider and think of someone's religion

---

[38] René Girard, *The Scapegoat*, trans. Yvonne Frecerro (Baltimore, MD: Johns Hopkins University Press, 1989).

[39] Taylor, *A Secular Age*, 424.

as the shape of their ultimate concern, then indeed, one can make a case that religion is as present as ever."[40] The meaning of grace in the theology of divine-human encounter exceeds the range of a miraculous supernatural.

The core of standard secularization theory is that in time people will just lose interest in religion. That's the truth behind the common experience of religious indifference. Once religious literacy and sensibility become so attenuated by the lack of practice and cultivation, the theory is that people will just forget all about it. After religion's role as a transcendent legitimation of social and political order is no longer required, religion would dry up in public life. This Durkheimian view of secularization holds that without strong social buttressing religion will pass away. Taylor disagrees with that premise, arguing that religious feelings and intuitions are in some respects universal and independent of society. Is St. Francis of Assisi delusional because he is religiously exceptional, or does he sense something real beyond the life of a wealthy cloth merchant? Is there something about religion that intuits a certain depth in the very nature of things and human relationships that cannot be reduced to economics or biology? In important ways, religious individuals who are grasped by that depth wind up with a mystical "take" on human experience. Jesus' pacifism can seem politically naïve until figures like Nelson Mandela in South Africa and Martin Luther King in America resurrect what Paul Ricoeur once called the "awkwardly historical" gesture of nonviolence.[41] In short, religious symbols survive the world which gave birth to them to find contemporary expressions in modern and secular contexts.

To summarize Taylor's long "master reform narrative" of the secular age, religion has continued to remain vital and creative despite the predictions that secularization would be its undoing. This creativity was not uniform at all. Classical Protestantism diversified until some vectors embraced Providential Deism to reconcile faith with the modern moral order of reason and human freedom. No sooner had that happened than the Nova Effect multiplied many possible religious and non-religious options. One could embrace forms of denominational Protestantism in America or choose agnosticism or atheism or some version of secular humanism or remain

---

[40] Ibid., 427.
[41] See the discussion on nonviolence by Paul Ricoeur in *History and Truth*.

Roman Catholic or simply wander among all the options in a continuous search for answers. Providential Deism morphs into a rationalist agnosticism with Kant before mushrooming into religious agnosticism and atheism. The nineteenth century begins with Ludwig Feuerbach's anthropological projection of God and ends with Nietzsche's humanistic nihilism. Nietzsche's death of God was meant to shock the elite despisers of religion as much as the devout, by announcing that the religious foundations of a genteel humanism were buckling under culture. After having drawn down the moral deposits in European culture left by centuries of Christian faith, how would liberal thought go about replenishing them when only power was left to settle values? Nietzsche doesn't just scandalize the pious; he cuts a huge assumption away from the humanist credo. This humanism is ungrounded in anything deeper or more stable than the markets or the political party in power. The deeper that science explores the human genome, the more it finds elementary particles of matter, even junk genes from Neanderthal ancestors. Where does human dignity lie? In the body's bio-chemical proteins? The very idea of human dignity looks suspicious.

The standard view of secularization is that the fading of religious belief started with elites who clearly saw the world for what it was before disbelief began spreading from them to the masses. Taylor sees the secular age as another stage in his master reform narrative, which stretches back as far as the sixteenth century. Religion is always embedded in a culture, and when culture changes from a hierarchical imaginary to a modern moral imaginary of freedom and rights, the religious spirit adjusts by drawing from its storehouse of wisdom new resources for understanding the enigma of human life in the world. Roman Catholicism has all the tools it needs in its toolbox to do this in and for a secular age. We only need to use them.

## The Secular Age and the New Evangelization

For well over a decade, significant developments have been taking place in the church's understanding of and dialogue with secularism. Earlier on, I mentioned that the year before Cardinal Ratzinger was elected pope, he and Jürgen Habermas met in Munich to address the "dialectics of secularization." The secular itself was evolving from a stance of arrogance to the realism of the post-secular. Ratzinger acknowledged that critical reason had an important role to play in identifying and curing the pathologies in religion. Violence was the one he mentioned. After clergy abuse, one could add hypocrisy. Habermas, for his part, admitted that religious intuitions about truth, meaning, and moral value could enlighten secular reason in the future as they had in the past.

The Pontifical Council for Culture has carefully surveyed the diversity of modern unbelief, ranging from atheism to agnosticism to mere passive religious indifference. The religious and secular worlds are cross-pressured worlds. The members and consultors to that pontifical council, meeting in plenary session in 2008 under its president, Cardinal Gianfranco Ravasi, addressed the topic "The Church and the Challenge of Secularisation." Benedict XVI offered brief remarks afterward where he drew attention once again to themes he had often mentioned in his diagnosis of secularism: the loss of a sense of God as if God's existence did not matter, the arrogance of reason that rejects faith, a barren cult of the individual, Western materialism, and a vague search for spiritual experience. He worried about cultural secularization invading all aspects of human life and even affecting the church itself. How was it possible to move beyond the impasse of such characterizations? In 2010, Benedict XVI gave his blessing to the Courtyard of the Gentiles movement where seculars, if they wish, can sit in silence in a church before an absent God.

On March 6, 2015, the Pontifical Council for Culture co-sponsored "The Piazza and the Temple—A Dialogue with Charles Taylor."[42] The aim of the conference was to find ways for believers and nonbelievers to coexist in equal freedom in secular society. A modest aim, perhaps, but very telling regarding conditions favorable to the new evangelization and religious freedom. This dialogue was defined by the Pontifical Council for Culture as a "postsecular dialogue" favoring a redefinition of secularization without religious prejudices. Prior to that event, the Pontifical Gregorian University in Rome and the Council for Research in Values and Philosophy jointly sponsored a

---

[42] See www.cultura.va: "The Piazza and the Temple—A Dialogue with Charles Taylor." Also, *Renewing the Church in a Secular Age: Holistic Dialogue and Kenotic Vision*, ed. Charles Taylor, José Casanova, George F. McLean, and Joao J. Vila-Cha (Washington, DC: The Council for Research in Values and Philosophy, 2016), 1. Charles Taylor's paper is titled, "Authenticity: The Life of the Church in a Secular Age."

meeting, "Renewing the Church in a Secular Age: Holistic Dialogue and Kenotic Vision," where Charles Taylor's monumental study, *A Secular Age*, was prominently discussed.

If there were such a genre as a philosophical catechism suitable to the new evangelization, Taylor's phenomenological narrative of the secular age qualifies. In my opinion, the ongoing debate about the secular age is a prologue for a fundamental and pastoral theology capable of supporting missionary discipleship.

The secular world is religiously unmusical in many ways. If the bells ring in European churches for the noon *Angelus* today, the tourists sipping coffee in cafes make no associations with the angel's annunciation to Mary. It's a quaintly romantic tolling of bells. Secular time comes as close to the temporality of sacred time when a funeral cortege bears the body of a slain American president down Pennsylvania Avenue or the sirens wail in Israel in remembrance of the Shoah (Holocaust). Taylor claims that modern consciousness is "disembedded" in culture because the secular world is "disenchanted."

Charles Taylor agrees with Marcel Gauchet's assessment that secularity in a certain way led to "the end of religion."[43] By that he only means that overpowering religious sensibility that the Christian faith conveyed in European public life for more than a millennium has passed. A modern believer must summon up that sensibility in other ways. But Taylor adds something to Gauchet that will be crucial for his argument in *A Secular Age* and for the new evangelization. The disenchanting secular age does not end "personal religion"; nor does it eliminate the effective presence of "religion in public life."[44] In effect, secularity, as Taylor defines it, has made possible a more authentic personal quest for religious experience even as it concludes religion's previous hegemony. In that respect, he anticipates a new social location for religious faith in the secular world, yes, vastly trimmed back from what it once was in medieval Europe, but still empowered by strong personal belief and corresponding concerns for the quality of human public life. Speaking in sociological terms, religion now exists in a post-Durkheimian dispensation where religious practice has become optional and detached from larger cultural scaffolding that both presupposed and that supported it in the past.

---

[43] Taylor, *Modern Social Imaginaries*, 187.
[44] Ibid.

Religious faith and practice is optional now and personal. It is unavoidably ecumenical and even, in some sense, "trans-confessional." We Catholics are the inheritors of all religious traditions. Eugen Rosenstock-Huessy foresaw in the mid-twentieth century that the task of Christianity in the next millennium would be to reconnect itself with its Jewish roots. That has already begun in biblical studies as well as in interreligious Jewish-Christian dialogue. Analogously, the church's other challenge will be to reconnect men and women, whom Genesis sees equally and conjointly as the "image of God." It needs to do this on the basis of a better archeology of its own traditions and on the secular premise of equal human rights. In the end, the new evangelization for a secular age means taking better account of the new conditions for belief today as someone like Charles Taylor has diagnosed them. It also requires proposing from within theology more thoroughgoing reforms for the Catholic Church, not only because of clergy abuse and other crises in the church, but because of the Gospel itself and the unexhausted power of the figure of Jesus Christ as God's revelation. Missionary discipleship demands nothing less.

*Chapter 9*

# The Joy of the Gospel

The various chapters in the book in various ways have set the table for this one. My first task was to lay out the stages of the new evangelization movement before setting that against the much longer narrative of the church since 1800 and at Vatican II. The council itself was the source for the fourteen ordinary world synods of bishops held between 1967 and 2015. As I write, the fifteenth world synod on youth and the faith is about to begin. "Vatican III," which progressives urged on the church after Vatican II, never came to pass. In its place were the world synods of bishops overlaid by the divisive interpretations of Vatican II, one of which adopted the slogan "reform of the reform." It implied turning back the clock on Vatican II. The apostolic exhortations of Paul VI, John Paul II, Benedict XVI, and Pope Francis written in response to those synods are a first draft of an agenda for any future ecumenical council. Meanwhile, these exhortations, along with the papal encyclicals, constitute the syllabus of the new evangelization movement for the church.

The book was not intended as a summary of the many themes that have come to expression in the new evangelization era from 1974 to the present. My sole interest was to provide a better philosophical exegesis of one theme: modernity and the secular age. I have already treated some of what Pope Francis wrote about secularism in the new evangelization and will briefly summarize some of it again here. But my main purpose in this chapter is to explain the deeper significance of the theme of joy in the ecclesial summons to missionary discipleship. My conviction is that what Charles Taylor has written about our secularity in *A Secular Age* would enable the new evangelization to better understand the "signs of the times." His master reform narrative of secularization takes us further toward understanding the scope and depth of the secular condition as regards religious belief.

It is almost impossible to take a detached view of one's own culture. The intellectual vista which a great treatise on secularity like Taylor's sets before us enables the preacher to understand more sympathetically the challenges facing evangelization in the secular age. It would be wrong to discount or belittle them or overestimate their ability to disassemble the grounds for religious faith.

Few serious scholars think the religious symbolisms that have powered Western civilization for three millennia, buttressed by metaphysics and textual hermeneutics, will disappear. On the contrary, many traditions are getting stronger. But Christians who don't even take themselves seriously as a factor in shaping history and culture will convince no one of anything. When their belief becomes no more than a leisure time activity with no worldview of social and moral implication, what's the point of it? Who needs the Scriptures, traditions, and liturgies of the church for values, like humane compassion and justice, when secular culture already subscribes to those without the crutch of the supernatural? On the other hand, the prophetic warning of David Foster Wallace to the graduates of Kenyon College that the gods of this age "will eat you alive" should give sanguine secularism a lot of pause. If the transcendent fulcrum of spiritual reference and moral conviction collapses in secular culture, what will succeed it?

In this chapter, I turn to the latest redaction of the new evangelization seeking to offer the language of the transcendent fulcrum, The Joy of the Gospel.[1] After a brief introduction, I will mention some of the themes in the document's five chapters. Then, I turn to the master theme of joy powering the evangelical concept of missionary discipleship. The joy *of* the Gospel (objective genitive) is the basis for the joy *of* the disciple's existence and mission (subjective genitive). What is evangelical joy and how does it relate to ordinary human joy? What is the passionate substratum in human emotional life which helps to power a faith anchored in a belief in the resurrection of the dead?

---

[1] In the body of the text I will abbreviate The Joy of the Gospel by the initials of its official Latin title *Evangelii Gaudium* or EG and paragraph number for a reference or quotation.

To start, I will indicate how The Joy of the Gospel positions the issue of secularism within the political and economic horizons of life today. Then I will take up a new expression, "thymotic joy," to distinguish evangelical joy from mere religious sentimentality. That will help to understand how a certain kind of conviction is capable of powering the *metanoia* (a life-changing reversal) which the Gospel of Mark puts on Jesus' own lips at the beginning of his public ministry. Evangelical joy and missionary discipleship make greater sense if we can graft them onto the passionate "spiritedness" of what Homer and Plato once called "*thymos.*" I will spend some pages explaining the place of that in a psychological spirituality of joyful discipleship for a secular age.

## The Context for The Joy of the Gospel

Vatican II's Pastoral Constitution on the Church in the Modern World (*Gaudium et Spes*) is the springhead of the new evangelization movement in its narrow sense as an evangelization of culture. The 2012 world synod of bishops on the new evangelization was carefully planned during the pontificate of Benedict XVI. He personally presided over the sessions, assisted by various cardinals. But when Benedict retired as pope in early 2013, Pope Francis assumed the task of summarizing its findings and putting the stamp of his own theological rhetoric and priorities upon them. That includes the pastoral rhetoric of the secular.

The organizational aspects of the synod fell to the general secretariat of the Synod of Bishops, which circulated a list of preparatory questions to all the bishops. Their responses were organized into a working agenda for the synod (*Instrumentum Laboris*). Conducted as much in an atmosphere of prayer as business, the 2012 synod was marked by international ecumenical participation. Ecumenical Patriarch Bartholomew I represented the Orthodox Communion of Patriarchates and the archbishop of Canterbury, Dr. Rowan Williams, also attended.[2] The recording secretary (*Relator General*) of the synod was Cardinal Donald Wuerl, archbishop of Washington, DC. He and his associates were tasked with reporting the results of the month-long deliberations that were summarized into fifty-seven proposi-

---

[2] In 2006, Dr. Rowan Williams delivered an address on secularism and religious faith at the Vatican.

tions.[3] These were written in relatively brief paragraphs and reflected the mind of the bishops at the synod. They served the pope as a collegial framework of concerns and priorities for his own apostolic exhortation. Unlike councils, synods have only consultative authority. The pope has the last word.

While this was happening, Pope Benedict himself was already working on a draft of what would have been his final encyclical on faith.[4] Then, quite unexpectedly, he resigned the papacy on February 28, 2013 (he had announced his intention to resign some two weeks earlier on February 11, 2013). *Lumen Fidei*, drafted in part by him and in part by Pope Francis, would become the new pope's first encyclical letter. Since retirement, Benedict XVI has lived a semi-cloistered life, writing and praying within the walls of the Vatican. The appearance of the new pope on the balcony of St. Peter's, the first pope from the Americas, certainly signaled to the church and to the secular world that, in electing Bergoglio from Argentina, the cardinals were reaching outside Europe for leadership and vision. The new evangelization that began in South America as *nueva evangelización* was going to Rome.

Pope Francis introduces The Joy of the Gospel (*Evangelii Gaudium*) on the new evangelization by placing his contribution to it within the new ecclesiology of Vatican II's Dogmatic Constitution on the Church (*Lumen Gentium*). The recommendations he makes for changes in the church's administrative organization are based on that ecclesiology. The pope builds his case of evangelization on other Vatican II documents as well, most notably *Gaudium et Spes* and *Unitatis Redintegratio*. What is barely mentioned in the pope's footnotes is the unremarkable Decree on the Church's Missionary Activity (*Ad Gentes*) at Vatican II. On the other hand, the pope draws heavily on Paul VI's *Evangelii Nuntiandi* (1975).

Where Francis sets himself apart from previous papal interpretations of evangelization is in placing greater emphasis on the Latino edition of the *nueva evangelización*. That is reflected in references to the Aparecida Document (June 19, 2007) of the Fifth General Conference of the Latin American and Caribbean bishops. This dependency accounts, I believe, for the shift in emphasis in Pope Francis from the

---

[3] www.vatican.va.synod: Thirteenth General Synod, Propositions.

[4] Pope Francis, Encyclical, *Lumen Fidei* 7. The letter was published on June 29, 2013, over the signature of the new pontiff based on a draft by his predecessor.

epistemological stress his predecessors put on secularism to the pastoral, social, and economic interpretation he prefers. The European assessment of secularism is present, but Pope Francis goes further. He joins a Latino interpretation to it. What makes this clear is the degree to which The Joy of the Gospel relies extensively on the Pontifical Council for Justice and Peace's *Compendium of the Social Doctrine of the Church*. The aim is to link religious indifference to the overwhelming influence on human religious consciousness of a liberal economic order.

The Thirteenth Ordinary General Assembly of the Synod of Bishops was held October 7–28, 2012. Its formal title was "The New Evangelization for the Transmission of the Christian Faith." The Pontifical Council for the Promotion of the New Evangelization provided the attending bishops with a massive encyclopedia of texts from Pius XII to Benedict XVI dealing with every conceivable aspect of the new evangelization. It included every mention of any conceivable aspect of mission and evangelization by a pope or council from World War II to 2012 in numbered paragraphs for easy reference. That was supplemented by a complete index of themes. The bishops also had the *Instrumentum Laboris* (working document) that was prepared by the general secretariat of the Synod of Bishops. The fifty-seven propositions that the synod fathers approved at the end of October 2012 as a digest of the previous month's discussions and proceedings are available on the Vatican website. If Pope Benedict made a draft of an apostolic exhortation on the synod, we do not have that text.

A post-synodal apostolic exhortation is the genre popes employ to communicate synod results personally in their own hand to the universal church. Paul VI wrote *Evangelii Nuntiandi* after the first synod on evangelization, which, as I mentioned, became the magisterial foundation for much of what Pope John Paul wrote and for Pope Francis's The Joy of the Gospel. The adjective "apostolic" refers to the ministry of the pope as the bishop of Rome (the Apostolic See). The magisterial authority of such a text is indicated by the noun "exhortation," suggesting a special rhetorical encouragement by the pope to the universal church that a matter of worldwide importance in the life of the church be undertaken.[5] In that sense, The Joy of the

---

[5] See Francis Sullivan, *Creative Fidelity: Weighing and Interpreting Documents of the Magisterium* (Eugene, OR: Wipf & Stock, 2003). See also the *Catechism of the Catholic*

Gospel was written precisely to stimulate theological reflection and pastoral action in all the local churches around the world whose mission of evangelization is to be carried out in communion with the pope and the universal church. A world synod of bishops is the broadest collegial consultation possible for the pope apart from an ecumenical council itself.

The synod is juridically defined in the new Code of Canon Law (1983) as a consultative body of bishops (CIC, Canon 342). "Synod" (Greek: *synados*, assembly) is ordinarily used for an assembly of bishops of regional churches who exercise their governance and teaching collegially or a diocesan bishop with the pastors of his local church. A general synod is either ordinary, when held at regularly scheduled intervals, or extraordinary, when called to treat a topic of special urgency and concern to the pope at the universal level. There have been fourteen ordinary world synods of bishops held in the Catholic Church since Vatican II. (The fifteenth will be held on Youth, Faith, and Vocational Discernment in 2018.)

When compared with previous apostolic exhortations written by the popes since 1970, The Joy of the Gospel is unique. Its style is more informal, personal, and emphatically pastoral than the usual Vatican genre. The reader quickly senses the pope's priorities and the tone of voice of his pontificate. The points the pope makes, his choice of imagery and phrasing, seem meant to stir to life the embers of religious passion still present in the cool indifference and quiet demoralization of many in the church. Pope Francis wants to equip his flock as joyful missionary disciples (Eph 4:12).

The pope's flair for metaphor in the text has caught the eye of Francis's admirers and critics alike. The "tide of secularism" (EG 65) touches the nerve of a culture warrior while taking on "the smell of the sheep" (EG 24) speaks to those critical of a late recrudescence of clericalism. As with all such personal and exhortatory texts, the temptation is to cherry-pick individual metaphors for personal reasons. Where some understand what "taking on" the "smell of the sheep" means for ministerial identification with the flock, others alter the verb "taking on" in commentaries to "knowing about" how the sheep smell! That's the difference between a shepherd and a tourist!

---

*Church*, no. 892, on the meaning of "religious assent" to non-infallible magisterial teaching based on *Lumen Gentium* 25.

One of the biggest changes that Francis has introduced into the new evangelization is the serious attention he gives to much-needed reforms in the church at the universal and local levels. The mission given to the church by Christ, and that alone, is what determines the shape and pastoral expression of ecclesial reforms. Reform serves the mission. And if the mission is a mission in the secular age, then it is crucial to fit the reforms to the conditions of the age without sacrificing the truths of the faith. To figure out where and how to reform the Vatican Curia, and to renew its structures in service to a more effective mission in the modern world, Pope Francis appointed a group of nine cardinals (commonly called C9). When this curial reform is complete, it will constitute the third post-conciliar reform of the Roman Curia since the first changes made by Paul VI in 1967, which were followed twenty years later by those of *Pastor Bonus* by John Paul II in 1988. The crisis of clergy abuse led Pope Francis to call a global meeting of the presidents of Catholic bishops conferences around the world to Rome in February 2019 to address the crisis more comprehensively than the Curia has been able to do.

## The Joy of the Gospel:
## Five Chapters on Joy, the Challenges of the Secular, and Christian Discipleship

What follows is a very general summary of the topics and themes found in the various chapters of The Joy of the Gospel. In its English translation the document is 211 pages, but the text moves easily and swiftly as the five chapters are conveniently divided into labelled subsections. The thirteen-page introduction to the text sets the motif of evangelical joy at the center of the church's evangelizing mission. The theme of joy came to express the rhetoric of post-conciliar Catholicism in 1965 with *Gaudium et Spes* (The Pastoral Constitution on the Church in the Modern World). For Pope Francis, joy first counts as a profound spiritual reaction to revelation and a mood woven through the Scriptures. The prophets in the Hebrew Scriptures and the various writings in the New Testament are the pope's primary biblical references for the religious reasons that make joy the proper response of faith. What I will try to show later is that joy is also a primary ontological mood of the human person. That provides faith and the secular identity with a common psychological tangent. The Greek notion of *thymos* ("spiritedness") will help explain why.

The Joy of the Gospel's five chapters are: (1) The Church's Missionary Transformation, where the ecclesiology of full lay participation in the evangelizing mission of the church comes squarely into view; (2) Amid the Crisis of Communal Commitment seeks to diagnose the chief factors that impede or discourage the joint missionary discipleship of clergy and lay together, one of which is secularism and secularization; (3) The Proclamation of the Gospel is where the text again emphasizes the joint communal efforts of clergy and lay in proclaiming Jesus Christ and his teaching to the world; (4) The Social Dimension of Evangelization attempts to guide faith away from a safe and sentimental interiority to a properly social expression in the concern for injustice, poverty, the common good, and dialogue with others of different faiths and worldviews who also wish to contribute to social peace; (5) Spirit-Filled Evangelizers returns again to thymotic joy and the missionary impulse in the church born of the Holy Spirit. That is followed by a Marian coda with the image "Mary, Mother of Evangelization" as exemplar of the disciple in the church and figure of intercession for those on mission.

Let me briefly select some of the points the pope makes in each of the five chapters. My focus is only on what is distinctive in them about joy and secularism.

## Chapter 1:
## *The Church's Missionary Transformation (EG 19–49)*

This is the most succinct way of putting what the new evangelization for Pope Francis is about—transforming the self-understanding of Christians themselves. The core ecclesial concept of "missionary discipleship" is introduced here. The underlying point of the expression is to change the understanding of the practice of faith from that of a passive religious consumer of sacraments to that of a disciple with a missionary purpose of some kind. For centuries, Catholics have come to consider faith largely in terms of obedience, dogmas, and sacraments. The modern consumer age has transformed these obedient recipients of grace into mere religious consumers of experience. Vatican II had emphasized the universal call to holiness and the sacraments of initiation. But imagining Christian faith as a summons to "missionary discipleship" goes further than making responses at Mass and receiving Holy Communion. The accent shifts from receiving Christ to encountering him as a personalized sacramental presence calling the recipient to witness and self-conscious discipleship in some way. It is meant to intentionally power a believer's moral and personal commitments in the public spheres of life.

*Chapter 2:*
*Amid the Crisis of Communal Commitment (EG 50–109)*

In this chapter the pope diagnoses the various challenges the contemporary world presents for faith understood proactively as missionary discipleship. This is where the pope does not hedge on where some of the most powerful challenges to discipleship and evangelization originate. The Enlightenment considered religious faith to be an entirely private and sentimental matter. The deepest challenges today to faith, however, originate in the economic spheres of life. So, the chapter opens with an emphatic prophetic refusal: "no to an economy of exclusion." If you missed the point, that is followed by two more negatives: "no to the new idolatry of money" and "no to a financial system which rules rather than serves." For Pope Francis, the deep inequalities in any society, including a liberal democratic one like ours, breed violence and dehumanization. This critique does not de-legitimate liberal economics, much less espouse some form of communism as some critics wrongly claim. Rather, it adds necessary evangelical caveats to some political ones Francis Fukuyama issued about capitalism in his exegesis of *thymos* as the passion for recognition, which I will treat in the conclusion to the book.[6] The economic and social themes Pope Francis weaves through The Joy of the Gospel create a Latino social justice orientation to missionary discipleship. The church has spoken often and regularly about economics since the nineteenth-century pontificate of Leo XIII. The culture war that many American Catholics associate with abortion is also the culture war with a capitalistic politics that sees few connections between life and market forces concerning the affordability of children, maternal leave, universal health care, and the prioritization of leisure over other human values.

---

[6] Francis Fukuyama, *The End of History and the Last Man* (New York: The Free Press, 1992). See also a sequel to Fukuyama's understanding of *thymos* and human recognition in *Identity: The Demand for Dignity and the Politics of Resentment* (New York: Farrar, Straus and Giroux, 2018).

What saves The Joy of the Gospel from being a mere rehash of magisterial references to evangelization is how the text refocuses the challenges of the secular order around the very matters that make that secular order what it is—a secular state, the malaises that attend all forms of social and technical progress, the culture of self-authenticity, and, overarching all of this, the dominance of global capitalism. Piercing through the usual papal exhortations and homiletic encouragements, what I see happening in The Joy of the Gospel is an entirely new way of conceiving the renewal of religious faith in a secular age. The consumer of religious sentiment is being called to follow a prophet. No evangelical mission will get far led by self-absorbed couch potatoes.

As one expects, to a certain degree the issues of secularization and secularism remain somewhat muddled in the exhortation. The "tide of secularism" or "the onslaught of contemporary secularism," in my view, are not helpful. Reducing the secular order to secularism and identifying it with only its amoral derivatives is not the way to go. If read more carefully, I believe The Joy of the Gospel seeks to bypass that to get at the heart of the challenges faith faces in a liberal democratic order.

The exhortation treats secularism as such, not in the larger sense I'm pressing for, but under the sections dealing with the specific cultural challenges, the challenges that make inculturating a Christian approach to life so difficult, and the challenges that arise specifically from urban cultures. The mention of secularization and secularism here should not lead us to think they constitute the full challenge of a secular age to missionary discipleship. The signs of it are more diverse than life issues alone: attacks on religious freedom on the one hand and religious indifference on the other, a soft moral relativism, the loss of deep cultural memory and heritages, globalization, the privatization of religious faith, a superficial approach to life fascinated more by things and fashions than deeper meanings. All of these challenges have been mentioned by the popes. To inventory them is not to tell the reader a lot about the larger processes in modernization that brought secularization to pass more as a byproduct than a strictly rational choice. After thirty years of this, the repetition of these symptoms without a more intentional philosophical exegesis of the causes can itself prove defeating. The pope himself worries about the "diagnostic overload" for pastoral ministry. But what choice do we have but to figure out more carefully where these phenomena that bother him all come from?

In the second half of the chapter, the effects of the cultural challenges on the inner life of the church and pastoral workers themselves are highlighted. This is a pastoral staff's examination of conscience for a secular age. The task will be to connect the symptoms of demoralization in the church to the cultural causes ordinarily concealed from everyday awareness. The pope focuses attention on positive values connected with a missionary discipleship instead of the privatized religiosity of the ordinary Catholic. One paragraph alludes to the maxim of Hugo Grotius that I explained earlier in connection with religious indifference—"As if God did not exist" (*Etsi deus non daretur*). Pope Francis turns the maxim in other directions. He applies it to other realities easy to ignore in social life: "Practical relativism consists in acting *as if* God did not exist, making decisions *as if* the poor did not exist, setting goals *as if* others did not exist, working *as if* people who have not received the Gospel did not exist" (EG 80). The secular age lets us see some things clearly while blinding us to others.

The default religious mind-set in a liberal economic culture is to see religion as one more object for consumption. A shallow spiritual consumerism is evident in those turning up only for Christmas and Easter Mass. The second chapter ends emphasizing the important roles of the laity, especially for women, youth, and religious vocations. Without reaching out in new ways with new opportunities for service and involvement for young men and women, the church risks losing the attention and energies of the next generation. The fifteenth ordinary world synod of bishops on youth concluded in October 2018 only a few months before the pope assembles the presidents of bishops' conferences around the world to the Vatican to try to address the catastrophic effects and internal ecclesial conditions of the clergy abuse crisis.

## Chapter 3:
## The Proclamation of the Gospel (EG 110–175)

This chapter turns attention to the important role preaching and catechesis play in the new evangelization. All the popes have stressed the importance of catechesis. Only Francis, however, has seriously emphasized the importance of preaching and the homily. The hand-writing is on the wall. Evangelization may involve a thousand things in the church, but preaching, and preaching alone, is the one action that constitutes a local pastoral gesture of credibility that will keep people worshiping a God they cannot see. No pope before Francis has so emphasized the preaching ministry of the priest in the context of the new evangelization. I wrote about this in an early chapter at some length, so I will not repeat myself here.

At the outset, the pope stresses that the whole "People of God"—not just clergy—is the subject of the church's proclamatory mission. There is a great diversity of gifts in the church; it is not "mono-cultural" or "European." The clerical interpretation of the church still prevents laity from seeing their proper role in evangelization. Like everything else, Catholics think: Can't evangelization be outsourced to the professionals who know how to do it? Too many lay faithful still see themselves as spectators of something ordained and non-ordained ministers do for them. The lay faithful are reduced by some clergy or reduce themselves to "mere onlookers" in the task of eccle-sial mission. It's a small step from concierge doctors to concierge religion and clergy!

## Chapter 4:
## The Social Dimension of Evangelization (EG 176–258)

This is the lengthiest chapter in The Joy of the Gospel. Building on a century of substantial papal social teaching on justice and rights, the text affirms that "the Kerygma has a clear social content" (EG 177). Redemption transforms interhuman social relations as much as it does the private ethical stances and commitments of the individual person. Human salvation in the most inclusive sense is encumbered and inevitably conditioned by the socio-cultural order. Reducing Christian faith to a private relationship with Jesus Christ is simply impossible if one understands Christ as the gospels do. Charity and justice are inseparable from salvation. The Gospel concerns all crea-tion and "every aspect of human life" (EG 181).

Pastors who lack competence in these secular spheres should be humble enough to admit it and not offer naïve solutions to complex problems. The pope remarks that the church's pastors must demon-strate competence by drawing on the results of the social sciences in presenting "opinions on all that affects people's lives" (EG 182). The document reiterates, "It is no longer possible to claim that religion should be restricted to the private sphere and that it exists only to prepare souls for heaven" (EG 182). This mistaken view effectively excludes any appropriate public role for the church in secular life. Faith, as the church understands it, is less a private consolation than a public witness for redemption, justice, and mercy not only in the lives of missionary disciples of Christ, but for the common good of all citizens.

The second part of chapter 4 begins: "In what follows I intend to concentrate on two great issues which strike me as fundamental at this time in history. I will treat them more fully because I believe that they will shape the future of humanity. These issues are first, the inclusion of the poor in society, and second, peace and social dialogue" (EG 185). Many Catholics eager to protect their rightful freedoms in the secular order remain unfamiliar with the evangelical premises of the church's social teaching. Increasingly, the right to an education, access to health care, and employment are being recognized as integral to an understanding of human rights in a modern social order. So is religious diversity and the freedom not to believe.

Pope Francis quotes the Congregation for the Doctrine of the Faith which took some in the church to task in 1984: "defenders of orthodoxy are sometimes accused of passivity, indulgence, or culpable complicity regarding intolerable situations of injustice and the political regimes which prolong them" (EG 194, n. 161). The wealth of the liberal secular order leaves Christians prey to a "new self-centered paganism"—an Epicurean cultivation devoid of spiritual substance (EG 195). Consumption can easily turn into the whole point of living. Those who lack the means of a humane existence are not mere objects of our pity and charity but from the point of view of the Gospel the vulnerable embodiment of a divine appeal. Had the racial and neurological lottery that benefitted us turned out otherwise, we would grasp that intuitively. Bill Gates does. The poor need more than money. They need presence and our ability to communicate the Gospel values that would deliver them from their own self-hatred and the hatred of others (EG 200).

At this point, Pope Francis goes even deeper into the exegesis of the economic challenges which demand a new evangelization. The critique of excesses in capitalism is not to praise some socialist utopia. In my reading, it is to assert the inherent strengths of a market-based economy to better serve an authentic humanization. The pope only rejects what some take as the "absolute autonomy" of markets (EG 202). In this ideology, free markets cannot bend to any ethical norms (EG 203) because an "invisible hand" guides them (EG 204). Political economy is a noble vocation, he says, that the church encourages and where micro-issues are grasped in the context of macroeconomic and social developments. The pope does not hesitate to say, "I am firmly convinced that openness to the transcendent can bring about a new political and economic mindset which would help to break down the wall of separation between the economy and the common good of society" (EG 205). To the sad sight of bewildered migrants escaping war, poverty, and malnutrition and the trafficking and abuse of women and children, the heart and conscience cannot help but respond. Furthermore, natural creation must not be ruined for the sake of profit. The euthanasia movement deems certain people to be living worthless lives. A throw-away economic culture values a death with dignity for those who have outlived their usefulness. It's sensible economics, seculars think, to make them realize that.

The chapter moves on to the second theme of the common good and social peace. The pope asserts principles for achieving peace as societies increasingly find themselves vulnerable to violence: (1) one must not relax the irresolvable tension between ideals and limited circumstances, not allow what is best to defeat attempts to do what is good; (2) conflict must not be allowed to take away from people a belief that unity and reconciliation to some degree are always possible; (3) language can be deceptive, so there must always be an appeal to facts, lest generalizations distort realities. "This calls for rejecting the various means of masking reality: angelic forms of purity, dictatorships of relativism, empty rhetoric, objectives more ideal than real, brands of ahistorical fundamentalism, ethical systems bereft of kindness, intellectual discourse bereft of wisdom" (EG 231). In one sentence, the pope captures many of the topics I have explored more analytically in the book. To gloss this single sentence with concrete illustrations would be an education for evangelization.

Pope Francis confirms the importance of dialogue across worldviews and beliefs as essential in evangelization, a dialogue that was first inaugurated at Vatican II. True dialogue is not easy between substantially different worldviews. But there are many overlapping interests and shared values between secular and religious worldviews. The secular view of the world in Providential Deism and secular humanism inherited biblical values and incorporated them into a nonbiblical view of social and political life. Humanistic traditions of every kind depend on proprietary translations, and each new one can create unforeseen possibilities in the older one. For seculars and Jews to see the Christian faith as not merely an adversarial religion but one that includes a humanistic tradition of its own can demand in return that Christians award equal respect to Judaism and agnosticism as a basis for dialogue. As a self-declared divine revelation, Christianity is also a humanism. The pope praises a "healthy pluralism" in the spirit of dialogue but warns of the threats to religious freedom by a secular intolerance as nothing less than "a new form of discrimination and authoritarianism" (EG 255). He adds: "The respect due to the agnostic or non-believing minority should not be arbitrarily imposed in a way that silences the convictions of the believing majority or ignores the wealth of religious traditions" (EG 255). The church needs to express its closeness to those who do not hold a religious belief. Many are "precious allies in the commitment to defending human dignity, in building peaceful coexistence between peoples and in protecting creation" (EG 257). Finally, the chapter concludes with the same overture to a renewed ecclesial dialogue with seculars and agnostics that Benedict XVI initiated toward the end of his papacy. "A special place of encounter is offered by new Areopagi such as Court of the Gentiles, where 'believers and non-believers can engage in dialogue about fundamental issues of ethics, art and science, and about the search for transcendence'" (EG 257).

## Chapter 5:
### Spirit-Filled Evangelizers (EG 259–288)

The final chapter in The Joy of the Gospel is important for what I will describe in the next section as the hyperthymic passion necessary for ecclesial mission. The spiritual motives for missionary identity are found in the (1) personal encounter with the saving love of Christ, (2) with the spiritual vigor gained from ecclesial communion, and (3) from the belief in the ongoing work of Christ in the Holy Spirit in the church and, in another way, in the world. I will offer further reflections on the pope's idea of a joyful missionary disciple in the next section.

The Joy of the Gospel ends with the customary Marian coda in papal documents (EG 284–88). Mary is the "mother of evangelization" and the "star of the new evangelization" in her role as mother of the church. Pope Francis ends the exhortation with a prayer he composed to Mary that recalls many of the themes he has presented earlier.

## Joy in the New Evangelization: The Meanings of *Thymos*

I briefly mentioned the opening references to joy in the introduction of The Joy of the Gospel. Pope Francis's spiritual translation of biblical joy in missionary discipleship draws on what I will call a motivational poetic of hyperthymic sentiments. Pope Francis begins The Joy of the Gospel by exhorting the church: "I wish to encourage the Christian faithful to embark upon a new chapter in evangelization marked by this joy, while pointing out new paths for the Church's journey in years to come" (EG 1). A joyless heart is characterized by opposites—a complacency on the one hand and a restless coveting on the other. These feelings belong in the leaky cistern of Greek legend. What someone pours in drains out almost as fast. Consumed by coveting things, it is easy to become indifferent to other people. This "is no way to live a dignified and fulfilled life; it is not God's will for us. Nor is it the life in the Spirit which has its source in the heart of the risen Christ" (EG 2). The resurrection of Christ from the grave is "always capable of restoring our joy."

The prophetic literature of the Bible supplies the poetics for the new evangelization. Isaiah 9:3 and 12:6 associates joy with messianic fulfillment. Nature joins this chorus: "Sing for joy, O heavens, and exult, O earth; break forth, O mountains, into singing! For the Lord has comforted his people, and will have compassion on his suffering ones" (Isa 49:13). The city sings, too, as Zechariah 9:9 adds, "Rejoice greatly, O daughter Zion!" The Wisdom literature teaches us about the ordinary joy in living: "My child, treat yourself well, according to your means. . . . Do not deprive yourself of a day's enjoyment" (Sir 14:11, 14). Were it not in the Bible, one would mistake such counsel as Epicurean, even secular. Later, I will complement Sirach with Ecclesiastes and the Song of Songs on enjoyment.

The Gospel of Christ adds an even more emphatic poetics of joy. The joy associated with Easter in the gospels spills onto the events associated with the beginning of Christ's life. The annunciation to the Virgin Mary opens with the summons of the angel Gabriel, "Rejoice." When Mary, pregnant with Jesus, visits Elizabeth, herself already carrying John the Baptist in her womb, the embryonic life of the great Forerunner of the Messiah leaps for joy in his mother's body (Luke 1:41). The hyperthymic poetics of Mary's *Magnificat* begin, "My spirit rejoices in God my Savior" (Luke 1:47). From birth to resurrection, Christ's presence is the occasion for singing.

These familiar Lukan figures of joy have their Johannine parallel in Jesus' Last Discourse following the Last Supper. "I have said these things to you so that my joy may be in you, and that your joy may be complete" (John 15:11). To that, the Lord adds, "But I will see you again, and your hearts will rejoice, and no one will take your joy from you" (John 16:22).

The poetics of joy are also present in the church following Pentecost in Acts of the Apostles (2:46; 8:8; 13:52). Pope Francis sums up the biblical poetics of joy with a rhetorical question addressed to us: "Why should we not also enter into this great stream of joy?" Disappointments, sorrows, and defeats, of course, constitute the daily prose of life punctuated by ordinary moments of joy. It is difficult to know which of these moments signify the true meaning and destiny of human existence. A response to that doubt comes in Jesus' Beatitudes, explicitly addressed to people deprived of the simple joys of life. The kingdom of God announces that joy is the destiny of human beings even in the state of sorrow. Pope Francis calls on the lessons of lamentation in the Bible to evoke joy, for Scripture itself sings the blues in its psalms of lamentation. Tears join the chorus of joy. The introduction to The Joy of the Gospel concludes that the human encounter with God is where human beings "attain the fullest truth of our being" (EG 8).

Turning to the fifth and final chapter of The Joy of the Gospel, Pope Francis says the new evangelization needs "spirit-filled evangelizers." At this point, the thymotic dimensions of joy come to fuller ecclesial expression. Spiritedness evokes the corporate fellowship and the loyalty to a cause that powers every social group (a business, research doctors, sports teams, churches, etc.) drawn together in passion for a mission. Dedication to a mission is often characterized by hyperthymic self-sacrifice. The Paschal Mystery of Christ is itself an incomplete revelation of *thymic joy* until the Holy Spirit enters the apostolic community at Pentecost, propelling piety huddled together into the street from the Upper Room. All this said, there is still more joy spoken in the Bible. Let me return to the Wisdom tradition, where the sentiments closest to those of secular consciousness are introduced.

## Spiritual Joy in a Secular Age

The Kerygma is the fulfillment of the existential mystery of human life. The Kerygma of Christ—the mystery of his birth, death, and resurrection—is an existential Kerygma in our lives as well. Such words are the existential boundaries that the philosopher Karl Jaspers calls "limit experiences."[7] No one transcends such radical existential boundaries as conception and birth, where two beings become the new being I am ("a monstrous collusion of chance, instinct and another's freedom have cast me on this shore," writes Paul Ricoeur[8]). No one transcends suffering in the insoluble universal questions, "Why me?" "Why her?" "Why now?" No one deciphers the uncanny restorations of life and the will to live that follow suffering and that do not cease even as the soul leaves the body (Remember me! Do not forget me!). The Kerygma of Christ responds to and fulfills the deepest mysteries and aspirations of human existence—life and death. That means there can be some aspects of the Kerygma sung in a minor key, in that of Leonard Cohen's "broken Hallelujahs."

The Bible has two testaments for a reason. They afford multiple perspectives on joy which can be joined to the poetic of the Kerygma. The Wisdom literature in the Old Testament includes the books of Psalms, Job, Proverbs, Sirach, the Song of Songs, and Ecclesiastes (Qoheleth). In them, evangelization discovers a unique poetics and rhetoric of suffering and joy. The love poem attributed to King Solomon (Song of Solomon) and sober reflections of an anonymous "Teacher" (Qoheleth) about the "vanity of vanities" in human life

---

[7] Karl Jaspers, *Philosophy*, vols. 1–3 (Chicago: University of Chicago Press, 1969). He treats "limit situations" or the boundary conditions which characterize human Existenz, as he calls it, throughout these volumes.

[8] Paul Ricoeur, *Freedom and Nature: The Voluntary and the Involuntary*, trans. Erazim V. Kohak (Evanston, IN: Northwestern University Press, 1966), 434.

offer evangelization in a secular age special resources for the joy of the Gospel. If eschatological and evangelical joy are the summit of the Kerygma, the ordinary enjoyments of life are its earthy analogues. Jesus' parables in the Gospel of Luke on the Lost Sheep, the Lost Coin, and the Prodigal or Lost Son are revealing. The Lost Son is the son who brings his father more joy than the righteous son because "there will be more joy in heaven over one sinner who repents than over ninety-nine righteous persons who need no repentance" (Luke 15:7). This is the joy of the Gospel—a repentance that transforms a person into a living parable of resurrection.

Wisdom is a distinct and respectable representative of biblical thinking which holds special insights into joy.[9] The Wisdom literature in the Bible is a special genre and the closest revelation that comes to secular experience. So, Paul Ricoeur observes,

> Nothing is further from the spirit of the sages than the idea of an autonomy of thinking, a humanism of the good life; in short, of a wisdom of the Stoic or Epicurean mode founded on the self-sufficiency of thought. This is why wisdom is held to be a gift of God in distinction to the "knowledge of good and evil" promised by the Serpent. What is more, for the scribes following the Exile, Wisdom was personified into a transcendent feminine figure. She is a divine reality that has always existed and that will always exist. She lives with God and she has accompanied creation from its very beginning. Intimacy with Wisdom is not to be distinguished from intimacy with God.[10]

The Hebrew name for Ecclesiastes is "Qoheleth," which means "The Teacher." In twelve chapters, Qoheleth repeats thirty-seven times his familiar refrain: "vanity" (*hebel*). This "vanity" is much more than pride. It is the empty and inconstant character of human desire and temporality. That is why this biblical book begins with a rhetorical chain of the enigmas of time that admit of no theoretical solution. True wisdom, therefore, involves bringing the soul's sense of

---

[9] The Lectionary of the Church only excerpts passages from Ecclesiastes 1 and 11 on a single Sunday of the year (C) and on one Friday and Saturday (Year II). The stunning poetry of the fragility of life in Ecclesiastes 11:9–12:8 has nothing to compare with it in the Bible.

[10] Paul Ricoeur, "Toward a Hermeneutic of the Idea of Revelation," *Harvard Theological Review* 70, nos. 1–2 (January–April 1977): 13.

itself into practical synchronicity with the unforeseeable uncanniness of time itself. The art of living well involves a recognition of the mystery of our temporality as finite creatures.

On seven separate occasions, Qoheleth recommends enjoyment as God's will for human beings. The human being needs to realize that enjoying life is wise, and it is wise to know that, in time, life's enjoyments will be taken away; it is wise to enjoy the present and keep expectations for the future as modest as possible; it is wise to live life fully while always expecting the unexpected; it is wise to keep options open to adjust to life's uncertainties; it is wise to make the inevitability of old age and death a reason for enjoying life while we are able, as long as we can. Some exegetes consider Ecclesiastes 9 to be Qoheleth's summation of his practical ethics of joy.

> Go, eat your bread with enjoyment, and drink your wine with a merry heart; for God has long ago approved what you do. Let your garments always be white; do not let oil be lacking on your head. Enjoy life with the wife whom you love, all the days of your vain life that are given you under the sun, because that is your portion in life and in your toil at which you toil under the sun. Whatever your hand finds to do, do with your might; for there is no work or thought or knowledge or wisdom in Sheol, to which you are going. (Eccl 9:7-10)

What value does this have for evangelization in a secular age? The spirituality of joy must begin in a simple honesty about the acceptance of human finitude. At the same time, Ecclesiastes is a biblical sentinel in a secular age warning against the excesses and hubris of that age. In Matthew 25:13 Jesus himself warns, "You neither know the day nor the hour." The acceptance of limits, for Daniel Bell, is the anteroom for the return to a new awareness of the sacred. The Eternal has inscribed something of eternity in the thirst of the human soul for the joy of living. In that sense, Ecclesiastes is an anticipation of the eschatology of the kingdom of God.

The Song of Songs is my second example of a Wisdom text where the poetics of joy in the form of human love come to expression. In this biblical love song, a wholesome eroticism serves tenderness and commitment. The Song of Songs sings of sexual rapture: "I come to my garden, my sister, my bride; I gather my myrrh with my spice, I eat my honeycomb with my honey, I drink my wine with my milk"

(Song 5:1). "I am my beloved's and my beloved is mine; he pastured his flocks among the lilies" (Song 6:3).

Traditional allegorical exegesis averted attention from such Middle Eastern candor. Its aim was to allow the poetry to speak only of a spiritual intimacy with God. Yet, exegesis can also peel back an unnecessary layer of allegory to find a spiritual dimension in the plain meaning of the love poetry. What is undeniable at first is that the Song of Songs does not attempt to place the couple's sexual intimacy within the context of marriage or the patriarchal family bond or the reproduction of offspring. Those values important to a Christian theology of married love must be recovered from the Song's canonical context in Scripture. What the insertion of the Song of Songs into the biblical canon does imply, according to one interpreter, is a genuine intuition that God's presence is already somehow at work in a faithful and tender sexuality based on love.

> Carnal love is perhaps consummated in 5:1 or 6:3, but this is not said in a descriptive mode. Rather it is sung. Hence, we can ask whether the veritable consummation is not in the song itself. And if, as I suggested above the true denouement is to be found in 8:6 ("set me like a seal on your heart, like a seal on your arm"), then what is important is not the carnal consummation, which is never described, never recounted, but the covenant vow. Signified by the "seal," which is the soul of the nuptial, a soul that would have as its flesh the physical consummation that is merely sung. But when the nuptial is invested in the erotic, the flesh is soul and the soul is flesh.[11]

The Song of Songs inclines to a nuptial theology of sexuality by the imprint of permanence and fidelity reflected in the enduring metaphor of "the seal" ("Set me as a seal upon your heart"). Pope John Paul II was the first pope to speak candidly of the "nuptial meaning" of the body. The Joy of Love (*Amoris Laetitia*) is the title of the apostolic exhortation Pope Francis wrote in 2015 on marriage and the family. To bypass the erotic dimension of human life in pursuit of an elevated, but unnecessarily excarnated, spirituality of joy, especially in a secular age, would be suspect. The Bible itself teaches that, and, now, so does the church.

---

[11] Paul Ricoeur, "The Nuptial Metaphor," in Andre LaCocque and Paul Ricoeur, *Thinking Biblically: Exegetical and Hermeneutical Studies*, trans. David Pellauer (Chicago: University of Chicago Press, 1998), 272.

## Renewing the Theology of Joy

In the early 1970s, some German theologians who had developed political theologies (Jürgen Moltmann and Johan-Baptist Metz) began writing about the theology of joy. Traditional theologies of joy in the church focused on the joy of heaven in the beatific vision (*visio beatifica*). But joy can equally evoke a sacramental, communal, and politico-ethical orientation in life. Even heavenly joy should not be confused with some kind of transcendent contentment. The Lord's invitation "to come share your Master's joy" does not imply what the river of "Forgetfulness" (Lethe) does in Greek mythology. Joy in Christianity is a divinely inspired social discontent on earth as well as the fullness of divine joy in God's presence after death. Joy gives life. It is not an escape from life or the inevitable sorrows that go with it.[12] For that very reason, Moltmann ridicules Germany's joyless "fun culture" and opposes it to spiritual joy understood as the "feast of life"—a social celebration of what is universal and essential for human beings. Joy binds up wounds and pulls people together. It is hyperthymic, not selfish and sentimental.

Marianne Meye Thompson writes about the different occasions and motives for joy in Scripture.[13] There is joy *because of* the world, joy *because of* seeing salvation in the world, joy *despite* suffering and, paradoxically, joy *on account of* suffering, and a protesting kind of joy *against* the world. N. T. Wright stresses that while hope is central to resurrection faith, joy, for Jesus and his disciples, saturates hope already.[14] Jesus' meals with sinners, his healings, his acts of forgiveness bring joy as the kingdom already in our midst. The body of Christ—born of the Virgin Mary and risen from the dead and received sacramentally in communion—is an unsurpassable symbol of hope realized in the incarnated experience of sacramental joy. The two solemnities in the entire liturgical year when joy is the dominant sentiment are Christmas and Easter. The celebrant vests in rose liturgical vestments instead of purple on Gaudete Sunday in the middle of Advent and Laetare Sunday in the middle of Lent. We are pursued

---

[12] *Joy and Human Flourishing: Essays on Theology, Culture, and the Good Life*, ed. Miroslav Volf and Justin E. Crisp (Minneapolis: Fortress Press, 2015).

[13] "Marianne Meye Thompson, "Reflections on Joy in the Bible," in *Joy and Human Flourishing*, ed. Volf and Crisp, 17–38.

[14] N. T. Wright, "Joy: Some New Testament Perspectives and Questions," in *Joy and Human Flourishing*, 39–61.

by joy even when we lack it. Its copies, the "knock off" non-patented counterfeits of a truly joyful life, distract us everywhere. The purpose of the church, one essayist says, is to be "training grounds for right rejoicing."[15] The church, reduced to its essence, is doxology (praise). It matters very much in living life joyfully that Christians assemble together to worship God in light of the death and resurrection of Christ.

The theme of joy is universal in religion too. Archbishop Desmond Tutu visited the Dalai Lama in Dharamsala, India, in April 2015 to honor the Dalai Lama's eightieth birthday.[16] They exchanged their thoughts and favorite practices for maintaining an inner quality of joy amid the sufferings and disappointments of life. Both agreed that a joyful sensibility is impossible for humans without strategies for coping with such overpowering emotions as fear, anger, loneliness, suffering, and sadness. There are, they advised, "eight pillars of joy" in life: gaining perspective, humility, humor, acceptance, forgiveness, gratitude, compassion, and generosity. These are human universals found in various ways in all wisdom traditions—religious or secular. Proverbial wisdom is transcultural. But the narratives, parables, and proverbs of the great spiritual traditions do not credit these pillars in the same way nor put the mood of joy in the same poetic context. In Judaism, the Exodus and Tanakh ground joy in social freedom, the search for justice, and the hope for national survival against enemies. Hope is not even mentioned in the eight pillars of joy, yet it is central to Judaism and the Gospel. The belief in the resurrection from the dead grounds it for Christians.

## Joy and Thymos:
### The Psychology and Ontology of Spirit

One approach to joy in building a philosophical foundation for the new evangelization is to link it to reflections on *thymos* in modern psychology and philosophy. I have already noted that, from this point of view, missionary discipleship is a hyperthymic faith. It is neither

---

[15] *Joy and Human Flourishing*, xiii.

[16] His Holiness the Dalai Lama and Archbishop Desmond Tutu with Douglas Abrams, *The Book of Joy: Lasting Happiness in a Changing World* (New York: Random House, 2016).

cynical nor consumerist. The Greek word *thymos* appears initially in the epics of Homer like the *Iliad*, where it demands that Achilles enact revenge on Hector for having killed Patroclus. At this stage, it is pure retaliatory passion based on justice and friendship. The hero in Homer is driven by indignation and anger to exact his revenge for his friend. What drives Achilles is an internal force in him that Homer calls *thymos*.

In Plato's *Phaedrus* and *Republic*, *thymos* is de-mythicized and becomes one element in the tripartite composition of the human soul or *psyche*. The composition of the Platonic *psyche* includes *logos* ("reason"), *eros* ("desire"), and *thymos* ("spiritedness"). The two prerational and irrational forces in the human soul (*eros* and *thymos*) provide reason with the energies needed to pull human purposes to expression. *Logos* on its own is powerless without *eros* and *thymos*. So much for rationalism. If *eros* and *thymos* unite without *logos*, we have unchecked passion. The idea of Platonic dualism of soul and body is undercut by the tripartite structure of the soul itself.

In terms of the meaning of missionary discipleship and joy in the new evangelization, I hold that *thymotic passion*, as Plato presents it, is the root principle involved. Paul Ricoeur returned to Plato's reflections on *thymos* in developing his anthropology of feeling and the passions. I will say more about that further on. The brilliant philosophical apology for liberal democratic capitalism written by Francis Fukuyama also drew on an exegesis of *thymos* as "the desire for recognition" which he borrowed from Alexander Kojeve's reinterpretation of Hegel.[17] I will take up what Fukuyama says about *thymos* as political and social "recognition" in the conclusion. To begin, however, let me start with *thymos* in psychiatry. If we are to grasp the joy of discipleship, this is where we must start.

The neurobiology of psychic emotional life is one of the fastest-growing fields in science. Modern brain scans display the neurobiological structures and processes of the living brain. We can see with our own eyes its labyrinthian pathways and circuitry, the intricate neural webbing and blood flows that make possible the involuntarily integrated sensorium of perception, movement, memory,

---

[17] Fukuyama, *The End of History and the Last Man*, 162–208.

cognition, and feeling.[18] A goal of neuroscience is to explain "a precise neuronal architecture for our conscious workspace."[19] Jean-Pierre Changeux points to the unique capacities humans have for recognizing the interior mental and emotional states in other human beings.[20] Neuronal factors make sympathy and compassion possible for us by virtue of the capacity to see and feel things as others do. The limbic system of the brain is composed of a reservoir of neurochemicals in glands that produce in us the effects we call feelings.

This neurobiological explanation of human feeling produced by glands and neurochemicals, absent a psychiatrist's and philosopher's sensibilities to the connections between those feelings and human meaning, is totally inadequate. Disconnected from a life narrative and the human relationships that knit purposes into us, what are they? Neurobiology demands the engagement with psychiatry and philosophy.

Neurochemicals may jump the synaptic cleft in the brain to adjacent neurons to bestow normalcy and calmness. They may restore in a patient the semblance of a normal human emotional state. But the highly integrated architecture of the self requires much more. There is no biochemical for meaningfulness, for *joie de vivre*, for the rational enthusiasm and exuberance that transforms the world. While psychiatry devotes much of its time to resolving emotional pathologies, there is a growing interest in hyperthymia—a word that describes the range of elevated human moods, moods like joy, that power the lives of successful and creative individuals.

---

[18] Jean-Pierre Changeux, *The Good, the True, and the Beautiful*, trans. and rev. Laurence Garey (New Haven, CT: Yale University Press, 2012), 76: "The human brain possesses an almost unique predisposition in the animal world. It can recognize intentions, desires, knowledge, beliefs, and emotions in other people. This capacity to attribute mental states, to put oneself in another's place, allows us to recognize possible differences from and similarities to our own mental states and to plan our actions vis-a-vis others in a way that agrees, or disagrees with the moral norms that we have internalized." Note the use of the personal and impersonal pronouns—the "it" of the brain and the "us" who do something with it. See also Jean-Pierre Changeux, *Neuronal Man: The Biology of Mind*, trans. Laurence Garey (Princeton, NJ: Princeton University Press, 1985).

[19] See Changeux, *Neuronal Man*, "Mental Objects," 126–69. Also see "To enjoy and to be angry," 107ff.

[20] Ibid., 74.

In *Exuberance: The Passion for Life*, Dr. Kay Redfield Jamison of Johns Hopkins writes extensively about this. Joy, she claims, is a primary human sentiment.[21] What most characterizes it are spiritedness, an exploratory agency, a light-hearted playfulness, and intense curiosity.[22] Happiness and contentment are pleasant feelings, but they fall far short of what Jamison means by joy. In joy, people find the capacity to mobilize psychic and social resources to resolve problems. In that respect, hyperthymic joy feeds off challenges; it does not seek to avoid them. But joy does much more: "Joyous states do other critically important things as well. They strengthen the bonds between members of a group and make more likely the group's participation in shared activities that will benefit the group as a whole; they fortify the ties between parent and child, teacher and student, leader and follower, lover and lover."[23] When I read Pope Francis's description of missionary discipleship, it sounds rather like what Jamison means by hyperthymic joy. Indifference? What's that?

Indeed, some people, Jamison says, are just "incapable of being indifferent." To illustrate her point, she recounts the story of President Theodore Roosevelt and John Muir who teamed up in 1910 to explore Yosemite together. Arriving there, they encountered a mystical place so majestically beautiful and untouched by human hands as to create in both of them something like awe. Roosevelt was not the type to spend all his time contemplating El Capitan (7,569 feet) or Yosemite

---

[21] Kay Redfield Jamison, *Exuberance: The Passion for Life* (New York: Knopf, 2004).

[22] All earthly life—whether vegetative, animal, or human—seeks propagation, adaptation, and flourishing according to the degree of its own capacities. Business, politics, and sports demand a high level of hyperthymic drive and special skills. Who could climb Mount Everest, El Capitan, and the north face of Eiger in Switzerland without an excess of skill underpinned by extraordinary thymic courage? Mastery of any skill in life demands months and years of dedication, but the focused and intense competition in sport makes hyperthymia in elite athletes something other than the couch potatoes watching them. David Foster Wallace wrote of watching Roger Federer play tennis as a "religious experience." St. Paul did not hesitate to compare mission and athletic competition in 1 Corinthians 9:24, which is reiterated in 2 Timothy 7 as "I have fought the good fight." Spectators and fans want the underdog to be competitive, the favorite to survive the challenge, the outcome to be delayed to the last second on the clock or the last putt. This exuberance needs to be translated into mission and ministry if the new evangelization is to be something more than rhetoric and outsourced turn-key programs.

[23] Jamison, *Exuberance*, 99.

Falls (2,425 feet) or the giant sequoias (up to 311 feet and 37 feet in diameter), marveling at them like an Indian yogi. The full shock of it all entered his soul and drove him on. A reporter once described the aftereffect that an interview with Roosevelt had on him: "You go into Roosevelt's presence . . . and you go home and wring the personality out of your clothes."[24] Well, he was an extraordinary man by any measure, but so are the great inventors, executives, elite athletes, and saints like St. Ignatius Loyola. They are all driven by hyperthymic joy and exuberance. This is what the new evangelization is searching for in ordinary parochial terms under the heading of missionary discipleship. To reduce church to peace of mind is to kill it.[25]

---

[24] Ibid., 11.

[25] Fortitude is the cardinal virtue for dangerous missions. Explorers cannot do without it. The book *Endurance* recounts Ernest Shackleton's expeditionary voyage in 1914 to Antarctica. Pack ice crushed the ship before they could explore the polar continent, yet Shackleton and his twenty-eight crewmen somehow made their way to Elephant Island. From that deserted godforsaken place, Shackleton set out with five crewmen in a twenty-foot lifeboat to sail across eight hundred miles of some of the roughest seas in the world to South Georgia Island where, upon landing, they were forced to hike over mountains and glaciers to a whaling station on the north side of the island to seek help. It is a story that leaves anyone, even by just reading it, breathless and exhausted. Soon thereafter, Shackleton returned to Elephant Island, where every member of his crew was rescued alive. Sea adventures are notoriously dangerous, but this one, given the circumstances, ranks among the most extraordinary. Getting a parish going? Are you kidding me? A thin line, of course, separates the foolhardy dreamer from the rugged explorer and creative visionary. St. Paul is the church's first and most famous missionary. His letters and Acts of the Apostles by Luke routinely recount the dangers he faced on mission. Nothing seemed to deter him. Similarly, the ninth-century Byzantine theologian-missionaries, the "apostles to the Slavs," St. Cyril and St. Methodius, are credited with the creation of the Glagolitic and Cyrillic alphabets to evangelize the Slavs who lacked a script for their language. St. Francis Xavier, the apostle of the Indies and the apostle of Japan, died before he could reach China in the sixteenth century. In the twentieth century, the great biblical scholar, Bach organist, and recipient of the Goethe Prize and Nobel Peace Prize, Dr. Albert Schweitzer, started a second career in medicine to become a humanitarian missionary in Lambarene in Gabon, Africa. Schweitzer once wrote, "Until he extends his circle of compassion to include all living things, man will not himself find peace." The Swiss Protestant Roger Schutz founded his ecumenical monastery at Taize in the Burgundy region of France in 1940 as France was defeated by Germany. Hyperthymic passion for God and humanity and hope is the essence of Christianity. Courage is the virtue of missionaries. The disengaged and hesitant pastor needs a way to get it. Therefore, let us not forget the lesson in the Parable of the Talents (Matt 25:14-30;

The New Oxford American Dictionary defines joy as "a feeling of great pleasure and happiness: *tears of joy/the joy of being alive*," and "a thing that causes joy: *the joys of Manhattan*." The etymology begins in the Old French *joie* from the Latin *gaudium*. *Joie de vivre* is a contagious cheerfulness. Enjoyment is *jouissance*. The French essayist Émile Chartier, known by his penname Alain, gave us some of the most insightful reflections we have on the human passions and the quest for happiness guided by a practical wisdom.[26] Joy seeks life, not death. Yet a tragic fate may power it into existence.

I believe that's exactly what happened to Irma Rombauer, whose story is an example of the redemptive potential in joy. Rombauer was the author of *The Joy of Cooking*. She wrote and published it privately with the insurance money she received after her husband's tragic suicide. The eighth and seventy-fifth-anniversary edition of *The Joy of Cooking* appeared in 2006. The death of her husband undoubtedly left Irma desolate. In that case, a work of mourning was not just psychological. It became literary and resulted in "the joy of cooking." Spirituality is the prayerful conjugation of all the modal verbs of surviving in everyday human life. A widow in 1930 felt the sting of death, and that sorrow restarted thymotic passion to publish the recipes her late despondent husband loved. Thymotic joy sustains the effort to exist in human beings tempted to abandon living at all. It is the power to undertake a new journey when the old one has ended or is likely to end. For Christians, joy recruits *thymos* as a recommencement of our lifelong apprenticeship to the Paschal Mystery.

Two twentieth-century philosophers in the phenomenological tradition have returned joy and *thymos* to their rightful place in the ontology of the human person. Paul Ricoeur and Emmanuel Levinas built these concepts into their philosophies. Levinas, a Lithuanian Jew who lived and wrote in France, and Ricoeur, a French Protestant,

---

Luke 19:12-27) where the frightened servant hides the one talent he is given in the ground for fear of failure if he invests it. His master repossesses the loan and awards it to the servant-entrepreneur who doubled the five talents he received. This is the parable a venture capitalist understands intuitively and that the church needs to understand better too. Modern philanthropy is right to expect a return on the gift that inevitably is an investment.

[26] *Alain: Alain On Happiness*, trans. Robert D. and Jane E. Cottrell (New York: Frederick Ungar Publishing Company, 1973). The French original, *Propos sur le bonheur*, was published in 1928.

made joy a central phenomenological theme. Both men served in the French army and were captured and imprisoned and survived. John Paul II bestowed the Paul VI Prize on Ricoeur in 2004 and referred to Levinas as a powerful influence on him in *Crossing the Threshold of Hope*.[27] In *Totality and Infinity: An Essay on Exteriority*, Levinas wrote a phenomenology of enjoyment.[28]

Philosophy begins properly for Levinas with the body and the embodied encounter with other persons. He did not share the priority of Descartes's mental *Cogito* or the withdrawn *Angst* in Heidegger's account of Dasein. For him, the truly primordial experiences are not thinking or solitude but those of embodiment and otherness. The face of the other person all by itself, for Levinas, is already an ethic without words. It says without even saying so: "Do not kill me; do not hate me." Intersubjectivity, for Levinas, has absolute priority over solitary subjectivity, the interior monologue of the solitary ego in us.

*Totality and Infinity* opens with an extended treatment of the Same and the Other. In its second and fourth sections, Levinas explores the primordial form of enjoyment (*jouissance*) found in the pure feeling of being alive. It makes itself felt in the experience we have of "living from" organic nature. Nature is the body's counterpart, the nourishment, a word, for Levinas, that suggests much more than a need or lack. Nourishment signifies a primary ontological reciprocity between the abundance in creation for which our hunger is the existential and organic counterpart. Therefore, human beings live not just in but physically "on the world," depend on the experience of nourishment and enjoyment at every level of their existence. From prenatal existence to the suckling newborn to senescence, we crave nourishment and, through it, experience joy. Spiritual transcendence builds its most elevated metaphors on the organic experience of "living from" what is outside and beyond the self—Grace and Love. The organic infrastructure of embodiment in food and drink can be metaphorically transferred to the homes we dwell in, to our personal possessions, to the kitchen table where nourishment and dwelling together are joined to sociality and hospitality. By making explicit the incarnated dependencies of the self, Levinas gives expression to the most original forms of enjoyment human beings know.

---

[27] John Paul II, *Crossing the Threshold of Hope* (New York: Knopf, 1995).

[28] Emmanuel Levinas, *Totality and Infinity: An Essay on Exteriority* (Pittsburgh: Duquesne University Press, 1969).

Finally, Levinas sketched the fuller dimensions of enjoyment (*jouissance*) in his reflections on love, *eros*, fecundity, and the family. The roots of love and family life lie in the soil of the body's enjoyment and nourishment. How could a Catholic at Mass fail to grasp such associations with spiritual fecundity in the church and the individual soul? An individualistic culture treats Communion like "fast food" taken at the window of MacDonald's before driving off on one's own. Final salvation itself is symbolized in the tradition as seeing the face of God and joining in a messianic feast. Even the "broken hallelujahs" of Leonard Cohen's lyric remind us that it is Hallelujah that we yearn for.[29] Hard to do that alone or without wine and song.

Let me complement Levinas's account of joy with Paul Ricoeur's phenomenology of *thymos* and the brief ontology of joy with which he concludes his study of the passions in *Fallible Man*. What Ricoeur borrows from Platonic *thymos* ("spiritedness") he connects to what Immanuel Kant wrote about the passions in his *Anthropology from a Pragmatic Point of View*. The specific genius of Kant regarding passions was to emphasize the unlimited urges bound to the three most potent human passions of all: the passion for power, the passion for possessions, and the passion for esteem or recognition. The word "lust," usually thought to be the most potent of the passions, is in truth recruited by the passion for esteem (love) or the passion for power (rape) or the passion for possession (jealousy).

For Ricoeur, these three passions—esteem or recognition, power, and having—are what drive human history itself. They correspond, one for one, with the great steering systems and institutions of political, economic, and cultural life.[30] Kant's observations on the human

---

[29] See the biblical lyrics of the song "Hallelujah" by Leonard Cohen.

[30] Paul Ricoeur, *Fallible Man*, trans. Charles Kelbley (Chicago: Henry Regnery Company, 1967), chap. 4, "Affective Fragility," 123–24: He calls *thymos* the "median function *par excellence* in the human soul. . . . It separates and unites vital affectivity or desire (*epithumia*) and the spiritual affectivity that the *Symposium* calls *eros*. In the *Republic*, Plato says that *thymos* sometimes battles on the side of reason, in the form of energy and courage; sometimes it enters the service of desire as an enterprising power, as irritation and anger." Ricoeur turned to Kant's *Anthropology from a Pragmatic Point of View*, where among the human passions and appetitive powers Ricoeur singled out three of them (*manias*): honor, domination, and possession (*Ersucht, Herrschsucht, Habsucht*). These are far different from what we usually think of as passions like lust, gluttony, or outbursts of anger. For one thing, the *manias* for honor or domination have no finite resolution in pleasure or satisfaction. They are open-ended and perpetually restless. Simply ask yourself when are we appreciated enough, or

passions (*manias*, he called them) for power, possessions, and esteem give concrete historical expression to what thymotic desire is all about. It is about a nuance of incompleteness attached to all craving. Human beings need and want power. But can anyone ever know how much power and control would be enough? Human beings need and want things. But when can anyone know if one has enough? Human beings need and want love and recognition. But when is anyone loved and respected enough? Thymotic desire is essentially restless because it is essentially limitless. It drives to excess of itself. This is the sign of what Ricoeur means by *thymos*.

Several twentieth-century existential thinkers made anguish (*angst*) the primary ontological mood. But, for Ricoeur, joy is more fundamental. He ended the first volume of his Philosophy of the Will, *Freedom and Nature*, by appealing to a Franciscan knowledge of necessity in creation rooted in a hope for reconciliation as opposed to what he called a Stoic or an Orphic solution to the human mystery of embodied existence. He wrote, "I am 'with' necessity, but 'among' creatures."[31] The preposition "among" suggests a communion in joy. In his phenomenology of embodiment, Ricoeur wrote, "Life is enjoyed (*erlebt*, *sentie*) rather than known: a certain diffuse affectivity reveals my life to me before my reason can explain it to me. . . . I can observe things, but I do not observe my life."[32] In life and death, presence and accompaniment are what we desire. This is why love is the fulfillment of the human spirit. *Fallible Man* ends on a similar note:

> If being is that which beings are not, anguish is the feeling *par excellence* of ontological difference. But Joy attests that we have a part of us linked to this very lack of being in beings. That is why the Spiritual Joy, the Intellectual Love and the Beatitude spoken of by Descartes, Malebranche, Spinoza and Bergson, designate, under different names and in different philosophical contexts, the only affective "mood"

---

when do we have enough money or possessions to feel secure and satisfied, or when is one's position in any hierarchy safe from betrayal? Why does a great talent need the audience's applause? Why did an American president authorize Watergate? These passions drive to excess by their very nature. And, yet they are the very same passions that also underlie the search for recognition in culture, for economic prosperity, and for political influence.

[31] Ricoeur, *Freedom and Nature*, 481.

[32] Ibid., 411.

worthy of being called *ontological*. Anguish is only its underside of absence and distance.

If man is capable of Joy, of Joy in and through anguish, that is the radical principle of all "disproportion" in the dimension of feeling and the source of man's *affective fragility*.[33]

For Ricoeur the very definition of human nature is the joy of living in the sadness of finite conditions.[34] Joy is irrepressible.

What I wrote about psychological hyperthymia—the passionate drive for excellence observed in explorers, researchers, successful executives, and elite athletes—has its psychological and ontological foundations in *thymos*. The same *thymos* Homer describes and Plato borrows from him is what Ricoeur reinterprets in the light of Kant's anthropology of the three passions responsible for shaping our public historical existence—the passion for power, having, and esteem. The thymic mood of joy is not defeated by life's challenges. If *thymos* guided by reason and rational purpose is there at all, struggle actually mobilizes it. At their very best, secular competition in the professions, politics, business, and athletics give us great analogues for the spiritual life. In the secular age, these pursuits may seem to have drawn down all the reserves in *thymos*, but that is far from the truth. The arts and humanities—all that STEM schools seem to overlook—will not cease. Religion is closer to the arts than it is to science. Christianity is a poetics of the possible as expressed in the Paschal Mystery. That poetics anchors itself in *thymos* in the case of a missionary disciple. Starting a family and sustaining a vocation or serving a parish or founding a monastery or a seminary takes more than a belief; they require thymotic passion. *Thymos* is what transforms the urge to give up for the joy of the final victory. It is the opposite of indifference.

The Joy of the Gospel is anything but a sentimental matter. It draws upon the psychic and ontological energies in the human person seeking something in the world to attach themselves to, something good, inherently worthy, and transformative for culture. The Gospel of Jesus Christ counts as that for Christians searching for a cause in which to invest thymotic passion. The task of the church is to make itself as transparently committed to that cause as it claims to be.

---

[33] Ricoeur, *Fallible Man*, 161.
[34] Ibid., 215.

In the conclusion, I will resume these reflections on *thymos* in relation to spirituality and to the social and political interpretation of thymotic recognition that Francis Fukuyama considers essential to liberal democracy itself.

# Conclusion

# The New Evangelization for a Secular Age

## Spirituality and *Thymos*

The World Synod on the New Evangelization (2012) coincided with the fiftieth anniversary of the opening of the Second Vatican Council (1962–1965). In five decades, the Catholic Church had reformed much of its internal pastoral life while strengthening the case it made for the Gospel of Jesus Christ as that relates to moral values in life, family, peace, and social justice. The analysis of modernity given in *Gaudium et Spes* became the pastoral and theological framework for the church's sense of mission in the post-conciliar period. But the meaning of modernity itself was in flux. The pace of progress in the technical spheres of life provided, as they often do, a giddy sense of cultural élan, but in the background was the loss of meaning, trust, and community. Cultural neo-conservatives bemoaned the loss of moral roots in American life. Daniel Bell traced much of the worry to the end of an industrial economy and beginning of a new technological communications revolution, to exhausted ideologies and to the feeling of a nihilistic view of life's purposes which had its birthplace in the philosophy of Nietzsche. Writing in the late 1970s, Bell offered those looking for hope this much comfort. "We stand, I believe, with a clearing ahead of us. The exhaustion of Modernism, the aridity of Communist life, the tedium of the unrestrained self and the meaninglessness of the monolithic political chants all indicate that a long era is coming to a close. The theme of Modernism was the word beyond: beyond nature, beyond culture, beyond tragedy—that was where the self-infinitizing spirit was driving the radical self. We are now groping for a new vocabulary whose key word seems to be limits: a limit to growth, a limit to spoliation of environment, a limit to arms, a limit to torture, a limit to *hubris*—can we extend the list? If we can, it is also one of the relevant portents of our time."[1] His argument on the future of religion was biblical in the sense that the Divine is what places limits on human freedom. But, after the death of God, only a storm of environmental, social, and economic crises could bring us to our senses. The "clash of civilizations"[2] has slowly edged toward "a world in disarray."[3] Beside the language of limits, there is also the anxious rhetoric of a possible apocalypse. Where should we turn for hope? The institutions of our political, economic, and social life in the West needed serious reform. The church itself has already embraced the arduous task of undertaking reform at the beginning of the 1960s.

Vatican Council II introduced the most far-reaching reforms in the Catholic Church since the Reformation and the Council of Trent (1545–1563). A century before Trent, Johannes Gutenberg produced the first Bible in movable type. Print technology would radically change the communicative conditions for Christianity from the sixteenth century forward. Luther published his famous "Ninety-Five Theses" (1517) on an early printing press. It took two weeks for them to circulate across Germany. Two months later, the text was being read all over Europe. The Lutheran Reformation was different from those eccentric medieval heretical movements that were suppressed by a local Inquisition. Print alone—modernization, if you will, in one of its earliest expressions—had changed the communicative conditions of an ancient faith and the nature of evangelization.

The church responded to this by invoking its authority. Forty years after Luther, the Council of Trent countered Gutenberg's printing press disseminating heresy with the church's *Index Librorum Prohibitorum* (*Index of Forbidden Books*, 1564). The Index was suppressed by the church in 1966 a year after Vatican II concluded. Evangelization by the censorship of books considered heretical became impossible.

New forms of Christian spirituality came to life in late medieval and post-Reformation Christianity. Two of the greatest were the ones

---

[1] Daniel Bell, "The Return of the Sacred? The Argument on the Future of Religion," in *The Winding Passage: Essays and Sociological Journeys 1960–1980* (Cambridge: Abt Associates, 1980), 353.

[2] Samuel P. Huntington, *The Clash of Civilizations and the Remaking of World Order* (New York: Simon & Schuster, 1996).

[3] Richard Haass, *A World in Disarray: American Foreign Policy and the Crisis of the Old Order* (New York: Penguin, 2017).

developed by the Jesuits and the Carmelites. The Carmelite mystic St. Teresa of Avila wrote great classics on the spiritual life. She also founded monasteries. The image of the soul in her *The Interior Castle* (1577) was modeled on the metaphor of seven mansions or stages in the spiritual life terminating in union with God. The post-Reformation contemplative was seeking a method of prayer which would bring her soul into the presence of God. Fifty years earlier, the *Spiritual Exercises* (1522–1524) of St. Ignatius Loyola were composed as a retreat program spread over twenty-eight to thirty days intended to engender in the participant who followed the recommended practices, prayers, and interior purifications a deeper awareness of God's will in one's life and a determination to follow Christ. It is, to speak in the language of the new evangelization, a "crash course" in missionary discipleship. These spiritualities, different as they are, were driven by a similar ardor for God and transformation. What I explained in the last chapter as "spiritedness" powered by thymotic desire is what these two religious geniuses had in abundance.

After Trent, Milanese Cardinal St. Charles Borromeo (1538–1584) created the first Catholic seminary in response to Trent's call for a reform of the clergy. That was a "spirited" gesture, as well, but in the sphere of pragmatic ecclesial imagination. He was not alone. Jean-Jacques Olier (1608–1657), *abbé* of the Church of St. Sulpice on the Left Bank in Paris, founded the so-called Sulpician method of priestly formation based on the idea of a *communauté éducatrice* (a formational community) of seminarians and priests living a common life in the seminary. For the Sulpicians, the necessary spiritual aptitude and theological competency as a priest had the best chance of success in the form of a living apprenticeship with priestly role models in a life of prayer, study, and pastoral experience.

Carmelite spirituality, Ignatian spirituality, and the French Oratory, despite their differences, brought to the church contemplative, educational, and formational spiritualities fed by diverse interests all powered by what psychiatrists and philosophers call *thymos*. In different ways, they were all missionary. The repressive *Index*, now suppressed, does not come close to telling the story of Counter-Reformation Catholicism.

In the manner of Trent, Vatican II initiated global reforms in the church because, like Trent, the world had changed radically. Pope John XXIII called the council praying for a "New Pentecost" for the church in the modern age. On the first Pentecost, the apostolic community of disciples in Jerusalem were filled with the Holy Spirit and began speaking in tongues the different nations could understand. It was a miraculous spiritual, evangelical, and hermeneutical event. The ecumenical, interreligious, and secular world needed to experience something like that again. The ideal of Christendom, enshrined in the slogan "throne and altar," which had dominated the ecclesial imagination of Catholicism from Charlemagne in the eighth century until the collapse of the Hapsburg Dynasty (1558) and the Peace of Westphalia (1648), would linger, but not for long. At Vatican II, biblical theology and doctrinal principles, more fundamental to revelation and Catholic ecclesiology than juridical canons and protégé monarchies, established the foundations for the new evangelization.

The political scaffolding once considered providential for ecclesial mission in the world had been removed. The church began to realize, often painfully, that Jesus Christ did not send his disciples on mission to establish a theocracy. Yet, in a certain sense, that is what happened by accident of one emperor's conversion and the birth of what later was known as Christendom. In the Nicene-Constantinopolitan Creed, the church confesses that Christ was "crucified under Pontius Pilate," an appointee of Tiberius Caesar to govern the Roman province of Judea. The Latin Christian apologist Lactantius would mark the military victory at Milvian Bridge in 312 of the first Christian emperor, Constantine, with the trope built on the ambiguity of the word "sign." He wrote, *in hoc signo vinces* ("in this sign you will conquer") because the hilt of Constantine's sword bore an uncanny resemblance to the cross of Christ. With the sixteenth- and seventeenth-century inter-Christian wars of religion, that trope became an unworthy conceit. For making that clear, one can thank Hugo Grotius and John Locke. The ideal of the nondenominational secular state began with their reflections on religious violence and civic peace.

In the same period of European history, the common noun "spirituality" (*spiritualité*) first began to be used in the seventeenth-century French Catholic tradition. The so-called "French School" of spirituality was born then. Like the nineteenth-century neologism of Charles Baudelaire, *modernité*, meant to characterize a radically new sensibility, *spiritualité* conveyed for French Catholics a distinctive religious self-consciousness. Today, the word spirituality covers the entire range of secular sensibilities in touch with different images of depth and meaning in human imagination, ranging from a deep attunement to personal depths in the self to the unspoiled natural world to social justice and rights of minorities.

In Catholicism, there are many spiritualities with images and metaphors drawn from the biblical tradition and the ambient culture and resourced from the writings of great theologians, spiritual masters, and founders of religious communities—Benedictine, Dominican, Franciscan, Ignatian, Theresian, Salesian, the list goes on. In our Catholic modernity, figures like the Trappist monk Thomas Merton, Dorothy Day of the Catholic Worker Movement, and the unbaptized French mystic Simone Weil, whose letters and essays were assembled in her spiritual masterpiece *Waiting for God*, capture the spiritual searching of a post-religious age.

Protestant spiritualities abound as well in modernity. From the meditative silence of Quakers to the ecstatic extroverted glossolalia ("tongues") in the Azuza Street Mission to the social gospel movements of the twentieth century, it offers a great diversity of expressions. Judaism has its Kabballah and Hasidic forms. Hindus may turn to Saivist (Siva) or Vaishnavist (Vishnu) in their spiritual practices. Buddhism even subdivides into Mahayana and Theravada types. Islam has Sufi mystics at one extreme and Al-Qaeda martyr-terrorists at the other.

From the perspective of average Sunday worshipers, such saintly figures and their followers constitute the "advanced placement" class for religious seekers and searchers and dwellers. These adepts sense something in the teachings, symbols, and rites of esoteric spirituality which is lost on the ken of much quotidian consciousness.

## The New Evangelization and the Secular Age

At the beginning of the new evangelization, secularism and the secular view on life were isolated as one of the major factors inclining some people toward religious indifference, agnosticism, or even a practical atheistic view of life. It was a short step from there to moral corollaries. Evangelization became morally tactical. But, the larger strategic assessment and comprehensive narrative of the secular age had not yet been written. The church lacked a fuller philosophical phenomenology of the modern self and the secular age. It was only natural that *Evangelii Nuntiandi* would be read against the fundamentalist horizon of the culture wars in the United States. The sexual revolution and the political debates over the right to abortion colored the responses of the church. In the aftermath of the 1968 encyclical of Paul VI on birth control (*Humanae Vitae*), the traditional image of Christianity as a religion overly-obsessed with violations of the sixth commandment was verified over and over as the sexual experimentation in society drove the culture war. Evangelization was fueled by the sense of resentment that American culture had been highjacked by the political left and by secular humanists. But, something much older in European and American culture associated with the birth of the idea of the secular order and the inventiveness of the denominational religious order was also at work. Moral relativism powered fundamentalism, and fundamentalism, like a low-pressure system in weather, powered relativism in turn. It was difficult to escape the moralistic interpretation of what Christian faith was all about. The new evangelization took the form of a catechetical recharge in the church, even a re-conversion of Catholics to the dogmatic and moral norms of their Catholicism. The hope was to reinvest Catholics in their faith by re-educating them about it. But, at that time, what Charles Taylor has articulated in his ideas about sources of the self, the conflicts of modernity, the modern social imaginary, and the secular age were not available. The problem of belief as such was not given a historical frame for the disturbing range of consequences of what was called secularism. While these ideas, by themselves, do not solve the pastoral problems which pastors are coping with, they do provide a rich vocabulary of sociological and philosophical categories with which to grasp our predicament as Christians in a secular age. The new evangelization movement, as I explained earlier in the book, was one movement in four papal iterations. Let me summarize them again as they related to secularism.

*Stage 1.* The Second Vatican Council did not use the word "secularism" in describing the modern world, though many of the cultural and moral issues it treated, especially in part 2 of *Gaudium et Spes*, relate to it. Paul VI first introduced the challenge of secularism in his closing speech at Vatican II. Later, in his apostolic exhortation *Evangelii Nuntiandi* (1975) the pope identified secularism as a major challenge in evangelizing the modern world. Much more work needed to be done, of course, in sociology, philosophy, ethics, and spirituality in parsing the social etiology and significance of secularism. But this early association of secularism with the crises of faith and morals after Vatican II became synonymous with evangelization for Catholicism as it was for Protestant Fundamentalism in the United States.

*Stage 2.* The new evangelization, properly so-called, began when the Latin American bishops coined the expression *nueva evangelización* in 1979 with the Puebla Document of CELAM. Its redaction of the changes would be as different as that culture and its challenges are different from those in North America or Europe. Shortly after his election as pope, John Paul II began to use the "new evangelization" image in speeches he delivered in Poland (1979) and Haiti (1983). For the next twenty years that expression would become the apostolic leitmotif of his pontificate. Everything he did and taught as pope was done to make the meaning and implications of the new evangelization plain to Catholics and to the world at large. When he died in 2005, he left a substantial body of papal literature on the meaning of it.

*Stage 3.* The first turning point in the church's assessment of secularism came at the 1985 Extraordinary World Synod of Bishops in celebration of the twentieth anniversary of the closing of Vatican Council II. Secularism became much darker and more menacing than what *Gaudium et Spes* called the "modern world." The final report of the synod even worried about a possible "secularization of the church." That view of the matter was reinforced in the pope's apostolic exhortation on the priesthood, *Pastores Dabo Vobis* (I Will Give You Shepherds), in which secularism also played a major part as an obstacle to evangelization. The formation of future priests in seminaries accordingly began to focus on secularism as some critics then defined it along with the ideology of atheism and moral relativism. Very little of redeeming moral, political, and social value in the secular order of modern life was noted.

*Stage 4.* The United States Conference of Catholic Bishops (USCCB) paid close attention to the strong links between the new evangelization and secularism developed at the Vatican. In the late 1980s, the USCCB chose the new evangelization as one of the top pastoral priorities for the United States. By 2012, the USCCB had developed a three-year strategic plan for the new evangelization, leaving bishops free to implement it locally as they saw fit. Gradually, theologians and commentators began to weigh in on the meaning of the new evangelization, which almost invariably included some critique of secularism. That critique leaned heavily on what Cardinal Ratzinger and John Paul II had published on the subject. Cardinal Francis George, archbishop of Chicago, who possessed a Ph.D. in philosophy, became a chief spokesman among U.S. bishops for the dominant anti-secular interpretation of the new evangelization. That earned him the nickname of "the American Ratzinger." Papal encyclicals of John Paul II such as *Fides et Ratio* (Faith and Reason, 1998) and *Veritatis Splendor* (The Splendor of Truth, 1993) carefully parsed the philosophical systems of thought which challenged the church's idea of moral and religious truth.

*Stage 5.* The attacks on the United States that took place on September 11, 2001, when four domestic passenger planes were highjacked and converted into missiles, two of them targeted at the Twin Towers of the World Trade Center in Manhattan, were essentially aimed at American secular society. Secularism was the "Great Satan," and it included American Catholics, Protestants, Jews, and Muslims. In 2002, when revelations of clergy abuse of minors and children and the diocesan cover-ups of that abuse became known, it was the secular press that made it known. Some Catholics felt the church was being unfairly targeted by seculars who despised its teachings. In 2004, Cardinal Joseph Ratzinger was lecturing on the same podium in Munich as Germany's leading secular philosopher, Jürgen Habermas, and remarking about pathologies in religion that secular reason had every right to critique. As Pope Benedict XVI, he chose to address the issue of religious violence in a lecture at Regensburg University but his imprudent reference to violence in Islam created a firestorm of criticism. Toward the end of the first decade of the new millennium, Benedict XVI returned from a visit to the Czech Republic to encourage the Pontifical Council for Culture to reach out in a new way to secular thought. The "Courtyard of the Gentiles" was launched in response to the pope's urgings. Perhaps, secular thinkers had something to teach the church not only about morality and the protection of children, but about religion itself in a secular age.

*Stage 6.* Pope Benedict XVI in 2010 formally established the Pontifical Council for the Promotion of the New Evangelization which he charged with preparing the Thirteenth Ordinary General Assembly of the Synod of Bishops on the theme of "The New Evangelization for the Transmission of the Christian Faith" to be held October 7–28,

2012. Pope Benedict presided over that synod and four months later, at age eighty, decided to retire as pope. His successor on the Chair of St. Peter was Cardinal Jorge Mario Bergoglio from Buenos Aires, Argentina, who took the name Pope Francis. In the fall of 2013, Pope Francis published his apostolic exhortation on the recent synod under the title *Evangelii Gaudium* (The Joy of the Gospel). The diagnosis of secularism in the edition of the new evangelization written by Pope Francis casts as much suspicion on globalization, consumerism, and economic factors as it does on relativism and life issues. It had a pronounced social justice orientation most evident in its fourth chapter. The Vatican would subsequently call two more world synods of bishops following the one on the new evangelization. The Fourteenth Ordinary General Assembly of the Synod of Bishops was on the theme "The Vocation and Mission of the Family in the Church and the Contemporary World," the results of which were met with intense criticism by a small group of bishops and theologians. The exhortation was entitled *Amoris Laetitia* (The Joy of Love). The October 2018 Fifteenth Ordinary General Assembly of the Synod of Bishops announced the theme as "Young People, the Faith, and Vocational Discernment." In light of the current crisis over the way Catholic bishops have managed reports about clergy sexual abuse and, in some cases, were abusers themselves, it will be interesting to see what kind of formal conclusions or propositions the participants in the synod will consider timely and urgent to pass along to the Holy Father. Abuse could just as easily incline the church to tip backward to a jurisprudence of religion than to an evangelical reform of it. How much of it do we attribute to the constitution of the clerical culture itself and how much to the permeation of religious sensibility by the culture of transgression?

These six stages summarize in some detail what I treated in the opening chapters of the book. They indicate two things. First, the need for a more comprehensive hermeneutic of the secular age to contextualize some of the moral and religious disturbances in society which, heretofore, had been isolated for criticism in a tactical way by the church. Evangelization under current conditions requires an interpretation of the "signs of the times" which place them in a much longer philosophical narrative. I have tried to show in the book what advantages such an approach has over mere indictments. Second, the new evangelization needed to make good on the claim that it would be new in ardor, messages, and methods. Pope Francis has tried to do that more than his predecessors preoccupied, as they were, with doctrinal and moral errors. One method of the new evangelization was to reform the church itself. Deep internal reforms in the church after clergy abuse have become unavoidable, but they will depend on the correct diagnosis of what created the conditions for this crime at the time it happened and the conditions which favored its cover-up. Pope Francis rejuvenated the rhetoric of joy as a mode of interpreting what John Paul II spoke of as "ardor." The culture of religious indifference today is now additionally burdened with a cynicism about the church itself. The changes proposed in the church must not only be according to the Gospel and tradition read in light of it, but proportionate to the damage done to Christian faith by the abuse crisis. One of the matters I had addressed in the book was the church's resistance for most of the nineteenth and twentieth centuries to the idea of religious freedom. With the belated recognition by the church that religious freedom was not only essential to the secular democratic order, but integral to our own belief in human conscience, the concept of religious freedom became a shared if controversial linkage between the church and the secular moral order.

## Religious Freedom without Resentment

When direct power over liberal democracy was removed from religious institutions, the sentiment of resentment became unavoidable for some of them. The long nineteenth century in the church was one reflection of it. Democratic liberalism was viewed by many as the archenemy of the faith. Today Catholic bishops in the United States appeal to the concept of religious liberty in defense of the church's right to dissent from secular moral worldviews.

To complete what was said earlier about its secular genesis and its late adoption into the official teaching of the church, let me briefly offer what Charles Taylor, Jocelyn Maclure, and Paul Ricoeur say about it. All agree that a post-secular, open, pluralistic, public sphere and state, one that is not demeaning of conscience, whether religious or secular, is needed. Jürgen Habermas holds the same opinion of the matter.

Thus it is in the interest of the constitutional state to deal carefully with all the cultural sources that nourish its citizens' consciousness of norms and their solidarity. This awareness, which has become conservative, is reflected in the phrase: "postsecular society."

This refers not only to the fact that religion is holding its own in an increasing secular environment and that society must assume that religious fellowships will continue to exist for the foreseeable future. The expression "postsecular" does more than give public recognition to religious fellowships in view of the functional contributions they make to the reproduction of motivations and attitudes that are societally desirable. The public awareness of a postsecular society also reflects a normative insight that has consequences for the political dealings of unbelieving citizens with believing citizens. In the postsecular society, there is an increasing consensus that certain phases of the "modernization of the public consciousness" involve the assimilation and the reflexive transformation of both religious and secular mentalities. If both sides agree to understand the secularization of society as a complementary learning process, then they will also have cognitive reasons to take seriously each other's contributions to controversial subjects in the public debate.[4]

Habermas not only means to grant religious citizens freedom of conscience, but also to admit, as part of an open secular outlook on values, in principle at least, that religious worldviews have something reasonable to say to secularism.

In 2011, Jocelyn Maclure and Charles Taylor co-authored a small insightful piece of political philosophy on conscience and secularism entitled *Secularism and Freedom of Conscience* (originally written in French since the authors are both Canadians and specifically concerned about the debates about faith and secularism in Quebec Province). It treats such topics as moral pluralism and neutrality, the main principles of political secularism, secular political regimes, life in the public and private spheres, and religious symbols in public life. The argument in the book begins with a discussion of moral pluralism, state neutrality about worldviews, and secularism in the philosophical sense. Moral pluralism in free modern societies is the universe in

---

[4] Jürgen Habermas, "The Pre-political Foundation of the Democratic Constitutional State," in *Dialectics of Secularization: On Reason and Religion* (San Francisco: Ignatius Press, 2006), 46–47.

which religious pluralism finds itself. Liberal states guarantee individuals the autonomy to decide for themselves what philosophical and moral worldviews they will hold and live by. Liberal states, by definition, grant freedom of conscience (each one may decide his or her own moral outlook) and freedom of religion (each one may believe and practice the religion of his or her choice). The state as such is obliged to remain neutral about worldviews and faiths. Deep moral convictions, whether religious or secular, are protected by the state's commitment to the individual's freedom of conscience and the state's acknowledged incompetency in such matters. In short, the state's neutrality about faith and morals is itself a new "moral ideal."

There is a limit to the state's neutrality, however. It cannot be neutral on a few core principles like human dignity, basic human rights, and popular sovereignty (democracy). These are not up for debate. They are axiomatic for a liberal democratic political system. If a society allows moral pluralism to exist in principle and if it protects it, the state cannot side with or force on conscience any religious or secular worldview. If it does so, it threatens to turn one or another group into "second-class citizens."[5] State neutrality is a "moral ideal" in liberal secularism, so states that declare themselves officially atheistic or theocratic have abandoned the secular ideal of moral neutrality.

Further on the authors raise the question of the "principles of secularism."[6] The principles are more fundamental than the ways and means by which a state ensures its moral neutrality. There are two major principles or aims in political secularism: (1) equality of respect and (2) freedom of conscience. These are always essential. The means or modes for realizing these essential aims are (1) separation of church and state and (2) state neutrality toward religions. There is often some confusion over the core principles of secularism and the different means for realizing them in any situation. Some principles underlying secularism are moral principles, like freedom of conscience, and other principles are only institutional arrangements, such as separation of church and state, to protect the deeper moral values involved. There are secular societies, like Britain and

---

[5] Jocelyn Maclure and Charles Taylor, *Secularism and Freedom of Conscience*, trans. Jane Marie Todd (Cambridge: Harvard University Press, 2011), 13.

[6] Ibid., 19–26.

Denmark, that have established churches but still protect freedom of conscience.

There are two types of secular "regimes." Type 1 is republican (not the party), and rigid, such as we find in France. Type 2 is liberal, pluralist, and open. The first type really has other aims in mind than mere freedom of conscience. It controls religion in public life precisely to substitute secular values for the values religion once supplied in society. "Civic integration" is the overriding secular aim in that case; diversity is dangerous. In other words, there is a certain worldview interest involved. Complete neutrality is sacrificed for the hegemony of some possibly contested secular values for the sake of civic harmony. Religion is driven by such states into the private sphere because it is often socially divisive. The second type of secular regime is described by Maclure and Taylor as open, pluralist, and liberal, "whose function is to find the optimal balance between respect for moral equality and respect for freedom of conscience."[7] In other words, secularism is not a static doctrine but a work-in-progress, negotiating a balance between freedom of religion and equal respect for different worldviews.

Republican secularism confines the practice of religion to the private sphere of life, where it may nourish personal meanings and motivations but where it cannot challenge other public secular meanings designed to ensure "civic integration." The word "public" can be ambiguous. It may refer to the state itself (the "republic") or to what philosophers today call the "public sphere," a civic concept where opinions are freely held and expressed. "Public" can mean what the state officially endorses (schools, the lawn in front of the courthouse as well as the courtroom) or it may refer to public spaces like streets, sidewalks, malls, and stadiums. In the open version of secularism, neutrality about religious conceptions of the good life is obligatory for state institutions. Individual persons retain the right to their moral convictions. In the republican conception of secularism beliefs are to be observed in private and kept out of the civic public sphere. Maclure and Taylor consider this view of secularism "morally suspect."[8] It cannot help but treat religious citizens as second-class citizens.

[7] Ibid., 34.
[8] Ibid., 40.

State neutrality in religion does not require that religious citizens "privatize their religious affiliation."[9] Are judges and teachers allowed to display the religious symbols of their private faiths on their person while exercising their public office? Open secularism still must weigh principles of personal freedom against principles of state neutrality in such cases. Where the power to punish is involved, as in courtrooms, it seems that visible displays of religious symbols should not be allowed. On the other hand, allowing reasonable accommodation for workers in public institutions to practice their religion does not compromise the neutrality of the state in religious matters. From questions about individual citizens or public officials wearing crosses to laws obliterating the religious heritage of a given society, like public displays of the Ten Commandments, pluralist secularism seeks to strike a balance of reasonable accommodation and respect for different principles. The calendar of a country is a striking example in which the state may recognize religious holidays and events without endorsing the particular beliefs those holidays represent for believers. These are the kinds of distinctions about religious freedom and secularism that Maclure and Taylor offer in their monograph on the subject. Though crafted in the light of the Canadian francophone issue in Quebec, the distinctions are also helpful in the American context which sometimes seems poised toward a French *laïcisme* and other times toward a more open pluralist secularism.

The philosopher Paul Ricoeur, in the French context, offered a set of parallel distinctions between a political "secularism of abstention," where the state maintains complete neutrality about religion, and a civil "secularism of confrontation," where the policy is to encourage public debate about ideas whether religious or non-religious. He asked secular individuals, who claim to be interested in religious tolerance, how they can expect their children to dialogue peacefully about different moral and religious ideas if those ideas and their sources are systematically ignored in public education. Before public schools end up secularizing children coming from religious traditions, it makes children coming from secular backgrounds ignorant of the religious foundations of Western civilization. Does it make any sense from an educational and cultural point of view for high school kids

[9] Ibid., 42.

to study the love life of Zeus in Greek myths but be kept ignorant of the biblical texts which are the source of the canon of Western literature from Dante to T. S. Eliot? This view of the secular censorship of education is itself intolerant. The prejudice that all expressions of religion are irrational and fundamentalist makes secularism narrow and ideological.

For dialogue to occur in a secular context in the confrontation of ideas, Ricoeur claims that three essential conditions are necessary: (1) those who speak for religion need to admit that its claim to truth *does not exhaust* all truth and that it welcomes the contributions of other viewpoints; (2) rationalist thought in stating its own view *must not deny that religion* can contribute in important ways to public life; (3) finally, between religion and science there exists a wide range of moral viewpoints whose *plausibility forces a generous agnosticism on everyone.*[10] The rules governing a dialogue between religion and secularism operate, then, with three self-imposed limits—the truth I know, which I can admit is not the whole truth; the contribution reason makes to society does not exhaust every possible contribution to public life, even and including those contributions coming from believers; a generous agnosticism must impose limits on any pretensions to absolute knowledge. Pastors could encourage such respectful virtues from the pulpit. Even families could put those rules into practice at home. The dialogue between religious and secular worldviews, to use the language of Charles Taylor in *A Secular Age*, is the condition for belief in the modern world.

Ricoeur proposes his own version of the "open and pluralist secularism" of Maclure and Taylor. Such openness simply acknowledges that there are "unresolvable differences" between convictions in the modern world. But that doesn't mean dialogue and reasonable accommodations in pluralist societies are impossible. The fear of fundamentalism is what drives secularism today to become more intolerant itself. The Catholic approach to faith and reason, its endorsement of biblical criticism and religious freedom as the condition for a reasonable religious faith in the secular age, should make it an ideal dialogue partner in the context of critique and conviction.

---

[10] Paul Ricoeur, *Critique and Conviction: Conversations with Francois Azouvi and Marc de Launay*, trans. Kathleen Blamey (New York: Columbia University Press, 1998), "Education and Secularism,"127–38.

## *Thymos* **and Public Life**

In my discussion of The Joy of the Gospel, I referred to the source of the image of *thymos* as the basis for the soul's "spiritedness" in Homer and Plato. *Thymos* in Homer's *Iliad* is the passionate instinct within Achilles that demands he take revenge on Hector for killing his comrade Patroclus—loyalty to a friend, instinctive justice, and revenge based on it. Plato transferred instinctively martial *thymos* to philosophy to the passion for the city's defense in the *Republic*. *Thymos* is one dimension of the tripartite human soul in the *Phaedrus*. In loyalty to its master, Plato makes the guard dog protecting its home and master an example of *thymos*. It is courage in the face of danger and in loyalty to a noble ideal. Paul Ricoeur borrowed Plato's philosophical translation of a Homeric image as a basis for his analysis of human passions as part of his larger philosophy of the will. He interpreted Platonic *thymos* through the lens of Immanuel Kant's anthropology of the human passions including the three which are most influential in the public sphere of our social and moral experience: the passions for power, wealth, and recognition.

The Platonic image of the charioteer of reason (*logos*) holding the reins of two powerful stallions pulling this way and that—desire (*eros*) and spiritedness (*thymos*)—gave him the symbol he needed to construct a threefold dialectic of passion instead of the twofold dualism of body and soul favored in the traditional tracts on the human passions from Thomas Aquinas to Descartes. *Thymos* is the restless passion par excellence that is the stallion's spiritedness in us to which religious faith and symbolism must be harnessed if faith is to make a difference in cultural life.

The spiritualities through the centuries much taken with the Stoic ideal of *apatheia*—the soul becalmed of all passion—like Quietism, are the opposite of the missionary discipleship harnessed to *thymos*. Apathy moves nothing. *Thymos*, and the "heart" which is the biblical seat for it, is inherently restless. It veers toward revenge as easily as it does toward courage. By extending the range of *thymos* from its seat in the soul, as it was in Plato, to the exteriorized human passions for power, possessions, and esteem, Ricoeur built a conceptual bridge from his anthropology of the passions to the passions that drive the most potent spheres of public life and meaning: politics, economics, and culture. He attached an Augustinian vision of the working of divine grace, not only in the soul itself, which is where it must be, but in the works of human culture where the incessant dialectic of good and evil plays itself out.

The Joy of the Gospel speaks explicitly in thymotic terms when the pope says the missionary disciple lives "fearlessly" and with "boldness" (Greek: *parrhesia*) (EG 259). God himself "desires" a transfigured life in us. The words of the missionary evangelist should "stir up" the heart. Pope Francis longs for a new chapter in ecclesial evangelization "full of fervor, joy, generosity, courage, and boundless love" (EG 261). These pages are a glossary of rhetorical images and religious synonyms for *thymos*. The pope complains that too many Christians lack "vigor and passion" (EG 266).

The Second Vatican Council adopted an Augustinian transformational approach to faith and culture. The church acknowledged the legitimate autonomy of the political, social, and cultural spheres of human action while upholding religious freedom and the mysterious working of grace in secular time. The recognition of human autonomy and the autonomy of nature was an acknowledgment by the church that at creation God had endowed the world with its own causality and the human person with choice. Human freedom itself was a gift of God that was both creative and destructive. The Lord did not rescind freedom after the first sin, or the second, or the accumulated evil that provoked the flood. To the contrary, God himself repented of a destructive impulse. YHWH is not Shiva. The odor of Noah's offering persuaded the Lord of the futility of divine rage: "I will never again curse the ground because of humankind, for the inclination of the human heart is evil from youth; nor will I ever again destroy every living creature as I have done" (Gen 8:21). Divine patience conquers fate. After Moses shattered the first tablets of the Law when he descended from Sinai and saw Israelites worshiping the Golden Calf, he re-wrote them a second time (Exod 34:1-4). In Ezekiel, God himself says to the prophet, "Moreover, I gave them statutes that were not good and ordinances by which they could not live. I defiled them through their very gifts, in their offering up all their firstborn, in order that I might horrify them, so they might know that I am the Lord" (Ezek 20:25-26). God loves human freedom which is his gift so he loves second chances as well.

From the book of Genesis and the first sin through Jesus' crucifixion, human freedom is not just fallible freedom but historically fallen freedom. Reason, as Luther never tired of saying, is equally damaged by Adam's fault. We know much about fallen human nature from St. Augustine's *Confessions*, his Anti-Pelagian writings, and the *City of God*. But created human nature is more originally good than freedom on its own can ever be bad. The *imago Dei* in the human being survived the Fall.

This "assimilation" and "reflexive transformation" of both secular and religious mentalities can only happen in dialogue and in the open public sphere. Habermas rejects the cavalier dismissal by secular reason of religious intuitions. Like Taylor and Pope Francis, he accepts the principle that the dialogue and encounter between nonbelieving and believing citizens will transform both in ways they can't presently foresee. The importance of religious freedom, conceived as a secular response to religious violence, has transformed Catholicism as much as the nature of the dignity and respect due to the human person is beginning to transform secular law. Exchanges between faith and reason are as old as Christianity itself.

In the beginning of the book, I mentioned a few examples of contemporary apocalyptic secular politics and religion. The rhetoric of Robert Heilbroner, Kurt Anderson, or Rod Dreher is an implicit recognition that the modern moral order is in jeopardy. Their views may be reasonably balanced by what Daniel Bell wrote for the OECD Interfutures project in Paris (later reprinted in *Foreign Policy* as "The Future World Disorder: The Structural Context of Crises"). Bell confirmed the worries of many that, along with its stunning progress, the modern world faced disturbing forces threatening the current world order. The essay aimed "to sketch the broad socioeconomic context which, at its loosest, will constrain policy-makers and pose, in direct form, as yet unresolved dilemmas."[11] Two years after the paper was published, the Ayatollah Khomeini left his exile in Paris and returned to Iran as its supreme leader. Bell hardly mentioned Islam.

As much as secular intellectuals may hope otherwise, religion will always remain a factor in the human search for meaning and truth. Best that it be good and healthy religion that can learn from secularism and responsibly transform the secular order in the future. The issue most alive now at the level of public philosophy is the debate between liberalism and communitarianism on the matter of religion.

---

[11] Bell, "The Future World Disorder: The Structural Context of Crises," in *The Winding Passage*, 211.

How can a liberal democratic order legitimately not impose its secularism upon the diverse cultural and religious cultures existing within it? Maclure, Taylor, and Ricoeur, as I indicated above, offer some fresh ways to think about that.

Bell wrote that the postwar period was unrivaled in terms of economic and political progress. Optimism on many fronts felt justified and the so-called religious optimism, widely evidenced at Vatican II, did not seem out of place. Europe had recovered from World War II. Hope had its reasons. In his essay, Bell identified a "second transformation" in the modern order that should have bothered policymakers more than it did. The international order, he argued, was ending. The emergence of new states and "a vast multiplication of new actors, new constituencies, new claimants in the political arenas of the world" were changing the conditions of international order.[12] This was accompanied by the astounding progress in technology, communications, and transportation. Bell labelled it the postindustrial age. Advanced societies would have to face and resolve four overarching issues in the years ahead. First, because economics was global, national economic policy has international repercussions. Second, national debt brings economic protectionism, which is isolationist. Third, a demographic tsunami of youth asking for education and work opportunities was growing in the First and the Third Worlds. Fourth, the distribution in the world of rich and poor nations, and the percentage of industrial production the poor countries would have to achieve by the end of the millennium just to keep pace, must be bridged by an ever-increasing middle class. Poverty breeds violence, and poverty plus local violence cause immigration. The Joy of the Gospel has good reason to put the accent on economics and poverty in relation to secularism as it does.

For the most part, these are economic issues, but they have major political and social repercussions. Bell suggested ominous similarities between the 1970s and the period after World War I. Four deserved attention: (1) in both periods, there is an "insoluble problem," (2) a "parliamentary impasse," (3) "an unemployed and educated intelligentsia," and (4) the phenomenon of "private violence."[13] Adjusting for the current situation, the "insoluble problem" is religious terror and nuclear threats; the governing impasse is a politics paralyzed by

[12] Ibid., 212.
[13] Ibid., 223–27.

ugly tribal partisanship; there is an overeducated, searching, underemployed youth class; and the constant story of local American news is drug violence while rogue militias consume the strategic security planning of nation states.

What Pope Francis offered us in The Joy of the Gospel, if seen against this canvas of concerns, points to analogous issues. Withdrawing into enclaves of wealth, piety, anger, or indifference will not solve poverty and violence much less its causes. The new evangelization needs a social ethic more capacious than the right to life.

When a single canopy of meaning covered human life, as in the medieval period, it was impossible not to believe in God or in Christ as our Savior and Judge. After Darwin, the torn canopy of religious symbols gave way to a new scientific canopy of evolution, which is thought to explain the genesis of all there is and can be in human beings. Twentieth-century political religions tore holes in a self-sustaining scientific canopy and the humanism it was expected to strengthen. Powerful political ideologies turned science and economics against human beings in Communism and Nazism. Things change, but they also remain the same. In the twenty-first century, Twitter brought down Egyptian President Mubarak in the Arab Spring of 2011. It may soon do the same to representative and deliberative democracy in the United States. Trust in public institutions like serious journalism and the responsible referees of events in news media is breaking down as authoritarian heads of state attack them. Is the Westphalian System itself breaking down?

The dualism of body and soul on which so much Christian teaching rests is, in this reading, formally clear and existentially incomplete. The metaphysical clarity of Aristotle and St. Thomas needs, indeed demands, a treatise on the passions to make sense of the human quest for the good. *Thymos* is one key to an answer. *Thymos* has more than a purely psychological and philosophical significance. It belongs in political theory as well. The argument for *thymos* interpreted as "the passion for recognition" was made in a controversial but brilliant defense of liberal democracy written by Francis Fukuyama, *The End of History and the Last Man*.[14] Written after the collapse of communism in 1989, Fukuyama's thesis was that the lone contender for a viable

---

[14] Francis Fukuyama, *The End of History and the Last Man* (New York: The Free Press, 1992). See "Part Three: The Struggle for Recognition" and "Part Four: The Last Man." See also Francis Fukuyama, *Identity: The Demand for Dignity and the Politics of Resent-*

economy left in the world was liberal capitalism. In that sense, and in that sense alone, the "end of history," meaning its "immanent goal," was more likely to be found in some version of free democratic capitalism than in a Marxist utopia. Still, the image "end of history" drew much criticism, including from Pope Francis in The Joy of the Gospel where he wrote: "Evil crystallized in unjust social structures . . . cannot be the basis of hope for a better future. We are far from the so-called 'end of history'" (EG 59). The pope and others misunderstood Fukuyama's point, but he was correct in the sense that democratic capitalist institutions are very far from meeting the full ideals of distributive and social justice. What Fukuyama wrote about the political factor of *thymos*, however, is very germane to the pope's intentions. For Fukuyama, *thymos* is the irrational ground in the human soul for political recognition in public life. A secular liberal regime ignores this at its peril.

Many contested Fukuyama's thesis. Whatever weaknesses the book may have had in terms of political theory and economics, the author's exegesis of the political implications of *thymos* as recognition was a *tour de force*. It complements Ricoeur's philosophical interpretation of thymotic passion amplified by Kant's understanding of the quest for honor (*Ehrsucht*) or esteem, which Fukuyama, following Alexander Kojeve's interpretation of the master-slave dialectic in Hegel, calls the quest for recognition. Fukuyama placed *thymos* as "recognition" at the heart of his political theory and a challenge to liberalism hooked exclusively on the acquisition of private wealth.

One cannot reduce democratic political life, he claimed, to free-market economics and the constitution of a free state in the balance of powers as many commentators do. Reducing capitalism to a calculation for benefits and personal satisfaction misses the essentially irrational components in the universal human desire for recognition. Human beings not only need and want order, security, physical goods, and prosperity. They need and seek to be recognized politically and socially for who they are—for their identities. In short, democratic politics was not just about partisanship and private property but about the conditions that make recognition and dignity possible in public life. Liberal democracy offered the best chance, Fukuyama argued, for realizing that desire. Despising certain races,

---

*ment* (New York: Farrar, Straus and Giroux, 2018) for a further examination of the meaning of *thymos* in contemporary U.S. political life.

creeds, and sexualities insults irrational *thymos* in pluralist societies. The ways in which some demands for the recognition of identity destabilize older moral regimes in society constitute the agenda for the current struggles in American public life.

## Pastoring the Sheep in a Secular Age

I believe that the new evangelization as outlined in The Joy of the Gospel provides a fresh starting point for the ecclesial renewal that began with Vatican II and will continue into the foreseeable future. The political order of life in the world today reminds some of the aftermath of World War I and the Bolshevik Revolution in Russia. Fundamentalisms and nationalisms contend for the passionate allegiance of human beings around the world. The moral capital of church leaders after the latest revelations about the clergy abuse crisis has never been lower. Some predict a hemorrhaging of trust in one of the world's greatest religious and moral institutions because of it.

In that context, let me return to the six challenges I mentioned in chapter 2 which affect the prospects of the new evangelization. My responses flow from a conviction that the secular age is not only with us but, in a paradoxical and ironic sense, was itself a providential development in Western history. It is time for the church to make the most of it even while it critiques its excesses and moral distortions.

*Declining numbers.* The numbers of people in many churches each Sunday send a sign of apathy about and indifference to religion. *Thymos* has moved elsewhere from religion to engineering, business, medicine, sports, and the secular philanthropy in our time. What is the parish for? The causes for declining numbers vary: location, weak pastoral leadership and liturgy, neighboring parishes that offer better religious services, and the rising indifference to religion itself as secular activities absorb everyone's attention. Weekends are full enough as it is. There's lacrosse practice. There's golf. The truth is that large crowds always matter in church, especially in a commercial age, as they do in every other marketplace. Numbers communicate an enterprise of serious intent and consequence for consumers. World Youth Days draw enormous crowds which because of mass media project the message into the public sphere. Jesus addressed crowds. The crowd is an empirical verification, whether assembled by a political candidate, pope, bishop, or pastor, that something important is going on.

For that reason, half-empty Catholic churches broadcast a failing mission and in fact demoralize the assembly itself. They must be either turned around or merged so that numbers in worshiping congregations are consolidated. "The medium is the message"[15] and the medium for public worship normally is the large assembly of voices. Numbers create the conditions for a contagious experience of missionary *thymos*.

Half-empty seminaries have carried the ball in training priests now for the past forty years. Merging two or three together has met resistance for many reasons. In place of the rational solution, the bishops have been forced to follow a Malthusian Law—the weak die off, small seminaries starve to death and vanish without a trace. There has been no national plan from the U.S. bishops to rationalize the seminary marketplace since vocations went into free fall in the late 1960s. An underreported financial scandal in the church would show the red-ink in the per-student costs of training seminarians by pursuing this Malthusian course. To disguise it dioceses have recruited seminarians from Latin America and Africa whose linguistic and cultural fluencies for the new evangelization here are normally quite poor. This was always a stop-gap measure. The church must find another solution to vocations. The Vatican has already approved the reception and ordination of married Anglican priests into the Catholic priesthood. The clergy abuse crisis cannot help but raise once again the question of ordaining married men to the Catholic priesthood. Every Catholic may be a missionary disciple, but competent spiritual and pastoral leaders are crucial for mobilizing the ecclesial spirit in the laity. If the mission of the church is primary and if the Eucharist necessary, then the church needs many more competent priests— celibate and married. The new evangelization demands more pastors and pastoral associates with spiritual *thymos* and imagination. The role of women in the church at every level must also be pursued at the same time. One cannot fail to see what moral disasters all-male sub-cultures in church and society have managed to tolerate.

*Finances*. Fewer seminarians in seminary, fewer faithful in church, and fewer Catholic kids in parochial school equal greater financial pressures and deficits. This cannot be kept up indefinitely with special collections because larger diocesan services will suffer. Lay parish

---

[15] Phrase coined by Marshall McLuhan.

finance committees notwithstanding, seminaries need to form future priests competent in managing the capital and personnel resources of the parish. Most newly ordained priests suddenly find themselves responsible for institutions whose capital worth runs in the millions of dollars. Many have never managed anything more complex than a personal schedule and studies.

But managing deficits and closing parishes alone is not to solve the problem. Downsizing the ministry means downsizing the mission at the same time. If parishes are merged, their budgets need to be combined with a larger percentage going to expansion efforts in outreach. Personal contact is crucial, but today the growing parish needs to attract more twenty- and thirty-somethings who get their information from new social media platforms. Evangelical churches are way ahead of most Catholic parishes on this. Some successful Catholic parishes are modelling their church organization on evangelical models of management and marketing. Technical expertise is absolutely required, and usually significant personnel and capital costs are involved. That adds to the strain. One of the most successful evangelical initiatives ever in denominational Protestantism was Methodism. Little white, framed Methodist "chapels" still dot the rural landscape of America. They fit in any neighborhood. Easy to build, pay for, and maintain, they match the uncertain character of contemporary American religious demographics. If the congregation falls away, such chapels are easily converted into another business. They're practical in a pragmatic and religiously uncertain age. The megachurch may become, in time, a white elephant itself. God traveled in the ark with his people in a tent in the Judean wilderness. The Son of Man had nowhere to lay his head. Downscaling construction of churches in missionary circumstances is just smart.

*Religious options.* The secular world is a world of choices—spiritual and otherwise. Catholics think less in terms of parochial geography and more in terms of parishes where they feel welcomed, needed, and spiritually nourished. Like it or not, competition and choice drive religion today as they do everything else. Parishes, despite themselves and the usual diocesan rhetoric, are competing with one another and with evangelical start-ups. Experimentation in pastoral life, within the norms of Catholic doctrine and identity, should not be discouraged. The mission today, in fact, demands it.

In 1965, the Holy See authorized the celebration of Sunday Mass on Saturday evening. The real meaning of a "Vigil Mass" had no purchase in the mentality of the average Roman Catholic. Who keeps "vigils" today except family members at the bedsides of the dying? Even Christmas Eve was not a vigil in the proper liturgical sense. Santa Claus came down the chimney then, not the Infant Jesus! The Saturday Vigil Mass has become a mainstay in church life by now and for very important pastoral reasons—some, like firemen, had to work on Sundays and could not easily attend Mass then. But the Saturday Mass was certainly never felt then or now as a real vigil—a way of anticipating the "Lord's Day." Rather, the Saturday Mass was and has always been a pastoral accommodation and sheer convenience liturgy, like the twenty-four-hour 7-Eleven or MacDonald's. An ancient liturgical tradition was co-opted by secular time. The "weekend" is how we speak, not the sabbath. It's free optional time yet increasingly encumbered for middle-class families with more things that must be done. It's one more workday in the workweek that is working seculars to death. The ancient sabbath was given by God to Israel to spare people from working all the time. Work is the religion of America and other global economies. Some people must work at night, like cops, so we can rest. In France, seculars are insisting that businesses not force them to do work by emailing tasks after work hours. On secular terms alone, the idea of the sabbath is trying to come back.

*Religious illiteracy.* Even after fifty years and enormous biblical catechetical efforts, many Catholics are effectively illiterate about the Bible and their own tradition. Liturgical tools for lectors and parishioners like *Give Us This Day* and *Magnificat* are helping to address this. The first illiteracy is in a secular media itself who announce that a priest is "holding" or "performing" a Mass. Searchers can find plenty of spiritual literature, but much of that is New Age, Evangelical, and Fundamentalist. The new evangelization began with a strong emphasis on personal spirituality, better catechesis, and active parochial involvement. Like a Jewish synagogue and its rabbi, the Catholic parish needs to see itself today as a "school of religion" as well as a place of worship and fellowship. Biblical literacy should be, as it was at Vatican II, the foundation and goal of adult catechesis. Serious Catholics should be reading serious popular Catholic journals of opinion about their religion and public life. A sermon cannot do this. You can't skim the cream off a religious tradition as rich as Catholicism and the biblical canon with ten minutes of bromides on Sunday morning. My earlier comments about the observations of the literary critic George Steiner on the collapse of biblical commonplaces in the mental universe of the average American apply here as a challenge to us. Supplementing the Liturgy of the Word with projected images and hymns is simply acknowledging the rhetorical conditions of a secular age. This can be done respectfully and prayerfully and reverently.

*Moral pluralism.* Pluralism, as I have stressed in the book, creates cognitive contamination in all populations. The diversity of the modern world is the future diversity of the local parish, if it isn't already. An active parish community is an antidote to an amnesia about one's own religious tradition. Faith cannot survive in a meaningful sense without that. The parish is a social statement of the significance of belief. The human lifeworld of faith has been and will continue to be colonized by the overpowering steering systems of public life. That's the path into post-religious experience.

The church has often spoken of relativism as an epistemic remainder from moral pluralism and religious toleration. Charles Taylor argues that relativism cannot be a serious moral stance. The moral doctrines of the church are well argued even if people might have disagreements with some of them. If they are true, perhaps better arguments are needed. The popes for a century have established a coherent moral continuity based on love (*agape*) and justice.

The moral issues in secularism have not been the subject of this book. My aim was to explain the conditions for belief, not moral beliefs or disagreements over them. But, morality has often been substituted for the Gospel message itself. One of the challenges of the new evangelization in America is to free itself from the Moral Majority version of the Gospel. Fundamentalists with political ambitions like the Rev. Jerry Falwell trapped well-meaning Catholics opposing abortion into a Protestant version of Christendom. The theological and ethical syllabus of the new evangelization is far deeper, much broader, and quite a bit different from that. The church in the United States lost several generations of young people by identifying itself too closely with moralistic Protestantism. Now, the crisis of clergy abuse may impose another fifty-year penance of evangelical recovery for the oldest surviving Christian tradition of the Western world.

*The new evangelization in a secular age.* In the book, I have argued that only by broadening our idea of what secularization means, along the lines of thinkers as diverse as Daniel Bell, Peter Berger, James Davison Hunter, and Charles Taylor, can the new evangelization avoid the hopeless alternative of a culture war in favor of a constructive mission of public persuasion and rejuvenation in Christianity. The secular state, for all its problems, was the only political remedy for inter-Christian violence after the Reformation hooked on power more than persuasion. It did mean, of course, that the political legitimation of religious belief and practice would cease, not immediately but eventually. Today, the secular state needs to be "worldview-neutral" and to accommodate different convictions of conscience and belief as much as possible. It cannot treat religious citizens, who disagree with secular worldviews on the meaning and purposes of human life, as second-class citizens. But, Christian citizens must also respect the rights of pluralist secular states to make laws based on constitutional principles, even as believers reserve the right to protest and not participate in practices which violate their moral principles and not be punished by the state for that. How to do this while respecting differences, human dignity, and the "unsocial sociability" of a liberal democratic order pressured by a new tribalism is a major challenge of our age.

The secularized public sphere no longer buttresses religious practice as it once did. More responsibility accordingly falls on churches, schools, parents, and the individual believer when it comes to maintaining and transmitting a faith and faith tradition. Apart from that, religious indifferentism in a secular context is all but inevitable. The open public sphere permits and oftentimes encourages indifference, but it also permits religious exploration and rediscovery. Finally, a closed secularism is just another ideology of the "blinkered Enlightenment" that is not agnostic enough to admit its answers to basic life questions are also contestable answers.

The kinds of tests which a secular age poses for Christian faith are formidable ones. The "immanent frame" of our human experience lacks a "sacred canopy" which all would accept as medievals accepted the hierarchical structures of the natural, human, angelic, and divine orders. The modern self is not the "porous self" Charles Taylor explains as the self of the twelfth century. It is a "buffered self" but no less threatened by forces beyond its control as the history of the twentieth century confirms and the apocalyptic scenarios of the present time confirm as well. How presciently we as Christians read the "signs of the times" determines to a large extent how we preach the Gospel of Christ. The hermeneutical revolution in Christian theology which was made possible by the critical Enlightenment and the romantic conviction that a single figure in history may hold the key to understanding ourselves and our longings in history and beyond—namely, Jesus Christ—has created new conditions for evangelization unavailable in the past. The Word of Christ who is Word of God himself is the basis for that hope.

> If you continue in my word,
> you are truly my disciples;
> and you will know the truth,
> and the truth will make you free.
>
> —John 8:31-32

The "signs of the times" demand that the church draw from the Scriptures and its tradition timely truths which people seeking God in any age, but especially in a secular age, can hear in a new way and without distortion. In each epoch of its two-thousand-year history, the church by the grace of the Holy Spirit has found the language necessary to translate the Gospel message into the vernacular of that age, drawing from culture, art, and philosophy the appropriate idioms which best express the mystery of Jesus Christ. This is a timeless truth which must be rendered, without sacrificing the ballast of tradition nor the creativity of the human intellect, into contemporary terms—new expressions of an ancient truth. It's all captured in sign and symbol in the Vigil of Jesus' resurrection (Holy Saturday).

In the liturgy, and after blessing the new fire in the darkness of the Vigil, the presider takes a knife and cuts the arms of a cross and two Greek letters into the wax of the large Paschal Candle—the symbol of Christ's sacrifice. At the top of the vertical arm of the cross he cuts the first letter of the Greek alphabet, *Alpha*, and at the bottom of that arm the last letter, *Omega*. While doing this, the presider says the following while tracing the numerals of the current calendar year around the central axis of the cross:

> Christ yesterday and today
> the Beginning and the End
> the Alpha
> and the Omega
> All time belongs to him [*Ipsius sunt tempora*]
> and all the ages [*et saecula*]
> To him be glory and power [*Ipsi Gloria et imperium*]
> through every age and for ever. Amen [*per universa aeternitatis*
> *saecula*. Amen.]

The repetition of the word *saecula* in the Latin prayer naturally leaves no echo in the English translation "ages." If it did, then the new evangelization for a secular age would not strike us as an oxymoron but as a new opportunity for faith. If the secular age also belongs to Christ, as much as the Hellenistic and medieval ages did, it will be the task of his disciples to show others how and in what particular ways it does. Is it even thinkable that the secular order of human life in general, and by God's mysterious Providence, has become the condition for a rebirth of the Christian faith? And, does that rebirth not require of the church new reforms, for its inner life and in the expressions it uses and in the example it gives to the secular age, a convincing image of Jesus Christ which is as timely as it is inexhaustible and everlasting?

# Bibliography

*Note: The bibliography includes more than those monographs and articles cited in the footnotes. I included many other titles for those interested in reading further and in greater depth about evangelization, secularization, culture, and the Christian faith. It is to be expected that faithful believers no less than scholars differ significantly on the nature and meaning of the secular age. I have learned a great deal from the most perceptive of them even when I finally disagree on what is to be said about it all and what is to be done to further the cause of the Gospel.*

## Catholicism, Vatican II, and the New Evangelization

Boguslawski, Stephen, and Ralph Martin, eds. *The New Evangelization: Overcoming the Obstacles*. New York: Paulist Press, 2008.

Douthat, Ross. *To Change the Church: Pope Francis and the Future of Catholicism*. New York: Simon & Schuster, 2018.

Faggioli, Massimo. *Vatican II: The Battle for Meaning*. New York: Paulist Press, 2012.

Fisichella, Rino. *The New Evangelization: Responding to the Challenge of Indifference*. Translated by Very Rev. G. J. Woodall. Herefordshire, UK: Gracewing, 2011.

Gaillardetz, Richard R. *An Unfinished Council: Vatican II, Pope Francis, and the Renewal of Catholicism*. Collegeville, MN: Liturgical Press, 2015.

Hahnenberg, Edward P. *A Concise Guide to the Documents of Vatican II*. Cincinnati: St. Anthony Messenger Press, 2007.

Hitchcock, James, *What Is Secular Humanism?: Why Humanism Became Secular and How It Is Changing Our World*. Ann Arbor, MI: Servant Books, 1982.

O'Malley, John W. *What Happened at Vatican II*. Cambridge: Harvard Belknap Press, 2008.

O'Malley, Timothy P. *Liturgy and the New Evangelization: Practicing the Art of Self-Giving Love.* Collegeville, MN: Liturgical Press, 2014.

Pontifical Biblical Commission. *The Interpretation of the Bible in the Church.* Boston: St. Paul Books and Media, 1993.

Pontifical Council for the New Evangelization. *Compendium on the New Evangelization: Texts of the Pontifical and Conciliar Magisterium 1939–2012.* Washington, DC: United States Conference of Catholic Bishops, 2015.

Tanner, Norman. *The Church and the World: Gaudium et Spes, Inter Mirifica.* New York: Paulist Press, 2005.

Weigel, George. *Evangelical Catholicism: Deep Reform in the 21st-Century Church.* New York: Basic Books, 2013.


## Papal and Episcopal Documents

Paul VI. *Evangelii Nuntiandi* (Apostolic Exhortation). December 8, 1975. www .vatican.va.

John Paul II. *Redemptoris Missio* (Encyclical). December 7, 1990. www.vatican .va.

———. *Tertio Millennio Adveniente* (Apostolic Letter). November 10, 1994. www.vatican.va.

Benedict XVI. Address to the Pontifical Council for Promoting the New Evangelization, May 30, 2011. Homily on the Solemnity of SS. Peter and Paul at the Basilica of St. Paul Outside the Walls, June 28, 2010. Other letters and addresses starting in 2011 dealing with the Year of Faith, Migrants, and so forth. www.vatican.va.

Synod of Bishops. XIII Ordinary General Assembly. The New Evangelization for the Transmission of the Christian Faith. Lineamenta. 2012. www .vatican.va.

United States Conference of Catholic Bishops. The Intellectual Tasks of the New Evangelization, 2011, 2012. (This amounts to talks given by various theologians, but none—except for Archbishop Di Noia [who relies on Edward Norman] and by Cardinal Wuerl—treat secularization. Wuerl's paper states the standard Roman Catholic position which needs to be superseded.)

———. Pastoral Plan for the New Evangelization. www.usccb.org/beliefs -and-teachings/how-we-teach/evangelization/go-and-make-disciples -a-national-plan-and-strategy-for-catholic-evangelization-in-the -united-states.

## Religion, Modernity, and the Secular Age

Barbieri, Jr., William A., ed. *At the Limits of the Secular: Reflections on Faith and Public Life.* Foreword by Charles Taylor. Grand Rapids, MI: Eerdmans, 2014.

Bell, Daniel. "The Return of the Sacred? The Argument on the Future of Religion." In *The Winding Passage: Essays and Sociological Journeys 1960–1980,* 324–54. Cambridge, MA: ABT Press, 1980.

———. *The Cultural Contradictions of Capitalism.* 20th anniversary ed. New York: Basic Books, 1996.

———. *The End of Ideology: On the Exhaustion of Political Ideas in the Fifties.* With a new afterword by the author. Cambridge: Harvard University Press, 1988.

Berger, Peter. *The Sacred Canopy: Elements of a Sociological Theory of Religion.* New York: Anchor Books, 1990. Originally published in 1967.

———. *A Rumor of Angels: Modern Society and the Rediscovery of the Supernatural.* Garden City, NJ: Anchor Books, 1970.

———. *A Far Glory: The Quest for Faith in an Age of Credulity.* New York: The Free Press, 1992.

———, ed. *The Desecularization of the World: Resurgent Religion and World Politics.* Grand Rapids, MI: Eerdmans, 1999.

———, ed. *Between Relativism and Fundamentalism: Religious Resources for a Middle Position.* Grand Rapids, MI: Eerdmans, 2010.

Browning, Don S., and Francis Schussler-Fiorenza. *Habermas, Modernity and Public Theology.* New York: Crossroad, 1992.

Bruce, Stephen. *God Is Dead: Secularization in the West.* Oxford: Blackwell, 2002.

Calhoun, Craig, Mark Juergensmeyer, and Jonathan Van Antwerpen, eds. *Rethinking Secularism.* Oxford: Oxford University Press, 2001.

Davaney, Sheila Greeve. "The Religious Secular Divide: The U.S. Case." *Social Research* 76, no. 4 (Winter 2009).

Dreher, Rod. *The Benedict Option: A Strategy for Christians in a Post-Christian Nation.* New York: Random House, 2017.

Flanagan, Kieran, and Peter C. Jupp, eds. "Symposium on Charles Taylor with his Responses." *New Blackfriars* 91, no. 1036 (November 2010).

Fodor, J., and W. T. Cavanaugh, eds. "Symposium: Charles Taylor: *A Secular Age.*" *Modern Theology* 26, no. 3 (July 2010).

Garbowski, Jan Pawel Hudzik, and Jan Klos. *Charles Taylor's Vision of Modernity: Reconstructions and Interpretation*. Christopher, Newcastle upon Tyne: Cambridge Scholars, 2009.

Greeley, Andrew M. *Unsecular Man: The Persistence of Religion*. New York: Delta Books, 1972.

Habermas, Jürgen, et al. *An Awareness of What Is Missing: Faith and Reason in a Post-Secular Age*. Translated by Ciaran Cronin. Cambridge, UK: Polity Press, 2010.

Heft, James L., ed. *A Catholic Modernity? Charles Taylor's Marianist Award Lecture, with Responses by William Shea, Rosemary Luling Haughton, George Marsden, and Jean Bethge Elshtain*. New York: Oxford University Press, 1999.

———, ed. *Beyond Violence: Religious Sources of Social Transformation in Judaism, Christianity, and Islam*. New York: Fordham University Press, 2004.

Himmelfarb, Gertrude. *The Roads to Modernity: The British, French, and American Enlightenments*. New York: Knopf, 2004.

Hunter, James Davison. *To Change the World: The Irony, Tragedy, & Possibility of Christianity in the Late Modern World*. Oxford: Oxford University Press, 2010.

Hunter, James Davison, and Alan Wolfe. *Is There a Culture War? A Dialogue on Values and American Public Life*. Washington, DC: Brookings Institution Press, 2006.

Levine, George, ed. *The Joy of Secularism: 11 Essays for How We Live Now*. Princeton: Princeton University Press, 2011.

Mendieta, Eduardo, and Jonathan VanAntwerpen. *The Power of Religion in the Public Sphere*. New York: Columbia University Press, 2011.

Norman, Edward. *Secularization*. London: Continuum, 2002.

Smith, Christian. "Introduction." In *The Secular Revolution: Power, Interests, and Conflict in the Secularization of American Public Life*, edited by Christian Smith. Berkeley, CA: University of California Press, 2003.

Smith, Christian, with Melinda Lundquist Denton. *Soul Searching: The Religious and Spiritual Lives of American Teenagers*. New York: Oxford University Press, 2005.

Taylor, Charles. *A Secular Age*. Cambridge, MA: Harvard Belknap Press, 2007.

———. *Sources of the Self: The Making of Modern Identity*. Cambridge, MA: Harvard University Press, 1989.

———. *The Malaise of Modernity*. Concord, Ontario: Anansi Press Limited, 1991.

———. *Philosophical Arguments*. Cambridge, MA: Harvard University Press, 1995.

———. *Varieties of Religion Today: William James Revisited*. Cambridge, MA: Harvard University Press, 2002.

———. *Modern Social Imaginaries*. Durham, NC: Duke University Press, 2004.

———. "Transcendent Humanism in a Secular Age." In *Reimagining the Sacred: Richard Kearney Debates God*, edited by Richard Kearney and Jens Zimmermann. New York: Columbia University Press, 2015.

———. "Recovering the Sacred." *Inquiry* 54, no. 2 (2011): 113–25.

———. "Religion is Not the Problem." *Commonweal* 138, no. 4 (2011): 17–21.

———. "The Sting of Death: Why We Yearn for Eternity." *Commonweal* 134, no. 17 (October 12, 2007): 13–16.

———. "Benedict XVI." *Public Culture* 18 (2006): 11–14.

———. "Risking Belief: Why William James Still Matters." *Commonweal* 129, no. 5 (March 8, 2002): 14–17.

———. "Foreword." In *The Disenchantment of the World: A Political History of Religion* by Marcel Gauchet. Princeton, NJ: Princeton University Press, 1997.

———. "Spirituality of Life—and its Shadow." *Compass* 14 (May/June 1996): 10–13.

———. "Religion in a Free Society." In *Articles of Faith, Articles of Peace: Religious Liberty Clauses and the American Public Philosophy*, edited by James Davison Hunter and Os Guinness. Washington, DC: Brookings Institution Press, 2010.

———. "The Person." In *The Category of the Person: Anthropology, Philosophy, History*, edited by Michael Carrithers, Steven Collins, and Steven Lukes. Cambridge: Cambridge University Press, 1985.

———. *Dilemmas and Connections: Selected Essays*. Cambridge MA: Harvard University Press, 2011.

Taylor, Charles, and Jocelyn Maclure. *Secularism and Freedom of Conscience*. Cambridge, MA: Harvard University Press, 2011.

Taylor, Charles, José Casanova, and George McLean, eds., *Church and People: Disjunctions in a Secular Age*. Washington, DC: The Council for Research in Philosophy and Values, 2012.

Taylor, Charles, José Casanova, George F. McLean, and Joao J. Vila-Cha, eds. *Renewing the Church in a Secular Age: Holistic Dialogue and Kenotic Vision.* Washington, DC: The Council for Research in Values and Philosophy, 2016.

*The Taylor Effect: Responding to A Secular Age.* Edited by Ian Leask. Cambridge Scholars, 2010.

Tracy, David. *Blessed Rage for Order: The New Pluralism in Theology.* New York: Seabury Press, 1975.

Warner, Michael, Jonathan VanAntwerpen, and Craig Calhoun, eds. *Varieties of Secularism in a Secular Age.* Cambridge, MA: Harvard University Press, 2010.

Wilson, Bryan R. *Religion in Secular Society.* London: C.A. Watts, 1966.

Wuthnow, Robert. *Rediscovering the Sacred: Perspectives on Religion in Contemporary Society.* Grand Rapids, MI: Eerdmans, 1992.

## Philosophical, Biblical, and Theological Studies

Abbey, Ruth. *Charles Taylor.* Princeton: Princeton University Press, 2000.

———, ed., *Charles Taylor.* New York: Cambridge University Press, 2004.

Bellah, Robert N. *Religion in Human Evolution: From the Paleolithic to the Axial Age.* Cambridge, MA: Harvard Belknap Press, 2011.

Bonhoeffer, Dietrich. *Letters and Papers from Prison.* Edited by Eberhard Bethge. New York: Macmillan, 1967.

Brague, Rémi. *Eccentric Culture: A Theory of Western Civilization.* Translated by Samuel Lester. South Bend, IN: St. Augustine's Press, 2002.

———. *The Wisdom of the World: The Human Experience of the Universe in Western Thought.* Translated by Teresa Lavender Fagan. Chicago: University of Chicago Press, 2003.

Brown, Raymond E. *An Introduction to the New Testament.* New York: Doubleday, 1996.

———. *The Gospel According to John.* Vols. 1 and 2. Garden City: Doubleday, 1966–1970.

———. *An Introduction to the Gospel of John.* Edited, updated, introduced, and concluded by Francis J. Moloney. New York: Doubleday, 2003.

Changeux, Jean-Pierre. *Neuronal Man: The Biology of Mind.* Translated by Dr. Laurence Garey. Princeton: Princeton University Press, 1997.

Changeux, Jean-Pierre, and Paul Ricoeur. *What Makes Us Think? A Neuro-scientist and a Philosopher Argue about Ethics, Human Nature, and the Brain*. Princeton: Princeton University Press, 2002.

Colorado, Carlos, and Justin D. Klassen, eds. *Aspiring to Fullness in a Secular Age: Essays on Religion and Theology in the Work of Charles Taylor*. Notre Dame, IN: University of Notre Dame Press, 2014.

Dreyfus, Hubert, and Sean Dorrance Kelly. *All Things Shining: Reading Western Classics to Find Meaning in a Secular Age*. New York: Free Press, 2011.

Girard, René. *I See Satan Fall Like Lightning*. Translated by James G. Williams. Maryknoll, NY: Orbis Books, 2002.

———. *The Girard Reader*. Edited by James G. Williams. New York. Crossroad, 2000.

Habermas, Jürgen. *The Future of Human Nature*. Cambridge, UK: Polity Press, 2003.

———. *Religion and Rationality: Essays on Reason, God, and Modernity*. Edited by Eduardo Mendieta. Cambridge, MA: MIT Press, 2002.

Jaspers, Karl. *Man in the Modern Age*. Garden City, NY: Doubleday, 1957.

Joas, Hans. *The Sacredness of the Person: A New Genealogy of Human Rights*. Translated by Alex Skinner. Washington, DC: Georgetown University Press, 2013.

———. *Faith as an Option: Possible Futures for Christianity*. Translated by Alex Skinner. Stanford: Stanford University Press, 2014.

LaCocque, Andre, and Paul Ricoeur. *Thinking Biblically: Exegetical and Hermeneutical Studies*. Translated by David Pellauer. Chicago: University of Chicago Press, 1998.

Leavitt, Robert F. "Raymond Brown and Paul Ricoeur on the Surplus of Meaning." In *Life In Abundance: Studies of John's Gospel in Tribute to Raymond E. Brown*, edited by John R. Donahue, 207–30. Collegeville, MN: Liturgical Press, 2005.

Levenson, Jon D. *The Death and Resurrection of the Beloved Son: The Transformation of Child Sacrifice in Judaism and Christianity*. New Haven: Yale University Press, 1993.

Levinas, Emmanuel. *Totality and Infinity: An Essay on Exteriority*. Translated by Alphonso Lingis. Pittsburgh: Duquesne University Press, 1969.

Meier, John P. *A Marginal Jew: Rethinking the Historical Jesus. Volume Two: Mentor, Message, and Miracles*. New York: Doubleday, 1994.

Metz, Johann Baptist. *Faith in History and Society: Toward a Practical Fundamental Theology.* Translated and edited by J. Matthew Ashley. New York: Crossroad, 2007.

———. *A Passion for God: The Mystical-Political Dimension of Christianity.* Translated and edited by J. Matthew Ashley. New York: Paulist Press, 1998.

Milbank, John. *Theology and Social Theory.* 2nd edition. Oxford: Oxford University Press, 2005.

———. *Beyond Secular Order: The Representation of Being and the Representation of the People.* Chichester: John Wiley & Sons, 2013.

Niebuhr, H. Richard. *Christ and Culture.* 50th anniversary ed. New York: Harper and Row, 2001.

Ratzinger, Joseph Cardinal, and Jürgen Habermas, *Dialectics of Secularization: On Reason and Religion.* Edited with a foreword by Florian Schuller. Translated by Brian McNeil. San Francisco: Ignatius Press, 2006.

Ricoeur, Paul. *Fallible Man.* Translated by Charles A. Kelbley. Chicago: Henry Regnery, 1965.

———. *History and Truth.* Translated with an introduction by Charles A. Kelbley. Evanston: Northwestern University Press, 1965.

———. *Critique and Conviction. Conversations with Francois Azouvi and Marc de Launay.* Translated by Kathleen Blamey. New York: Columbia University Press, 1998.

———. *Memory, History, Forgetting.* Translated by Kathleen Blamey and David Pellauer. Chicago: University of Chicago Press, 2004.

———. *The Course of Recognition.* Translated by David Pellauer. Cambridge: Harvard University Press, 2005.

———. *Figuring the Sacred: Religion, Narrative, and Imagination.* Translated by David Pellauer. Edited by Mark I. Wallace. Minneapolis: Fortress Press, 1995.

———. *On Translation.* Translated by Eileen Brennan. London: Routledge, 2006.

———. "Rhetoric—Poetics—Hermeneutics." In *Rhetoric and Hermeneutics in Our Time: A Reader,* translated by Robert Harvey, edited by Michael Jost and Michael J. Hyde, 60–72. New Haven, CT: Yale University Press, 1997.

Rosenstock-Huessy, Eugen. *Out of Revolution: Autobiography of Western Man.* Norwich, VT: Argo Books, 1969.

————. *The Christian Future or the Modern Mind Outrun.* New York: Harper Torchbooks, 1966.

————. *Lifelines: Quotations from the Works of Eugen Rosenstock-Huessy.* Edited by Clinton C. Gardner. Norwich, VT: Argo Books, 1988.

Senior, Donald. *Raymond Brown and the Catholic Biblical Renewal.* New York: Paulist Press, 2018.

Smith, James K. A. *How (Not) to Be Secular: Reading Charles Taylor.* Grand Rapids, MI: Eerdmans, 2014.

Tracy, David. *The Analogical Imagination: Christian Theology and the Culture of Pluralism.* New York: Crossroad, 1981.

Volf, Miroslav, and Justin E. Crisp, eds. *Joy and Human Flourishing: Essays on Theology, Culture, and the Good Life.* Minneapolis: Fortress Press, 2015.

Volf, Miroslav. *Flourishing: Why We Need Religion in a Globalized World.* New Haven: Yale University Press, 2015.

Witherup, Ronald D. *Biblical Fundamentalism: What Every Catholic Should Know.* Collegeville, MN: Liturgical Press, 2001.

Wright, Addison G. *The Literary Genre Midrash.* Staten Island, NY: Alba House, 1967.

————. "Ecclesiastes 9:1-12: An Emphatic Statement of Themes." *The Catholic Biblical Quarterly* 77, no. 2 (April 2015): 250–62.

## Political and Social Science Studies

Anderson, Kurt. "How America Lost Its Mind." *The Atlantic* (September 2017): 76–91. This is adapted from *Fantasyland: How America Went Haywire—a 500-Year History.* New York: Random House, 2017.

Connolly, William E. *Why I Am Not a Secularist.* Minneapolis, MN: University of Minnesota Press, 1999.

————. *Pluralism.* Durham, NC: Duke University Press, 2005.

Fukuyama, Francis. *The End of History and the Last Man.* New York: The Free Press, 1992.

————. *Identity: The Demand for Dignity and the Politics of Resentment.* New York: Farrar, Straus and Giroux, 2018.

Heilbroner, Robert L. *An Inquiry into the Human Prospect: Looked at Again for the 1990s.* New York: W. W. Norton, 1991.

Hitchcock, James. "The Dynamics of Popular Intellectual Change." *The American Scholar* 45, no. 4 (Autumn 1976): 522–35.

Huntington, Samuel P. *The Clash of Civilizations and the Remaking of World Order*. New York: Simon and Schuster, 1996.

Kissinger, Henry. *World Order*. New York: Penguin Press, 2014.

Manent, Pierre. *A World Beyond Politics: A Defense of the Nation-State*. Translated by Marc LePain. Princeton: Princeton University Press, 2006.

Markus, Robert A. *Christianity and the Secular*. Notre Dame: University of Notre Dame Press, 2006.

Putnam, Robert D., and David E. Campbell. *American Grace: How Religion Divides and Unites Us*. New York: Simon and Schuster, 2010.

Walzer, Michael. *The Paradox of Liberation: Secular Revolutions and Religious Counterrevolutions*. New Haven, CT: Yale University Press, 2015.

Weber, Max. *The Protestant Ethic and the Spirit of Capitalism*. Translated by Talcott Parsons. New York: Charles Scribner's Sons, 1958.

## Occasional Essays and Poetic Works

Alain. *Alain on Happiness*. Translated by Robert D. and Jane E. Cottrell. Evanston, IL: Northwestern University Press, 1989.

Dalai Lama and Archbishop Desmond Tutu with Douglas Abrams. *The Book of Joy: Lasting Happiness in a Changing World*. New York: Avery Press, 2016.

Dale, Peter. *Richard Wilbur in Conversation with Peter Dale*. London: BTL (Between the Lines), 2000.

Eliot, T. S. *Collected Poems 1909–1962*. New York: Harcourt, Brace, 1963.

Frankfurt, Harry G. *On Bullshit*. Princeton: Princeton University Press, 2005.

Herbert, Zbigniew. *The Collected Poems: 1956–1998*. Translated by Alissa Valles. New York: HarperCollins, 2007.

Jamison, Kay Redfield. *Exuberance: The Passion for Life*. New York: Alfred A. Knopf, 2004.

Riley, Naomi Schaefer. *Got Religion? How Churches, Mosques and Synagogues Can Bring Young People Back*. West Conshohocken, PA: Templeton Press, 2014.

Steiner, George. *On Difficulty and Other Essays*. Oxford: Oxford University Press, 1978.

Wallace, David Foster. "Joseph Frank's Dostoevsky." In *Consider the Lobster and Other Essays*, 255–74. New York: Little, Brown, 2006.

———. *This Is Water: Some Thoughts Delivered on a Significant Occasion about Living a Compassionate Life*. New York: Little, Brown, 2009.

Yeats, W. B. *The Variorum Edition of the Poems of W. B. Yeats*. Edited by Peter Allt and Russell K. Alspach. New York: Macmillan, 1973.

# Index

agnosticism, 16, tolerant agnosticism, 24, civil agnosticism, 86; in *The Catechism*, 143; Joseph Ratzinger on, 145, n. 14; magnanimous agnosticism, 231; Pontifical Council for Culture on, 235; Paul Ricoeur on "generous agnosticism," 285, n. 10

Anderson, Kurt, 8, 10, n. 10; as example of secular apocalyptic, 288

atheism, in *Pastoral Constitution on the Church in the Modern World*, 33; Pontifical Council for Culture on, 82, 139, 235; Institute for Advanced Studies in Culture on, 211–212, n. 7; in Paul VI, 34, 82, 136; in John Paul II on "state-sponsored" 57; Joseph Ratzinger on, 145, n. 14, 146; Dietrich Bonhoeffer on, 93; religious violence and, 85; dogmatic v. pragmatic, 83; types of, 83–85; in Pierre-Simon Laplace, 88; secular atheism, 136; David Foster Wallace on, 78; Charles Taylor on, 213, 214–215, 229–230, 234

Augustine of Hippo, St., homiletics and rhetoric, 77; experiences of transcendence, 98; on *intellectus*

*fidei* v. *sacrificium intellectus*, 115; influence on Joseph Ratzinger, 146; in *Sources of the Self*, 159; an example of Christ above Culture, 164–165; and imperial Christianity and the *saeculum*, 195–196; Charles Taylor on, 180

authenticity, birth of the idea of, 42; Charles Taylor on, 159, 180–183, 220–227, 232, 235, n. 42; The Joy of the Gospel on, 247

Axial Age, the meaning of, 107, 199–202

Baudelaire, Charles, on *modernité*, 42, 159, 172, 176, 179, 216

Bell, Daniel, ix, on Nietzsche, 91, n. 6; on the culture of modernity, 170, 173–179; "The Return of the Sacred," 178–179, 203; culture as a *ricorso*, 204; the exhaustion of substitutes for religion, 207; on secularization and profanation, 175–176, 179; the significance of the language of limits, 272; challenges of the post-industrial age, 289

Berger, Peter, 20, n. 14, 14, n. 17; on the "sacred canopy," 39; on pluralization theory, 202–205, 216, 297

Bin Laden, Osama, 29; *See* Islam

37, context for, 238–244, analysis
of, 244–253, on missionary
disciples, passim, 140, 243;
on dialogue, 288, on the homily,
74–75, on *etsi deus non daretur*,
97, n. 14, on the "apologetics of
beauty" 206; joy and *thymos* in,
253–255, 263, 287; Ross Douthat
on, 74–75; Richard Gaillardetz
on, 300
power, power in religion, passim;
*See* Christendom, clergy abuse,
religious freedom, secular state
Protestant Reformation, 2; and the
rise of the secular, 109, 156, 89,
n. 8, 232
Putnam, Robert, on *American Grace:
How Religion Divides and Unites
Us*, 24, n. 1, 54, n. 3

Quietism, *apatheia* versus *thymos* in
spirituality, 286

Ratzinger, Cardinal Joseph, passim;
28, 30, on "dictatorship of relativism" 60; 2004 Munich address,
61; colloquy with Jürgen
Habermas, 61, 108, 145, n. 15,
146, 234, 278
relativism, and truth, 84, 173;
dictatorship of, 50, 60–61; and
moral pluralism, 296; and fundamentalist reaction to, 276; in
The Joy of the Gospel, 97, 248;
and Charles Taylor, 222, 231;
*See* Harry Frankfurt
religion, *See* Evangelization, Pope
John Paul II, Pope Francis,
*thymos*
Republican Party, on religion, 54
Robinson, Marilynne, 46
Ricoeur, Paul, passim; ix, on joy
and *thymos*, 37, n. 9, 261, 265,
267, n. 30, 268–269, 286–291;
on language, 45, 174, n. 27; on

revelation, 100, n. 16, 115, n. 9;
on Wisdom literature, 256, n. 10,
258, n. 11; on Charles Taylor, 182,
n. 43; on modernity, 171, n. 14,
172–173; on religious freedom in
a secular state, 189; and Paul VI
Prize, 266; on non-violence, 233,
n. 41
Rorty, Richard, on religion a
"conversation-stopper," 55

sacred and profane, 40–41, human
rights as the secular sacred, 41
*saecula*, 186, 194ff., in liturgy, 299
Saunders, George, on Buddhism,
25; satire on post-truth era, 46
Scruton, Roger, on the secular,
Mohammed Atta and Septem-
ber 11, 2001, 28–29, n. 4
searchers and seekers, 24–25, 53, 79,
224, 275
secular (and *saeculum*, secular age,
secular order, secular state,
secular time, secularism, secular
humanism, and secularization),
*See* modern and; *See* Bell, Berger,
Casanova, Habermas, Hunter,
Joas, Manent, Ratzinger, Taylor
on; meanings and distinctions,
ix, 1, 3–4, 11–12, n. 14, 13, n. 16,
14, n. 17, 24, 186–191; history
and origins of, 2, 85ff., 112,ff.
191–197; analysis of, 37–48,
202–206; belief and unbelief in,
82–95; dialogue with, 145–155-
New Evangelization and, 19–21,
27–37, 50–51, 56–62, 64, n. 8,
121, 155–156, 234–252, 275–279,
292–299; religious freedom and,
280–285; Taylor and, 208–234;
bibliography about, 302–305
*A Secular Age, See* Charles Taylor
seeds of the Word, 3–4
self, selfhood, *See* Charles Taylor on
modernity